BURT FRANKLIN: RESEARCH & SOURCE WORKS SERIES 582
Selected Essays in History, Economics and Social Science 242

THE ENGLISH CATHOLICS
IN THE
REIGN OF QUEEN ELIZABETH
1558-1580

QUEEN ELIZABETH

German School, Galleria delle Belle Arti, Siena

THE
ENGLISH CATHOLICS

IN THE REIGN OF

QUEEN ELIZABETH

A STUDY OF THEIR POLITICS
CIVIL LIFE AND GOVERNMENT

BY

JOHN HUNGERFORD POLLEN, S.J.

1558–1580
FROM THE FALL OF THE OLD CHURCH TO THE ADVENT
OF THE COUNTER-REFORMATION

WITH ILLUSTRATIONS

BURT FRANKLIN
NEW YORK

Published by LENOX HILL Pub. & Dist. Co. (Burt Franklin)
235 East 44th St., New York, N.Y. 10017
Originally Published: 1920
Reprinted: 1971
Printed in the U.S.A.

S.B.N.: 8337-27982
Library of Congress Card Catalog No.: 71-153897
Burt Franklin: Research and Source Works Series 582
Selected Essays in History, Economics and Social Science 242

Reprinted from the original edition in the Louisiana State
University Library.

INTRODUCTION

THE number of Protestant writers who have described for us the history of the Reformed Church of England is considerable; they have studied their subject from many points of view, and enriched their histories with excellent collections of contemporary documents. On the part of the English Catholics there have been but few publications to set by their side. We have indeed many volumes about our heroes, our martyrs and confessors, about the last members of our ancient hierarchy, and about the leaders of the Catholic revival. But about our history considered as a whole it has been impossible for us to learn much, chiefly because of the dearth of contemporary evidence before the general opening of State archives in the last century. Then we gradually became acquainted with the rich stores of papers still preserved in Spain and at Rome, which were our chief protectors during bad times, as well as with the records of the persecutors, at our Record Office. The arrangement of all this material is still very imperfect, and the publication of its chief treasures is far from complete, but it is now possible to follow, with far greater certainty than before, the main course of events by which the fortunes of the English Catholics as a body were determined. The object of the present volume is to recount their corporate history, and it dwells rather on their public and political life, than on the achievements of individuals.

In passing over what is personal, I am omitting, I know, many of the brightest and most interesting pages in our history. But in the acts of the martyrs, and in lives of the religious leaders, a good beginning of the personal history has been made, while it was impossible in those particular studies to give full care and attention to broad questions and underlying principles, which those lives everywhere presupposed, yet never treated adequately. I am here endeavouring to supply an historical background, against which the work of others will be seen in due proportion. I am furnishing principles, and mapping out the flow of main currents, which will enable readers to unite smaller studies into a harmonious whole.

And here some pertinent questions may be put to me. Why, it may be asked, begin with Queen Elizabeth's accession, and not with her father's revolt from the Church? For the latter was the cause of the former, and, indeed, the origin of all the subsequent troubles. Again, it may be asked, if you do begin with Elizabeth's long reign, why commence before the middle or end? For the new life of the Catholic party only began to throb and grow articulate in the latter decades.

To this I would say that Henry's revolt is indeed the proper starting-point for a history of the Reformation taken as a whole; but Elizabeth's accession is better, if one is primarily considering the political and civic life of the post-Reformation Catholics. Reform and counter-reform under Henry, Edward and Mary were transitory. The constructive work of each was immediately undone by their successor. But the work done under Queen Elizabeth, whether by Catholic or Protestant, lasted a long time. There have, of course, been many developments since, but they have proceeded on the lines then laid down. On the Catholic side the work of reorganisation began almost immediately after the first crash, though it was only in the middle of the reign that the vitality and permanence of the new measures became evident.

However cursorily one surveys the period, one cannot help seeing the collapse of the old Church at the beginning of Elizabeth's reign, and its return to life after her second decade. These two points mark the beginning and the end of this volume (Chapters I and IX). Midway between these extremes stands out conspicuous the Excommunication (Chapter V). Its contrast to the depression which prevailed at the end of the first decade (Chapter III) is very marked indeed. But the advent of Queen Mary Stuart in England had created a new situation. The extreme respect for the Crown, on which the Tudors traded, now told strongly in favour of the legitimist heiress, who was also a Catholic. Close prisoner though she was, the North soon rose in her support (Chapter IV).

Though both Rising and Excommunication were political failures, they were successful from the religious point of view, in having given to the Catholics a new aspiration to resist the tyranny of the State Church. The Catholic revival, already powerful on the Continent, begins to produce permanent good fruit, especially among the Catholic exiles (Chapter VII). In contrast with this permanent good stand the shifting gains and losses caused by the religious wars in France and Flanders and the royal courtships between Catholic and Protestant Powers (Chapters VI, VIII), all of which leave the English Catholics in a slightly worse position than before. Success, however, comes at last, without the support of any temporal power, with the return from the seminaries of new missionaries, breathing a fresh enthusiasm for the ancient cause.

HISTORICAL SOURCES

The sources from which this history is drawn are very scattered. But as so much has been published of late years, it may now, or soon, be possible to go through almost the whole story relying on the printed sources mentioned in the footnotes. To ensure finality of judgment, however, or security against partial views, considerable manuscript studies are still requisite.

I. The Spanish dispatches are, upon the whole, of the greatest importance for this volume, for they alone continue in an unbroken series to give news of the English Catholics throughout the whole period. Mr. Hume, in his invaluable *Spanish Calendars*, follows chiefly the *Coleccion de Documents inéditos para la historia de Espagna*, vols. lxxxix. to xcii., Madrid, 1886, etc. (in the British Museum under Fuensanto del Valle), and the Froude Transcripts (B. M., *Additional*, 26,056, etc.). These may often be supplemented by the ample publications of Baron Kervyn de Lettenhove, M. Gachard, and M. A. Teulet. There is also at Paris (Ministère des Affaires Etrangères, Mémoirs et Documents, Espagne, 270, etc.) a fine series of transcripts made by M. Tiran at Simancas, much used by Mignet and others. At the *Archives Nationales*, the *fonds Simancas* comprise almost all the Spanish diplomatic correspondence with France for the whole of our period, under the reference K., 1500, etc. Simancas itself, moreover, is no longer so inaccessible as it used to be; and though the fondo "Inglaterra" is fairly well represented by our *Spanish Calendars*, much fresh matter may be found elsewhere, *e. g.* in the sections for Rome, for Flanders, etc., etc.

II. The Vatican Archives contain even more about England than does Simancas. But the papers are very scattered, instead of being in a few well-marked series, and the writers are of every class, instead of being predominantly diplomatists. During this period there was no official intercourse between London and Rome : all correspondence is circuitous and intermittent. The *Roman Transcripts* at the Record Office give a

very good idea of what is to be found in Rome, and since this book was
written, the first volume of the Calendar for them has appeared, entitled,
" Rome, 1558–1571." While we earnestly look forward to the continuation of these volumes, we must also remember that, owing to the
nature of the records, our Calendars do not altogether absolve us from
the duty of occasionally re-consulting the originals. Besides the general
principle, that one must never regard a translation or the calendar form
of a document as an equivalent to the original, these Roman papers are
often anonymous and undated; intelligible perhaps only by their surroundings in the correspondence to which they belong, or by some minute
official sign, endorsement or reference. But our Government Calendars
usually arrange all papers in one large chronological series, and do not
attempt to indicate details of diplomatique, such as seals, handwriting,
water-marks, endorsements and the like, on which, when doubts arise,
so much may depend.

III. *French Diplomatic Papers* suffered most seriously during the
Republican period. The correspondence with England no longer exists
for most of our present period. I have made much use of Fénelon's
Dépêches, 1568–1575, edited by Purton Cooper in 1838, and of the dispatches of Castelnau de Mauvissière in the Baschet Transcripts at R. O.,
1578–1581 (from Fonds Français, 15, 973). See also *Inventaire Sommaire
des Archives du Département des Affaires Etrangères*, 1892.

IV. *English State Papers* are chiefly at the Record Office, with smaller
sections at Hatfield (Cecil MSS.) and Lambeth (Carew MSS.). All are
now well calendared, though generally in a much abridged form. It
must, however, be remembered that these papers are generally so hostile
that they must often be read in a sense very different from that in which
they are written. They do not even attempt to describe the civil or
political estate of the Catholics. These deficiencies explain their in-
feriority for our purposes to the papers of Spain and Rome. Moreover,
during most of our period, persecution made it impossible for the English
Catholics to keep any records of their own. It is only at the conclusion
of our volume that English Catholic institutions came into existence
abroad, and were able to preserve evidence regarding England. Their
archives are now represented by those of the Cardinal Archbishop of
Westminster, the English College, Rome, and Stonyhurst College.
Some useful pieces are also quoted from the now scattered collections of
the Jesuits on the Continent. We shall hear more of these sources in the
ensuing period.

This book has been for several years upon the stocks.
Preliminary sketches and special studies appeared in *The
Month* and elsewhere as far back as 1897; and the war
has held up the publication since 1914. It would be
impossible to name in particular the many friends and
helpers without whose aid during all these years, and
earlier also, I should never have completed these pages. I
can only say, therefore, that their kind services are still
gratefully, and even proudly, remembered, and that this
book itself is the best thank-offering which it is in my
power to make them.

J. H. POLLEN, S. J.

31 *Farm Street,*
   London, W.1.
   November 1919.

CONTENTS

LIST OF ILLUSTRATIONS

THE ENGLISH CATHOLICS IN THE REIGN OF QUEEN ELIZABETH

CHAPTER I

THE OLD CHURCH AND HER ENEMIES
(1558–1559)

§ 1. *The Old Church*

WHEN Elizabeth came to the throne, she found herself face to face with the venerable Church which St. Augustine had founded close on a thousand years before, which had grown with the people, and had become an integral part of the national life. The laws of the Church ranked with the laws of England, if not above them, for it was to Rome that the final appeals were made. Her Bishops were among the greatest lords of the land, and were then holding some of the highest offices under the Crown, while the clergy governed and taxed themselves. The Church, moreover, derived still further power from her intimate communion with the other great Churches of Christendom, while the Pope, the common head of the Faithful, was in a special way her loving father and powerful protector. Her external greatness seemed the more remarkable, when contrasted with the trifling opposition which was offered to her in holes and corners by small gatherings of insignificant dissentients.

Yet all was not well with that great body. Free though she seems to have been from flagrant abuses, she was little better than the rest of the people in the matter of servility. Five and twenty years before she had fallen with the fall of her King, and shameful had been the facility with

B

which she had capitulated. It is true there had been some opposition. A handful of heroes had refused all compromise, and a considerable number had offered temporary resistance. It was, at all events, made clear that she only yielded to violence; that if liberty of choice had been permitted, the ancient order would certainly have been retained.

Still the ignominious surrender was made, and first schism, then heresy, had dominated the land. Queen Mary had, indeed, re-established Church government in its ancient pride of place; but she had done so by an exercise of the same royal power which had previously abrogated it.

Thus, while at first sight the Church seemed as great and strong as ever, on closer inspection the difference from the times of St. Thomas, St. Anselm and St. Hugh is found to be very considerable. Then the Church had stood inviolable. From time to time, it is true, some stark, imperious baron or monarch had made rude, even murderous attacks on individual priests, Bishops and Church liberties. Periods of absolute peace were never very long. But public opinion would reassert itself in one way or another, and the violated liberties would be confirmed more effectively than ever, in consequence of the martyr's blood or the confessor's heroism. But the Marian Church had plainly lost the old character of inviolability. The courage and self-respect of the clergy had given way before Henry and Edward. Friend and foe regarded them as waverers, a generation of Vicars of Bray,[1] who had gone before their flocks into errors, which they had denounced, until force had made them eat their words.

The sovereign—instead of being a protector, who

---

[1] As the changes of side made by the Vicar of Bray are stated in a well-known song to have been occasioned by the political revolutions of the late seventeenth century, it may be worth recalling that the original vicar is said, by Fuller (*Worthies*, p. 18), to have held the living of St. Michael's, Bray, Berkshire, during the religious revolutions of Henry, Edward, Mary, and Elizabeth. Want of documents prevents our testing this in all particulars; but it cannot be exactly correct, for one vicar, Simon Symonds (possibly the person intended), is known to have died in 1551. But Thomas John, Vicar of Blisland, Cornwall, instituted in 1529, continued there for fifty-two years. There are similar cases at Brighton, Pontefract, etc. The popular song, however, has also some foundation in fact. See *Notes and Queries*, Indexes to series v. and vi.

accepted Church authority *in spiritualibus,* and her ecclesiastical legislation—had become a tyrant, who would not hear of any law but his own whim. Though he still respected ecclesiastical forms, he altered them autocratically, and made their administration entirely subservient to his will.

The laity, far from fighting the battle of the Church, had robbed her, and feared nothing so much as having to disgorge their prey. The spoils had been sold, bought and passed from one to another with such feverish haste, that there were now hardly any whose hands were clean. Restitution was already an impossibility. So perverted had the public conscience become, that Michiel, the Venetian ambassador, says that people became positively angry with Mary for restoring lands to the cathedrals, which after the dispensation of December 1554 she was not bound to do.[1]

The politicians in authority, too, were not the men under whom any decided change for the better was to be expected ; they were turn-coats, who stuck to power without any respect to principle. Indeed, amidst all the revolutions, voluntary resignations of office were very rare. Lord Paget, for instance, so influential under Mary, had been in every administration, save one, since the schism. Nor did the Crown itself find it necessary to make many changes among its advisers, even after radical changes of policy. The Privy Council, for instance, which played so important a part in executing the royal wishes, remained much the same in *personnel* even during the periods of greatest change of policy. The successive Parliaments, which almost unanimously confirmed first one revolution, then another, were made up in large measure of the same men.

With such a spirit of obsequiousness running through clergy and people, it had been, of course, impossible for Pole and Mary to re-establish Catholicism in a way that should be proof against all future attack on the part of the Crown. Yet their work was in many respects sensibly and well done,

---

[1] Michiel's Relation, May 13, 1557, in Albèri, *Relazioni degli ambasciatori Veneti* (1839), i. 328 and 361–65. English translation, *Venetian Calendar,* VI. ii, n. 1058. Giovanni Michiel had left England in January 1557, which makes his forecast of what might happen if Elizabeth succeeded the more remarkable. In some points, however, he is misled by his undisguised dislike of the English on racial grounds.

so far as it went. It was begun in moderation, and relied for development on a good educational scheme.

The first steps of the re-establishment were broad-minded, though without any compromise. For the burial of King Edward VI a solemn requiem was sung before the Queen in the church of the Tower, then the royal residence, while Cranmer conducted at Westminster a funeral service according to the Protestant rite. This was on the 7th of August, 1553, and soon after this the Catholic reaction received a great impetus from the recantation made at his execution by Northumberland, who had so lately been the chief of the reforming party. In the middle of December a royal proclamation gave formal sanction to the re-intro-duction of the Mass, which had already been restored in many churches by private initiative. Wyatt's rebellion (January–February 1554), with other riots and disturbances, had the effect of introducing, here as elsewhere, the note of bitterness. The Convocation in May 1554 requested a re-enactment of the laws against heresy; but this was not acceded to. The married clergy, however, were now removed, and Catholics were substituted for Protestant Bishops. On St. Andrew's Day (November 30, 1554) Pole solemnly pronounced the absolution of the realm, an important engagement having been previously given—that Church property, which had been appropriated in the late reigns in opposition to Church law, should now be alienated by the Church and confirmed to the present holders. This was done by Pole's *Literæ Dispensatoriæ*, on Christmas Eve.[1]

Next St. Andrew's Day a legatine synod was opened,

[1] The *Literæ Dispensatoriæ* are in Wilkins' *Concilia Ecclesiæ Angli-canæ* (1737), iv. 112–14. They are based on the Bull, printed *ibid.*, p. 102. Pole prescribed no formula for this alienation, and Pope Julius appears to dispense from one (*ibid.*, p. 103). But next year Paul IV, by a Bull of July 6 (*Bullarium*, 1745, vi. 319), revoked all alienations of Church property made without forms of law. Though Pole's dispensation was not hereby revoked, this decree gave rise to suspicions and to some agitation, and some conscientious people took out letters to fortify their titles. Father Persons (*Memorial for the Reformation of England*, pp. 20–24), writing in Spain in 1596, says ironically that he who did so " was considered a great Catholic." But in view of Julius's Bull, which Persons probably did not know of, this irony seems misplaced. Persons's authority for this period is probably Sir Francis Englefield. See also *Julius III to Pole*, November 6, 1554; Arch. Vat. *Lettere di Giulio III a diversi* 1550–1554, vol. 393, p. 123, and Bib. Vat. Ottoboniana, 3166, 377 b.

which may be considered as marking the highest point of
Pole's reforms. The decrees were worthy of the occasion.
Church reform, they declare, must begin at home; the
duties of Bishops must, therefore, be regulated first, the lives
and conversation of the clergy next. The Decree for the
Erection of Clerical Seminaries is especially noteworthy. It
was passed eight years before that of Trent, and was probably one of the earliest synodal decrees on that subject.
Well adapted, again, to the needs of the day were the provi-
sions for the regular catechising of children, and the examination of candidates for orders. Nor are these decrees marred
by that harshness and severity to offenders which were so
habitual with rulers of that age.[1]

It took just half of Mary's short reign to think out and
formulate these reforms. The other half, just two and a
half years, was all the time they were allowed for introduction and practice, a period far too short to enable us to
test them by results, for they were based on an educational
system, under which a whole generation should have been
trained before we could fairly estimate the merits of the
reform. One good reason at least remains for believing
that this counter-Reformation was genuine and efficient.
That is, that the Marian Church, in spite of all disadvantages, resisted Elizabeth's tyranny incomparably better than
the pre-Reformation Church had resisted Elizabeth's father.[2]

Turning to the weak side of Pole's reforms, we cannot
fail to see that excessive reliance on royal support was their
greatest danger. It would have been difficult, indeed, to
guard against this even if Pole had always recognised it;
and he probably did so at the end. Even during Mary's
life the Queen's influence, however well intentioned, had
not by any means been always felicitous. That Pole was

---

[1] Wilkins, iv. 121–26, esp. d. 11.

[2] Father Persons took a different view. He says that " the reconciliation was huddled up in Queen Mary's days by a certain general absolution
only. . . . Priests that had fallen and married were admitted presently
(*i. e.* immediately) to the altar, without other satisfaction than only to
send their concubines out of men's sight."—*Memorial for the Reformation
of England,* ed. E. Gee, 1688, p. 20. Persons was not a contemporary, and
his statements, though shrewd, and drawn presumably from well-informed
sources, are sometimes unreliable. The lamentable defections of 1559,
however, of which more in § 6 below, warn us that he *may* have had good
reason.

long denied entrance into the country; that England soon found herself at war with France, and, in consequence, on the most difficult terms with the Pope, the ally of France, were misfortunes that befell the Church through the closeness of her alliance with the Crown. There is no reason to suppose that Pole was less far-seeing than, for instance, the Venetian ambassador, who wrote of Elizabeth's probable accession several months before it took place, and of her probably changing the religion of the realm. When the news of Mary's death reached Pole, he declared it was " a grievous final catastrophe." [1] He evidently then feared the worst, and had no remedy to suggest; nor does he seem to have ever prepared one.

Something must now be said on the persecution of Protestants, so far as we are at present concerned with it, that is, in so far as it affected the balance of parties at the time of Elizabeth's accession. That it was a failure and a bad policy, was then generally recognised.[2] In London, where it had begun and had been warmest, it had been given up for several months. On St. Andrew's Day, 1557, Cardinal Pole had alluded to the subject in a sermon, which is still extant.[3] This part of his discourse does not do him much credit. He shows himself out of touch with a large section of the people, and at this he is vexed; but he is wanting in the true leader's gift of taking hearts by storm. He complains that the executions have " scandalised " many, especially of their younger men; but the feeble conclusion is that parents and schoolmasters should exert themselves more to bring up the young in the old way. There is no taking the audience into his confidence; no attempt to gain their support by strong persuasive reasoning : nothing but an appeal to mediæval standards, as if they seriously influenced men of the Renaissance.

This want of genuine leadership, so natural where royal power is excessive, explains how the Church had originally

---

[1] " A grievous final catastrophe."—*Venetian Calendar,* VI. iii. 1550, November 27, 1558.

[2] M. Surian, Venetian ambassador, reports to the Doge, April 3, 1557: " The affairs of religion are regulated with less severity to avoid further exasperation of the public mind."—*Venetian Calendar,* VI. ii. 1004.

[3] Pole's Speech, Strype, *Ecclesiastical Memoirs,* ed. 1721, III. ii. 237–56.

drifted into the persecution policy, and had been carried along to lengths unheard of in England before. It was not that Bonner and his *confrères* were cruel, but that they had not the instinct to see where to stop. Hardly any one in those days would have denied that the teachers of new and revolutionary doctrines should be punished in the most striking way. Elizabeth and Cecil claimed and exercised the power of burning heretics [1] as well as Mary and Bonner. But the former were careful not to go beyond what public feeling would support; the latter, working mechanically, according to the letter of an ancient law, found out too late what a mistake they had made in not taking the course which their kindly natures had often suggested.

The impression which " the Martyrs " would make on public opinion was not foreseen by Pole in 1557. Political writers on both sides during the crisis that ensued after Elizabeth's accession paid little or no attention to the subject, and Protestant statesmen could not, considering their own claims, afford to speak very strongly. The immediate effect of the persecutions was not so deep as we might have imagined. In those days, when no medicine was trusted, unless it half killed before it cured, mere severity did not create the same revulsion of feelings that it would now. It was only when Foxe's *Acts and Monuments* had been set up in church beside the Bible, that the poor sufferers acquired the halo of canonisation, and the name of " the Martyrs " became a war-cry to their co-religionists.

The harm which the persecution had done so far, was that it had increased unrest and irritation and impeded the popularity of the Church, an object at which the Catholic Reformers should have aimed from the first. For the position of Catholicism had never been secure; and security, rather than rapid extension or rigid uniformity, ought to have been their first aim. Mary's health had always been precarious; the number of tumults and risings had been

---

[1] Francis Kett, clerk, educated at Corpus College, Cambridge, was burnt in the castle ditch, Norwich, 1589, for heresies, which affected, or seemed to affect, the divinity of Christ.—*D.N.B.*, s.v. Kett. James I burnt others. The last execution for heresy was in Scotland, that of Thomas Aikenhead, 1697.

disquieting; a possible counter-change from Elizabeth could not be lost sight of. How inopportune then the rigour which kept the two parties in active opposition at the moment when it was all-important to encourage the idea that the past was buried, and that the Church lands would never be reclaimed; when the only stable foundation for the Church (humanly speaking) lay in her acquiring wide and active popular support. Sander recounts that the Earl of Bedford mockingly thanked Bonner in the debates, of which more later, for having " by his zeal advanced the cause of the Queen's (Elizabeth's) religion." [1] Bonner turned off the sneer by the sincerity and generosity of his reply. That there was much truth in the insinuation cannot well be gainsaid.

Another misfortune which befell the Church at this moment was the unusually large number of deaths among the Bishops. It was a time at which a full and united bench of Bishops would have presented a front of great importance, round or behind which many waverers might have gathered. Now the Bishops not only lost their leader, Cardinal Pole, but before the year was out, no less than ten out of the twenty-six of their number who had seats in the Lords. Heath, Archbishop of York, who was left with the leadership, was not, as we shall see, the man for that very difficult post; and Bonner, who should have been the next in influence, was so unpopular that he, too, was ʾquite disqualified from taking the foremost place. In the rank and file of the Bishops we shall find much to praise. Their heroism forms the brightest incident in the sad story of the fall of the ancient Church.

§ 2. *The Enemies of the Old Church*

Elizabeth adapted herself so well to the work of separating England from the ancient Church, that many have

---

[1] Sander to Cardinal Moroni, *C.R.S.*, i. 39. The agitation against Bonner, though not unnatural, was also in part fictitious. See Phillips' *Extinction of the Ancient Hierarchy*, 1905, p. 320.

considered her, as it were, born to the task. This, however, ignores the years of her childhood, passed in " Henricianism," and her Catholic period under Mary. Either periods might, but for external and accidental causes, have been prolonged through life, and she probably ever retained some preference for her father's settlement of religion. Elizabeth was, therefore, by no means constrained, either by birth or by nature, to that particular form of Protestantism which she established in this country; but a tendency there certainly was to break with the old Faith.

She was born of a union which, according to canon law, then universally received, made the offspring incapable of claiming the inheritance of the father, and this incapacity is explicitly mentioned in the Bull of Excommunication against Henry passed in 1535.[1]

Cranmer and the English Parliament, at her father's desire, had gone much further than the Bull. The former had declared, without explaining his reasons, that the marriage was " absolutely and intirely null, invalid, void, without force, consequence, moment, or effect at law." Parliament had actually proclaimed Elizabeth to be " illegitimate . . . utterly preclosed, excluded and barred to claim, challenge or demand any inheritance as lawful heir to your Highness . . . anything to the contrary in any wise notwithstanding." [2]

If Elizabeth had shown resentment at the brutal way in which she had been treated by her father and his Court, Parliament included,[3] she would have had good reason.

---

[1] The Bull was dated August 30, 1535, but not issued till after the destruction of the Shrine of St. Thomas, December 17, 1538. Wilkins, *Concilia*, 1737, iii. 792, 840.

[2] Wilkins, iii. 803; *Statutes of the Realm*, iii. 658; 28 Henry VIII, c. 7, § vi.

[3] The treatment of the marriage of Anne Boleyn by the Irish House of Commons has a curious history. It had first to declare, as the English Parliament had done, that Anne was " the most dear and entirely beloved wife " of the King, and that " to utter anything to the prejudice of this marriage should be misprision of treason." A proclamation to this effect was to be made in every town of Ireland (28 Henry VIII, c. 2. *Statutes at Large, passed in Parliaments held in Ireland*, Dublin, 1786–1801, i. 80, 81).

But, owing to unforeseen delays, the Act only got through the Parliament of Dublin, while that of London was declaring Anne an adulteress and her marriage null. (Letters of May 17 and June 1, 1536, saying that the Act has passed. *Letters and Papers*, x. pp. 373, 426.)

But she could now make Parliament pass just such an Act as she pleased, whereas Rome was an independent power. No decree had been pronounced against her personally; on the contrary, there was every disposition to deal with her handsomely.[1] But the evil effect of her father's sin was not easily overcome. She felt compromised. To ask for recognition was not altogether pleasant, and the form in which it would be granted might not have been flattering.

Elizabeth, however, was at first prepared to submit to this ordeal, as we shall see; and this she would have done, partly perhaps from a feeling of necessity or convenience, partly because she was always inclined to a conservative course. These tendencies and instincts were strong, the controversies about her birth making her insist all the more on her undoubted royal descent and its consequent honours, which seemed best ensured by following custom and tradition. Such principles, however, so far as they went, made against a new religious revolution.

Birth, therefore, had not created an *a priori* impossibility of remaining Catholic, nor yet had the events of Mary's reign, though the latter had left many bitter memories. Mary was reported to hate her; and even if that was not true, there was no question that Mary had the greatest aversion to considering her as successor to the throne. It is said that Mary thought of having her executed, when the repeated charges of complicity with Wyatt and others had most vogue. The political morality of the day would

---

Upon hearing this Cromwell wrote that the King's pleasure was that the Act should be stayed, if not " thoroughly " passed. If it was so passed, the Parliament was to be kept in session till the King wrote again (*Letters and Papers*, x. 436; *State Papers*, ii. 330).

After this there is no further information in the Calendars. That the Act had received assent before Cromwell's letter arrived seems probable (cf. Letters of May 17 and June 1, quoted above). But as the Parliament was kept together for some time, there would have been no difficulty in another change. The printed *Statutes passed in the Parliaments of Ireland* cite this Act, as if it had never been invalidated. The Parliament Rolls should be consulted again, for it is evident that Anne cannot have been proclaimed according to the Act, when she had not a head upon her shoulders. It may be that, as Parliament left Dublin at this date for Kilkenny, the subsequent corrections may have got lost, and so omitted in the printed edition.

[1] See the next Chapter, § 1.

have condoned such an execution, and Elizabeth herself took her cousin Mary Stuart's life under circumstances less excusable.

Philip II of Spain, however, had interfered in Elizabeth's favour. He was most averse to the Queen of Scots, who was then also Queen of France, becoming heiress. But for this fixed idea of the King, Elizabeth's life would perhaps have been forfeit, or at least she would have been sent to Spain, or to some other distant country, and a different arrangement for the succession would have been taken. Philip, however, did not share his wife's strong aversion to her half-sister.[1] He cannot have believed in her being constrained by birth to Protestantism. Had he come over for his wife's last illness and death, and afterwards proposed to Elizabeth in person, instead of by proxy, there is no saying how great the effect might not have been.

If the Catholic party had been well organised, if Elizabeth had had one good Catholic friend and adviser, the resultant policy of the Queen would probably have been different.[2] When Catherine de Medici came into power two years later, when Maximilian became Emperor three years later still, the fear that they would turn Protestant was much the same as in the case of Elizabeth. On each occasion it was the people, the Court or the ministers who played the decisive part in the development of the situation. The mass of the people were in all cases in favour of the old religion, but in England, since the late religious troubles, their voice, and still more that of the nobility and the Court, spoke with little certainty. The final decision was taken in England by the Queen's selection of her Councillors.

This is not the usual conclusion of orthodox and popular

---

[1] Before Mary's death seemed nigh, Philip had proposed the Duke of Savoy as Elizabeth's husband, a fine match, which Elizabeth afterwards refused; but by that time her accession was looking much more probable.

[2] De Feria wrote on the 19th of March : " Cecil and Knollys have managed the Bills in Parliament for their own ends. . ·. . Cecil is a cursed heretic, and he governs the Queen in spite of the Treasurer (Parry) . . . who is not a good Catholic, but behaves better than the others." On the 24th of March, 1559 : " It is a great pity that the Queen has no one near her, man or woman, to advise her, except to her injury." On the 11th of April he added : " I, for my part, believe that the Queen would be glad not to have gone so far in the matter of religion."—*Spanish Calendar*, pp. 37–39, 45, 50.

Protestant historians, who generally consider that the initiative in the Reformation was wholly Elizabeth's. Lord Macaulay, for instance, describes "the opinion generally held by judicious readers" as amounting to this, "that there was not room in one Government for an Elizabeth and a Richelieu." [1] Many have described her predominance in still more ample terms.

Very different from this was the language of the English Catholics. Like the rest of their contemporaries, they were king-worshippers to excess, and it was natural for them to excuse their sovereign by laying the whole blame for the heresy on her ministers.

The truth seems to lie between these extremes. Elizabeth was a woman, and it was natural for her to govern through men, and to take her ideas on politics and religion from them. Her initiative was shown in her choice of advisers, and in her deliberately keeping to them. Sometimes she insisted on modifications, sometimes she would even stand out against them, and would have taken other advisers and followed a different course, had there been men at hand of sufficient capacity to carry out a different policy.

But eventually, as the crisis became grave, she would accept the advice offered her, and finally adopt her ministers' policy as her own. Thus in one sense it is true that the working-out of the Reformation was almost entirely the handiwork of others. But in a truer sense it was the work of Elizabeth. For not only was there eventually very little which she did not either know of beforehand, or authorise or support when done; but she deliberately, and from first to last, entrusted her fortunes to the hands of these men. This is what really decides the matter. Transitory, and sometimes unpleasant differences there were; but these do not affect the main question.

Thus it was that the fate of England was decided at a time and place unknown to us, when Elizabeth took Sir William Cecil as secretary and chief councillor. If the responsibility for the English Reformation lies chiefly with

[1] Macaulay's *Essays* ("Lord Burghley and his Times"), 1870, p. 225.

Elizabeth, Cecil was certainly the most active and efficient of her co-operators. Indeed, so ubiquitous, so decisive, so forceful was he, that it seemed natural to hostile critics to call him ironically " the King." [1] In our pages he appears, alas! almost always in an unfavourable light. Everywhere he is the instrument of ruin, the inventor of frauds, the agent of cruelty. Yet it would be an entire misconception to picture him as primarily cruel or fraudulent. The Count (afterwards Duke) of Feria, writing of the situation in England even before Mary was dead, describes Cecil to Philip in a few vigorous terms, which are worth considering with care. Elizabeth, he notes, though she had not yet changed her creed, " seems inclined to govern through men held to be heretics," and coming to Cecil, he writes his first impression (which, however, he modified later) : " They say he is a man of intelligence and virtuous, but a heretic." [2]

Cecil's intelligence needs no encomium here. As a thinker and a writer he was undoubtedly an eminent man, while his vast and varied correspondence shows him to have had a knowledge and mastery over all the details of government which is truly astonishing; and his foresight was not less remarkable, in its way, than was his insight into the significance of what was actually going on. Looking back at the length of his rule, the opposition he had to face, the complete triumph of the great revolution he

---

[1] " Cecilio che si puo dire Ré d'Inghilterra" (Arch. Vat., *Inghilterra*, i. f. 391).

[2] Kervyn de Lettenhove, *Relations Politiques des Pays-Bas et de l'Angleterre*, Brussels, 1882, i. 282. *Apuntamientos para la historia del Rey don Felipe II*, Madrid, 1832, p. 8. Baron de Lettenhove could not find this dispatch of November 13 at Simancas. In December de Feria wanted a pension for him (*Spanish Calendar*, p. 11), but Cecil eventually either refused, or at least did not get it (p. 59); and de Feria, irritable as usual, afterwards calls him, " maldido hombre," and " tan pestilential bellaco." Fuensanta del Valle, *Documentos Inéditos*, pp. 138, 157; *Spanish Calendar*, pp. 38, 49. About 1572, when the strife with Spain had become acute, a much harsher judgment was passed by Gerau Despes, then ambassador: " Burghley, a man of low origin, but very cunning, faithless, mendacious, full of guile. He is a great heretic, and so brutally English that he thinks all the princes of Christendom would not make a league that could injure the lord of this island. He therefore treats the ministers of other powers with great arrogance."—Teulet, *Relations Politiques*, 1862, v. 47. A modern writer says: " In a very true sense the reign of Elizabeth was the reign of Cecil."—H. D. Traill, *Social England*, iii. 311.

inaugurated, we cannot help seeing at a glance that he was a genius of a very high order.

" Virtuous " too in a sense he was, and it is important to keep this steadily in mind. Some of his triumphs were, to be sure, brought about by means that were mean and dishonourable. Still, broadly speaking, every one who had to do with Elizabeth and her Court knew that in an atmosphere of extreme worldliness and insincerity, of avarice and baser vices, he gave an example of religious and moral virtue, of humanity, moderate ambition and general honesty. If he did not escape blame, that cannot be thought wonderful, considering the immense ruin he brought upon so many innocent men. Still we notice in the chief books written against Elizabeth's Government, as the *Treatise of Treasons* (1572), *Leicester's Commonwealth* (1584), and the various answers to the Proclamation of 1591,[1] that the terms of reproach used against Cecil are far less condemnatory than those flung against Leicester, Nicholas Bacon, Walsingham, and other dominant politicians.

The following account by the ambassador next but one to de Feria, was written at one of those rare periods when the relations between England and Spain were friendly :—

" When I first arrived here, I imagined Secretary Cecil, judging by the accounts given me, to be a·very different man from what I have found him in your Majesty's affairs. He is well disposed towards them, truthful, lucid, modest and just, and although he is zealous in serving his Queen, which is, I think, one of his best traits, yet he is amenable to reason. He knows the French, and, like an Englishman, is their enemy. . . . With regard to his religion, I say nothing, except that I wish he were a Catholic, but to his credit must be placed the fact that he is straightforward in

---

[1] *A Treatise of Treasons against Queen Elizabeth,* s.l. 1572. The chief villain here is Sir Nicholas Bacon, who is called " the hen " (p. 89). But Cecil, " Suttle Sym " and " Second Synon," sig. i. 1; ff. 70, 74, 86 b, etc., is also very severely and powerfully criticised. This very rare, and hitherto almost unused book, the writer of which is unknown, is catalogued in the British Museum under " Elizabeth." See also *Leicester's Commonwealth* (catalogued there under " Parsons ") and the controversial works of Southwell, Verstegan (the most severe upon Cecil), Stapleton, Creswell, and Persons.

WILLIAM CECIL, LORD BURGHLEY

From the portrait by Marc Gheeraedts in the National Portrait Gallery

affairs, and shows himself well affected towards your Majesty." [1]

When Drake returned to England in 1581, laden with the spoils of a country with which England was at peace, Sir William Cecil, as the Spanish ambassador himself notes, was the only one to refuse the great sailor's costly presents.[2] The French ambassador likewise, writing to Mary Stuart in 1584, answering her warnings against Walsingham and Leicester, advises her to address Cecil, for "*il est à la fin le meilleur.*" [3] A more elaborate study of Cecil's character would not pass over his avarice, his vanity, his deceitfulness. But de Feria was right in directing his master's attention first to the better side of the Secretary's character; for it was the virtues, not the foibles, which made him so successful.

"*Pero herege*" (" But a heretic "), added the Spaniard, and he doubtless meant the exception to be emphatic. " Heretic " did not merely mean for him one who held the Reformed doctrines. In de Feria's mouth it also signified one who would stick at nothing to injure the Church which he had deserted. And such, too, was William Cecil. If in so many things respectable and amiable, he wished for nothing but war to the death in regard to the Church in which he was baptised and educated, and which he had joined again in manhood under Mary,[4] after having acted as Secretary of State to John Dudley, Duke of Northumberland, in his endeavour to oust both Mary and Elizabeth Tudor from the succession in favour of a Protestant claimant. He could, indeed, restrain the fanatical Puritans, who called for the blood of the Bishops, when it seemed to him probable that Catholicism would fail in any case; but his humanity ceased to act, when the Church began to

[1] Fuensanta del Valle, *Documentos Inéditos*, lxxxix. 71.   English translation, *Spanish Calendar*, January 2, 1565, p. 401.
[2] *Spanish Calendar*, 1580–1586, p. 75.
[3] F. von Raumer, *Elizabeth and Mary Queen of Scots*, 1836, p. 267.
[4] P. F. Tytler, *Edward VI and Mary*, 1838, ii. 445, quotes the " Easter Book of Wimbledon, 1556," now R.O., *Dom. Mary*, viii. 1, and shows that it " establishes on evidence that cannot be controverted . . . that he (Cecil) confessed (and received communion), with his wife, Lady Cecil, and he brought up his son, Thomas Cecil, in the profession of the Roman Catholic faith."

show signs of recovering again, in spite of the grievous injuries he had inflicted. There is no doubt that he cordially supported Walsingham's great effort to extirpate the old faith.

His special part in the persecution, however, did not lie in the execution of savage laws, but in drafting and passing them through Parliament, and in issuing proclamations or even pamphlets in which those infamous measures received a constitutional air and a look of specious plausibility. It was he who devised, or at least defended and developed, the use of " the bloody question," of which more in the chapter on persecution.

He had not played a courageous part under Queen Mary; nevertheless, he was a firm believer in the policy of doing violence to the consciences of others. Quite late in Elizabeth's reign, after the courage of the Catholic martyrs had inspired all Europe with respect, he could still write : "Papists, who, truly I know, being straightly pursued, are but cowards, like their father the pild priest of Rome." [1]

" Intelligent, virtuous, they say, but indeed a heretic," was he whom Elizabeth now made supreme in her councils, and by so doing ensured the eventual triumph of the new religion. For the time, however, they were both outwardly dutiful Catholics, and the old Church was still standing with apparent firmness throughout the land. She must be treated at present with great respect, and the first adverse measures will need much precaution.

§ 3. *The First Step in Schism*

Not long before Mary's death the Privy Council, warned that her disease was very serious, asked her to recognise Elizabeth as heir (November 6, 1558). Mary consented, and sent two of them to Hatfield to communicate this to her, requiring of her certain conditions, one of which was

---

[1] Strype, *Annals*, 1824, iv. 45.

"that she should maintain religion as she, Mary, had restored it." [1]

The precise words of Elizabeth's answer are not recorded, but they were at least very reassuring. To Philip's representative she recounted a day or two later that, "being questioned by the Queen (Mary) on certain points," she had promised that, "beginning [her reign] in whatever estate God granted, she would entirely and in all particulars act in conformity to your Majesty's will." [2] To d'Assonleville, who had already reported the "certain points," such an answer signified the fullest assent.

A fuller but later account is given in the *Life of Jane Dormer, Duchess of Feria*, who was with Mary at the time. Elizabeth is here said to have answered [3] :—

> "'Is it not possible that the Queen will be persuaded I am a Catholic, having so often protested it?' and thereupon did swear and vow that she was a Catholic."

Allowance being made for some unconscious colouring, due to lapse of time (for the words were not put down till much later), this report probably truly represents the strong assurance which Elizabeth gave of her Catholicity before her accession.[4]   Indeed, even if it be exaggerated, its

[1] D'Assonleville to Philip, November 7, 1558, in Lettenhove, *Relations Politiques*, 1882, i. 277; *Spanish Calendar*, 1558, p. xii.

[2] D'Assonleville to Philip, November 14, *ibid.*, p. 283. The Venetian ambassador at Brussels confirms this: "(Elizabeth) sent a most gracious reply." For Sandys' version see his letter (20 Dec.) quoted p. 19, *n* 3.

[3] H. Clifford, *Life of Jane Dormer, Duchess of Feria*, ed. Stevenson, 1887, p. 90. Clifford, who wrote somewhere between 1608 and 1643, adds that this is "confirmed" by the Duke of Feria's letter to the King: "He certified him, that she did profess the Catholic religion, and believed the Real Presence, and was not like to make any alteration for the principal points of religion." No precise quotation is attempted, and the words must not be strained. In the hitherto published letters of de Feria, however, no passage of this exact import is to be found. They go further than his letters written *after* Elizabeth's accession, when he was, even from the first, very anxious about the issue. But they may represent his view *before* Mary's death.

[4] It seems that Elizabeth never went through any form of renouncing Protestantism. Thus King Philip, when proposing to marry her in 1559, lays down (to de Feria) as one of the conditions on which he would have insisted, "She will have to obtain secret absolution from the Pope, and the necessary dispensation, so that when I marry her she will be a Catholic, which she has not been hitherto."—*Spanish Calendar*, p. 22; Lettenhove, p. 400.

Elizabeth always wanted to style herself "Catholic." Her treaty with

duplicity is still as nothing to that with which the Oath of Coronation was taken soon after.

The day that Queen Mary died Cecil wrote a list of *Memoranda*, mentioning, amongst other things, the sovereigns to whom special messengers should be sent, and first among these stands the name of the Pope.[1] Such messengers to the Pope at the opening of a reign carried messages of warm devotion and allegiance to the Holy See. We see, therefore, that Cecil himself at first contemplated going that far. But next day the *Memoranda* were re-written, and the name of the Pope was omitted. We must not lay too much stress on an omission, the circumstances of which are not definitely known. No great change had happened yet, but the straw shows which way the wind was veering.

Next day came the first of Elizabeth's Royal Orders about religion. They forbade any change whatever, and that under threat of penalties the most extreme.

" The Queen straitly charges and commands all manner our subjects of every degree not to attempt upon any pretence, the breach, alteration, or change of any order or usage, presently established within this our realm upon pain of our indignation, and the pains and penalties which thereto may in any wise belong." [2]

What could be more conservative and reassuring to the supporters of the old Church? The terms " pains and penalties which thereto (*i. e.* to heresy) may in any wise belong," might include even the now extinguished fires of Smithfield. Priuli, Cardinal Pole's Secretary (who notes that Elizabeth had " even before her sister's death evinced

---

France in May 1559 began: " Nos Elizabetha . . . in fide principis christiani, ac catholicam et apostolicam fidem profitentis." At the same time she told the Protestant Duke of Schleswig-Holstein that she embraced " the religion set forth in the Confession of Augsburg " (*Foreign Calendar*, 1558–1559, p. 218). Yet as late as the Proclamation of 1591 she maintained that her religion was " Ancient, Apostolic, Catholic."—Persons, *Philopater*, p. 273, § 297.

[1] *Foreign Calendar*, 1558, 1559, nos. 1 and 5.

[2] Strype, *Annals*, i. ii. 389. This proclamation is not to be confused with that of December 28 following.

her intention of not making any further change in the affair
of religion "), understood the proclamation as " an edict
announcing that the (new) Queen did not intend to change
anything which had been ordained and established by the
(late) Queen her sister." [1] But men soon learned how to read
between the lines. Though all change was forbidden to
subjects, the suspicion soon arose that the Crown did
not thereby mean to shackle itself. The Venetian envoy
wrote ten days later : " People interpret the prohibition to
change religion by private authority as a sign that it will
be done on royal authority. Not to be in fear is impossible,
for all the people about her are suspected." [2]

Next week (November 23) the Queen came from Hatfield
to London, and the Bishops went out as far as Highgate,
doubtless in pontificals, to welcome her, and swell the procession. Elizabeth stopped to receive their greetings, and,
according to custom, gave to each her hand to kiss. It is
said that she refused this courtesy to Bonner, and if it is
true, we may regard it as part of a plan to divide, especially
among the Bishops, those who might perhaps be won over
from those from whom opposition was to be expected.

Next Sunday (November 27) occurred what we may
regard as the first skirmish in the campaign. William Bill,
an ecclesiastic whom Mary had rusticated for his heterodoxy,
was sent for by Elizabeth to preach at Paul's Cross. While
blaming the excesses of the fanatics, who had always
abounded in London, and were now breaking out afresh,
Bill showed himself clearly unCatholic in doctrine. Next
Sunday Christopherson, Bishop of Chichester, mounted the
same pulpit and boldly refuted Elizabeth's preacher.
Elizabeth sent for him, and he was eventually committed
to prison, where he soon died.[3] As the Catholics took little
note of the affair, we infer that the cause of complaint was
the ordinary one, that is, the implied disregard of the
Queen's authority involved in answering her preacher.

Bishop White of Winchester was punished in a similar

---

[1] *Venetian Calendar*, vi. i. ii. n. 1287.
[2] *Ibid.*, n. 1293.
[3] Sandys to Bullinger, December 20, 1558, *Zurich LL.* Parker Soc.,
i. 3. Sandys describes Bill's sermon as preached " the Sunday after
Elizabeth's accession." But Elizabeth was then still at Hatfield.

way for his sermon preached at Mary's funeral (December 14). There was nothing in it which could be definitely blamed as injurious to the new Queen, but his theme throughout had been a warning against coming change, and this was considered " an offence." Finally, a proclamation was issued (December 28) forbidding all preaching, either by Catholic or Protestant, as the question of religion was to remain untouched until it was decided in Parliament.

Thus by degrees did it become more and more probable that Elizabeth would " settle religion " in her own way, though up to the end of the year the Catholics, it would seem, could not bring themselves to that unwelcome conclusion. " Until now," wrote the Mantuan agent, Il Schifanoya, the most penetrating and best informed of the Catholic correspondents known to us, " I believed that religion would continue, her Majesty having promised this many times with her own mouth. But now I see they are little by little returning to the bad way." [1]

While the Catholics, without a leader or a plan, were the prey of uncertainty, irresolution and fear, the Court, though keeping up an appearance of Catholicity, was making every preparation for the coming struggle. The first important step was to put into office as many of Elizabeth's known supporters as possible under the circumstances; and this was done so well that on the 14th of December de Feria wrote, with characteristic vehemence: "The kingdom is now entirely in the hands of young folk, heretics and traitors." [2] Another and still more important measure was to agree on a plan of campaign.

We have three of these schemes of policy, and they deserve our close attention. The Reformers, as men are wont to do who have long been out of office, describe the present situation in gloomy terms. Change will be beset with difficulty and danger, cannot be attempted openly, and may (according to the two first) take a long while to introduce. None of the schemers apprehend danger on the side of Spain or of Rome, though they do from France

---

[1] *Venetian Calendar*, 1558–1580. Dispatch of December 31, 1558.
[2] *Spanish Calendar*, 1558, p. 7.

and Scotland. The real difficulty lies at home, and is to be overcome by the use of royal authority; not, however, by employing rigour and cruelty, but by bending the constitution gently but firmly until the desired change is effected. In details there are many differences. Armagil Wade's *Distresses of the Commonwealth* does not go very far, but it opens out to us a view of the situation which is too often neglected. It is not so much religion which interests him, as its spoils. He groans over the poverty of the Queen, and feels "distress" that the meaner sort are too wealthy. He may be taken as a representative of the class who had risen on the plunder of the monasteries, and his chief anxiety now is to seize the residue of the Church property, which he proposes to do so thoroughly that Bishops and Archbishops would be left a pittance of 1000 or 500 marks a year only. For the verity of the new creed this Reformer expresses no care whatever. We are apt to forget that men of this class exerted very great influence in the Elizabethan settlement of religion.[1]

Goodrich's *Diverse Points of Religion* [2] is the work of a much more sincere mind, full of argument against papal supremacy, which, however, he would be very slow to resist openly. He would have been content to begin by repealing the laws against heresy, then to have the Litanies said in English, then to omit the elevation at the Mass, and to wink at a married clergy. Homilies should be read in the parish churches in lieu of sermons by Catholics, and some Catholic prelates and leaders should be sent to the Tower to frighten the rest. The Queen's agent with the Pope should be continued, but new business should be protracted and delayed until the Reformation had taken good hold. Goodrich's advice was adopted by Elizabeth in almost every detail, and Carne was for the time left on in Rome, but without anything to do.

The Device for the Alteration of Religion [3] is a more important paper still, and describes beforehand the policy

---

[1] Printed in H. Gee, *Elizabethan Prayer-book*, 1902, p. 206, from R.O., *Dom. Eliz.*, i. 66.

[2] Gee, *ibid.*, 202, from *Dom. Eliz.*, i. 68, also in Dixon, v. 28.

[3] Gee, *ibid.*, 195, also in Strype, Tierney's edition of Dodd's *Church History, Foreign Calendar*, 1558, etc.

of the leaders in graphic terms. With statesman-like vigour it begins by going straight to the root of the matter. " When shall the alteration be first attempted ? At the next Parliament, so [*i. e.* provided] that the dangers be foreseen and the remedies therefor provided." The success of the Settlement was undoubtedly assured by this bold and careful assumption of constitutional forms, here put in the first place. The writer, or writers, then go on to treat the problem in all its bearings and with careful attention to detail. For example, that " provision of wood, coals and drink, and two messes of meat, must be laid in " at those places where the " learned men " sit, who are to revise the services and arrange reforms. As to broader questions, the insular security of England is noted, and that no opposition from Spain need be apprehended. There was danger from France and from Scotland, but " by kindling controversy of religion," and " helping forward their divisions," these countries may be partially or wholly paralysed—a policy which was unblushingly carried out, and with complete success. From the Pope " nothing is to be feared but evil will, cursing, and practising." The chief end was to crush the opposition in England. The followers of the old Church must be overwhelmed *per fas et nefas*. They must be " based, discredited, and proceeded against . . . involved in the law and not pardoned . . . till they put themselves wholly to her Highness's mercy, abjure the Pope of Rome, and conform themselves to the new alteration." Nor must they ever again be allowed liberty, for whenever the occasion offers they will probably once more " maintain and defend their ancient laws and orders."

This hatred and resolution to destroy Catholicism is emphasised by the different treatment to be accorded to advanced fanatics, and to the unruly who might " conspire and arise " against increased taxation. The latter were to be won over by " gentle and dulce handling." On the former there was to be " severe execution of the law, at the first," which will " so repress them that there is great hope it shall touch but a few." But for the men of the old religion, even their children at the schools and universities are to be robbed of their faith.

§ 4. *The Coronation*

The final scene in the *Interim* period was the Coronation. On the previous day Elizabeth had made her solemn entry into London, and the pageant was significant both from a political and religious point of view. It showed that Elizabeth was a mistress in the art of evoking popular enthusiasm, and that she would appeal from the Church and from the nobility to the people. She stopped the procession repeatedly to receive, amid thunders of applause, a nosegay, or a petition, from some old woman in the crowd. She bowed to the bystanders, answered every speech, and held up her hands to those at a distance. At one point an English Testament was offered her. " But she, as soon as she had received the book, kissed it, and with both hands held up the same, and so laid it upon her breast, with great thanks to the city therefor." [1] The new religionists, who were numerous in London, and invaluable allies at this juncture, were, of course, ravished with loyalty and fervour ; and, indeed, considering Elizabeth's objects, what could have been more cleverly contrived or more happily executed ? The coming changes had been indicated, not emphasised, and the populace brought into a temper in which they would accept any creed their sovereign might impose. Catholics, however, saw things in another light. " In my opinion," says the Mantuan Agent, " she exceeded the bounds of gravity and decorum." [2]

The Coronation took place on Sunday, the 15th of January, and here the Queen played a part, the ambiguities of which go to the greatest lengths. On the one hand, she is the dutiful child of the Church, kneeling before its altar, obedient to its minute observances, offering her gold for its support, giving and taking the kiss of peace, swearing to maintain the liberties of the clergy conceded by Edward the Confessor. On the other hand, her chaplain ostentatiously omits from the Mass the sacred (but not essential) ceremony of elevation, and worse still, her ministers must already have decided upon those bloody laws, introduced

[1] Holinshed, *Chronicles of England*, 1808, iv. 168.
[2] *Venetian Calendar*, p. 17.

a week or so later, by which those whom she now swore to protect were reduced to ruin or misery, and might perhaps have been butchered on the scaffold.

A difficulty had been found in persuading a Bishop to crown her. Heath, who had proclaimed her accession at Mary's death, and was still of her Privy Council, now refused to officiate; so did his brethren. This refusal is the first sign of independence shown by the Catholic party, and must be remembered to the Bishops' credit, for very great pressure must no doubt have been brought to bear upon them. At last Oglethorpe of Carlisle consented, as Sander tells us :—

" Lest the Queen should be angry if no one would anoint her, and be more easily moved to overthrow religion. Nor at this time were things so desperate but that many hoped it might still be possible to turn her from her purpose." [1]

At Oglethorpe's hands then she took the Coronation Oath, and it will be well to recall its terms :—

Bishop. " Will you grant and keep, and by your oath confirm . . . the Laws, Customs and Franchises, granted to the Clergy by the glorious King St. Edward, your predecessor ?

Queen. " I grant and promise to observe them.

B. " Will you keep peace and godly agreement entirely according to your power, both to God, to the Holy Church, to the Clergy, and to the people ?

Q. " I will keep it.

B. " We beseech you to grant us your (general) pardon, to preserve unto us and to the Churches committed to our charge all Canonical Privileges and due Law and Justice; to protect and defend us, as every good King in his Kingdom ought to be Protector and Defender of the Bishops and Churches under their Government.

Q. " With a willing and devout heart, I promise and grant my pardon, and that I will preserve and maintain to you and to the Churches committed to your charge all

[1] *C.R.S.,* i. 31, cf. 35.

Canonical Privileges and due Law and Justice, and that I will be your Protector and Defender to my power, by the assistance of God, as every good King in his Kingdom ought in right to protect and defend the Bishops and Churches under their Government.

" This done, the King (or Queen) doth confirm that he will observe the premisses by his Oath, taken immediately upon the altar before all." [1]

It is, indeed, hard for us to qualify Elizabeth's duplicity over this oath with the severity it deserves. Taking it in connection with the new laws, which had been resolved upon in *The Device*, and which were brought into the Houses of Parliament so soon after the service, it reveals to us a mind whose perfidy and cruelty it would be very hard to equal.[2]

At the close of the ceremony Elizabeth's title was proclaimed as " Defender of the true, ancient, Catholic Faith," and she proceeded to hear Mass in state. When, however, her chaplains came to the consecration, they said the words aloud in English, at the Queen's command. Hereupon, as she had left the church at Christmas, when Bishop Oglethorpe had insisted on elevating, in spite of her command, so now the old Bishops withdrew from the Queen's service,[3] and after Mass a sermon was preached which indicated still greater changes to come.

[1] The *Liber Regalis* is reprinted by L. G. W. Legge, *English Coronation Records*, 1901. A comparative table of the Coronation Oaths at p. xxxi. That the *Liber Regalis* was exactly followed is agreed to by all historians. Elizabeth did not wish any doubt to arise later whether the full formalities had been used. It is also distinctly affirmed by Il Schifanoya (*Venetian Calendar*, p. 17). His authority, impugned by Mr. Bayne (*E. H. R.*, xxii. 650), is entirely confirmed by the restoration of the true text (*ibid.*, xxiii. 533). The short English account of the ceremony, though it does not give the words of the oath, testifies that the *Liber Regalis* was exactly used (Bayne, as above, xxii. 654, 655). Sander in 1575, *Lib. iii de Schismate* (MS. English College, Rome, f. 120), says that Elizabeth debated for some time whether she should take the oath, and finally took the advice of those who counselled her as above.

[2] Elizabeth could plead the binding force of her oath when it served her purpose. Thus, when asked by Maitland to confirm Mary Stuart's accession, she answered : " If there be any law against her (and I protest to you I know none, for I am not curious to inquire), but if any be, I am sworn, when I was married to the realm, not to alter the laws of it."— Pollen, *Letter of Queen Mary to the Duke of Guise* (Scottish History Society, 1904, xliii. 41).

[3] Episcopi affuerunt donec aliquid de ritu antiquo Sacrificii Missæ immutatum videbant.—Sander, 1562, *C.R.S.*, i. 7.

Elizabeth's Catholic period was closed. She had been "sacred" by the Bishops of the old Church, and she had nothing more to gain now from consorting with the orthodox. Never again would she use the ministrations of a priest in union with the Church universal. Schismatics and crypto-heretics would henceforth conduct her services. Yet the Roman Mass was still the official form of Divine worship, until such time as she made it treason to celebrate it any more. The reason for this is given quite frankly in *The Device*, § iv.:—

"It is thought most necessary that a straight prohibition be made of all innovation until such time as the book [of Common Prayer] come forth [from Parliament], as well that there should be no often changes in religion, which would take away authority in the common people's estimation, as also to exercise the Queen's subjects to obedience."

And for her Highness's conscience in this prolonged hypocrisy it would be sufficient, continues *The Device*, § v., "if there be some other decent sort of prayers or memory said [*e. g.* Litanies in English], and the seldomer Mass."

§ 5. *The Supremacy Bill*

When the authors of *The Device* resolved to make the alteration of religion "at the next Parliament," they knew beforehand that they could get a Parliament to carry out their plans, though the greater part of the country was Catholic, and though the Parliament, which had been elected only a few months before, was distinctly Catholic also. Those used to Tudor methods of government knew that neither people nor Parliament counted for very much. Once the offices of Sheriff, and Lieutenant of the Shire, and the like, were well in hand, all others could be controlled with little difficulty. It was not necessary in those days to bribe very heavily. The peremptory assertion that you had the Crown favour behind you was generally sufficient. Cecil had worked the machinery before, and the whole gist of *The Device* was that it must be worked again, and with the utmost vigour and enthusiasm. All those who had sided with Elizabeth hitherto, all " who are known to be sure in the [Protestant] religion, each one according to his ability," is to be " set in place throughout all England." " None such " as the late Queen promoted " to be on commissions of peace in shires, but rather men meaner in substance and younger in years (so that they have discretion) to be put in place. Lieutenants to be made in every shire, one or two men known to be sure at the Queen's devotion. Musters and captains appointed, viz. young gentlemen which earnestly do favour her Highness. No office of jurisdiction or authority to be in any discontented man's hand," etc.

There is, indeed, no specific mention here of packing the Parliament with party men. But if party spirit, and party spirit only, was to qualify for every " office of jurisdiction or authority," we could not conceive Cecil and his followers omitting to apply the principle to the elections of members of Parliament, when they could control them, to a considerable extent, with very little effort.

It will be noticed that *The Device*, while giving the greatest favour of all to " sure " Protestants, does not confine its party to them, but accepts any who " earnestly do favour her Highness." Cecil and Elizabeth knew perfectly how to attach such vigorous youth to their side, whatever their religious traditions and preferences,[1] and it was in this that their undoubted genius for politics was most clearly demonstrated. This also made the task of finding partisans infinitely easier. There was no necessity for pressing Protestant fanatics upon the electorate. Indeed, it would have been contrary to the policy of the hour to do so, when strict proclamation had been sent forth that nobody was to talk, or even " to give audience " to discussion of the religious problem.

The members who were eventually elected did not differ much in class or connections from those of previous Parliaments; indeed, nearly half of them had actually sat in one

[1] An interesting example of religion *à la mode* is offered by young Mr. Thomas Sackville, afterwards Lord Buckhurst. Compare the account given of him in *D.N.B.* with the notes and documents in *C.R.S.*, ii. 1–11.

or other of Mary's Parliaments.[1] And yet, when the questions of religion were mooted, they accepted the measures of Cecil and his followers with such alacrity that the defenders of the old order were at once reduced to a mere handful.[2] Exactly the same thing happened in the Lords, where only two or three (besides the Bishops) dared to resist the Government action.

It was an extraordinary change from the preceding year, but we are not to presume that there must have been much bribery or other elaborate malpractices in order to account for it.[3] The weakness of Parliament in Tudor times is notorious. It is not necessary to go further.

The next stage in the Reformation was the passing of the Supremacy Bill, which naturally overshadows every other interest during the next three months; for, when properly understood, this Bill gives the clue to the whole of English Protestantism. England did not leave the Church on a question of dogma, but of jurisdiction, though changes of dogma, of course, followed immediately.

The course of the Supremacy Bill was much more laborious and chequered than is commonly supposed. Dearth of documents prevents our giving as clear an account

---

[1] Bayne, *ut supra*, p. 645.

[2] The chief defenders of the Catholic side were John Storey, the future martyr (see Bede Camm, *Lives of the English Martyrs*) and Sir Thomas White (see Simpson's *Campion*, p. 5); Phillips, *Life of Pole*, ii. 144, mentions " Lord Montacute in the Upper House and Mr. Atkins in the Lower "; but this may possibly be a confusion for Mr. Atkinson, who spoke in the Parliament of 1563 (Phillips, *Extinction*, p. 223, from Strype, i. 263). The Catholic minority was praised by Harding, *Confutation of* [Jewel's] *Apologie*, 1565, p. 276, *apud* Bayne, p. 459. See also Camden's *Elizabeth*, p. 36.

[3] There is, however, a distinct tradition that the Government exerted unusual influence to introduce Protestants in large numbers. So de Feria, on the 20th of February, 1559, *Spanish Calendar*, p. 32. Camden says this was stated in Parliament by Catholics at the time (Bayne, p. 457). Sander, writing in 1571 and 1577 (*ibid.*, p. 458), gave it currency among all subsequent Catholic historians, while writers so diverse as Strype (Bayne, p. 462), Lingard and Dixon, all affirm it. Moreover, there is found also among the Clarendon Papers at Oxford a seventeenth-century note which states that lists of names of the candidates to be elected were sent round to the sheriffs, from which the electors had to choose. Mr. C. G. Bayne has examined this particular statement with minute care, and has arrived at the conclusion that it is " a fable " (*English Historical Review*, July–October 1908, xxiii. 455–76 and 643–82). Though this conclusion may be somewhat strained, there is no question that the Clarendon document cannot be true as it stands. Further than this it does not seem to me safe to go. The policy of *The Device* must make us most suspicious of Government influence; but the Government nominees need not have been all Protestants.

of its fortunes as could be wished, but we may say in brief
that it went through four different forms.

1. In its first form it was introduced by the Government
on Thursday, February 9, but was soon either withdrawn
or rejected at the second reading on the following Tuesday.

2. It was then remodelled by a committee of the
Commons, and eventually sent up to the Lords (February 22
to 25).

3. The Lords, however, cut out a very large portion of
the second form, and in this third form it passed both
Houses, and was on the point of becoming law, when
Elizabeth changed her mind and refused to sign it, March 15
to 24.

4. Again altered to suit her, it took the form which we
now know, passed the two Houses, April 10 to 25, and
received royal assent May 8, 1559.

These changes of fortune were not the work of the
Catholic party by itself, which was very weak in both Houses.
They were due to a variety of causes. To begin with the
new Supremacy Bill itself was at first a sort of "portmanteau"
measure, comprehending a good many sections afterwards
incorporated in separate Bills, and the Act of Uniformity
itself was presumably one of these sections. This com-
plexity was a source of weakness. The Uniformity Bill
divided opinions more than the Supremacy by itself.
Indeed, it would seem that the passing of the Supremacy
articles, in some form or other, was always a foregone conclusion, as Parliamentary parties then stood; whereas there
were many, including the Queen, as it was said, who preferred
the old religious rites.

Another reason for going cautiously was due to external
causes. It will be remembered that, though Elizabeth had
nothing to fear from the English Catholics, if not driven to
desperation, there was certainly reason to beware of
hostilities from Scotland, and France her ally, because of
Mary Stuart's claim to the English throne, a claim so strong
that Cecil himself in later years spoke of her having on
her side "the universal opinion of the world for the justice
of her title." [1]   The English Catholics, indeed, had not so

[1] S. Haynes, *State Papers*, p. 580.

far recognised this title, for she was already wedded to the Dauphin of France, a country with which England was at war. But the new religionists, and also the Spaniards, feared that they would change. On the other hand, if the war spirit should die down, if the new religion were to be imposed in such a way as to drive the majority to revolt, what was to prevent them in their desperation from transferring their loyalty to the Catholic princess who had such claims upon them? Finally, until peace with France was made there was the suspicion that the King of France might be actually encouraging a party of his own.

Thus there were many reasons why the Court party, and the Protestants themselves, should go slowly, and not insist on advanced Protestant rites, nor on the cruel penalties to enforce their observance which had been at first proposed. The Queen, too, was wavering, as we shall see, and this would be soon whispered in the House.

Influenced, then, by considerations of this sort, the Lords made great changes in the Bill, leaving, for instance, the whole liturgy much as it had been at the end of Henry's reign, or rather at the beginning of Edward VI's; and they eliminated the "many extraordinary penalties against delinquents." [1]

Elizabeth, we must also remember, was on the point of confirming this; and, as Easter was near, she wished to do so at once, in order that her Mass might be legally celebrated with communion in both kinds. A proclamation enjoining this service everywhere was prepared, printed, and ready to be sent out as soon as the Queen's assent should be given. [2] But at the very last minute Elizabeth changed her mind. It is hardly necessary to add, that if she had confirmed that form of the Act which went back to the first, not the second Act of Edward VI, the constitution, and perhaps the history, of the Established Church of England would have been considerably different from what they are.

This change in Elizabeth's mind was presumably due

---

[1] *Venetian Calendar*, p. 52. Dispatch of March 21.

[2] A copy of this proclamation is in the British Museum, G. 6463, from which it has been reprinted by Gee, *The Elizabethan Prayer-book*, 1902, p. 255. It can never have been issued, as it states that Elizabeth had already confirmed the Act restoring the settlement of Edward VI.

to her having passed for a time from the influence of Cecil to that of the Spanish ambassador. She had already intimated to him that she did not intend to take the title of " Supreme Head," and now he had been with her again, and had reproached her for failing to act up to her declaration that she would restore religion " as her father had left it."

" She knew her father had burnt Lutherans, whilst all those who were preaching now to her were either Lutherans or Zwinglians. She denied this, and was much surprised. I told her I would send her notes of the abominable and bestial things they had preached. She asked me to do so (and I have sent them). I think when I left her on that occasion she was rather kinder than she had been last time. . . . Next day I wrote, begging her not to take any step in the Parliament business until I had seen her again after the (Easter) recess. I am doing everything I can to lengthen the life of this sick man." [1]

Excellent as de Feria's intentions were in attempting to " lengthen the life of this sick man "—that is, of the Catholic Church in England—it is an interesting speculation whether it would not have been a less evil for the Church if the Bill had become law in the form in which it then stood. At that moment the Catholic and conservative influences had done their best, the Puritan influence (to use a term that became common later) was on the decline. But the latter, with Cecil to help them, had many chances of recovery, and at this moment two incidents occurred which turned out fortunately for them. In the first place, news arrived that peace was finally signed with France, and this freed them from dread of foreign complications. In the second place, an opportunity was found for involving the Bishops in a false position, akin to the bogus conspiracies in which Tudor statesmen so much delighted. The occasion was this :—

The absence of debating power on the side of the Protestants in the Lords had been conspicuous. Sander, writing from a Catholic standpoint, says : " The Lords

---

[1] *Spanish Calendar*, p. 44. The uncertain course of Parliament was complained of by Grindal, *Zurich Letters*, ii. 19.

temporal had nothing to say on any point. Though they confessed that they admired the Bishops, they always dissented from them, their reason being no other than this—that the Queen, so they understood, wished otherwise." Jewel, looking at the same thing, but from a very different point of view, says : " The Bishops rule as sole monarchs, and easily over-reach our little party." Then Jewel goes on to say that it had therefore been decided that the Bishops should now hold a disputation with some champions of the Protestant side, in order that they might not complain that they were put down by force. A somewhat droll idea, when one remembers the sequel.[1]

When the first conference opened at Westminster (Friday, March 31) the Catholics were told to begin, and this they did, though at some disadvantage, for they had had short notice, and the method of debate had been frequently changed, *e. g.* first that they should dispute in Latin, then in English; first by word of mouth, then in writing; at one time in private, eventually before a lay audience. They could not, therefore, get their paper ready in time, whereas the Protestants had everything prepared, and declaimed their paper " to the gallery," as we should say.

When the disputants next met (Monday, April 3) the Catholics had come prepared to answer the arguments advanced against them, and it appears from Jewel's letter that this had been previously arranged. Sir Nicholas Bacon, however, whom the Government had appointed to preside, called upon them to proceed to the next point, as if the first were now settled. The Catholics demurred, " and pleaded that this left an enormous advantage to the other side, who, after all, were the opponents only, not defenders of the doctrine in possession." Bacon peremptorily answered that they must argue " in the order appointed for you to keep," a decision which virtually called upon them to accept the royal supremacy over the teaching Church. Under these circumstances the Bishops refused to go on, and Bacon departed with the threat : " For that you will not that we should hear you, you may perhaps shortly hear of us."

[1] *Zurich Letters*, i. 9; and *C.R.S.*, i. 8.

It was not long before the Bishops heard of the quite incontrovertible reason which Bacon had on his side. That very afternoon they were summoned before the Privy Council. Two of their number (White of Winchester and Watson of Lincoln) were instantly thrown into the Tower. The rest were punished with overwhelming fines, amounting in all to £3380, with the additional humiliation of having to appear daily before the Council till further order was taken.

To justify such severity the Government took the characteristic precaution of publishing a pamphlet, which has been often reprinted.[1] Here we read the story recounted above, coloured, of course, as might be expected from Elizabethan statesmen, but they do not charge their victims with any other acts than those already recited. At the end of the draft Cecil added a sentence in his own hand, which states that the punishment of the Bishops was " condignly " inflicted " for their contempt so notoriously made . . . and for having obstinately disobeyed common authority."

In a similar spirit, Jewel treats the fate of the Bishops as a joke. Strype's comment is : " Thus gently did those Bishops and divines feel the displeasure of the Lords of the Council," and Sir Simon d'Ewes breaks into an exclamation of wonder at " the great lenity and mercy of this great Queen in not having at once ejected and silenced the heretical and obstinate papist Bishops." When one studies the circumstances and sentiments of the time one sees that there was nothing inconceivable in the Government's own story of its harshness. It meant to be exceptionally, not incredibly severe.

This severity was due partly to cruelty, partly also to fear. Cecil and his followers knew well enough that the Church had cause to treat them as heretics, and they probably induced the Queen to think that the Bishops meant to excommunicate her. The Government said that their " meaning was in part understanded," and what else was

---

[1] *The Declaracyon of the Procedynge of a Conference begon at Westminster the last of March*, 1559, *etc.* (Jugge and Cawood). Reprinted by Holinshed, Stowe, etc., and in Burnet, ed. Pocock, v. 524–39. There are also MS. copies at R. O., one of which, No. 53, is a draft with MS. corrections by Cecil.

D

the Government likely to have " understood " except the infliction of censures? As *The Device* shows, they had made this conjecture from the very first.[1] And no wonder. Similar surmises were then in the minds of many. It is not so much the surmise, as the acting with such cruelty and violence upon surmise that we must condemn. If the Government had had evidence, they would, without fail, have told the public that they had it. Jewel and others would have described it to their Genevan correspondents. If the Bishops had entertained the project of excommunication, that, too, would have been known. The excommunication of a sovereign and a Government is the declaration of war on a very large scale. To say nothing of other improbabilities, it is impossible to suppose that so vast a project would be resolved upon off-hand, in the course of a few minutes' public talk.[2]

The little band of Bishops having been thus publicly bullied and set at naught, the Supremacy Bill was re-introduced. Cecil stated that the reason why Elizabeth had lately refused to accept it was her humility, which scrupled at the title " Supreme Head." At this some of his hearers became a little restive. Why had they been made to declare the headship a matter of life and death, and clearly contained in the Word of God, if, after all, the Queen would not accept it?[3] However, as she was now not unwilling to assume the title " Supreme Governess," the Bill was ere long amended to her satisfaction, and sent up again to the Lords. Here the Bishops, in spite of the Government's tyranny, continued their courageous and unanimous opposition. The Bill, however, was of course carried, and royal assent was given on the 8th of May. The division of England from the Church was now an accomplished fact. The Act of Uniformity ensured the gradual Protestantising of the land.

[1] *The Elizabethan Prayer-book*, §§ i. iii. pp. 195, 197. It is true that censures were then expected from the Pope, rather than from the Bishops, and this was the normal course. But once suspicion on this subject was roused (and indications of this suspicion are frequent) every possible source would be dreaded.
[2] See note at the end of the chapter.
[3] *Spanish Calendar*, p. 52.

§ 6. *The Fall of the Old Church*

The passing of the Bills of Supremacy and Uniformity was immediately followed by their execution, and in a very short time the ancient Church ceased to exist as an open, organised association. True it lived on in secret, somewhat like the ancient Christians in the catacombs. Not only was it never entirely extirpated from the hearts of many, it soon began to revive by slow degrees. Never was it without sacraments and sacrifice and a priesthood united to the centre of Christendom; but considered as a visible, public, hierarchic body, with its ancient rites, courts, privileges and jurisdiction, it was violently suppressed, and ere long ceased to exist. If episcopal government was still in force, this was not in virtue of the ancient hierarchy, whose survivors were entirely cut off from their flocks, but by reason of the Apostolic authority of the Western Patriarch, who is Bishop in all lands, as well as Bishop of Rome. Hierarchic government, a system for the granting of spiritual jurisdiction and the like, would have to be built up again anew, and by the same Apostolic See which had sent Augustine to England of old, as we shall see in due time.

The day on which the new ritual was to come into operation was fixed by the Act of Uniformity for June 24, 1559, St. John the Baptist's, or Midsummer's Day. But the London churches were attacked at once, and none save St. Paul's could resist the onslaught. Even the courageous Bonner could only hold out for a month, and the Blessed Sacrament was removed from St. Paul's on the 11th of June. Bishop Bonner had already been pressed three or four times before the end of May to resign his See. He was then deprived, and took refuge in the sanctuary of Westminster, to avoid the annoyances with which he was now incessantly harried. When called before the Council he had maintained his rights with spirit and constancy, and he even carried war into the enemy's camp by exposing the illegality of the procedure against him.[1]

---

[1] Phillips, pp. 103–6, 311. Gee, *Prayer-Book*, p. 124.

This boldness was not without its effect. There was a little show of independence in the middle of June, when a large number of Justices were offered the Oath of Supremacy, which, however, was refused by many, and no immediate steps were taken against them.[1] There was for the moment a good deal of division even in the Queen's Council. Those who had hitherto compromised their Catholic and conservative principles, thought and said that matters were being carried too far.[2] But the Protestants were not to be denied, and on the 26th of June, at Westminster, no less than seven Bishops, those of Carlisle, Chester, Chichester, Lichfield, Lincoln, Llandaff, and Worcester, were deprived together. The hierarchy was already so reduced in numbers that this audacious stroke almost extinguished it. There only remained the invalid Bishop of Exeter, who was away from London (deprived August 10), and the three wealthiest Sees of York, Durham and Ely. A last effort was made to win their holders, but in vain. Ely and York were deprived on the 5th of July, and finally Tunstall of Durham on the 28th of September. He had been spared at first in the vain hope of persuading him to consecrate Parker.[3] Thus in the course of three months a violent end was made of the ancient hierarchy. The Bishops were all in restraint, under the custody of the new State Bishops, or some other keeper. Intercourse with their dioceses was henceforth impossible; an occasional message is the most that can have passed between shepherd and flock in this moment of sorest trial.

All things considered, the Marian Bishops must be said to have given an example of magnificent courage and splendid unanimity. Amidst general defection and tempting solicitations, in spite of the ever-increasing severity of the persecution, they stood manfully to their posts, speaking aloud, so long as they could do so, then voting uniformly against the new measures; finally protesting, without avail, at the injustice done to their rights and to their persons. We cannot detect any duty they left undone, nor any

---

[1] This was expected in *The Device*, Gee, *Prayer-book*, pp. 196, 199.
[2] *Spanish Calendar*, p. 77.
[3] R. O., *Dom. Eliz.*, vi. 41. See Gee, *Elizabethan Clergy*, p. 38.

cowardice which might have encouraged, nor any indiscretion which might have needlessly irritated, their foes. Their misfortune was that they, men of good, though only average abilities, were called upon suddenly to fight with Cecil, a political genius of the first rank, supported by the might of the Tudors, which no English statesman or party, however strong, had ever succeeded in thwarting. They were, in consequence, entirely outgeneraled and overthrown.

It must be confessed that in leadership they were deficient. We see no trace of plan, organisation or provision for the future; no alliances, no combinations, no idea of keeping part of their forces in reserve in case the rest were defeated. They do not know how to appeal to the people, how to make or lead a party. Sander records that before the Conde de Feria left England, he sent to ask Archbishop Heath what could still be done. The answer was : " Nothing can be done, but we can suffer whatever God wills." [1]   A Christian, a noble sentiment, no doubt; but not the maxim of a great and inspiring leader.

It is not, however, to be imagined that the heroic courage of the Bishops was fruitless and without any effect, though it failed in its primary object. To say nothing here of the Catholic elements remaining in the Anglican establishment,[2] which are largely due to the party of which the Bishops were the head, they at least succeeded in making Elizabeth's tyranny visible to all who had eyes to see. They could not prevent her wresting the consciences of her people, but they could and did frustrate her plan of keeping on the mask of Catholicism while she did so. This was much, for it was part of the secret of her power to pretend that she was always conservative, and always acted according to ancient precedent. Many were the misrepresentations circulated about the ancient Church, but no one could colourably maintain that the Elizabethan Settlement had been passed by the Catholics, though that would certainly

---

[1] *C.R.S.*, i. 15.

[2] " The pseudo-Bishops [*sic*] opposed with all their might the pious designs of the Queen, and caused many things not to terminate in the way that good men wished."—Parkhurst to Gesner, Phillips, *Extinction of Ancient Hierarchy*, 1905, p. 71.

have been done unless the clearest possible protests had been made.[1]

As it was, every one knew that the Church had resisted strongly, while still free to do so, though always treating Elizabeth's Government with the greatest possible deference. To some it may perhaps seem that they ought to have gone further, and have proceeded to pronounce those excommunications which Elizabeth and her officials so richly deserved. The Protestant party, no doubt, feared this, and Catholics not perfectly in touch with the situation might have admired it. But such a course would surely not have been prudent, for it would have been to pronounce sentence, in spite of a quasi-certainty that it could not be executed, but would, on the contrary, impede the restoration of law and right.

The Bishops appreciated that Elizabeth's power was overwhelming. The Queen and her ministers really feared the potential dangers that surrounded them, and their enemies on the Continent fully believed that the danger signals portended an imminent downfall.

But the Catholics who lived under her sway, and who saw and felt her power, had no such illusions at any time. To be sure they could not scientifically define the secret of her might—it is only recently that sea power is generally recognised and defined—but it has always been appreciated aright in practice by those who knew its results, as all living in England did.[2] Thus the English Catholic Bishops always felt clear about Elizabeth's great power, both within her realm and against foreign foes, and did not offer her the least cause for irritation.

While the fall of the Bishops is at least relieved by their sturdy devotion to duty, there is little consolation to be

[1] Thus the still-born Proclamation of Easter, referred to above, states plumply that the new laws had been passed by " the Lords Spiritual and Temporal," and the Supremacy Bill is still said in the preamble to have been asked for by the Lords Spiritual and Temporal, etc., though the Lords Spiritual are not mentioned afterwards. Similarly, in the Act of Uniformity, part of the phrase remains, showing that it was only dropped in the later corrections of the Bill. Gee, *Prayer-book*, p. 255; *Elizabethan Clergy*, pp. 9, 23.

[2] When Philip's envoy, Gerau Despes, asked Elizabeth if she did not respect Philip's power, Elizabeth curtly replied: " *Nescis quod domina sum maris.*" Lettenhove, v. p. vii, quoting B. M. Titus B., iii. 26 (*sic*).

found in the short, sad story of the fall of the clergy and the laity. Protestants, no less than Catholics, must feel ashamed of their immediate surrender. So long as they were at liberty their protests against the new religion were uncompromising, as the Convocations of March clearly showed. But the two commissions sent out to North and South by Elizabeth's Government in August passed rapidly round the country, and returning to town in October, could boast, and with truth, that they had entirely overset the ancient order. "The ranks of the papists," wrote Jewel, "have fallen almost of their own accord." Nowhere now could you see Mass, nowhere sacraments, nowhere profession of Catholicity. The great Church had collapsed almost like a house of cards; and, saddest of all, the great mass of the clergy had allowed themselves to be impressed into the enemy's army. Unwilling, but submissive, they read the schismatical homilies from the altar, at which they prayed according to a rite which in their hearts they condemned. There is no getting away from the shame of that great defection.[1]

There was also a minority which resisted with various degrees of courage. It is, however, very difficult to speak about them with satisfactory precision, so very defective are the registers and other records on which we have to rely. We cannot, for instance, tell how many priests there then were in England, nor how many actually subscribed to the Oath of Supremacy. Without security on these two fundamental points, all our calculations must needs be left somewhat indefinite.[2] Speaking, therefore, with intentional vagueness, we may estimate the total of the clergy in 1559 at about 8000, and of these the great majority, roughly about three-quarters [3]—that is, some 6000—accepted

[1] This defection may, perhaps, lend plausibility to the view of Father Persons, above, p. 5 note.

[2] For the fallacy that 9208 of the clergy took the oath, see Additional Note II. to this chapter.

[3] The figures given by Gee, *Elizabethan Clergy*, pp. 95–8, show 1453 signatures for five dioceses, London, Norwich, Ely, Coventry and Lichfield, Oxford. The number of clergy, however, is very uncertain; it would seem about 2200. This makes about two-thirds subscribe. But the subsequent visitations make it clear that some whose signatures do not appear in 1559 must have submitted soon after.

the changes, with the outward man [1] at least. Protestant inquirers calculate the number of those who resisted strongly and were turned out by violence at about 200; Catholic inquirers estimate them at about 700; in any case a very low figure. We may here rate them at 600. Then two approximate figures, 6000 and 600, will give us the classes we have principally to bear in mind. The Vicars of Bray, whose weakness led to such deplorable results; and the men of courage, who, though few, were not altogether despicable.

Between these come two groups, whose example, broadly considered, should tell on the side of the old Church. The first group were those who, on the one hand, were not so weak as to perjure themselves by signing the new oath, and, on the other, had not the courage to face the consequences of refusing it. They would simply have forsaken their charges and retired. The second group, though they yielded at first to violence, gathered courage later on, and forsook the dangerous occasion which had at first been too strong for them. This latter class must be added to the army of the Vicars of Bray, so far as concerns the first impression produced by their cowardice. But their subsequent retirement, or even return to the unity of the Church, would tend to counter-balance the original bad impression. The former group, though certainly wanting in zeal and devotion, did nothing actually wrong.

How many were they? We must not expect to find in the registers of the visitors any regular notice of these cases. As a rule the rallying priest's name would fall out without comment. In fact, Father Birt has counted, in the accessible registers, no less than 1934 unexplained disappearances during six years, 1559 to 1565. Deducting 700 or 800 for disappearances possibly due to other causes (e. g. deaths during six years, promotions to other dioceses, etc.), we may still point to 1100 or 1200 "disappearances" in the extant registers, a remarkable figure, inexplicable

---

[1] There were some who said Mass in private at home, and read the Protestant service in the public church. Allen to Vendeville, F. Knox, *Letters of Cardinal Allen*, p. 56; Rishton, the Third Book of Sander, *De Schismate* (ed. Lewis), p. 267. Persons, *Three Conversions of England*, 1603, i. 603, but he refers primarily to the time of Edward VI.

unless the two groups above mentioned had been extremely numerous.[1]

Thus a more minute examination of the materials, while it does not diminish the shame of the great defection, at least shows that cases of individual bravery, on a smaller scale, were more numerous than might at first appear. Two or three hundred of the clergy probably left the country, while a much larger number retired upon patrimonies, or pensions, or took to lay occupations. Only a few were active in looking after their flocks, in secret and without any organisation; and this gave the impression that few were left anywhere. But this was not so : they were living quietly in the background. As soon as a system was introduced some came forward again. As late as 1596 there were said to be some fifty Marian priests still at work.[2]

The Church had now disappeared as a visible, active, self-governing body. But every one knew that this disappearance was not extinction. It was in the interest of the defeated to hide; it was in the interest of Elizabeth's Government not to find more than it could deal with or replace at the moment. In private letters the Reformers fully confess that the Church was not at all eradicated from the land;[3] and no sooner had the first Royal Commissioners completed their work than a new commission was appointed to do the same work again more thoroughly. The task was only begun, not completed. All heads were bowed, like a cornfield by a tempest. If fair weather should follow, they would soon arise again. It is also to be remarked that we know the story from Protestant authorities almost exclusively.

---

[1] Father Birt, p. 203, following Simpson, thinks (and apparently with good reason) that the clergy who sooner or later refused to conform amounted to some 2000, that is, about a quarter of the whole.

[2] So Father Holt, S.J., Knox, *Douay Diaries*, p. 378. "Queen Mary priests" appear even during the Appellant controversy, which was later still.

[3] Examples have been gathered by Father Birt (pp. 140, 177, 178, 192), *e. g.*: "The whole body of the clergy remain unmoved . . . Of the clergy none at all range themselves on the side of the Reformers" (Cox, May 22). After the visitation : "If inveterate obstinacy was found anywhere, it was altogether among the priests, those especially who had been on our side" (Jewel, November 2). "The ranks of the Papists have fallen, almost of their own accord . . . but it is no easy matter (for us) to drag the chariot without horses (*i. e.* ministers), especially uphill." The complaints made by the Protestant Bishops in the ensuing years frequently contain references to "lurking" priests.

There were, as yet, no houses of English Catholics beyond seas in which the records of the faithful could be preserved. Had there been any such place, we should probably know many tales of individual heroism now utterly lost.

It is not to be thought that in their want of independence the clergy were notably behind their age. The prepotency of the Crown during the Tudor period over every estate is too notorious to need fresh demonstration. Too many instances of it have been alluded to already, and too many more will follow. The previous submission under Henry and Edward does, no doubt, explain much; but it is not to be forgotten that the Reformers themselves note with some surprise that the staunchest defenders of the Catholic restoration were those who had been most compliant but a few years previously.

§ 7. *The Laity*

The large majority of Englishmen were Catholics at the time of Elizabeth's accession. It was only in London, and a few other ports and larger cities, and in the counties that lay north and south-east of London, that Protestantism had any considerable following.[1] Yet even in London, the stronghold of Protestantism, with the Court actively favouring the new religion, the old nevertheless resisted until force was used. Il Schifanoya writes:

" The acts and decrees of Queen Mary and Cardinal Pole [*i. e.* the old legal safeguards and obligations to Catholicism] have vanished in smoke, but it is really surprising to witness the very great fortitude of many persons," etc. " Mass is said in all the churches in London before numerous congregations, who show much devotion. So it is evident that religion is not on such a sorry footing as was supposed [*i. e.* in the previous dispatches]; for everybody is now at liberty to go or stay away." [2]

[1] *Venetian Calendar,* p. 52; *Spanish Calendar,* pp. 39, 67; Sander; *C.R.S.,* i, 45.
[2] *Venetian Calendar,* February 6, 1559, pp. 26, 28.

There are some cases of courage on record. The Justices at first, as we have heard, generally refused the oath. The Universities, too, showed a good front, and are lucky in having had some one to chronicle their good deeds. Dr. Sander records that not less than 300 had resigned good posts at Oxford or Cambridge in the early years of the change. We hear, too, of individuals who acted with courage, like Dr. John Storey. But the list is not a long one. Perhaps the strongest resistance of all was made by Winchester College. Sander, himself a Wykehamist, tells us that after the imprisonment of Thomas Hide the boys continued to refuse attendance at the new services. Eventually soldiers were called in, from Southampton apparently. The main body then reluctantly yielded, but twelve ran away.[1] In a later chapter we shall find Winchester men taking a most surprising lead in the literary controversies of 1564 to 1568.

Nevertheless, the opposition of the laity was, on the whole, very faint. They raised no protests, organised no resistance, and looked on with little show of disapproval while the clergy were transferred in numbers from one camp to the other. Though they stood off longer than the clergy, it must be remembered that they were not exposed to the same pressure. Owing perhaps to the changes introduced into the laws by the Lords, there was, as yet, no necessity for them to take the oath. If they were office-holders, they would, indeed, lose their posts on refusal, and they would be denounced if they stayed away from church. But it would not be very difficult for the great country landowner in these first years to live on as before, keeping his priest in private, and disregarding the denunciations of the parson.

But no one, it seemed, could come within the influence of the Court without being compromised. The Lords were the most powerful estate after the Crown; very many were Catholics; and what little opposition was made to the new settlement, apart from that of the Bishops, was made by them. Yet how little it was ! De Feria did not exaggerate much when he said that " the Queen has the entire disposi-

[1] *C.R.S.*, i. 45.

tion of the Upper Chamber, in a way never seen in previous Parliaments."[1]

Indeed, so entirely were they enthralled, that Elizabeth actually put upon the first commission for administering the Oath of Supremacy to the clergy both Thomas Percy, Earl of Northumberland, and Henry his brother, the next Earl. Yet both these men were Catholics, and both eventually suffered imprisonment and even death, from which they might have freed themselves if they had then been willing to support Protestantism. Now,[2] however, they lent, without protest, the support of their authority to the overthrow of their ancestral Faith! The majority simply kept away from church, and waited for another change of the royal whim, of which they had experienced so many. Three creed-compelling sovereigns had died in eleven years, and the reigning Queen was far from strong. Or, again, she might marry a Catholic, for there was as yet no Protestant prince who was her peer. Again, the Catholics in England were so numerous that many thought there was no danger of the Faith failing.[3] But in the meantime, the new men held all the churches, all public education, all offices, and the irresistible forces of the Crown. Against such advantages mere numbers availed little from the first, and ever less and less as time went on; while, with a man like Cecil at the head of the Government, fresh measures were sure to follow for finally disposing of those who at first only meant to yield on a few points.

[1] *Spanish Calendar*, p. 32.
[2] Both Earls were considered, for this reason, as martyrs by contemporary Catholics (Bridgewater, *Concertatio*, p. 410 b). But even Lord Thomas's cause is not free from difficulty (*see below*, Chap. V), and there is much obscurity in regard to Lord Henry's death, which, by Protestants, is stated to have been suicide. Broadly speaking, however, there is no question that both were ready to suffer much, and did suffer much, for the Catholic cause in later years.
[3] " I am sure religion will not fail, because the Catholic party is two-thirds larger than the other. . . . Things cannot last at the present rate. . . ."—*Spanish Calendar*, p. 39.

ADDITIONAL NOTES TO CHAPTER I

I. *Alleged project of Excommunication at the Conference of Westminster*

So long as we keep to contemporary records the story is clear. But writers of later period have inadvertently opened the door to some not inconsiderable confusion, and this time the blame seems to rest with no less a person than Cardinal Allen. Lord Burghley had written in 1585 his *Execution of Justice in England,* and in this he had (quite inconsistently with the language used in 1559) made much of what he described as the peaceful spirit of the Marian Bishops, in order that he might depreciate the Seminarists, newly arrived from Dr. Allen's Seminary.

Dr. Allen, as he then was, thought it necessary to emphasise the other side of the question, and to dwell on the independence shown at the Conference of Westminster, and he hereupon asserted that some of the Bishops " were of a mind it should be good to use the censure of excommunication against her Highness and some of her leaders . . . but the wiser sort of Bishops, or at least the milder, persuaded the contrary," etc., etc.[1]

Not long after this, Father Persons, while revising Rishton's edition of Sander's *De Schismate Anglicano,* inserted the above words of Allen's into his new edition (p. 267 in edition of 1628), which became immensely popular on the Continent. Camden, a widely read man, found that this story was still unknown to his Protestant fellow-countrymen, as, for instance, to Haywood (*Annals of Elizabeth,* Camden Soc., 1840, p. 23), who wrote in 1612. He therefore inserted it into his *Annals,* published in 1615. From Camden it has descended to most Protestant historians down to Dr. Gee (*Elizabethan Clergy,* p. 32), and it is still supported by Bayne (*Anglo-Roman Relations,* 1913, p. 54), Father Bridgett having shortly before shown its legendary character in his life of Bishop Watson (*Queen Elizabeth and the Catholic Hierarchy,* p. 161). But none of these writers note that Allen is its source.

Allen wrote twenty-five years after the event, which he did not know at first hand. We cannot, therefore, accept his word as a contemporary evidence, and slow as I am to believe it, I cannot help thinking that he, or his informant, somehow took the idea from the phrase in the official report that " the Bishops' meaning in some part be understanded." Excommunication is doubtless hinted at here, and Allen probably combined this with what he did know, that excommunication rumours were then common. Far from regarding the project as a crime, he would at that time have considered it highly laudable.

It was a controversial age, and what is more common among controversialists than to argue from what is conceded? " Your official report," Allen seems to say, " hints at excommunication as though that were something too terrible to mention. On the contrary, we are proud of the Bishops who dare such things. You, then, cannot contradict my conclusions." Camden does the same. The threat of excommunication helped on his view. It was alleged by the other side.

Father Persons, as we have seen, at first (1587) only knew what he had read in Allen. To insert the passage into Sander with so little warning was a very unscientific way of writing history, but one which the age condoned. Rishton, the previous editor (see Lewis's edition, 1877), had acted even more unfortunately, for he had cut out Sander's own accurate account of the Conference (the text of Sander's original *Liber Tertius De Schismate* is at the English College, Rome) and left the subject in absolute silence. Persons was not wrong in introducing the subject, but his faulty method has caused us some trouble.

---

[1] Allen, *True and Modest Defence,* p. 52, reprint of 1914, p. 69, *apud* Phillips, p. 150. Latin translation in Bridgewater's *Concertatio,* p. 118.

When writing his *Memoirs* twenty years later he carried his defective method further still—he had meanwhile picked up some new details (conceivably from Sir Francis Englefield). He again combines them all into one, without specifying authorities for any. He now adds the name of one of the would-be excommunicators (Bishop White), and tells us that he offered to proceed to Paul's Cross and deliver the censure from there, a circumstance which cannot have been accurate (*C.R.S.*, 1906, ii. 59 ; Phillips, 1905, pp. 93 and 150). This story, however, has only recently been published from the MS.

Thus we see there is a tradition, both among Catholics and among Protestants, that is at variance with contemporary authorities. Such a thing is rare. It may be that further explanations will come to hand some day. But whether they do or not, we must not swerve from the only sure historical method—adherence to first-hand witnesses.

II. *Camden's Fallacy on the Conformity of the Clergy*

Camden seems to have been the first to offer definite statistics for the numbers of clergy who accepted or rejected the Settlement. But his method was utterly unscientific. Finding in Sander a list of 192 clergy who rejected the Settlement, he assumed (against Sander's own protest) that this must be the maximum which the Papists could claim. He also found a paper which gave the number of benefices in England as 9400, and he again assumed that there was a curate for each benefice. Then he contrasts the two figures, and infers that 9208 clergy had accepted the Settlement, a statement which has been, and is still, frequently repeated, as, for instance, by a scholar like Bishop Creighton.[1]

In reality, however, the number of clergy in England was far less, possibly not more than 7500, probably somewhere about 8000. (Birt, *ibid.*). And then Sander is not handling the question of clerical conformity, but he is treating in general of all whom *he knew* to have shown fortitude. In this class he names or enumerates some 700, 192 (or thereabouts) being the number of superior clergy (Bishops, Canons, etc., etc.). Yet this last number has been arbitrarily picked out as the number of *all* clergy who would not conform !

The honour for detecting the origin of this last number belongs, I think, to Mr. Gee (pp. 218, etc.), that of ascertaining the number of the clergy to Father Birt (p. 189). The information and tables given in R. G. Usher, *The Reconstruction of the English Church* (New York, 1910, pp. 241, 243), excellent as they are for the Protestant period which followed, throw no light at all on the Marian period. See also p. 96.

---

[1] *Queen Elizabeth*, p. 53, *apud* Birt, p. 188.

CHAPTER II

POPES PAUL IV, PIUS IV AND KING PHILIP II
(1559–1565)

THE last chapter described what looked to the outside observer like the sudden and complete fall of the Catholic Church in England. This chapter and the next will show us the first sparks of political life returning, after a period of utter lethargy. When a man has been felled by a stunning blow, his friends, if they be at hand, will run to his assistance and endeavour to revive him. So here, the Church being crushed to the ground, we see that the first to move are her friends abroad, the Popes and the Kings of the neighbouring Catholic countries. England's insular position prevents their doing much; and their own lamentable quarrels and rivalries—quarrels in which the Popes themselves take part—form a greater obstacle still. Nevertheless, they take the first steps, and that should count for much.

The English Catholics themselves play an almost entirely passive part. But the Bishops are still persevering, united and firm, though in greatly reduced numbers; and their constancy—ignored, insulted, persecuted at home—is abroad regarded with honour and as a pledge that the Faith will survive.[1]

§ 1. *Pope Paul IV*

Gian Pietro Carafa is one of the most disappointing of the Popes (1555–1559). A man of strong and austere virtues, it might have seemed that he had just the gifts

---

[1] C. G. Bayne, *Anglo-Roman Relations*, 1558–1565 (Oxford, 1913), treats this period in detail, and with great wealth of material. Though writing from an Anglican point of view, he describes Catholic affairs with insight and sympathy.

necessary to purge the Church of those corruptions which the excessive love of culture and luxury had lately introduced; nor were expectations altogether falsified in this regard. Where he failed was in want of moderation (usually so superabundant in the Popes) and in nepotism, allowing his nephew, the mischief-making Cardinal Carlo Carafa, to stir up that war against Spain (1557) which led to England being drawn into the war against France, to Pole being deprived of his status as legate, and to a general disgust with the Holy See. By the time, however, that Elizabeth was beginning to show her policy, the old Pope had discovered the greatness of his mistake, and was verging towards the other extreme—of doing nothing. He died in August, saying to Father Laynez, with a remorse which clearly exaggerates his responsibility : " From the time of St. Peter there has not been a pontificate so unfortunate as mine." [1]

Whatever truth may underlie this humble confession, we may at least nowadays absolve him from a charge which was freely made at the time among Protestants and has been frequently repeated since. It was stated that he had precipitately declared Elizabeth a bastard, if he had not pronounced her excommunicated ; [2] and that he had formed a great papal league for the extirpation of heretics.

Before, however, we look into these assertions historically, it will be worth while to inquire further into the nature and meaning of such charges. The excommunication of princes, and papal leagues against heretics, are—or at least have been—fiery, passion-moving topics; and as they will frequently recur in these pages, it will be well to take stock of them at once, especially as different and conflicting views about them were taken, not only by Catholics and Protestants, but also among different schools of Catholics.

The excommunication and deposition of princes who

[1] Oliver Manare, *Commentarius de rebus Soc. Jesu*, Florentiæ, 1886, p. 125. For his obstinate refusal to do anything for the legation to Scotland, see my *Papal Negotiations with Queen Mary* (Scottish Hist. Soc., 1901), pp. xxiv, etc.

[2] If a Bull had been then issued against Elizabeth, it would certainly have declared her heretical in the first place. But in this chapter we have to deal with a transitory period and confused ideas. The more general (though erroneous) charge is that the Pope declared against Elizabeth's legitimacy, but did so because she was a heretic.

had sinned enormously against God and man, was an outcome, an almost inevitable development, of legislation during those ages when the laws of the Church were most intimately united, like woof with warp, with the laws of the land. Here in England, as in every country of Christendom, this union was established and seemed permanent and immutable—one of the things every one took for granted; a postulate which entered into calculations of every sort. Trials for breaches of Church law were regularly referred to Rome in final appeals; and everybody was as interested in the execution of her sentences as they were in the execution of judgments pronounced in the King's Courts. Church law was the acknowledged, the efficacious international law of Europe. Regalists might indeed say: *Princeps legibus solutus est;* yet if he too could be sued, even in his own courts, still more was this the case at Rome. But if that were done, with the public mind thinking as it then did, there could be no logical stopping short, either between suing and judgment or between sentence and the execution of the sentence—although, in very extreme cases, that might involve the upset of a kingdom, and even its invasion by other Powers who were on the side of law. This, we note, followed, not as the result of some treaty (such, for instance, as the recent " League of Nations "), nor as a duty of religion. It was the natural, logical sequence of one great legal system.

Sentence in such extreme cases had to be severe, that is, one of *excommunication* from all the graces and privileges of the Church. This punishment, though it might be restricted to the delinquent alone, was generally extended so as to affect all the participators in the offender's guilt. In the former case civil life in the state would go on as before, in the latter all the ministers of the Crown would be affected; and the sentence tended to paralyse the government. This paralysis would be heightened if the kingdom were laid under an *interdict*. Then all the workings of the Church, in the service of the altar and the administration of the sacraments, as well as of the law, would cease, and an unbearable deadlock would be produced, which was likely to unite the whole state in a serious effort

E

to bring about a reform.   But since it was rare that subjects had sufficient force to coerce a prince, who had already won the upper hand and stopped at nothing to maintain his position, the only logical climax to the mediæval system was to *depose the tyrant* and to *invoke external powers to execute the sentence.*   There are in all between twenty and thirty cases on record of such extreme measures having been taken in Europe during the Middle Ages.   The case of King John, in our own history, may be taken as a fair sample of the class.

It is important to notice that these punishments were not deductions from religious dogma : they were legal measures, and they could only remain in honour and efficiency while Christendom was united in honouring and sustaining one system of law—that is, canon law—as Western Europe did all through the Middle Ages.   Men might, while retaining one Faith, have rejected the unity of the Church's legal system.   Indeed, they were on the way to do so by the time of the Reformation, though that evolution was not yet complete.   National systems of law were growing independent and jealous of each other and of a superior ecclesiastical jurisdiction.   Then, as canon law began to suffer eclipse, the ordinary layman in time lost his esteem for canon law as a great and important system, and the sentences of the canon law lost power to move the many.   One might respect sentences of canon law sincerely ; but the feeling that one ought to risk everything for their execution died down and passed away ; and when that state of mind became general, the deposition of princes had become automatically a matter of the past. It was not that the power to pass such sentences had been intermitted or given up by the Church.   It was that the international legal system had become suspended with the passing away of the universal voluntary acceptation of the old code.[1]

At the period at which we have arrived, the process of change was not complete, but it had made very great advances ; and, in consequence, there was much variety of

---

[1] On the authority of canon law, even in England, see Maitland's Essays, *Roman Canon Law in the English Church*, 1898, also *English Historical Review*, 1901, p. 44.

opinion. The Renaissance had led to disrespect for canon law, on the plea of its being Gothic and out of fashion; while enthusiasm for the classics had led to the veneration of Roman law, with its idea of the State and secular ruler being absolute. The Reformation, too, suggested and encouraged the idea of absolutism in every kingdom, the growth of which idea naturally tended to weaken the prestige of a central ecclesiastical authority. We shall find Philip of Spain and other Catholic sovereigns still upholding the ideal of excommunication and deprivation, but not with the old fervour and confidence in its general acceptance. In their minds it was not to come into play until some Catholic sovereign had established his superiority by force over the heretics. After this, the spiritual arm would appropriately come in to give the *coup de grâce* to a defeated foe. To every other use we shall find them strongly averse. Whether in this they were right or wrong, their attitude at least shows that the old respect for the sentence was in full decline.

On the other hand, there were also some who, in their zeal to revenge the work of the Reformation, were prone to look back to mediæval times even for the practical remedies to be applied to their own. Thus we shall frequently find good, zealous Catholics, especially when not in touch with the actual state of affairs in those countries where the Reformation was spreading, who thought that the excommunication of the Prince was the palmary remedy for the evils of the day, and who regarded the caution of those who were in contact with the Reformers as somewhat worldly and reprehensible.

The Popes occupy a midway position. They believed in the remedy, as Paul IV plainly showed by his Bull *Cum ex Apostolatus*.[1] On the other hand, they were well aware that in those autocratic days, and, of course, in lands which were half or wholly Protestant, the old reverence for canon

---

[1] This Bull, dated February 16, 1559, declared that all heretical sovereigns fell from their right by the mere fact of their heresy. This was, however, general legislation, intended for all Catholic countries. The fact of heresy would have to be proved in each case, before the law could be applied to any particular prince. The Bull was not a personal sentence against any individual, as, for instance, Elizabeth. But coming, as it did, so near her accession, it may have been represented as aimed at her.

law had greatly diminished or ceased. A sentence of excommunication could, therefore, as a rule, only be executed
by some neighbouring monarch or monarchs.[1] Without their
knowledge and assistance, no such thing could be attempted;
for the attempt would, to say the least, only make the
eventual execution more difficult.

Though the punishment of excommunication was retained
by the new religionists, and was even sharpened by Elizabeth's Government, we cannot wonder at Protestants, in
their intense hatred for the Popes, misconceiving and mis-
representing many parts of the papal discipline in this
matter. Excommunications were issued, according to
Protestant reports, with a frequency far in excess of truth,
and on the lightest grounds. Again, they believed that
Catholics regarded them as dogmatic, sacrosanct, religious
decrees, whereas they were legal sentences only, which
depended on evidence, were liable to many exceptions, and
did not in any way affect the infallibility of the Church as a
judge of dogma.

Finally, Protestants of that day indulged in a curious
exaggeration as to the method by which excommunication
would be executed. The idea of *a papal league for the
extirpation of Protestants* has now fallen into desuetude,
but at the time which we are studying it was much in
vogue, one of the stock political cries for exciting Protestants
to a warlike mood.

The reader will remember that in mediæval times foreign
princes did, on some occasions, combine for the execution
of sentences of excommunication. The violent suspicions
of the sixteenth century were at work, in season and out of
season, conjuring up the possibility (which was called an
ascertained fact) that some new confederacy had been made
between Catholic princes, and that the allies were about
to take the field against the followers of the Gospel.

It is not my object to maintain that this suspicion of
leagues was unnatural and incomprehensible; perhaps it
was just the contrary. But few, however, who have not

---

[1] We shall see that Pius V passed his sentence relying on information
that the Rising of the North was imminent, and he hoped for aid from Alva.
Sixtus V passed no sentence at the time of the Armada, because he waited
to know the success of the Spanish arms.

looked into the subject, can realise now how frequent, how wide of the mark, those rumours were in all countries where the Reformation held sway.[1]

Catholics may have been equally unreasonable in their apprehensions; but they were not likely to adopt rumours of Protestant leagues as their popular bugbear, because Protestants differed so much one from another. On the other hand, Catholics being at one on so many points, it was not unnatural for non-Catholics to regard with special dread the possibility of alliances between them.

Negatives are always difficult to prove, and it may not be easy to disprove the existence of this or that alleged Catholic league. As historians, however, we are bound not to believe in the existence of any confederation of nations, when an examination of their respective archives gives no ground whatever for suspecting that such a league had been formed. Leagues of this nature are necessarily preceded by, and accompanied with, much negotiation. It follows, therefore, that we must now, when the archives of all nations are open to inspection, regard as apocryphal all alleged papal leagues of Catholic Powers for the extirpation of Protestants. They rest only on the allegations of religious or political adversaries without support from contemporary diplomatic papers.

With these explanations before us of the ideas then prevalent in regard to excommunications and to papal leagues for their execution, we may return to the history of Paul IV, and to the prevalence of such ideas in his time.

At the moment of Elizabeth's accession, as we have heard, Cecil had intended to send a special envoy to the Pope, but this plan was soon given up. Goodrich had advised that Sir Edward Carne, who was already in Rome as Mary's ambassador, should be left there to send advertisements, but that no new powers should be given him.[2] This advice was not followed to the letter, for a message to the Pope, hinting at a new agent to be sent to him, was

[1] I have mentioned several belonging to this period in the *Month*, March 1901, *Mary Stuart and the Great Papal League*.

[2] Gee, *Prayer-book*, p. 206.

posted on the 20th of December. But when, on the 31st, Carne requested his recall, an order to return was dispatched, on the 9th of February.[1] Before he received this, however (March 10), the Pope had already heard of Elizabeth's first steps in schism, and spoke angrily to Carne on the subject (March 27), forbade him to leave Rome, and appointed him (as his commission from England had run out) to be Warden of the English Hospice at Rome.

Meantime, France and Spain, energetic rivals for predominance in the Papal Court, were taking part in the English question, each urging their own interests, though neither desired to push the matter to an immediate decision. Philip, who was offering to marry Elizabeth,[2] desired to keep the Pope in a conciliatory mood, while Henri of France, who felt keenly the preponderance which Spain had won by the English alliance during Mary Tudor's reign, was anxious to prevent the proposed match. His commission to his ambassador at Rome was confined to this point, and on it the ambassador's letter, of the 25th of December, must have reassured him. This assurance was not long after turned to certainty, by Philip proposing to marry Henri's own daughter, Elizabeth of France, the engagement being published in March.

Then there was also the question of the right of Mary Queen of Scots to the English throne, or at least to be declared heiress to the Crown. We may take it for certain that the French urged this upon the Pope. But unfortunately we have no official information as to the extent of the French claim, or as to the papal answer.

So far we see that the Pope has been distinctly forbearing on the subject of Elizabeth's heterodoxy. But it is difficult to make out what followed. When Philip's engagement to Elizabeth of France was known, the ostensible reason for moderation to the English Queen was gravely

---

[1] B. M. Cottonian MSS., Caligula, B. IX. f. 208; *Foreign Calendar*, 1558-1559, nn. 161, 333; Tierney's Dodd, *Church History of England*, vol. iv. advert. vi., vii. Lingard does not notice the message sent on the 20th of December. Its tenor, however, is not known. It may be that the Government empowered Carne to continue urging the Chetwood marriage case in accordance with 1 Eliz., c.l., fin.

[2] But no formal application to do so had been made yet (*Spanish Calendar*, p. 23).

affected, and it was likely that so frank a man as Paul IV would say this at once to Cardinal Pacheco, Philip's ecclesiastical representative at Rome. " He was certainly angry with Elizabeth," wrote Carne on the 27th of March, "because of her leaving his obedience, as he was now informed."

Paul accordingly opened up the question of Elizabeth's deposition to the Spaniard, and " desired to proceed against her immediately, to deprive her of her kingdom, and to give the investiture of it to King Philip." This is Philip's story; but he sent to beg the Pope that for the time he should neither declare her a heretic nor deprive her, and " put before him such reasons that he suspended the business." Moreover, Paul wrote direct to Philip and told Pacheco by word of mouth that he was " very satisfied, and would expect my information, and be as reserved as possible, without prejudice to his authority."

These are not the Pope's own words, which have not so far been brought to light, but their general authority cannot be gainsaid, for they are taken from two letters of King Philip sent back to Cardinal Pacheco himself later on.[1] It is not possible to question the general reliability of such statements, the more so as there are no official letters which weaken their force. They must, therefore, be maintained, even though this lead us to refuse credit to the very persistent rumours that proceedings against Elizabeth had been an affair of the French, not of the Spaniards, and that they had actually obtained a sentence against her. Cecil went so far as to assert this strongly in a State paper addressed to the Privy Council. But this and similar statements are all ultimately based on hearsay, whereas Philip's words show us that the negotiations followed a different line. The French diplomatic papers (which support the Spanish) will be discussed immediately, but first we must follow the interchange of ideas between Paul IV and King Philip.

Paul IV, we see, thought that the excommunication and deposition of Elizabeth would be a necessity, and that the sooner it could be done with justice the better. That was a common opinion; we find it in the only letter from

[1] Philip to Cardinal Pacheco, Frexelingas (? Flushing), August 22, 1559, and Madrid, July 16, 1561. Simancas MSS., printed by Mignet, *Marie Stuart*, i. 402, 404.

England to the Pope which has come down to us.[1] Cecil
had taken it as a matter of course in one of the first State
papers of the reign.[2] Nevertheless, Paul, abrupt and fearless of consequences as he ordinarily was, has not taken the
step. He has asked King Philip if he shall take it, and
when the King will execute the sentence. Philip refused.
On the 24th of April, as soon as he had received his
ambassador's letter, he wrote urging the Pope to continue
his previous passive attitude.[3] Here again the Pope's
answer is not available, but the summary of it given by the
King himself cannot be questioned. His Holiness declared
himself satisfied with King Philip's plan, and that he would
await the issue of the Spanish negotiations before going any
further. Philip's report on his negotiations was sent from
Belgium on the 22nd of August (quoted above), but the
Pope had sickened and died on the 18th, before the dispatch
could have reached Rome. This correspondence brings us
nearer to the inner minds of the persons chiefly concerned
than any other papers yet available; and the conclusion
from it clearly is that excommunication was talked of
indeed, but never decided upon.

The French Government was not aware of the above
negotiations between Philip and the Pope; and so the
French diplomatic papers cannot be expected to support
the above evidence directly. Indirectly, however, they do,
in so far as they give no support to the popular English
account of strong measures having been taken by France
against Elizabeth at Rome. If she had indeed been deposed
and Mary invested with her kingdom by a Bull, that would
have involved war on a large scale, and we should inevitably
have found ample evidence of it in the French diplomatic
dispatches of the times. In point of fact, however, the
great French scholars and writers who have investigated

---

[1] "Spes nostra post Deum sita est in patre nostro sanctissimo, pastore
nostro, Romano Pontifice, ut ille . . . cum omni festinacione et auctoritate
sua precipiat reges christianissimos, videlicet regem francorum ac regem
philippum opem ferre fidelibus Anglis," etc. [This plainly involves the
deposition of the Queen, though the excommunication is not asked for
specifically.]—MS. *Deflebilis status Anglicanæ gentis*, Jesuit Archives,
Anglia Historica, i. 57.

[2] *Device for the Alteration of Religion, Foreign Calendar*, 1558, p. 19.

[3] Philip gave a summary of this letter to de Feria at the time he wrote
it. *Spanish Calendar*, p. 61.

this period—De Thou, Le Laboreur, Ribier, in earlier times, and later on A. Teulet, Le Croze, De Ruble, L. Paris, De Bouillé, A. Chéruel, H. de la Ferrière—have not come upon any evidence of such a design. On the contrary, M. Mignet, while studying this subject, has collected and published the papers showing how the excommunication was suggested to Philip, but rejected by him.[1]

Another strong argument might be drawn from Henri's conduct in regard to the war in Scotland, so important for France. If we listen to the English, or to the Spanish, who were both in this case the enemies of France, we should believe that Henri was ready to make every sacrifice in order to prosecute the war. If we turn to French State papers, we shall see that Henri was entirely bent on compromise, and would hardly bring himself to face the possibility of a new war.[2] If in June the French King was intent on nothing but compromise, delay and pacification in dealing with the smaller troubles of Scotland, what likelihood was there that in February or March, when his exhaustion had been greater, he would have solicited or welcomed the incomparably more difficult task of invading England? We should also remember that the French navy had been practically swept from the seas by the English in the late war, as Henri himself confessed to Elizabeth.[3] Under the circumstances we can hardly believe that the French did more than obtain from the Pope the promise that he would admit nothing to the prejudice of Queen Mary's title.

Finally, what explanation can be given of Cecil's statements? He was too clever to speak without some founda-

---

[1] Mignet, *Marie Stuart*, pp. 399–404. It is unfortunate that the correspondence of Henri II with Babou de la Boudaiserie, his ambassador in Rome, is not fully explored. De Thou and Ribier quote from it and Mr. Bayne prints three further letters of importance. But until the negotiations are adequately set forth, we cannot tell what the French actually did do in Rome during this period. We may be sure they would have lost no opportunity of protecting the interests of Mary Stuart and of preventing the aggrandisement of Spain. I have examined a collection of transcripts of Babou's letters covering this period, but found no reference to any Bull of Deprivation. Turin, Archivio di Stato, *Raccolta Balbo Seniore*, n. 276. There is another collection of his letters, Paris, *Bibliothèque Nationale*, 500 *de Colbert*, n. 343.

[2] This is clearly shown by the documents quoted in *Papal Negotiations with Mary Stuart*, pp. xxxii–xxxvi.

[3] *Foreign Calendar*, 1558, p. 52.

tion, and in this case there had been the speeches of the French deputies, when treating about the peace of Cateau-Cambrésis, declaring for Mary's rights, which some said should be urged at Rome; and Carne too had written from that city several times, that the French were working towards the same object, at first unsuccessfully, afterwards (March) with some success, though he could not discover the details. De Feria, moreover, had spoken of Philip's "good offices with the Pope in order that he should not proceed against her." [1]

With this and other information of the same sort before him, Cecil wrote in an instruction for the English ambassador in Spain, of " the quarrels at Cateau-Cambrésis, and of the French practices with Paul IV against Elizabeth's right to the crown of England, in both of which she thanks Philip for his earnest and brotherly friendship." [2] But in a paper drawn up in order to urge the Queen and Privy Council to make war upon the French in Scotland, he bade them remember " what means they made at Rome to have the Queen's Majesty declared illegitimate, is manifest, and so, as it is known, that the same sentence is brought into France under the Pope's Bull." [3] On the 8th of April, 1560, a proclamation was issued containing the same statements, except that no mention is made of a Bull. It might, indeed, be that this omission was made to save the Queen's honour, but it is more likely that Cecil here felt uncertain of his ground. If he did so, we can now see that he acted with his usual sagacity; if he only omitted the words out of consideration for the Queen, he was either entirely misinformed, or else perhaps he had in mind some reports about the Bull *Cum ex Apostolatus*, already referred to.

It is impossible to look on Paul IV's pontificate without being struck by the great confusion then rife, of thought, of standards, of rumours. The world was changing rapidly. No one knew what to expect next, whose word could be trusted. Old traditions were passing; new ones were being formed. History was being made rapidly, but its records

---

[1] *Spanish Calendar*, April 29, 1559, p. 62.
[2] *Foreign Calendar*, 1559–1560, p. 316 (January 1560).
[3] *Ibid.*, 1558–1559, p. 521, repeated briefly p. 524.

how confused, how often false ! Two of these historical
fictions need mention here, for they have been frequently
repeated ; and as they probably originated spontaneously
out of the welter of true and erroneous ideas then current,
they are not wanting in a certain appearance of truth.   One
of these relates to the Pope, and tells us that when Paul IV
heard of Elizabeth's accession he sent for her representative
and imperatively required that his mistress should forth-
with submit her right of accession to his arbitrament; that
Elizabeth brought this before her nobles, who at once refused
the test, and the change of religion was therefore introduced.
As there is no doubt that Paul IV was sometimes both
high-handed and imprudent, this story gained considerable
credence, among Catholic as well as Protestant writers, and
was quoted by Cardinal Pallavicino and by Rinaldi, the
continuator of Baronius, as well as by von Ranke.
Lingard did so too, in his earlier editions, but then it was
found that the above story was a mere travesty of
the facts of the case. Paul had, in fact, been quite
moderate; the initiative in the Reformation was altogether
Elizabeth's own.[1]

The second popular fiction was of different origin.   It
was not based on any shrewd knowledge of the parties
concerned ; it only won its wide popularity because
it appealed to the incredible hatred for Rome current
among the Reformers. They took it for granted that
Catholics must be always plotting the slaughter of the
Gospellers. Accordingly, when the Catholic powers combined to make peace at Cateau-Cambrésis, the rumour went
abroad in Reformed countries that a great league had been
formed for the extirpation of Protestants, and the story
has been popularised amongst us through *Melville's Memoirs*,[2]

[1] The story is first found in the Protestant Paolo Sarpi (Polaco
Soave), *History of the Council of Trent* (London, 1620, p. 411), though it
may be older.   It has had a very wide vogue, and impressed the great
Italian historian L. A. Muratori so much that he declared that he " turned
cold " every time he read of the Pope's " inopportune unearthing of his
odious pretensions " (*Annali d'Italia*, x. 318). A long list of errant
historians will be found in Tierney's edition of Dodd's *Church History*
(iv. advertisement), who was the first to publish its refutation.   See also
Maitland, *English Historical Review*, xv. 324, *Queen Elizabeth and Paul IV*
(April 1900), and the *Month*, October 1900.
[2] *Sir James Melville's Memoirs*, Bannatyne Club, 1827, p. 76; *L'Apologie
de M. d'Orange*, Leyden, 1583, p. 53.

and other contemporary writers. When allowance is made for the fierce feelings of the time, there may not be much to wonder at in the origin of such popular rumours. But in that case the blame that rests on our historians is increased, for so often crediting a story whose unreliability they ought always to have suspected.[1]

§ 2. *The Spanish Alliance Fatal to France*

One unexpected consequence of the late extraordinary changes, was that France rather than Spain became for the moment the natural defender of the Catholics in England through the intimate connection of their cause with that of Mary Queen of Scots. For a generation France had played a very different rôle : she had consistently aided the cause of Protestants against Charles V, and had befriended Henry VIII, in spite of all his quarrels with the Popes. It is true that this had been done for political reasons only, and the political horizon had now changed. Mary Stuart was now in their hands, and her claim to the English throne, or at least to the English succession, they felt bound to assert; and they could not do so without supporting the Catholic cause.

France had, therefore, herself to undertake the same part as Spain and to act with her. Yet this opened the door to new dangers. For as they had only made peace because both were exhausted (the rivalry and distrust of the two remaining as strong as ever), it was almost inevitable that one would leave the other in the lurch when the opportunity arrived. The opportunity was bound to arrive, for France in her destitution, especially in her want of a fleet to meet that of England, was constrained to lean upon Spain, and Spain let her fall heavily in her moment of need, a disservice which afterwards reacted disastrously on Spain herself.

---

[1] I fear there is not a single modern writer who has rejected, or at least shown reason for rejecting, this fable. Writers of high repute, like P. F. Tytler (*History of Scotland*, 1837, vi. 110) and J. L. Motley (*Rise of the Dutch Republic*, 1875, i. 180), down to Dr. Philippson and Major Hume, accept it without any question. The two latter, however, do not (so far as I can see) explicitly allude to it at this crisis. For further references see *Papal Negotiations with Mary Stuart* (1901), pp. xxxviii–xliii, and the *Month*, March 1901.

We have already seen that France perhaps took some action against England at Rome about March 1559, probably only extracting from the Pope a promise not to allow Mary's rights to be passed over. At the same time England was executing a much more effective counter-stroke. From the first Cecil had laid down the principles, " If controversy of religion be there among them, to help to kindle it . . . and especially in Scotland, to augment the hope of them that incline them to good religion." [1] Before Elizabeth had been six months on the throne the Protestant preachers were gliding in numbers across the borders, and in May the flag of religious revolution was raised all through the Lowlands. It was no longer time for the French to think of protecting the English Catholic party; it was all they could do to preserve any sort of power in Scotland. The French alliance with Scotland had for many generations been a regular factor in the European balance of power. Again and again had the aspirations of English Kings to play a great part on the Continent been kept in check by demonstrations and raids on the Scottish borders. Now all this was threatened, and the Scotch throne itself seemed insecure. And where was the remedy, with the fleet destroyed and France in utter collapse ?

.Henri II answered as a man of lax principle might be expected to do in his difficulties. He used big words, he threatened to spend his crown in suppressing the revolution ; but he sent no men, and in money only 20,000 livres, less than £2000. Moreover, he instructed Mary of Guise to temporise in every way she could ; to the Protestants he made offers of freedom of conscience ; to the Pope (from whom he requested a large subsidy) he promised a thorough Catholic reform. But these offers satisfied no one, and the Reformers continued to progress rapidly, when Henri's sudden death (July 10, 1559) brought Mary Stuart to the throne of France, and the Guises into power. The Guises were the most capable and most willing men in France to push the Scottish expedition, yet how little could they achieve ! They managed, indeed, to send off some reinforcements,

---

[1] *The Device for Alteration of Religion*, 2. *Foreign Calendar*, 1559, p. 19.

but not until the end of the year; and when the greater part of their fleet perished in a gale, they could do no more.

The hour had now come when the idea of a Spanish alliance became a strong temptation to France. Philip had just married a French princess, and made all sorts of promises of mutual assistance; and it might have been thought that, if he could agree with any Frenchman, he would agree best with the thoroughly Catholic Guises. They on their side perceived that Philip with his Spanish and Flemish fleets would be the only possible intermediary who might overawe England, or lend ships in the last resort. Elizabeth, too, was at first not averse to accept Philip as an intermediary, in fact she begged him to act as such.[1]

Here, then, was Philip's chance. He might have united with France on his own terms, and have dealt a great blow by diplomatic pressure, or by force of arms, to the advance of the Reformation, the ultimate effects of which blow might have been very far-reaching. At least he might have saved Catholicity in Scotland, and so maintained the balance of power in Europe and have bridled the expansion of English Protestantism. But he did not even attempt to avail himself of his opportunity. So far as we can penetrate his mind, we may suggest that he did not realise the problem before him, and therefore left himself in the hands of the Duke of Alva and of Margaret of Parma, governess of the Low Countries, both of whom had the most persistent distrust and dread of France and the lowest ideas of the strength of England.

Alva's advice to the English was cynically outspoken : " Let Elizabeth keep strong at sea, for at sea she can most effectively bar the passage to Scotland." He added, too, a parable :—

" If thy enemy be in the water to the girdlestede, lend him thy hand and help him out. If he be in to the shoulders, set hold on him and keep him down." He meant, if the Queen were able to drive the French out of Scotland in

---

[1] *Foreign Calendar*, 1559–1560, pp. 315, 317, 321 : " She [Elizabeth] is best content to accept him [Philip] as a judge."—Instructions for Lord Montague, January 23, 1560.

avoiding peril to herself, to do it without asking further counsel or aid.[1]

This was not spoken out of love for England, but out of genuine fear for the consequences of her supposed weakness. He wrote to Philip :—

" For the defence of your States, it beseems you to ally yourself with England, a country that is weak, without armies, without soldiers to guard itself, without leaders that can defend it, poor, with a Queen such as neither she nor any of her Council understand the danger in which they are. She does not comprehend your Majesty's favour and aid. On the contrary, she is suspicious, on her guard, and is governed rather by whim and fancy than by reason. Nevertheless, in spite of all these difficulties it is necessary to defend her, until your Majesty has a convenient opportunity of offending her." [2]

It is clear, in fact, that Alva was wholly obsessed with the idea of the facility with which France might conquer England.[3] In the following December, talking to Chamberlain, the English ambassador at Madrid, he interjected : " What thinks the Queen ? Has the French King no party in England ? " [4] " Yes " (quoth he), " I fear me I may say as great as the English Queen's or greater." He also owned that if Elizabeth had seized all Scotland, Spain would not have interfered.[5]

Here he was simply misinformed. The French and Spanish diplomatic dispatches (Alva would not have had regular access even to the Spanish correspondence) show

---

[1] *Foreign Calendar*, 1560–1561, p. 67.

[2] Parescer of Alva, August 2, 1560. *Papal Negotiations with Mary Stuart*, p. 456.

[3] Alva's fixed idea of the danger from the French was due to his experience of their recuperative powers, which he had often witnessed. There was also the mistrust born of prolonged hostilities with them. He had very little knowledge of England.

[4] The Spanish State papers afford strong evidence that there was practically no English Catholic party supporting France (*Spanish Calendar*, 1558, pp. 76, 85, 124). At the latter page we find a Catholic alliance with France set on a par with an alliance with Turks !

[5] *Foreign Calendar*, 1560, n. 817.

this clearly. Alva's fears were illusory, and the policy which Philip followed at his advice was most injurious to Spanish interests. He assumed the rôle of arbitrator, but acted with such slowness that pushful Cecil had free scope and ample time to bring matters to a conclusion in his own way. Now to resume the thread of affairs from the time when the survivors of the French fleet reached Scotland.

With their advent, or even before it, the loyalist party began to recover power rapidly, and it seemed possible that they would be entirely victorious, when Elizabeth again intervened. An English fleet entered the Firth of Forth, and from that moment the cause of the French again declined. An English army was sent to complete the victory, but against them the tiny French force made a prolonged and most heroic resistance. But at last, after half a year's fighting, France being unable to send them the least help, they were forced to submit to the Treaty of Edinburgh (July 6, 1560), after which the French left Scotland for ever. Five months later Francis II died (December 5), and therewith Mary's reign in France ceased, and with it all the power of the Guises. Catherine de Medici, as Regent, advanced the Protestant party in France to counterbalance the Catholics, leaving herself the miserable satisfaction of being able to sway the see-saw. Henceforth Elizabeth could have no fears of France. On the contrary, by fostering its religious dissensions she brought the power of the country so low that in England apprehensions in its regard were altogether at an end.

If during the six months that the French held out in Scotland, Philip had come to their aid, he would have been fighting for the existing balance of power in Europe, and a victory might have meant the eventual predominance of Catholicism in these islands. By his abstention from action, after encouraging the French to hope for his intervention, he may be said to have kept the ground while Protestantism secured its final triumph throughout these islands.[1] That

[1] Dr. E. Bekker, who has worked out the details of this episode with great pains, says in conclusion : " For her military and diplomatic disasters France had, in the first place, to thank her request to Spain for intervention and aid."—*Beiträge zur Englischen Geschichte im Zeitalter Elizabeths*, Giesener Studien, 1887, iv. 62.

was for Philip a disaster of the first importance, which could never again be repaired. Who shall say where its consequences ceased ?

To return to the English Catholics, whose fortunes were so sorely affected by the failings of their friends. The efforts of the French, far from bringing them any relief, occasioned a new outbreak of persecution at home. No sooner was there the possibility of war with France than the French ambassador's house was put under observation, and on the Feast of the Purification (February 2, 1560) his chapel was raided, and the English present were carried off as prisoners.[1] The ambassador might protest, but Cecil was glad of this occasion to make the quarrel with France deeper; and it was his steady policy to increase persecution whenever any hope of aid to Catholics from without might arise.

Nor did matters stop here. Asked by Elizabeth to mediate, Philip could hardly have done less in reply than to raise a word of warning, when she began openly to assist the Protestant insurgents in the Netherlands. In reply the cry of *Christianos ad leones!* was at once raised by the English Government. Philip's co-religionists must pay the penalty.

" Since his Majesty," wrote the Spanish ambassador, " warned the Queen not to help the rebels, the Catholics have been persecuted worse than ever, and all those that are known are cast into prison. Oxford students and law students in London have been taken in great numbers. They have also arrested those that came to my house at Easter Day to hear Mass, and have declared my house suspect." [2]

The English and Scottish Protestants had, no doubt, a far easier task in shaking off the French protectorate in Scotland than Catholic France and Spain had in maintaining it. Still, however their failure is explained, it was chiefly their want of union at this moment, and in particular Spain's distrust of France, which left Elizabeth free to take a dominating position in Northern Europe.

[1] *Spanish Calendar*, p. 126.
[2] De Quadra to the Count de Feria, May 23, 1560. *Ibid.*, p. 156.

F

§ 3. *Pope Pius IV and the Council of Trent*

While the English Catholics expected little good from France, and, in fact, received some harm, they did hope much from the new Pope, Pius IV, elected on Christmas Day, 1559; yet from him too they received but little. The Pope's best endeavours at assistance all failed. His less laboured attempts, however, were more successful, and under him the first signs of new life among the English Catholics make themselves evident. They would also have been greatly encouraged by the chief work of his pontificate, which was the completion of the Council of Trent. Before its re-commencement the whole Church seemed to be in danger. Germany and England were already gone. France and Austria appeared as good as lost. Some said the borders of Spain and Italy would fall away too. Certainly all seemed bent on frustrating the Council. But the Pope's moderation and great diplomatic ability gradually prevailed. The Council began; and the splendour of its unanimity in all matters of faith and morals re-animated every heart. The Church as a whole was once more recognised as being in an obviously invincible position, and by degrees new courage and a new spirit permeated the whole body. The Counter-Reformation was in full tide.

The cry for a General Council to reform abuses in the Church had resounded in every country, and had been taken up by all parties, by Elizabeth and Cecil no less than by Mary and Pole. In reality they did not all have in view quite the same thing. The Protestants, to use Cecil's words, August 5, 1559, wanted " a free general Council, where the Pope of Rome hath not the seat of judgment." [1] In other words, they wanted a Council to judge the Pope, while the Catholics wanted one that would give the Pope the opportunity of teaching the Church in the most authoritative way.

But however this might be, both Protestants and Catholics agreed, in something more than words, in desiring a Council—

[1] R. Keith, *History of Church of Scotland*, 1844, i. 369.

PIVS IIII.PONT. MAX.

POPE PIUS IV, GIOVANNI ANGELO MEDICI

Painter unknown, Milan

and that as a practical measure of reform. The insuperable obstacle hitherto had been the European wars. But now that exhaustion at last had brought about a pause, now that the treaty of Cateau-Cambrésis had cleared the ground, it was resolved that invitations to the *Concilio* should be issued to all, Protestants as well as Catholics. Special congregations of Cardinals were appointed to deal with the affairs of different nations, and the five names on the committee for England are reported (28th of March) to be the Cardinals Moroni (Protector), de Carpi, of Tournon, of Trent (Madruzzi), of San Clemente,[1] and they had selected, before April 27, 1560, as messenger, Vincenzo Parpaglia, Abbot *in commendam* of San Solutore in Turin (commonly, but less correctly, called San Saluto or San Salvatore), to treat with Queen Elizabeth.

This mission turned out a failure. Parpaglia never got further than Brussels, and therefore had no direct influence on the English Catholics. We may, therefore, pass over the history of his mission briefly, though there are abundant materials for describing it in detail, and the interesting story would throw a curiously vivid light on many important topics, especially on King Philip's fixed idea that France was on the very point of overthrowing England. Suffice it to say, that he imagined the mission to be a step in some French scheme for the immediate excommunication of Elizabeth, the execution of which sentence would give France a handle for invading England. Parpaglia was, therefore, told to wait until Philip's negotiations about Scotland were settled; and settled they doubtless were by the Treaty of Edinburgh in July. There could then be no objection to Parpaglia writing to Elizabeth on September 8, and as no correspondence followed, he left Brussels early in November for Italy.

There was a certain amount of mystery in Philip's conduct in this matter, which has not yet been entirely cleared up. But it is probably of no great importance, because Philip was acting under impressions which did not last. At first he was entirely carried away by his mania against France. Our documents make the negative toler-

[1] Vat. Arch. *C. T.*, 79, f. 196. Cf. *Foreign Calendar*, 1560–1561, n. 74.

ably sure, viz. that neither France nor the Pope entertained the projects which Philip feared. Indeed, the plan of sending Parpaglia, instead of being first suggested by France, was, in fact, communicated by the Pope to Spain (March 5), and to France afterwards (March 15 or 27), and with the request that the two might co-operate.[1]

Philip's extreme nervousness could not have lasted beyond the retirement of the French from Scotland in July 1560; and if after that he still objected to Parpaglia's mission, it would either have been because he was always slow to change, or because there was some private grudge between Parpaglia and the Spaniards.[2]

When this year, 1560, ran out, Philip's anxieties were still further allayed by the death of Francis II and the end of the close alliance between France and Scotland. Catherine de Medici had seized the Government, and the balance of power was altogether changed. If Pius still wanted to send a nuncio to Elizabeth, the old objections could no longer hold.

The Pope did wish to send. It was part of his policy at this time to invite every one. Legates, nuncios and envoys were going to every crowned head, and to the princes of Germany; special messengers were even dispatched to the Bishops of Scotland and of Ireland.[3]   In December 1560 the Abbate Girolamo Martinengo received orders to visit Elizabeth.

Still the Pope would not this time take any steps " without first communicating with his Catholic Majesty." [4]   Philip

[1] Brief to Philip of March 5, 1560, commending Parpaglia is partly printed in Raynaldi's continuation of *Baronius's Annals*, with three other briefs. There are full copies in R. O. *Roman Transcripts*, etc.   The messages to France are given in *Papal Negotiations with Mary Stuart*, pp. 45–47.   See also Bayne, pp. 42–60.

[2] There was another Parpaglia, who apostatised and fought for the French Huguenots.   It is conceivable that the two were confused.

[3] Father de Gouda, S.J., was sent to Mary and the Scottish Bishops, Father David Wolfe to the Irish Bishops.   For the former see *Papal Negotiations with Mary Stuart*, pp. li, etc., for the latter, P. Hogan, *Distinguished Irishmen of the Sixteenth Century*.   As the Council of Trent dominates the whole of this period, so the correspondence of the Pope and his staff with the heads of the Council from now, 1561, onwards is of first-rate importance.   This gives great weight to the excellent edition of that correspondence by Josef Šusta, *Die Roemische Curie und das Concil von Trient unter Pius IV*.

[4] *Papal Negotiations*, p. 51.

now made no difficulties; [1] indeed the project fell in excellently with a Court intrigue in which his ambassador, de Quadra, was deeply interested. De Quadra, the Bishop of Aquila, whose ecclesiastical dress seemed somewhat out of place at Elizabeth's Court, had by this time given up hopes of influencing Elizabeth's Government directly, and he was endeavouring to advance the Earl of Leicester, and to promote a marriage between him and Elizabeth, in order to outweigh the influence of Cecil. It was not a dignified policy and not altogether for the advantage of the Catholics. " I determined," wrote the ambassador on April 12, " of two evils to choose the least . . . Although this pretended understanding with Leicester might somewhat damage the Catholic cause . . . it would damage the Queen much more." By means of this not very edifying intrigue he managed before long, with consummate skill, to get Elizabeth to consent to receive the nuncio.[2]

But Cecil's resources were many, and he now practised a trick, destined afterwards to be employed again and again, and almost always with the effect desired. He fabricated a bogus plot, inflamed therewith the fanatics, and alarmed the Queen, who immediately put herself again into his hands.

The details are imperfectly known. A priest, presumably Cox, *alias* Devon, was seized at Gravesend on April 14, and his presence of mind gave way during examination. He confessed that he was the chaplain of Sir Edward Waldegrave, that he had said Mass daily in his house, and that he was then starting for Flanders to distribute some

---

[1] That is, none which affected the course of events. In April, however, he induced Pope Pius to order Martinengo to wait (April 12, 1561). But before this could become effective the mission had worked itself out. Bayne, pp. 88, 269.

[2] De Quadra wrote, April 14, 1561, to Cardinal Granvelle :—

" [Queen Elizabeth] said to me, of her own accord, that she was pleased at his coming, but that she would inform me that, in conformity with the laws of this kingdom, he would be styled Ambassador of the Roman Pontiff only, as it was forbidden to give the title of Universal or Supreme Pontiff. I said that I did not know how he would come, and did not intend to examine that point now, but that . . . if she desired to unite her Church to the Church Universal, she should not trouble to introduce doubts into matters where there were none, etc. She nevertheless repeated something about this law of her kingdom, but showed herself greatly inclined to bring difficulties to accord, and completely contented with the coming of the nuncio. . . ."—K. de Lettenhove, *Relations Politiques des Pays-Bas et de l'Angleterre*, Bruxelles, 1883, ii. 548.

money in alms among the poor exiles for religion. About the same time a letter from one of the imprisoned Bishops was intercepted which breathed the hope that, through the good offices of the Pope's nuncio, he and his episcopal brethren might at last recover their liberty. Finally, from Ireland there came the oft-repeated rumour of disturbances.

It was Cecil's special gift to combine details such as these into a plausible plot-scare; but even he found difficulties on this occasion. " The way was full of crooks," he owned. Anyway, he filled the prisons with unfortunate Catholics, and this was sufficient, in those suspicious days, to make his followers believe something very serious must have been afoot. Sir Edward Waldegrave had been one of Mary's Council; it was assumed, therefore, that he must have been plotting for a restoration of the *ancien régime*. Disturbances in Ireland might be matters of daily occurrence, but now that Father Wolfe, S.J., had gone there from Rome, the troubles must clearly be attributable to him.

By these rumours the Queen was at last alarmed. It was at once perceived in Court circles that she would return to Cecil's guidance, and the crypto-Catholics and their friends were paralysed. The crisis came over the vote in Privy Council for the admission of the nuncio, on the 1st of May, 1561. Cecil, backed up by Sir Nicholas Bacon, declared that any one who voted for his admission would be guilty of treason. " By this one word ' treason ' Cecil brought it about that, though many wished that the nuncio should be heard, he was, in fact, refused by the common vote of all." [1]

Cecil's letter to Throckmorton, after he had won the day, lets us see clearly his view of what had occurred. His ideal of inter-relations between the Divinity, her Majesty and himself, and his use of the " We " of majesty, are all noteworthy :—

" Sir —— [sends him copies of the official answer to the Bishop of Aquila]. Howsoever the end is, the way was full of crooks. I found my Lord Marquis [of Winchester],

[1] *De Nuntio Apostolico*, in Dr. Sander's hand. *Arch. Vat.*, Arm. xliv., v. 28, f. 335; Bayne, p. 272.

my Lord Keeper [Sir Nicholas Bacon] and my Lord of Pembroke [1] in this matter my best pillars. Yet was I forced to seek byways, so much was the contrary labour by prevention. This Bishop of Aquila had entered into such a practice with a pretence to further the great matter here (meaning principally the Church matter), and percase the other also [*i. e.* the Leicester match], that he had taken faster hold to plant his purpose than was my ease shortly to root up. But God, whose cause it is, and the Queen, whose only surety therein resteth (the one by directing, the other by yielding), have ended the matter well. If it may so continue, I shall be in more quietness. . . . Your letters, though they came late, yet did they confirm the Queen and others in the former resolution.

" I have imported this answer for the nuncio to sundry places,[2] lest our former inclination had been too hastily spread by the adversaries.

" When I saw the Romish influence toward, about a month past, I thought necessary to dull the Papists' expectation by discovering of certain Mass-mongers and punishing them, as I do not doubt you have heard of them. I take God to record I mean no evil to any of them, but only for the rebating of the Papists' humours, which by the Queen's lenity grow too rank. I find it hath done much good." [3]

Such, however, was the man's hypocrisy,[4] that while " calling to God to record that he meant no harm to any of them," he was keeping scores in prison, some to remain there for months, some for years, some for life.[5] Those

[1] The Marquis of Winchester and the Earl of Pembroke had belonged to the other party during Mary's reign. Sander, as quoted above, had reason for naming Cecil and Bacon only.

[2] That is, to the Protestants of Germany. Three Latin copies, and two French, as well as several in English with Cecil's emendations, remain in the Record Office.

[3] R.O., *Foreign Elizabeth*, May 8, 1561, xviii. 103. For the episode of Martinengo see Bayne, pp. 73–116, and Šusta i. 172, 222.

[4] Mr. Bayne, starting from a different point of view, differs from me here, and thinks Cecil acted " honestly." To this I would quote Macaulay's words: " The great stain on [Cecil's] memory is that for differences of opinion, for which he would risk nothing himself, in the day of his power he took away without scruple the lives of others," etc. (*Essays*, 1870, p. 225). Such unscrupulosity was the reverse of honesty, and so were his cruel measures of this period.

[5] The number of prisoners in London alone was about thirty; those indicted in Essex alone amounted to thirty-eight (*C.R.S.*, i. 50–52). De

capable of paying were not freed without the fine of 100 marks, a large sum for those times; nor even then could any go free without taking the Oath of Supremacy.

No sooner did Philip hear of the rejection of Martinengo, than he again wrote to his ambassador at Rome, to prevent any steps being taken for Elizabeth's excommunication, which might lead to a French invasion. The time was not ripe, he said,[1] for restoring religion by force; when the occasion should come he would not hesitate to expose himself and his armies. The ambassador was to see whether the Pope would, at this, offer to confer on him the English crown. I have not seen the Pope's answer, but we may be sure that no such offer was made, for papal diplomacy was beginning to lean more and more openly to the policy of regarding Mary Stuart as the Catholic claimant to the English throne.[2]

No proceedings were taken against Elizabeth for refusing to admit the nuncio, though that refusal was in effect a rejection of the Council itself, and was accounted as such. It brought excommunication a step nearer, but it was not yet certain that this extreme measure was inevitable. By November there were new changes on the political horizon, and these had developed by February 1562 into a crisis somewhat similar to that of May 1561. The chief actors on the Catholic side were now the Cardinal Legate in France, Hippolito d'Este, brother of the Duke of Ferrara, and Bertino Salaro, Signor di Moretta, agent of the Duke of Savoy, a good Catholic and a good diplomatist, who passed not unfrequently at this period through Paris and London to Edinburgh and back. His chief business was in reality

---

Quadra gives the total of prisoners in April, as far as he can hear, at sixty gentlemen (Lettenhove, *Relations Politiques*, ii. 560). An anonymous writer in July puts them at about 200 in all (Arch. Vat., *C.T.*, 64, xxviii. 335); Sander, in 1562, at 160, *C.R.S.*, i. 45. A good many further details about the fines, etc., in R.O., *Dom. Eliz.*, xviii. nos. 7, 8, 19. Bekker, *Giessener Studien* (1890), v. 105–24, gives the fullest account of the whole incident. The future martyr, Thomas Woodhouse, now began his imprisonment, which only ended with his execution (*C.R.S.*, i. 42, 48, 50, 52, 54). There was also a confessor Thomas Woods, see *Cath. Encyclopedia*.

[1] *Philip to Vargas*, Madrid, July 16, 1561. Mignet, *Marie Stuart*, i. 402.

[2] Instructions to Cardinal d'Este, n.d., but certainly of this period. *Papal Negotiations with Mary Stuart*, p. 58.

to suggest marriages to Elizabeth and Mary with various princes and dukes, the Duke of Ferrara among them, and this, again, brought him into the confidence both of Cardinal d'Este and of Elizabeth. He was also able to trade upon an intrigue in which Throckmorton and the Earl of Bedford had taken part, during some negotiations with Catherine de Medici. She was at first, as has been said, in favour of the Protestants, and had declared that she did not want the Council, or only with certain restrictions and delays. Hereupon the English diplomatists had joined her, and declared that they, too, wanted the Council, but with the same conditions and delays.[1]

This will be enough, without going into further details, to show that Moretta had good opportunities of opening the subject and keeping the negotiation warm. His chances were still further improved in February 1562, when the Legate persuaded Catherine de Medici to abandon the favour which she had shown the Reformers, and to support the Council. This change had in France great and far-reaching results, but what concerns us here is that the Cardinal of Ferrara hoped with her aid to bring round Elizabeth to a similar change of policy, especially as Cecil was, for the moment, once more in an unsafe position.[2]

Though the Pope regarded the renewed negotiations with distrust at first, nevertheless, as Cardinal d'Este's success in France became more marked, so did hopes rise in Rome for England also. Thus, on the 3rd of January, 1562, the Pope would only praise the general idea.

" Our Lord the Pope," wrote the Cardinal Secretary, " has heard with pleasure of your negotiation, and of the circumspection with which you are conducting it. Not that he now hopes for any direct good result. His two attempts to send her nuncios have proved her obstinacy (*durezza*). But we shall at least have a further satisfaction to conscience, that we have not omitted any measure we could take."

---

[1] Numerous references to Moretta's negotiations will be found in the *Foreign* and the *Spanish Calendars*, pp. 219–22.

[2] Throckmorton's Dispatches of February 16 and March 20, 1562, *Foreign Calendar*, 1561–1562, pp. 525, 560.

But on the 15th of March, hearing that Catherine de Medici would back up the negotiation, a brief was sent, couched in cautious terms, which formally accredited the Cardinal to " our dear daughter, the Queen of England," for certain negotiations about which he will write.[1]

This brief was never presented, though the negotiation lingered on for several months. The English, presumably in order to keep in touch with the French, instead of refusing brusquely as before, proposed a delay of the Council until all Protestants could come to an agreement. Even upon this point the Legate was at first inclined to offer a compromise, but on May 9, 1562, the Pope wrote to him that this would be impossible, now that the Bishops were actually assembling. Still—

" If the Queen of England really wants to send, and to persuade the Protestants to appear, she may be herewith assured that all will be welcomed, and cherished with all possible affection and charity, in everything that may be service of God and of the Christian religion."

On June 1 the Pope wrote *manu propria* to Catherine in the same sense. But the correspondence was now near its end. A new war of religion was about to break out in France in which Elizabeth would side with the Protestants against Catherine. The alliance of the two Queens and any good to come from it were fast becoming negligible quantities. Accordingly, when M. de Lansac, ambassador from France to the Council, begged (May 21, 1562) that the next session might be postponed till August, vaguely promising that Elizabeth would then free the Bishops she had in prison, and send them to the Council, and that delegates would come from various German Protestant States, St. Charles Borromeo, then Cardinal Secretary, answered (May 27) refusing to delay even for an hour.[2]

---

[1] A summary of the whole correspondence, with references to the originals, will be found in *Papal Negotiations with Mary Stuart*, pp. 58, 81–84. The briefs are printed *ibid.*, p. 93. The letters from Rome are in Vat. Archives, *Germania*, iv. The letters of Cardinal d'Este are printed in Baluze-Mansi, *Miscellanea*, 1764, iv., 384, etc.

[2] Arch. Vat., *Concilio di Trento*, 58 f. 79. *St. Charles's Answer*, 54 f. 80. Šusta, *Curie und Concil von Trient*, etc., ii. 157, 176. *Rome Calendar*, i. 84–87.

Meanwhile the Council of Trent had recommenced its sessions. There was but one representative of the English hierarchy, Dr. Thomas Goldwell, formerly Bishop of St. Asaph, who had escaped from England when the rest were put under restraint; and he eventually arrived at Trent in June 1561. Dr. Nicholas Sander, afterwards so well known as a writer and an ecclesiastical leader, was also there in capacity of theologian to Cardinal Hosius, one of the presiding Legates, who probably also extended his hospitality to Goldwell.[1] Very few English affairs came before the Fathers of the Council, but before the end of the year 1562 a small committee was selected to report on the question whether it was lawful for Catholics to go to Anglican services in order to escape the Recusancy fines, a subject to which we shall return immediately.

Next year, 1563, on the 10th of May, the Council were greatly pleased at the receipt of a letter from Mary Queen of Scots. The Cardinal of Lorraine, with his usual eloquence, introduced the subject in a striking speech, giving an account of his niece's courage and perseverance in the face of great trials. Then he read the Queen's letter, dated March 18, 1563, welcoming the Council, and regretting that owing to the religious revolution her Bishops could not possibly attend. The Council answered " in regular form," praising her constancy very highly.[2]

It may be that this letter from Mary drew attention to Elizabeth, at all events the Legates received next month two letters almost simultaneously, referring to the excommunication of the English Queen. One letter was from the Cardinal Secretary in Rome, who approached the subject in a very matter-of-fact, business-like way, as though every one would expect the Council to declare against the greatest heresiarch then living.

" His Holiness says that, as the decrees of the Council ought to condemn the Queen of England, the Protestants

---

[1] S. Merkle, *Concilium Tridentinum ii., Diariorum Collectio,* 1910, p. 868; Šusta, p. 33. Stapleton's presence is rumoured, R.O., *Dom. Eliz.,* xi. 25.
[2] The letters, speeches and correspondence will be found fully, or in abstract, in *Negotiations with Mary Stuart,* pp. 167–73. Here, too, may be found a detailed account of the documents and bibliography for the ensuing paragraphs on Elizabeth's excommunication (pp. 173–176).

and the Huguenots, your Eminence ought to begin to think what steps you will take. . . . Let us know your opinion as soon as possible, especially about the Queen of England " (Rome, June 2, 1563.[1])

The second letter was from the English exiles at Louvain, a long memorial, pressing for a sentence and going into the details of the subject, even into the recognition of the Queen of Scots as rightful Queen of England.[2] The English exiles, we shall soon hear, were gradually growing into a little community at Louvain and in its neighbourhood, and having passed through the fire themselves, they had lost much of the Englishman's usual dread of extreme remedies. In fact we shall find them all through this volume more outspoken in complaint, more earnest in advocating strong measures, than those who were actually in the fiery furnace at home. The latter, one and all, had to practise patience so assiduously that they could hardly break themselves of the habit.

In the case of the exiles a reaction had set in. They heard others speak out, and there was nothing to prevent them doing the same. The miseries incident to exile kept their old wounds from healing, while new ones were being daily added through their sympathy with sufferers at home. No wonder that they wrote with bitterness, and counselled drastic measures which men less deeply moved would consider impolitic.

The first of such utterances preserved to us are from the pens of Morris Clenog and Nicholas Sander, who wrote, after the refusal to admit Martinengo (July to December 1561), various suggestions to Cardinal Moroni, the Cardinal Protector of England. They at first proposed moderate reforms—for instance, that five of the fifteen English Sees now vacant through the deaths of Catholic holders should be filled up, and that these new Bishops should represent England at the Council. If encouraged in this way, and

---

[1] Arch. Vat., *C.T.*, 68 f. 41; Šusta, iv. 48. This, and seven other notes from Rome, are printed in Meyer, pp. 408–11. *Rome Calendar*, i. 130.

[2] This document, beginning *Videtur valde*, is printed by F. B. von Bucholz, *Geschichte der Regierung Ferdinands des Ersten*, Wien, 1838, ix. 701. There is also a copy in Pallavicini's MS. materials for his *History of the Council of Trent*, iii. c. 22.

especially by alms, the Catholics in England might, they hoped, cause Elizabeth to " change her mind." But stronger measures were soon advocated,[1] and finally there came a note by Sander, that much might be effected " if these three easy [!] measures be taken," viz. if the English are absolved from their allegiance to Elizabeth; if Mary's title is confirmed; if some English exiles are sent to Scotland to proffer Mary the English crown. The memorial closes with the words: " Totum amittitur quidquid in illa dejicienda omittitur." [2]

After reading this we cannot wonder at the paper on the same subject addressed to the Legates. The Cardinals, whatever they thought of it, conceived that it would, at all events, serve as a convenient *ballon d'essai*, to see how far people were ready for the measure proposed by Rome. So they summoned the ecclesiastical representatives of the chief Catholic Powers, of the Emperor, Spain, France, Poland and Savoy, June 11, 1563, read them the English proposal, and inquired what their respective Governments would say to it. They also informed the Pope what they had done.

An interesting interchange of letters now followed. The Emperor and Spain condemned the proposal very strongly; from France I find no answer, which is, perhaps, to be explained because of the war with England, which was still in progress. But whether they would have liked it or not, the objections raised by the Emperor Ferdinand were so urgent that the whole project was immediately dropped.

It appears that the envoys of the Emperor received not only the paper about Elizabeth's excommunication, but also a further proposal for acknowledging Mary as Queen of England. This had been sent them later by Cardinal

---

[1] The first dated English scheme advocating strong measures is from Clenog in November 1561, Arch. Vat., Arm. lxiv., t. 28, f. 62. In the paper (Jesuit Archives, *Angl. Hist.*, I. 57) *Deflebilis status Anglicanæ Gentis* of April 1559, the prayer for help from the Kings of France and Spain had already been raised, but only in a passing phrase.

[2] Arch. Vat., Arm. lxiv., t. 28. f. 174 (printed in Bayne, p. 274). This volume contains the correspondence of the Protector Moroni. Unfortunately very few of the pieces are dated. If, however, the papers above referred to are studied in the following order, viz. folios 335, 167, 341, 96, 169, 50, 62, 45, 174, they will be found to form a regular sequence.

Hosius, and we cannot help suspecting that it must have come through his theologian, Sander. The Emperor was simply furious. " Never have I seen him so moved," wrote the Nuncio Delfino.[1] The measure would, he thought, so irritate the German Protestants, who were with difficulty kept quiet, that they might make bloody reprisals. Certainly the outcry and excitement would do the greatest harm. The Legates, at this, were all apologies; they denied all knowledge of the paper given in by Hosius, and declared that they had only sent the other for the purposes of inquiry; and as we now see, they were in reality only feeling their way towards the much more moderate proposal of the Pontiff, which, however, they now resolved to abandon.

When the Pontiff first heard that the Legates had inquired the opinion of the Catholic Powers, he expressed complete satisfaction. He evidently did not at all expect the strong rejection of the proposal by Austria and Spain. When, however, he did hear of it, he took exactly the same line as the Legates, and revoked his letter of the previous week.[2] In the Council the anathema was eventually pronounced in general terms on all those who rejected the definitions. But we now know whose name might have come first if ancient precedent had been followed.

The whole incident, and especially the immediate withdrawal, both by the Cardinal Legates and by the Pope, of the proposed excommunication of Elizabeth, at the complaint of the Emperor, shows clearly that great diversity of opinion existed on the subject of the excommunication of princes, on which we have lately dwelt (§ 1). The exiles return boldly to the mediæval idea, while the politicians, in touch with a broader world, reject its proposal with anger, or treat it as quite inferior to their own plans. The Pope and Legates, though inclined in its favour, have so little confidence in its practical utility, that they abandon the project at the first opposition. Still, none of them considers the measure as entirely antiquated and inapplicable under

---

[1] Delfino to Moroni, Arch. Vat., *C.T.*, 31, f. 13, June 17, 1563.

[2] Arch. Vat., *C.T.*, 68, f. 61, and f. 69. In the latter he says the excommunication was desired by " *Infinite persone et Inglesi proprii.*" The documents have now been printed by Meyer, Appendices 2 to 11.

any circumstances. The possibility of its coming into force some day is not at all precluded.

The Pope, while yielding to the representations of Austria and Spain, took the opportunity of pointing out to those Powers that they ought now to press Elizabeth, with all the instance they could, to relax her persecutions (August, September, 1563). They both accepted the duty. Ferdinand wrote,[1] with great courtesy, proposing that the Bishops should be set free, and that some such toleration should be given in England to Catholics as had been granted to Huguenots in France, where they had a church in almost every large town.

Elizabeth's refusal was characteristic. As for tolerating any other religion, her laws forbade it. It was she who held the ancient Catholic faith. The insolent breakers of her laws (*i. e.* the Bishops) were confined because they would not do what they had readily done in King Henry's reign. Still she had spared them at the Emperor's request (November 3, 1563).[2] The truth was that, out of fear of the plague, many of those imprisoned in London had lately been sent into confinement out of town. But they were in most cases not recalled to prison afterwards, and this good result may, perhaps, have been due to Ferdinand's intercession. He made no further requests.

Pius IV took no other public action against Elizabeth.[3] On the contrary, he continued in private to show his kindness and his desire to deal gently with her as with all Englishmen. This was manifested in a somewhat remarkable manner towards Thomas Sackville, afterwards Lord

---

[1] The original of Ferdinand's letter is in the British Museum, Vesp. F. iii. f. 64, September 24, 1563. Philip had already written on the 15th of June. He told his ambassador to apply again in January 1564, but no opportunity to do so presented itself (*Spanish Calendar*, pp. 334, 353, 384). To appreciate Elizabeth's reply to Ferdinand, we must remember that it was her style to pose as a Reformer when corresponding with Reformers, and to call herself Catholic when writing to Catholics.

There had been some previous correspondence on this subject, see Bayne, pp. 196–199, and his Appendices, pp. 51–54. In April 1562 the matter had been mooted at the Council, but nothing was done. In April 1563 representations were made against the new laws of that year, and in effect they were not enforced.

[2] See Bayne, pp. 202 and 306.

[3] In his instructions given to Visconti, October 1563, the Pope maintained the propriety of eventually excommunicating her, if all other means of helping the Catholics failed : Baluze-Mansi, *Miscellanea*, iv. 455–9.

Buckhurst and Earl of Dorset. He has been already mentioned as an example of the young men whom Elizabeth won over without difficulty at her succession. Now we see another side of the picture. He is at once won back at Rome, if not to Catholicism, at least to friendliness. Sackville and William Travers had been making a tour through Italy, and passed Christmas at Rome, where their English Catholic friends had entertained them (the date is not certain) at the English Hospice. But it is easy to see that some would have opposed this hospitality, for Sackville had voted for those laws of Elizabeth which had overwhelmed Catholicism in England. Sackville was denounced to the Civil Governor of Rome and imprisoned. His friends, however, stood by him and sent up a petition in his favour, subscribed by Bishop Goldwell and many of the most respected English in Rome.[1] Sackville was soon free again, and the Pope interested himself in the case, and even discussed the English question with him, and gave him definite and ample promises of the favour he would show the Queen in case she would rejoin the Church.[2]

We must not consider this as a formal diplomatic mission. Martinengo was the only envoy who was sent with due formalities; Parpaglia had started, but was recalled; and Cardinal d'Este's envoys never delivered credentials or attempted regular diplomacy. But though the Pope acknowledged that he could not send Elizabeth a public message, even though friendly, he was on that very account the more anxious that his love and kindliness should be well attested. Elizabeth had placed herself in the hands of Cecil and his party, who hated, maligned, and misinterpreted him and all that held by him. All the more need for endeavouring to win a man like Thomas Sackville, a relative of Elizabeth's and not a dependent on Cecil, to act as witness of his sincere benevolence. If there was an obvious danger of his seeming too anxious for Elizabeth's friendship, that was a far lighter error than acquiescing in Cecil's gospel— that the Pope was a monster of malice and hatred.

Regarded in this light, the messages sent through Sack-

---

[1] Reproduced in facsimile in *C.R.S.*, ii., frontispiece.
[2] *C.R.S.*, ii. 1–11, and vii. 53; Bayne, pp. 205–7.

ville were not undignified nor unnecessary, though his want
of character prevented their having any notable result.
On his return [1] he passed again under the Cecil yoke,[2] gave
up his letters from Rome to the Court controversialists,[3]
and at this price he kept place and property. Nay, he
prospered, and advanced notably, until, years later, in
1608, he died suddenly at the Council board.[4] Yet it
was believed that he had been received into the Church
before his death, and Catholicism certainly retained its
hold among his children.[5] He did, indeed, much dirty work
for Cecil, as, for instance, taking Queen Mary the sentence
of death. But he was employed in such cases precisely
because he was known to be a moderate man, a standing
argument that, under the Tudors, even those most respected
for humanity must support the dictates, however savage,
of their absolutism. Though Sackville no doubt adapted
himself entirely to circumstances, the love of the older faith
did not die, but slept, as was shown by its periodical awaken-
ings, and in this, too, he was a man of his age.

To return to the doings of Pope Pius IV. In the last
year of his pontificate he spoke again of Elizabeth in Consistory, June 8, 1565, and once more asserted his preference
for a policy of reconciliation. He was, no doubt, thinking
chiefly at that time of her resistance to the Puritans on the
subject of the crucifix and the surplice, and he would also
have borne in mind that the year 1564, peaceful throughout
Europe, had brought to the English Catholics a welcome
relaxation from the extraordinary troubles of the two

---

[1] He returned in consequence, probably, of his father's last illness,
not, as I have said, *C.R.S.*, ii. 2, after his death. The correspondence,
which preceded his return, is described *ibid*.

[2] He perhaps did not yield immediately. De Silva wrote, February
25, 1566: Sackville " was in Rome a year and a half ago. When he left
here he was a heretic, but now, *they tell me*, he has reformed." The
punctuation in the *Spanish Calendar*, p. 527, is evidently wrong, and the
words in italics are omitted. Cf. Fuensanta del Valle, *Documentos Inéditos*,
lxxxix. 274.

[3] They were in the hands of Bartholomew Clerke, who refers to them
in his *Fidelis Servi Subdito infideli Responsio*, 1573, sig. k. ii.

[4] Cf. J. Morris, *Troubles of our Catholic Forefathers*, i. 197.

[5] See *C.R.S.*, ii. 2. H. Thurston, *Two Lady Margarets*, in the *Month*,
June 1900. Southwell's *Funeral Tears* was dedicated to his grand-
children; his son Thomas was at one time an ardent Catholic, who visited
Rome, much as his father had done, but he reverted to Protestantism in
1625 (*C.R.S.*, i. 101). Mistress Sackfilde had been imprisoned with Lady
Carewe for hearing Mass—between 1562 and 1567 (*C.R.S.*, i. 49).

previous years, and he would, perhaps, have had in mind some such plan for her marriage as that with the Austrian Archduke Charles. The Pope's words were :—

" From England the news is that Catholics are treated more mildly by the Queen ; that she is less bitter every day and seems milder. We must not, therefore, altogether despair that, should she marry a Catholic, she may with him bring back the kingdom to true religion." [1]

This hopeful mood was, indeed, disturbed ere long by Elizabeth's conduct during the revolt which followed the Darnley match, as is clear from another speech in Consistory, on the 12th of October following :—

" As for himself he was never desirous of war, which, indeed, he greatly detested ; but when others began in the name of religion, he would take his part in defending Catholics (when they were attacked), and he hoped the other princes of Christendom would do the same." [2]

Thus the last words of Pius, while foreshadowing changes soon to come, remain true to his well-tried preference for the policy of peace.[3] It had been extraordinarily helpful in the cases of France and of Austria, and in the wonderful success of the Council of Trent, despite the insuperable obstacles which threatened at first to be its ruin. In regard to England his success was not so obvious, but the opposite policy would probably have been even more infelicitous. Some have thought that, considering the bitterness of Elizabeth's Government, his readiness to treat was unwise. The Spanish ambassador said so at the time,[4] and a curious

---

[1] Printed in Mazière Brady, *Episcopal Succession*, ii. 327.

[2] *Negotiations with Mary Stuart*, p. 228. Though Pius died December 19, 1565, before doing anything to substantiate his words, they did, in fact, lead to the papal subsidy to Mary in 1566. *Ibid.*

[3] During the last years of this Pope and the early years of Pius V there had been some obscure dealings between Gurone Bertrano at Rome and Sebastiano Bruschetto in Elizabeth's Court. They were gentlemen correspondents, somewhat like Ridolfi later on, who often assumed the air of authorised diplomatists. Their letters reflect the gentler and more conciliatory sides of two Courts. They say much about pensions, the Dudley match, etc., but eventually all is inconclusive. See Bayne, pp. 208–17. There was another such correspondent, Bernardo Ferrario of Pavia, who wished to engage in similar work in 1565. See *Foreign Calendar*, March 6, 1565, and *Arch. Vat.*, 64, xxviii. 110–113.

[4] *Spanish Calendar*, p. 219.

legend remains to show how much the Pope's desire for conciliation was abused. It became a favourite assertion of Queen Elizabeth's, that the Pope had been ready to approve the Anglican service if she would admit his supremacy.[1]

But it must be remembered that steadfast hatred of Catholicism like Cecil's was the exception, not the rule, among the English nobility, and even among the courtiers. The kind messages sent to Elizabeth might, it was hoped, receive support from these quarters, and Martinengo's mission actually did obtain an amount of favour that was surprising. The experiment was very well worth making. Broadly speaking, the policy was a good one. And, as we have seen, Pius was ready to change it when a change seemed requisite.

Besides the public action of the Pope, which we have considered in this section, it must be remembered that by new grants of missionary faculties, by alms and other ways, the Holy Father was trying to revive the interior spirit of the Faithful. Of this more will be said in the next chapter.

---

[1] See the *Month*, September 1902, and the next chapter. The oldest record of the legend appears to be after the excommunication, an assertion by Walsingham, June 21, 1571 (*Foreign Calendar*, p. 477), who alleges Sir Nicholas Throckmorton as his authority, and he in turn refers to the Cardinal of Lorraine. There is no such statement in Throckmorton's actual dispatches, but between August 1, 1561, and January 1562, various rumours are reported by him, which, if pieced together and a little embroidered, would quite sufficiently account for the story in its subsequent form. See *Foreign Calendar*, 1561–1562, nn. 461 (3), 618, 751 (3), 789 (7), 833 (2, 4), 855.

CHAPTER III

§ 1. *King Philip II*

THOUGH King Philip II of Spain appears so frequently in the history of the English Catholics, and plays in it so important a part, it is curiously difficult to discover and to express the truth about him. The reason is that few men have divided opinions more deeply. If you saw him, lived and dealt with him, you were charmed. Dignified, devout, generous, laborious, affectionate, fearless, high-principled, there seemed to be no kingly virtue, no claim to loyalty, which he did not possess. He was revered, admired, and served by all about him with the sincerest enthusiasm. Many were the good priests and religious in Spain who considered him more Catholic than the Pope, because more aloof from intercourse with sinners, heretics, and trimmers. Many were the acute thinkers and speculators who hailed him as *El Re Prudente*. Many the faithful followers who, after all his failures, considered him almost omnipotent.

But put on the spectacles of his English, French or Italian rivals, and how different the aspect ! Bully, tyrant, fool, selfish, weak, cruel, faithless—these are the more parliamentary of the reproaches levelled against him. The abuse contained in the *Satire Menippée de la vertu du Catholicon d'Espagne* knows no restraint at all of civility or even of probability. *L'Apologie d'Orange* and the diatribes of Antonio Perez are but little more moderate.

The truth is that Philip was born to a very great but very difficult position, and that his talent for government was only moderate. Had he had the genius of a

PHILIP II, KING OF SPAIN

From the portrait by Titian, Florence

Napoleon, or even the energy of his father, Charles V, he might have played a wonderful rôle. But Philip had no other considerable gift beyond that of being a good plodder. He would have made a conscientious secretary, a good second in command, where perseverance and endurance were the chief requisites. When originality and adaptability to circumstances were needed, he was quite inefficient. He was a bad financier, for, though in frequent receipt of huge sums from the Indies, he was always embarrassed, and never had money for present needs. As a manager he was deplorably incompetent; his naval administration, for instance (where foresight is so necessary), was hopeless. Another deficiency, which increased his incapacity for great achievements, was the slowness with which he made up his mind. It was not that he was always wavering and undecided in the usual sense of the word, but he could not arrive at a new decision for months. During the whole decade with which we are engaged his attitude with regard to England remained as it had been in the time of Mary Tudor. Through all the momentous changes of Elizabeth's accession, the revolution in religion and suppression of the old Faith, during the remarkable tragedy of Mary Stuart, his policy remained—I do not say unaffected—but substantially unaltered. He long hoped against hope that England would yet come back of its own accord to the old position, and when this hope faded, he did not think of any innovation to make in his policy.

In studying a statesman so extremely conservative as Philip II, it is important to remember how political ideas took their place in his mind; for, once implanted, they were sure to work uniformly, varying only with the circumstances that presented themselves for consideration.

Philip had inherited the tradition of a pacific policy in regard to England from his father, and this policy, after many years of failure, seemed to be rewarded with permanent success, when, as husband of Mary Tudor, Philip himself bore the title of King of England. It was a providential interposition, which would, he trusted, one day repeat itself. Whilst King he had endeavoured, as well as he could, to throw himself into his part; and well would it have been for him if he had thoroughly educated himself in his new life. But he was almost immediately called to Flanders to receive it as his portion of the inheritance of Charles V. It was an unfortunate inheritance, for here, too, he was incapable of entering into the ideas of the people he was called upon to govern; and from this mutual incomprehensibility ensued by slow degrees that ever-widening breach which was so injurious to Spain and to the interests of Catholicism in all Northern countries.

Philip never returned to England, except for a few weeks in March 1557 to drag Mary into war with France. This war, too, the only one in which Philip took part personally, affected his ideas deeply. He was impressed by the loss of Calais and by the feebleness of the English attempts to recover it, while he failed to appreciate the great services of the English fleet, which entirely drove the French from the sea, and actively contributed to the defeat of Marshal de Termes at the end of the war. The erroneous conclusion formed by Philip, Alva and his other Spanish Councillors, was that England was at the mercy of France, and that unless he acted as its protector, France (especially now that the Dauphin had married the Queen of Scotland) would bestride the Channel and effectually cut him off from the Low Countries. This anxiety dominated all other considerations, and led Philip to act as Elizabeth's jealous protector during the first two years of her reign, until she had firmly established her power in England, and had finally driven the French from Scotland. That she had in the meantime also established heresy throughout the British Isles was a consequence which Philip sincerely regretted, but his slow mind never perceived how that could have been prevented.

Philip's most trusted adviser at this time was probably the Duke of Alva, and his " parescer," or opinion on this subject, has been quoted in the last chapter. The view taken by Margaret of Parma was much like that of Alva :—

" If England lose the bridle of Scotland, which has often hitherto checked English enterprises, there is reason to fear that Elizabeth will act much more boldly. . . . Moreover, in this way religion will be lost entirely, throughout the whole island, which cannot but lead to the most serious injuries to these [Low] countries, which lie so near and have such mutual intercourse.   Worst of all, there is little hope of her defending herself against France, and if the French do set foot in England, all those disadvantages will follow of which you and your Council have so often spoken. . . . What I think most necessary is that you should use every means to pacify them." [1]

Philip certainly knew what would be the result of a complete victory by Elizabeth, yet, spell-bound by fear of France, he looked on with but few protests while the heretical Queen crushed the old order in England.   He hardly raised a finger when Ireland was similarly dealt with, and he almost encouraged her to do the like in Scotland.

When Ireland had been taken in hand, his ambassador, Bishop de Quadra, for once could not restrain himself from saying that his master's policy was wrong.   He wrote to de Feria :—

" The Catholic religion has been suppressed in Ireland, although not without great opposition.   I cannot write about this as I should like, as I am so troubled, and perhaps it would make your Lordship more troubled still if I were to inform you what I suspect about it.   Suffice it to say that, if we are content to let God's cause go by the board, it will not take much to drag us down with it." [2]

Philip continued his policy of protection and peace at any price all through the first decade of Elizabeth's reign, and it is no exaggeration to say that the price he had to pay was licence for English piracy at sea.

There had been naval war with France at first, and the English sailors (whom an ill-judged system of monopolies shut out from freedom in the shipping trade), after making prizes of French ships in the Channel, went on to prey upon the Flemings and others whom they could meet   During

[1] Margaret of Parma to King Philip, Brussels, January 6, 1560.   A. Teulet, *Relations Politiques*, v. 64.

[2] *Spanish Calendar*, p. 127.   De Quadra to the Count de Feria, February 12, 1560.

the first four months of Elizabeth's reign, actions had been brought before the Privy Council (but in vain) to recover property taken by piracy to the value of 150,000 ducats.[1] The depredations went on increasing with ever bolder daring and over an ever-widening area, as the instructions sent to de Silva [2] five years later abundantly show. It was not that Elizabeth did nothing. Though she came in time to connive openly at piracy in foreign seas, she began with efforts, which, if weak, were not insincere, to suppress it in home waters. Everybody admitted that the evil was serious; but it was impossible to get justices, or vice-admirals, or juries at the sea-coast, to convict or punish transgressors. But as time went on, the difference in treatment between home and foreign piracy became more and more marked. As to the latter, the high officials, nay, the Queen herself, spoke with two voices, and the voice of encouragement, of course, prevailed.[3]

It is not necessary to go into further details on a subject which did not affect the Catholics very directly. The important point is to note the tendency of events from the very first. When we compare the years 1558 to 1569 with 1588, we see it is the same quarrel, the same contest, the same conclusion. In scale and in circumstances the differences are great. But a dispassionate consideration of Elizabeth's early years, when Spain was her best friend, shows that the sailing of the Spanish Armada should really be attributed to the policy which England adopted from the first.

Though the relations of England and Spain did not radically alter during the first decade, 1558 to 1568, the process of deterioration is sufficiently evident. Philip gradually became more inclined to negotiate with the party opposed to Cecil in the Council; Elizabeth became bolder and bolder in attacking Spanish interests. In January 1560, when the war against the French in Scotland

---

[1] *Spanish Calendar*, p. 56, April 18, 1559.   [2] *Ibid.*, p. 355.
[3] Mr. Dasent, in his introduction to the *Registers of Privy Council*, vol. vii., 1558–1570, which covers the change of religion, tells us: " It is scarcely an exaggeration to say that the keynote of the present volume is piracy," and indicates, p. xviii, the ineffective measures taken against it. Elizabeth gave the Royal Standard to Stukely in 1563 (*Spanish Calendar*, p. 335) and lent ships to Hawkins in 1564.

was in progress, the most critical moment in the whole of Elizabeth's reign, Elizabeth sent to Philip two ambassadors, one a Catholic, Lord Montague, and Chamberlain, a moderate Protestant, and gave them a dispensation, written by Cecil with his usual cunning, " from all pains and censures of her laws " in case they conform to the uses of the Church of Spain, supposing there is danger in the contrary course.[1] Lord Montague, during the short time of his stay in Spain, probably availed himself of the dispensation; Chamberlain did not.[2] Challoner, the next ambassador, tried to get the dispensation renewed, but presumably without success.[3]

Thus Chamberlain had a better chance than any other English ambassador of judging Philip fairly, and his reports are very favourable. He wrote on December 3, 1560 : " I dare warrant the indifferent [unbiassed] friendship of the King and something more," and he wishes the Queen would write but two words of her own hand to the King. Next week " he again certified the King's inclination to peace, and other inclination he is not able to judge [*i. e.* recognise] in him." Challoner similarly describes him as " a good, gentle prince, a lover of rest and quiet, delighting in hunting and retired solitariness with a few of his familiars." [4]

These early representatives, though Protestants and not fond of Spain, were at all events gentlemen who could discharge their duties at the Spanish Court without giving offence. But in 1566 Elizabeth sent Dr. John Man, an apostate priest, now Dean of Gloucester. One would think there must have been some hidden purpose unknown to us in the selection of so very unwelcome a representative. The Spanish ambassador reported at the time that he was a bitter heretic, and that his only qualification was facility in Italian, though Elizabeth, with her usual regardlessness for veracity, afterwards declared that " when she sent him

---

[1] *Foreign Calendar*, 1559, 1560, p. 318 (January 23, 1560). *Ibid.*, 1561–1562 (February 9, p. 521).

[2] He got into a passing difficulty with the Inquisition (November 1560), which was understood to rule that, though the ambassador was exempt from their jurisdiction, his servants were not. But there was no disposition shown to urge the claim. *Foreign Calendar*, 1560–1561, pp. 488 n. and 543.

[3] *Foreign Calendar*, 1561–1562, p. 521 (February 9, 1562).

[4] *Ibid.*, 1560–1561, pp. 418–427, and 1561–1562, pp. 493, 567.

she considered him rather an adherent of the old religion than a Protestant." Still Philip received him without open protest, and matters went on somehow till early in 1568, when during dinner he said, in the hearing of many, that the Pope was a wretched little monk only kept up by the King of Spain, but that the French Huguenots would eventually overthrow him. Philip naturally refused to see him again, and ordered him to leave Madrid for a neighbouring village, from whence Elizabeth in time recalled him.

On the whole, she behaved during this little crisis with a larger sympathy for her brother-in-law than might have been expected, while Cecil and his party, with their mean endeavours to throw the blame for their agent's misconduct upon others, and their unceasing vindictiveness, make a proportionately bad impression.[1]

King Philip's relations with Mary Stuart, as his relations with Elizabeth, are now generally recognised to have been very different to what they were traditionally supposed to

[1] The incident of John Man brings out so clearly the contrast between the English and Spanish Courts that the leading facts (too often misstated) may be usefully summarised. Man was appointed in January 1566, and de Silva's report on him is studiously moderate (*Spanish Calendar*, 1558–1567, p. 517). Afterwards, however, he hears from Lord Arundel that he was a person " of low position, bad and unworthy " (p. 525). In Madrid public feeling soon revolted, and the Papal Nuncio, Castagna, Bishop of Rossano, requested Philip to refuse him (Dispatch of April 29, 1566, Vat. Arch., Borghese i. 606, f. 37). Philip, on consideration, declined to do this, but sent him warning through the Conde de Feria and Duke of Alva that he must keep strictly within the ambassador's privileges (*ibid.*, fol. 88, cf. 56). It is clear that some misunderstanding arose over this oral message. When persons like Man are supposed to deal with Catholics like Alva, there is small chance of inevitable misconceptions getting cleared up. Man understood that, though he might practise Anglicanism, his servants must attend Mass (*Foreign Calendar*, 1566–1568, p. 446). The Spanish officials afterwards told him " it was possible that he, Man, mistook Alva's saying " (*Foreign Calendar*, ibid. This is Man's version of their words). Philip himself declared that it was an " utter falsehood to assert that the ambassador's household was forced to hear Mass," and, on the contrary, he complained of Man's servants disturbing Catholics by coming to church (*Spanish Calendar*, 1568–1579, p. 20). Whatever the truth, the matter went on for two years without coming to a head, until Philip heard of the words spoken at dinner, reported above, and they were attested even by Hogan, one of Cecil's spies at Madrid, who had, indeed, written home in the previous September to warn Cecil of Man's imprudence and quarrelsomeness (*Foreign Calendar*, pp. 417, 435). It was only after this that Man's complaint about his servants being forced to Mass is brought forward.

Bearing all this in mind, we must either think that Cecil's anger with de Silva was feigned, or, what is more probable, that it pointed to bigotry deeply irritated at Man's failure, though in words he declares that he " always had been averse " to his mission (*Spanish Calendar*, p. 35).

have been. Instead of having been the persistent foe of
the latter and enthusiastic friend of the former, he showed
an extraordinary and (as far as his own deeper interests
were concerned) an infatuated friendship for the English
Protestant and an unreasonable distrust of the Scottish
Catholic. " If the new Queen [of France] were to die,"
he wrote to his trusted minister Granvelle—" and her health,
you say, is very bad—it would rid us of great embarrassments,
and of the right which they assert to England." [1] Later
on, when she had become weak and powerless, there is,
indeed, less of harshness, but no help, actual or moral.   There
was no envoy at her Court in Edinburgh, not even a correspondent. Lethington's grandiose scheme (in 1562) for
marrying her to Don Carlos of Spain probably made a bad
impression on the hyper-cautious Spaniard, but he eventually favoured the plans for marrying her to the Archduke
Charles. After he had been fully informed about the Darnley
match, he not only favoured it, but actually sent her by
Yaxley a small subsidy, though it was lost by shipwreck
on the Northumbrian coast. It is to be noted, however,
that this favour did not involve any new principle in Spanish
politics. The Darnley match would have weakened the
alliance of Scotland and France; while England united with
Scotland would be more independent of the Continent than
before, both in politics and in power of defence, as Alva
had noted long before.[2] When, however, Darnley was dead
and Mary was powerless again, the Spanish ambassador
was constantly warning Elizabeth to take care lest the
infant James should be carried off to France, or the deposed
Queen escape thither.

In future chapters we shall find Philip's policy in Mary's
regard somewhat altered; but the old leading principle,
the predominant fear of France, is never laid aside.

For the English Catholics Philip did and could do but
little. No one, except the Pope, reminded the English
Government so immediately, by his mere title, that the

---

[1] " Se la reyna nueva se muriesse, que diz que anda muy mala, nos
quitaria de hartos embaraços, y del derecho que pretenden a Inglaterra."—
Philip to Granvelle, August 24, 1559. Weiss, *Papiers d'État de Cardinal
de Granvelle*, v. 643.

[2] *Papal Negotiations*, pp. 224, 233, 461.

great changes lately made were a revolution which the nation had not yet fully got used to. This was an irritant, and Philip perceived that he could effect most, especially as he had chosen patience for his policy, by saying little. His ambassadors occasionally remonstrated at the persecution, but in their own names, not in the King's. They made stronger representations when the liberty of the ambassador's house and chapel were violated; but it was always clear that Spain never meant war on such grounds. To the Catholics Philip's envoys spoke always of patience and submission, the policy which he followed himself:—

" I have advised the Catholics to avoid all occasion for this accusation (*i. e.* of speaking against the Queen), as it is not prudent to offend her. Rather let them treat matters which are not against their conscience with moderation and reserve, since they owe to God a respect for superiors. Even if they had the strength to resist them with arms in their hands, it would not be wise to do so, and much less now that they are in such evident peril." [1]

What shows the peculiarity of the situation in England, is the way in which the ambassador often goes on almost immediately to suggest that, although he does preach patience, it is also tempting to think of the facility with which a different line of action might be followed. Three weeks after the above letter he wrote :—

" The number of Catholics is always growing. . . . Certainly if they [the Protestants] knew or had any suspicion that the reduction of the country to the Faith was to be undertaken in earnest by those who could do it, there would not be much difficulty. The alarm is great, and with good reason, seeing the current of feeling and the dissensions among themselves and other troubles." [2]

On the 28th of March, 1568, de Silva, having been asked by Philip to help the Archbishop of Cashel, answered : " The worst of it is that your favour to these good folk does them more harm than good, so that it is necessary to act with the utmost caution." [3] This is a pregnant passage.

[1] *Spanish Calendar*, 1558–1567, p. 389.   [2] *Ibid.*, p. 390.
[3] *Ibid.*, p. 16.

Philip was the most powerful friend of the English Catholics, and yet to display any favour does them more harm than good. What could show their forlorn condition more clearly? Of course the ambassador's phrase is not to be taken quite " at the foot of the letter." If one had questioned the English Catholics of the time they would certainly have said that Spain was their best friend. If it gave them up, they would have been in despair.

If one had pressed them for the particulars in which help had been given the answer might not have been very clear. Flanders, it could be said, was the chief resort of the exiles. It was there that they could settle in peace, there Philip could best bestow alms, pensions and other favours, there the Seminaries were eventually founded which saved the Faith in England. But Spain's best service to England was probably the silent moral support of her example. Spain stood firm. The campaign of calumny and misrepresentation kept up against her did not, after all, prevent her maintaining her dignified position. It was, in fact, an unwilling confession of Spain's greatness and of the persistence of Catholicism; and the English Catholics recognised through the example of Spain that patience and forbearance in the cause of religion worked no disgrace, and were no sign of interior weakness or of abandonment by Providence. Later on we shall see the wonderful moral effect of Queen Mary Stuart's Catholicity, and the support of Elizabeth's example to the side of Protestantism is again an obvious parallel.

And looking back, as we now may, we can also recognise that Philip's policy towards England was at all times capable of a much stronger defence than the admirers of Elizabeth have hitherto been willing to admit. In the abstract, to be sure, we can see that very much more might have been done. If Philip could have organised a navy sufficient to protect his own ships from being robbed in times of peace and on the regular waterways, the fortunes of Spain would never have declined, as they did, under his rule. But he was by nature far too pacific and too incapable as an organiser to brace himself for such an effort. Indeed, in days before permanent fleets were usual, the idea could hardly be expected to suggest itself. It is not usual to blame people for falling short of greatness, yet this was what lay at the root of Philip's mistakes. It was, for instance, not due to any deliberate misjudgment on his part that he left Elizabeth (as we have seen) free to ruin the cause of Mary Stuart and all that she stood for. It was only that he was not large-minded enough to think out and carry through, in spite of his advisers, a really great change of policy.

§ 2. *The English Catholics*

Though nothing could be more interesting to us, or more germane to this history, than a detailed and documented account of English Catholics themselves at the beginning of Elizabeth's reign, particulars about them are, alas, hardly to be recovered now. Under stress of persecution the Catholics were retiring into the catacombs. Correspondence became rare, records were no longer kept. They dared not show themselves openly; in fact they endeavoured (with, unfortunately, much too much success) to pass as non-Catholics. So much so, that it becomes at once exceedingly difficult to tell who are Catholics, who are not. We must begin, therefore, by considering what extension we are to give to the word " Catholic."

It is evident that we can no longer restrict the name, as one would ordinarily do, to those who practised openly the duties of their religion, for there were no churches, and very few priests, considering the extent of the country. Even a return of those present at Mass on Sundays (if one had been obtainable) would have helped but little. Lists of those who attend Protestant churches tell us under modern circumstances whom to exclude from our lists of Catholics. But in days when attendance was enforced under heavy penalties—while it was alleged that no account would be made of inward assent,[1] so long as there was exterior observance—the numbers of those who attended English churches did not at all necessarily correspond

[1] To Maitland, Elizabeth said: " In the Sacrament of the Altar some think one thing, some another; *unusquisque in suo sensu abundet.*" *Mary's Letter to Guise*, Scottish Hist. Soc., xliii. 39.

with the number of those who should properly be counted Anglicans. Not only Catholics, but also all whom we should now class as Nonconformists, were then forced to appear at the new services, and the latter so far did so without protest.

This being so, we must for the present take account of intention not less than of profession, and we must class under the heading of Catholics, not only those who openly professed, but also those who were interiorly convinced of, the truth of Catholicism, *and who would have confessed it, if they had been free to do so.*

Under ordinary circumstances it is not necessary to insist upon the latter clause, for at present every one, broadly speaking, has enough liberty to confess his faith. But it was not so then. No one might confess his faith : every one was forced to go to the Protestant church. The legal fine, it is true, though heavy, was not crushing,[1] but a Tudor Government was little trammelled by legality. It had only to say that there was a suspicion of treason, and then they could, and they did, take any vengeance they desired, as we have seen in the cases of Sir Edward Waldegrave and others. It cannot be denied by those who understand how great was the influence wielded by the Tudor sovereigns over the comparatively simple—in many cases childlike— characters of the men of those days, that the profession of Protestantism was enforced by means which men of ordinary constancy could not resist. Hence the necessity of our studying the interior conviction.

The criterion of conformity in those days was attendance at Anglican services, and it is necessary to look more closely

---

[1] The penalty for non-attendance under the Uniformity Act of 1559 had been a fine of one shilling to the poor, and excommunication. The latter punishment, however much its spiritual effects were despised, still had its terrors, for it made the victim liable to arrest and imprisonment. The process, however, was cumbersome, and so far as we know rarely enforced, though a special Act *de excommunicato capiendo* was passed in 1563. The fine, though it sounds small to us, was a heavy one then, and ruinous to poor people. We have, however, as yet hardly any details as to the working of the Acts. Gee, *The Elizabethan Clergy*, 1898, p. 190.

Since the above was written, a commencement has been made in investigating this subject by W. P. M. Kennedy. He shows that the fines "did not attain their object," and that the best field for further research would be the diocesan registers. *English Historical Review*, 1918, ii. 517–28. Punishment for actually hearing Mass was much more severe.

at the subtle or ensnaring character of that test. We should notice that, while there was so far no obligation to do more than to be present at service, that mere presence did not involve renunciation of Catholicism. Protestant communion was not yet required, nor explicit submission to the new legislation. The service itself was taken from the Scriptures and the old Catholic formularies. The Lords, as we have heard, had taken pains that the liturgy should be as Catholic as possible, and, though they did not have their own way altogether, they succeeded to a considerable extent. Elizabeth and her ministers stated (when it served their purpose) that they did not care about interior assent; what they wanted was obedience to the laws.

There can be no question, therefore, that the test was, for the men of those days, insidious and deceitful in no ordinary degree. Nor was it less dangerous than specious. According to the law, it might not be necessary to be present at the sermon, but in practice that could rarely be escaped. It had to be listened to with external acquiescence, and external acquiescence in what the conscience condemned could hardly go on without grave breach of honour and duty to God, to say nothing of the scandal to others. Man is the creature of habit; and those who regularly yielded so far as to conform exteriorly, in time blunted their consciences and conformed interiorly. All through our period this sad but inevitable process was working itself out. Enforced church-going was not a proof of Anglicanism, but it was the most powerful means of uprooting the ancient Faith.[1]

One, perhaps the smallest, of the inconveniences which

---

[1] It may be well to add for completeness' sake that, while church-going was the test for the people at large, the test for the clergy, for officers of State, and generally for all those who wished to get on, was the Oath of Royal Supremacy and submission to the laws. Hence church-going might be considered as " the thin end of the wedge," for the time being. Later on, as people's ideas became clearer, its function was taken by new snares, such as " the bloody question " and " the Oath of Allegiance." In King Henry's reign the Oath of Supremacy had played this part. For many people, when Gallicanism was common, thought the oath was merely a royal flourish which, like other regal pretensions, should not be scanned too closely. They would not take its schismatical character seriously. Under pressure, Catholics sometimes relapsed into this frame of mind even in Elizabeth's reign. See, for instance, the description of Lord Hastings of Loughborough and others being forced to take the Oath of Supremacy in July 1561 (R. O. *Dom. Eliz.*, xviii., n. 19; cf. nn. 7, 8).

ensued was (and still is) the difficulty of calculating the numbers of those who should be considered Catholics. By some they are estimated at ninety per cent. of the population at this time, by most at over fifty per cent.[1]

It is only even between such wide limits that we can reach any certainty, and this because we have to guess at *interior* beliefs (a matter always extremely difficult); and this we must do, not for one or two only, but for large multitudes, who are outwardly giving the signs of opposite convictions. Such men were in reality weak Catholics, but the Catholics of that day styled them " Schismatics," [2] and all calculations turned on their supposed proclivities. Catholics in high hope, and despondent Protestants would add them to the Catholic side, and so give the old Church a great majority. Then the mood might change, and similar, or even the same statisticians might, with an eye to the future, reckon the waverers with the Protestants. The number of " Schismatics " was, of course, largest during the early parts of the reign. They then gradually diminished, and are hardly heard of after the end of the century.

To return to the historical sequence of events. The English Catholics began, unfortunately, with a complete collapse. The new Church service was everywhere introduced ; the old disappeared from view. Priests who remained faithful gave up their clerical dress, and seemed to be absorbed by the laity; the Bishops and other leaders were placed in confinement. The few religious houses were scattered ; some communities managed to escape to Flanders, where they were received by their Flemish brethren, and so were at first lost as separate English establishments. It would seem that at the end of Elizabeth's first year the only

[1] *Sander's Report to Cardinal Moroni* deals on the whole with facts within the writer's cognizance; yet he says (1561): " The firm opinion of those capable of judging is that hardly one per cent. of the English people is infected " (*C.R.S.*, i. 45). Again " Infinita multitudo tam nobilium quam popularium " (Anon. 1563, *Papal Negotiations*, p. 175). Generally, however, the estimate given is that *the majority* is Catholic. Thus, April 17, 1559: " Maior pars Anglorum in divi Petri nave navigat " (*Deflebilis Status Anglicanæ gentis*, Jesuit MS., *Anglia Historica*, i., f. 57); " Molti signori principali di quel regno, et la maggior parte delli populi " (*Memorial* of about January 1560, Meyer, p. 403).

[2] I do not know of any authoritative explanation of the term. They never united into any schismatical body. I suppose they were thought to continue the position of the Schismatics under Henry VIII.

H

vestiges in the world of the Church of St. Augustine and St. Thomas were to be found in the little hospices for English pilgrims and sailors in Rome and some foreign ports, as Seville. Nor was this severance one of appearance only. For the time being correspondence had ceased, broadly speaking; and with correspondence, government.

But every one knew that the old Faith was living on in secret and would find new ways of renewing its vitality by re-connecting itself with the Church universal. Unfortunately, the imprisonment of the whole hierarchy and the ambiguous position of Paul IV retarded the process; and nothing seems to have been done till after the election of Pius IV (Christmas 1559). The earliest project of which we have record was probably made at the beginning of the next year, and suggested that the Pope should endeavour to put himself into communication with the Queen through Sir Francis Englefield, who was then at Padua. Nothing seems to have come of this, but on the 2nd of March papal correspondence began again, and it is noteworthy that the letter is addressed to the Spanish ambassador in London, not, indeed, as such, but because he was a Bishop, and the only Bishop in England who was at liberty to look after the Catholics and to protect them.[1]

A few weeks later Pius resolved to send Parpaglia to Elizabeth, and in spite of his failure Girolamo Martinengo was sent next year, 1561, as has been seen, though his mission proved as barren in direct results as the former. But the indirect results were not inconsiderable. Not only did both envoys keep attention and sympathy fixed on the English question, they also became the channels for supplying Rome with reliable information gathered from the English Catholics in Flanders; and they gave liberal alms from the Pope, and spoke for them to the Spanish Governors of the Netherlands. When they returned, the English Catholic exiles in Flanders, in spite of great poverty and the dejection caused by defeat, had become a reorganised

---

[1] Memorial, *Sopra li negotii d'Inghilterra*, Meyer, p. 403. Though anonymous, it is official, in so far as it is found among the papers of Cardinal Moroni, the " Protector " of England, *C.T.*, lxiv., tom. 28, fol. 299. Pius's letter of March 2, 1560, is Arch. Vat., Arm. lxviii., *Epistolæ Pii IV.* l. f. 227. Pius had heard of de Quadra's efforts through Vargas, Spanish ambassador in Rome.

body, destined to take a leading part in the maintenance of the Faith at home. Pius IV appealed to King Philip for them on August 19, 1560; Mgr. Commendone wrote to Rome for them November 30, 1561. Regular alms had been given by the Pope before December 10, 1564, when their " continuance " was promised. In a petition dated March 8, 1566, their numbers are given as : Priests 68, religious men 40, nuns 25, students 37, seven families totalling 30 persons, and 13 others, in all 213 persons.[1]

This increase in numbers is but too sure a proof that in England things were getting 'worse. On the day that Martinengo was forbidden entry—May 5, 1561—a new commission to persecute the Catholics was issued to the Ecclesiastical Commissioners, and the prisons were soon filled. In July many were released, after being fined and forced to take the Oath of Allegiance. But the persecution continued. On November 13 six Oxford students were sent to the Tower,[2] and on April 2, 1562, de Quadra writes that the Tower was still full. Of the prisoners at the latter date, some, he suspects, were confined out of fear of Mary Stuart, who had just returned to Scotland.

These severities had the indirect effect of making a pronouncement by ecclesiastical authority upon " churchgoing " very urgent; for attendance at service was perhaps in every case a *sine qua non* for escape or release. Moreover, Elizabeth was now priding herself on the reception of her liturgy by the *politiques* of Catherine de Medici, and alleging that the Pope himself might approve of it, or

[1] Pius's appeal is made in the dispatch to the nuncio at Madrid, Arch. Vat., *Germania*, iv., f. 75. This probably enclosed the list of seventeen exiled clergy, now preserved in Arm. lxiv., vol. 28, f. 281, which was perhaps sent on by Parpaglia in July 1560. Commendone's dispatch is, Arch. Vat.. f. *Barberini*, lxii., vol. 58. fol. 159. Another copy B.M., *Egerton*, 1078. Pius's promise of December 10, 1564, was in answer to an address by an Oxford scholar, preserved at Stonyhurst, *Anglia*, i., n. 2. The petition of Chauncey, Sander, and John Rastel to Father [Polanco] is Arch. Vat., Arm. lxiv. v. 28, f. 338. See below, p. 248.

[2] They had resisted the removal of the crucifix from their college chapel (*Spanish Calendar*, p. 218). The news was conveyed to the Pope by Commendone (see last note). Cardinal Moroni wrote from Trent, August 9, 1563, that some students had escaped to Louvain, though some had perished of prison treatment (Arch. Vat., *C. T.* xxvii., f. 120). These may be a different set; one may hope that the poor fellows confined in 1561 got out sooner. Many details about the ejection of the Catholics from Oxford will be found in Wood's *Antiquitates* (ed. 1674, pp. 281–4); but a connected account of the movement has not yet been attempted.

perhaps had already done so. It is easy to see how dangerous the temptation for the English Catholics was, when told that all their suffering was for a point on which the authorities of their own Church did not support them.

Under such circumstances it can cause no wonder to find that about Midsummer 1562 a letter was sent by some English gentlemen to Mascareynas, the Portuguese ambassador at Trent, for him to lay before the Legates, which he did on the 2nd of August. The petition asked that the opinions should be sought about the English case from men at the Council who were noted for piety and learning, and this in preference to a decree properly so called. Accordingly a congregation of thirteen was arranged, presumably by Mascareynas, for the Portuguese were in a majority. The President was Cardinal Hosius, a German Pole, one of the Legates, and the representative of Northern Catholics; he had also in his following both Bishop Goldwell and Dr. Sander. The Vice-President was Don Bartholomew of the Martyrs, the saintly Archbishop of Braga. There were also another Archbishop and two more Bishops, the two first of the Pope's theologians, Peter de Soto, O.P., who had taught at Oxford in Mary's reign, and Alphonso Salmeron. All four theologians representing Portugal were also of the number, and Father Diego Lainez, S.J. They eventually issued a longish exhortation to courage in resisting the new services, which they declared could in no way be tolerated, and they warmly praised the noble example already given by the English Catholics: " Where else in the world has the Faith, under bitter persecution and vehement opposition, been defended by men of religion and piety with more constancy, strength and courage ? " [1]

While this case was being discussed at Trent, the same petition (with one further clause) was proposed anew to

---

[1] I have searched in vain at Rome for this *Responsum*. We know it through an edition secretly printed by Father Garnet about 1600, *The Declaration of the Fathers of the Councell of Trent concerning the going unto Churches, at such time as hereticall service is saied or heresy preached*. This is an appendix to his *Treatise of Christian Renunciation*. For the circumstances of publication see his letter to Persons, June 2, 1601, *Month*, 1898, i. 465. From Garnet it has been reprinted by H. More, *Historia Provinciæ Anglicanæ*, St. Omers, 1660, pp. 66–73; also by Eupator (= James Mendham), 1850. See also Bayne, pp. 163–73.

Bishop de Quadra.[1] He preferred to refer it to Rome, accompanied by a letter, in which he says that the case is an extremely difficult one. The " case " sent in was rather remarkable, for it did not present the circumstances precisely according to the terms of the English law, but in a stronger form. The penalty for non-attendance at church, for instance, is stated roundly as death; and without mentioning " the communion," the service is described, for the sake of the argument, as " entirely made up from Scripture and the prayers of the Church, without any false doctrine or impiety "; the sermon in support of heretical doctrine is, however, admitted to be inevitable. The question proposed from England on August 7, 1562, asked whether under such circumstances attendance was a deadly sin.

The answer of the Holy Office, given on the 11th [2] of October following, was in the affirmative. Attendance, it was said, even though " not so much *communicatio* with heretics," is commanded solely in order to maintain " the life of heretics," that is, the Tudor fiction that Catholicism had expired on St. John's Day, 1559 (see Chapter II), and that now all lived as Protestants. This can never be licit; moreover, men of authority cannot be present without giving scandal to little ones. Studiously mild as had been the description of the Anglican service, and studiously emphatic the representations of possible excuses for yielding, this strong official answer shows plainly how extremely far Pope Pius really was from having approved the new service.[3]

With the answer from the Roman Inquisitors, one of whom was the future Pope Sixtus V, there had come a brief

---

[1] *Spanish Calendar*, April 3, 1562, p. 258. De Quadra probably acted in these matters through his chaplains. Of these Stephen Hopkins had been imprisoned and released again before the end of 1561 (Gee, p. 183); and he may have been the priest " who knows every Catholic in the place, and has absolved and administered the sacraments to many," and who was, therefore, obliged to fly in 1563, for receiving Storey (*ibid.*, p. 324). Matthias Rodarte remained with the ambassador till his death (*ibid.*, p. 362).

[2] This is Froude's date (B.M., *Add.* 26,056 A, p. 182). But October 2 is more likely—the day on which de Quadra's faculties were signed: ii is often miscopied as 11.

[3] Maitland, *English Historical Review*, 1900, pp. 530–2, and *Collected Papers*, iii. 179. A better text of the answer from Rome in Bayne, p. 296; but his narrative, p. 176, is somewhat over-stated.

to de Quadra,[1] answering the second half of his petition.
It empowered him to sub-delegate powers for absolving
those who had fallen into heresy and desired to be reconciled. This was normally an episcopal faculty, and its
concession to de Quadra is the first record we have of the
Holy See exercising its " apostolical " jurisdiction to supple-
ment the " ordinary " jurisdiction of the local Bishops,
now so reduced in numbers and in power to rule. *The
Resolution of Trent* was the earliest legislation on the
Catholic side to remedy Elizabeth's Settlement.

De Quadra wrote to ask Philip if he might use the faculty,
pointing out that, though the Queen would be very angry
if she came to know of it, there was very little danger of
her finding it out, as he had leave to sub-delegate, and could
keep secret the fact that he was the channel of the jurisdiction.[2] We unfortunately do not know what King
Philip answered. In any case, as de Quadra died August 24,
1563, he could not have exercised the faculties long.

His last months were among the most trying of his
embassy. Elizabeth was helping the French Huguenots in
their revolt against their sovereign and the Catholic party;
and it was in accordance with Cecil's methods to act the
provocateur, and to encourage his co-religionists by showing
his power to bully both the English Catholics and the representatives of the great Catholic Powers, the Spaniard even
more than the French, because Spain was supposed to be
the champion of Catholicism. Durham House, where de
Quadra lived, was therefore raided several times, and early
one Sunday morning those at Mass there were led away
captive, though they were all Spaniards or Flemings,
Philip's subjects.[3]

The inoffensive English Catholics were still worse used
by the enactment of new persecuting laws, called the
" Assurance of the Supremacy." These measures were
resolved upon in November and December; and when
Parliament met, in January, the preachers, even in the
Queen's presence, exhorted her " *to kill the caged wolves*,"

[1] Arch. Vat., xliv., xi., n. 419, dated October 2, 1562, printed in
Bayne, p. 297, from Simancas.
[2] *Spanish Calendar*, p. 267.
[3] *Ibid.*, January and February, 1563, pp. 280, 295, etc.

i. e. the imprisoned Bishops of the ancient hierarchy.[1]   The Lord Keeper Bacon told the Commons at the beginning of the session that " for want of discipline it is that so few come to service, and the Church is so unreplenished, notwithstanding that at the last Parliament a law was made for good order to be executed.   Therefore if it be too easy, let it be made sharper ; if already well, then see it executed." The Commons, thus urged, assured the Queen in return that they would " employ their whole endeavours to devise and establish the most strong acts of preservation of your Majesty . . . and the most penal, sharp, and terrible statutes."

The Lords had cut out the worst penalties from the Supremacy Act originally introduced ;[2] they were now restored, and the machinery for working the Religious Settlement made more stringent and effective.   The new Bishops were given enlarged powers for searching out those who were supposed to have sympathy with the old Faith, and for tendering them the Oath of Supremacy, the third refusal of which was now made a capital offence.

The prospect for the persecuted Catholics was indeed dark.   Bishop Scott, abandoning his bail, and Dr. Storey, breaking prison, escaped from the country ; Bishop Bonner was tendered the oath, which was understood to be the prelude to bloodshed, when fortunately the fury of the fanatics cooled.   It had been aroused by the prospect of Protestant victories in France.   When, however, the Huguenots collapsed, and actually turned against the English, the lust for persecution subsided.   The ejection of the English from Havre in July was followed in August by an outbreak of what was then called " the plague," which the soldiers may have brought back with them. There was a scare and a general exodus from London. Even some of the prisoners were sent away with their keepers for the time, and the year 1563 closed far more peaceably than it had begun.[3]   The next year, 1564, was also relatively calm, not for England only, but for the whole of Europe.

[1] *Spanish Calendar*, p. 291.   [2] *Venetian Calendar*, p. 52.
[3] Archbishop Parker's moderation perhaps contributed to this.   Gee, p. 192 ; Bayne, p. 199.

Then came the "vestiarian controversy," and the Government, no longer keen on pleasing the Puritans, left the Catholics for the moment in greater peace. Elizabeth publicly snubbed Nowell, the Dean of Westminster, for his sermon against Dr. Martial's *Treatise of the Cross*, of which we shall hear more immediately, and she told de Guzman, the new ambassador, " we differ from other Catholics only in matters of small importance." [1] Nevertheless the persecution was continued in less violent ways, and in particular Catholics were being steadily eliminated from the magistracy.

During this lull further progress was made in the distribution of faculties for confession.[2] About the middle of 1564 Cardinal Ghislieri, then head of the Holy Office and afterwards Pope Pius V, gave to Doctors Nicholas Sander and Thomas Harding, and to Thomas Wilson and Thomas Peacock, priests, full faculties for the reconciliation of those who had lapsed into heresy. It is noteworthy that they would not at first refuse absolution to laymen who went to Protestant services "*proper dissentientes multorum sententias.*" That is, according to modern terminology, there was still a probable opinion excusing the practice from grave sin. In other words, as there were many different opinions, therefore the law was not yet clear. But some time in the summer of 1566 Pope Pius V spoke strongly in Consistory against the toleration of such a practice, and Laurence Vaux, one of the foremost of the English clergy, was afterwards admitted to audience, at which the Pope ordered him to convey to Doctors Sander and Harding the substance of what he had said. The two Doctors, on receiving the message, moved Vaux to go into England himself and there to make the Pope's message known to those whom it most concerned. He did so, and we have a deeply interesting letter of his written in England,

---

[1] *Spanish Calendar*, March 10, and April 26, 1565, pp. 405, 425, cf. pp. 406, 416.

[2] The paragraphs which follow are drawn principally from two letters : (1) That of Sander and Harding to Cardinal Moroni (printed in Meyer, pp. 412–14), June 11, 1567. It records the steps taken during the last four years. (2) The letter of Laurence Vaux, November 2, 1566 (printed in T. G. Law's useful *Introduction to Vaux's Catechism* (Camden Soc., N. S. iv.) 1885, pp. xxxii–xxxviii). Their concurrence is not always obviously clear, because Vaux dwells chiefly on the faculties which had been granted, Sander on the practice of church-going, which was to be condemned.

and dated November 2, 1566, in which he speaks very strongly indeed against the common failing both of the laity and of the clergy at this time.

Next year, 1567, it was necessary to urge the matter still further. After the new orders had been promulgated and were being received with good effect, some recalcitrants suggested that Vaux's authority could not be very great, for he had not one word in writing to substantiate or explain his powers. Sander and Harding, appealed to by Wilson, wrote again to Rome (June 11, 1567), and asked Cardinal Moroni to procure them a definite *pagella*, the original of which they would keep in Flanders, and give notarial attestations of it to their representatives in England. This petition was granted on August 14, 1567, and authenticated copies of it were sent to England, where one was found by the Government after the Northern Rising, when it was printed by the English Government with a fiercely Calvinistic *Declaration* by Thomas Norton.[1]

About the same time that these faculties began to be renewed through the English theologians at Louvain, similar powers were entrusted to, and used by, certain English Jesuits. The Society of Jesus, then just coming into view as a protagonist against the advances of Protestantism, was sure to attract the English Catholic fugitives, who were often young men inclined to the clerical state. By the time of the last sessions of the Council of Trent some thirty or forty had been already enrolled, and a few had completed their religious training and were at work, generally in the country in which they had entered. Father David Wolfe, moreover, had been sent to Ireland, and Father William Goode afterwards worked with him there, and Father de Gouda had been to Scotland. But the

---

[1] *A Bull graunted by the Pope to Doctor Harding and other by reconcilement and assoyling of English Papists to undermyne faith and allegiance to the Quene, etc.*, no date or place. A broadside edition of this is in the Vatican, *Varia Politicorum*, lxvi. 258, and in the British Museum (c. 37, d. 36), an edition with the same type broken up in 8vo. The edition, with the rabid " declaration " that follows, is attributed to Thomas Norton, barrister and afterwards rack-master in the Tower. The date, from internal evidence, and from the entry in the *Stationers' Company's Register* (ed. Arber, i. 413), must be June 1570.

The document printed is not a Bull, but a petition to the Holy Office, made up by faithful quotations from Harding and Sander's letter above cited, with the answer of the congregation, given on August 14, 1567.

rigour of persecution had prevented their organising in either country missions that could be worked regularly. Father Simon Bellost, who preached in Flanders, was more successful, and he was given faculties for the English there, even that of receiving back heretics, as early as 1562.[1] During the quiet years, 1564, 1565, Father Thomas King was actually sent into England, but under some difficulties, as he was an invalid, destined to live a few months only. He received, however, full faculties,[2] and started zealously the career of a missionary, going about in secular dress, which caused some comment among the clerics of the old school. His death, however, ensued so soon that we hear nothing of the results of his labours, which were remembered chiefly as precedents for later imitation.[3]

§ 3. *The Controversy of* 1564–1567

Another advantage which followed from the greater peace of 1564, was the first publication of English Catholic books in defence of the Faith.[4] When Sander wrote his summary of the Catholic achievement in 1561, he made no claim for success in controversy. When he wrote his *De Schismate* twelve years later, he said of the controversy which had meantime intervened, that " nothing during the last fifty years had advanced the Catholic cause more." [5]

But as the Royal Commissioners kept driving out priests and scholars from churches and universities, the exiles began to gather in ever-increasing numbers at the nearest points in Flanders and the north of France, especially in the great port of Antwerp and at the University of

---

[1] Cardinal Moroni refers to this June 21, 1563. Arch. Vat., *Concilio di Trento*, xxviii. 97.

[2] The Jesuit General wrote, February 19, 1565, to the provincial in Flanders (*Flanders Register*, p. 254 b), sending faculties for Father King to reconcile heretics.

[3] Foley, *Records of the English Province of the Society of Jesus*, vii. 1437. He may be the Jesuit of whom Allen speaks, *Letters*, p. 33.

[4] Dr. Richard Smith, first Chancellor of the University of Douay (died in 1563), was the first English Catholic to publish books on the religious problem. But he wrote in Latin, and addressed himself primarily to the Reformation leaders, to English Reformers only occasionally and in the second place. Ninian Winzet began to publish in Scots in 1563, 1564.

[5] *English College, Rome, MS.*, lib. iii., f. 136.

Louvain, as we have already heard. In the course of 1562 or 1563, they were joined by Thomas Harding, D.D., once chaplain and confessor to Bishop Gardiner. He was also an influential Wykehamist, and the lead which he took at this time may account for the surprising rally of Winchester men who now combined to work with him.[1] To understand this we must go back a little.

John Jewel, a clever scholar, and faithful disciple of Peter Martyr, had been at once promoted to the See of Salisbury by Elizabeth, and not without reason from her point of view. His sermons, too, were esteemed at Court, and he was certainly skilful in representing the religious ideas of those who had the making of the new creed, in forms that were gratifying to them. A feature in his sermons was the defiance he hurled at the Papists. Only let them prove that this or that Roman practice was found in the first six centuries and he would himself submit to the Pope. Thrice did he issue his challenge, to the great comfort of all who desired nothing better than reasons for yielding to the Queen's injunctions. The Catholics, remembering the violence done to Jewel's opponents at the Westminster Conference, held their peace; indeed many of them were under bond to do so. Dr. Henry Cole, however, late Dean of St. Paul's, though also bound to silence, attempted an ingenious diversion. He wrote Jewel an adroit letter of inquiry, which by insinuation effectively laid bare the weakness of Jewel's cause. " Why not," said the Catholic, " prove the essentials of your creed ? After all, what does it matter about the points of modern Catholic discipline whose antiquity you deny if the underlying doctrine is certainly true ? " Jewel declined to explain, which had

---

[1] Of the eighteen English Catholic writers who brought out books at this time ten were Wykehamists : Thomas Dorman (3 books), John Fenn (1), Thomas Harding (5), Nicholas Harpsfield (1), John Martial (2), Robert Poyntz (1), John Rastell (5), Nicholas Sander (6), Thomas Stapleton (6). To these should be added John Fowler, the printer, who also wrote one book. The other writers were William (afterwards Cardinal) Allen (2), George Bullock (1), Alan Cope (1), Louis Evans (afterwards apostatised) (2), Thomas Hoskins (1), Robert Johnson (edidit Henry Joliffe) (1), Richard Shacklock (1), Laurence Vaux (1). The Winchester men were not only more numerous, but they also wrote more and better books, that is, about thirty-one books (or, counting new editions, thirty-five) to ten by the rest. Biographies of nearly all will be found in the *D.N.B.*, and in Gillow's *Biographical Dictionary of the English Catholics*.

inevitably, for Catholics, the appearance of shuffling. Cole thereupon showed the correspondence to a friend, and it was soon discovered by the lynx-eyed Protestants. Cole was haled before Elizabeth's inquisitors and badgered, perhaps punished; and Jewel was now bidden to publish an answer, which he did in that *de haut en bas* style so irritating to those who knew the answer, but were restrained by force from uttering it.[1]

This was in 1560. Next year the irritation was still further increased by the attempt made by Throckmorton in Paris to display the Elizabethan Settlement as a sort of *Via Media* between French Calvinism and Catholicism. In these intrigues Jewel's pen was frequently employed by Cecil,[2] and at the end of the year his *Apologia* for Anglicanism began to be circulated abroad. In 1562 it was published in English as well.

When Harding reached the Netherlands, therefore, there were very powerful inducements for him to do all he could to defend the Catholic side in the controversy, which had thus far been forcibly kept in silence. He had originally intended to circulate his answer in manuscript, a frequent practice in those days, but he eventually found means to print it, under the title : *An Answer to Maister Juelle's chalenge, by Doctor Harding* (Louvain, Jean Bogard, 1564). It was very well received, ran through three editions, and evoked many supporters and opponents, the most successful of the former being John Martial, whose *Treatise of the Cross* made an even greater impression, because of the vestiarian controversy with the Puritans then in progress. The Government were, nevertheless, instant in forbidding by Royal Proclamation the importation, circulation, even the reading or possession of the new books of controversy, and a special Act against them was proposed in 1566.[3]

---

[1] *Works of John Jewel*, Parker Society, 1845.

[2] Cecil made him "feign an epistle sent from hence thither." It was printed secretly in England, and Throckmorton was asked to get it also printed in France, to give it "more probability." All very characteristic of Cecil's sharp practice (*Foreign Calendar*, 1561–1562, p. 104, cf. pp. 481, 504).

[3] No copy of the proclamation seems to survive; but it is referred to as early as April 1564 (*Dom. Cal.*, p. 239). There is a copy of the proposed act, R.O., *Dom. Eliz.*, xli., n. 25, cf. n. 29.

But this repressive legislation, though often repeated, was never effective. These books awakened in the Catholics, perhaps for the first time, a widespread enthusiasm, a resolve to run risks; and over forty issues of fresh volumes or editions was made in two or three years. Though these issues were probably not large, the grand total must have been quite considerable, and proves that there must, already at this time, have been much more mutual understanding and correspondence between Catholics all over the country than we should otherwise have thought.

The movement grew rapidly. In 1564 five volumes (or editions) were published, in 1565 fifteen, in 1566 twelve. Then came an even more rapid decline; in 1567 nine, in 1568 four, in 1569 none. This cessation, however, was due to causes altogether extrinsic to the English Catholics. The Reformation was spreading even to the Netherlands. " The printing has been confused by Flemish Gospellers," says Harding in his *Rejoinder* (Antwerp, May 1566).

The imprints tell the same story. With only two or three exceptions, all the printing was done at Antwerp,[1] until the outbreak of "the Iconoclasts," whose violence, just alluded to by Harding in May 1566, came to a head in August. After this English Catholic printing at Antwerp was practically reduced to a standstill, and the work was transferred to Louvain, where the interesting Wykehamist and Oxford scholar, John Fowler, opened a press, and issued about a dozen volumes (some Latin), before the great troubles began in 1568; and then amid the general distress printing ceased altogether for some time. The more notable students, like Sander and Stapleton, continued to write, but they had to use Latin in order to find a sale among the *literati* of Europe. The Catholic book market

[1] The Antwerp printers were Christophe Plantin, who printed one volume (Harpsfield's *Dialogi Sex*) in 1566; Gillis van Diest, eight volumes, 1564–1565 (Sayle's *Catalogue of Early English Printed Books, University Library, Cambridge*, ascribes them to Gillis the younger); Hans van Laet (nine volumes, 1564–1566); Willem Sylvius (two volumes, 1565, 1566). John Fowler printed four volumes at Antwerp in 1566, then migrated to Louvain, where he printed twelve more in 1566–1568. Hans Bogard at Louvain printed four volumes, 1566–1567. The ecclesiastical imprimatur is generally given by Cunerus Petri de Browershaven, parish priest of St. Peter, Louvain, even when the books are printed at Antwerp. He declares that the book has been read and approved by English theologians. —See F. Olthoff, *Boekdrukkers in Antwerpen*, 1891, pp. 25, 33, 97.

in England was all but closed for some time. It is also possible (though the evidence is scanty) that William Carter (afterwards a martyr), the only Catholic who dared to print in England before the arrival of the Jesuits, set forth some book in English at this time, but we do not know what it was.[1]

Though we cannot analyse here the theological and patristic arguments employed on either side,[2] or pronounce judgments on their merits, there can be no question, historically speaking, that the fruits of victory remained with the Catholics. Never again was a challenge so shallow as Jewel's to be put forward with such solemnity. Moreover, it was obvious that, if the Catholics could fight with such good effect, in spite of poverty and ruin, and with the risk of the most cruel reprisals, what would not they have done had they had behind them all the resources of the English Church and universities, which they had founded and endowed? Neither side, it must be confessed, shows remarkable controversial skill. The patristic knowledge does not seem unusual, and the literary effect is confused by handling numerous objections in scholastic form. However praiseworthy this system in actual debate between two persons, it is unconvincing when the writer argues with himself, as he always appears to do when he writes an argument in dialogue form. Again, both sides were too grimly in earnest to take thought for the amenities of literature—for style, illustration, ornament. They were also too intent on parry and thrust, too anxious to transfix their adversaries, to devote much time to the outside public and to make their appeal quite frankly to them. They habitually set forth their opponents' errors in the blackest colours. Harding, for instance, claims to enu-

[1] He was charged by Bishop Aylmer with having printed a book written by Harpsfield. But Aylmer's diatribe was delivered nearly twenty years later, and it is not always reliable. Bridgewater, *Concertatio Ecclesiæ Anglicanæ*, 1594, f. 131 b.

[2] A list of the Protestant writers in this controversy will be found in Fulke's *Confutation of Stapleton and Martial*, 1580 (reprinted by Parker Society, 1849), pp. 3, 4, but his quotation of titles is unsatisfactory, and he does not distinguish between this and later controversies. The writers were Bishops Jewel and Bridges, John Barklet, James Calfehill, Robert Crowley, Edward Dering, Abraham Hartwell the elder, and Alexander Nowell. Lives of all will be found in *D.N.B.*

merate 1000 lies in his *Rejoinder to M. Jewel's Reply* (1566), and Edward Dering in his answer attempts to return the compliment.

But though all were too vehement to do justice even to themselves, the Catholics were distinctly the more restrained. Their books are frequently dedicated with all due respect to Elizabeth herself; and they endeavour to write so that their books may not be unwelcome to moderate men. In earnestness, and in appreciation of the real point of difficulty, their superiority can hardly be questioned; and their success in confirming their own followers was great. They awakened among the Catholics the first enthusiasm they had felt since the fall of the Church. A new zeal for Catholic truth, says Sander, " made the Catholics dare everything in order to learn about their Faith and to defend it : so much so that (in spite of all penalties) not less than 20,000 of these books were imported into England and secretly sold." Cardinal Allen considered them the harbingers of the great Catholic revival which came twenty years later : " Books opened the way." [1]

But however considerable the success of these publications, it lasted but a short time, and cannot conceal from us the sad truth that the Catholic party was on the whole failing, and dwindling rapidly. With no friends or protectors, very, very few and very scattered priests, what wonder if the faith of many grew cold, and hope died down? But at the moment of their deepest despondency, Mary Stuart, escaping from close prison in Scotland, fled to England, only to find herself again in confinement, which, if more honourable, was more effectual than ever. Yet the advent of that fugitive lady, to whom we must devote some space, was to contribute powerfully to the political and spiritual awakening of the Catholic body.

§ 4. *Mary Queen of Scots*

The next great leader whose influence on the fortunes of the English Catholics we have to examine is Queen Mary

[1] Sander, *De Schismate*, lib. iii. in MS., English College, Rome, f. 136 b. Allen, *Apologie of Two English Seminaries*, 1581, p. 26.

Stuart, but it is only under this aspect, *i. e.* with her influence upon the English Catholics, that we are at present concerned. Her intensely interesting fortunes and adventures need not at present occupy us.

We have already heard of the intrigues of the French in 1559 at Rome, either to obtain a declaration of her rights to the English throne, or at least to prevent those rights from being injured and over-ridden, as the Spaniards, with their jealous fear of French ambition, were evidently ready to do. But we have been unable to trace any real adherence to her among the English Catholics. France having been the ally of Protestantism for so long, and being actually at war with England at the time of Mary Tudor's death, it was obviously improbable that the English Catholics should straightway advocate the Queen of France's accession to the throne.

But when Francis was dead, and Mary was almost entirely without resources, the queen of a country which had revolted, supported only by the pension paid her as Queen Dowager of France, her position at once changed. There could be no reason now for letting fear of her power obscure the consideration of her rights by birth.

Accordingly, after another year, we find Sander and Maurice Clenog, English exiles at Louvain, in their dealings with papal negotiators, speak openly of Mary as heiress to the English throne; and in their dreams for the future, they consider that Philip of Spain should undertake the enterprise of England, and that Mary, wedded perhaps to the Archduke Ferdinand of Austria, should be set on the English throne. The same idea was formulated, probably by Sander, as we have heard, at the time of the Council of Trent, in 1563, only to be most solemnly rejected as a matter of practical politics by the great Catholic Powers concerned.

When the Catholics in England began to look to Mary as their future sovereign, it is hard to say. With proofs before their eyes of the power of Elizabeth and of Philip's weakness, their hopes and fears were naturally different from those of their exiled brethren in Flanders; but Elizabeth on the one hand and the Spanish ambassador on the

other, both recognised that she had a considerable party
in England by 1563. Elizabeth's anxiety was displayed
most clearly in her refusal to let Mary pass through England
in 1561, or to visit her at York or in the North in 1562 or
1563. But the inference to be drawn must be qualified by
the consideration of Elizabeth's extraordinary aversion to
any mention of the word heir or successor, or even husband
(when spoken seriously). It was partly a womanish whim.
Just as some ladies (and Elizabeth also among them)
affect never to grow old, so she made believe that she would
never die, that her sun would never pass the meridian; she
would never need an heir; and her cousin, Lady Catherine
Grey, was kept prisoner or under guard till death, in truth
only because some regarded her as heiress. Hence it
follows that we must not necessarily conclude, as we might
otherwise have done, from Elizabeth's incivility to, and
jealousy of her cousin, that she had actual evidence of a
strong propension in Mary's favour among Englishmen.
But she was certainly very afraid of affection for her
spreading.

When Elizabeth was thought to be dying of smallpox
in November 1562, nothing was heard in official circles of
Mary's succession, not even by the Spanish ambassador,
who reports that the Catholics (*i. e.* those whom he knew at
Court) were supporting either Lady Catherine Grey or
Lord Huntingdon. This is noteworthy, but not very
important, for the crisis was light and short. In March
1563, de Quadra thought her party stronger than that favouring a Protestant heir, and that Cecil's futile manœuvres to
get Parliament to exclude her really tended to her advantage.

Her gradual advance in English public opinion was
further illustrated by what passed between de Quadra
and Maitland of Lethington in March, during the negotiations for the pretentious but impracticable match between
Mary and Don Carlos, Prince of Spain. One of the arguments Lethington used was to extol Mary's influence with
the English Catholics, and he even professed to have lists
of " Catholics and others " who could raise troops in her
service. But Lethington's unreliability prevents our giving
to this statement the significance it might otherwise seem

I

to have, as an indication of the favour with which the English Catholics regarded Mary. De Quadra, however, was impressed, and desired that an English gentleman might go to Mary at once, in order to represent the English Catholics. But the ambassador sickened and died soon after this (in June or July), and Maitland's scheme for the Spanish match was rejected by Philip, and was heard of no more after the end of the year 1563.

Before we come to the tragic period of Mary's fall, it may be well to remember that the English Catholics of those days had no reason to think that if Mary did succeed to the English throne (say in the year 1565, at the height of her popularity), she would have come as the Pope's champion. At the period of which we are now writing, she appeared to the world as a Catholic indeed, but as a Catholic opportunist. She had governed Scotland through Moray and Lethington, and it was only to be expected that she would have governed England through Cecil and Bacon. She would have surrounded herself with moderate Protestants like the Howards and the Sidneys. In time, no doubt, she might have improved the position of Catholics much, as she did in Scotland. The era of toleration and religious liberty might have begun some centuries before it actually dawned, but she would not have risked any sudden changes either in foreign or domestic policy. English interests would, of course, have predominated in her councils.[1]

We do not find that Mary ever intrigued, or sought to intrigue, with the English Catholics before her marriage with Darnley. She seems to have ever remembered what Philip of Spain was always repeating to her, that a peaceful policy was for her the safest and most direct means of obtaining the throne of England.

Mary's marriage with Darnley presumably strengthened to some not inconsiderable extent the ties of sympathy between her and the English Catholics. Darnley was perhaps the nearest male heir to the English throne, and this gave him at once a position of no little importance. The Spanish ambassador lets us see that the English

[1] *Papal Negotiations*, p. 252.

Catholics had long looked to him as a possible saviour. That they really gave him any assistance, however, is nowhere on record, though I dare say that if his mother, Lady Margaret Lennox, had been left at liberty, she would have effected some diversion in his favour, for she was an able and devoted diplomatist. Elizabeth, however, promptly consigned her to the Tower, and none of Darnley's other friends durst show him any favour.

The English Catholics, then, were not concerned in any of those struggles in Scotland out of which Mary at first emerged victorious. To put the same thing in a different way, they attempted no diversions against Elizabeth to prevent her from assisting Mary's rebels. They rejoiced, no doubt, in Mary's victories, and grieved at the news of the murder of Darnley, which was followed soon by the rumours of Mary's complicity. These seem to have been at first believed, so the Spanish ambassador writes, by the former well-wishers of Darnley, but rejected by the old friends of Mary. Her credit, however, was " greatly weakened " by the event in the minds of all Catholics. Though for the two first months after the murder " the heretics wished to defame Mary and separate her from her friends " in England, the latter " say they are sure . . . that the Queen was in no way cognisant." But finally, when she married Bothwell, all " were disgusted, particularly those who had hoped that religion here (in England) might be restored through her instrumentality." [1]

If no one else but the English Catholics had felt disgust, the misgiving might not have been lasting. Unfortunately similar feelings lay heavy on the hearts of most of her Catholic contemporaries. For long, ever since she had returned to Scotland, she had seemed, as it were, lost to her old friends. They knew she was surrounded by strong Protestants, fanatics who hated all that she respected. The Jesuit, Father de Gouda, who was sent to her by the Pope in 1562, wrote : " She has not a single protector or good councillor. There is no mistaking the imminent peril of this good lady's position." He meant primarily, no doubt, peril for her faith, but he also intended to comprise

[1] *Spanish Calendar*, pp. 623, 632, 637, 639.

all those dangers which unscrupulous advisers are wont to bring to their patrons. Still for a long time everything seemed to go on fairly well. With the coming of Darnley there was evidently a change, and Pius IV in Consistory sounded a note of warning.[1] Still, in spite of some very serious trouble, the atmosphere seemed to clear again, especially at the baptism of her baby, the future King James.

This was the greatest Court ceremony she had yet kept, and it was also the first time when the Catholic rites had been used publicly and with honour. She hoped it might prove a pledge of the eventual liberation of the Church, and it seemed a sort of tacit recognition of her son as heir to the Crown of England, as well as to that of Scotland. So friends were summoned and had come from all sides. Philibert du Croc and M. de Clerneau represented France, Moretta was there for Savoy, and Father Hay, a Jesuit, was at hand in place of the papal nuncio.

Everything went off well, except that Darnley was away, but before all these friends and envoys returned a terrible tragedy had taken place. Darnley had been murdered, and there were ugly rumours afloat that his wife knew something about it. Being on the spot, and in actual touch with Mary's Court, her friends would have made every inquiry, would have asked for, and received, whatever was to be said on Mary's behalf; but they all went away with minds inclined to condemn her, and when they heard of her marriage with Bothwell (and that according to Calvinistic forms), which followed immediately, they "gave her up in disgust," as we have heard the Spanish ambassador say. The nuncio whom the Pope, St. Pius V, had sent to her, wrote to him that, "with this last act, so dishonourable to God and to herself, the propriety of sending her any sort of envoy ceases," and the Pope's Secretary answered :—

"His Holiness has never hitherto dissembled about anything, and he will not begin to do so now, especially in this all-important matter of religion. Therefore, in regard to the Queen of Scots in particular, it is not his intention to have any further communication with her, unless indeed, in times to come, he shall see some better sign of her life and religion than he has witnessed in the past." [1]

The disgust of the English was at the time shared on all sides by Mary's Catholic friends, as well as by her enemies. But the extraordinary misfortunes which immediately befell her not only began to create some sympathy for her, they also showed that her religious principles, contrary to what had been reported, were after all firm. Her friends breathed again; and they soon saw, from the methods followed by the party in power, that they were keen on preventing the real truth from coming to light. Thus a reaction in her favour was beginning at the time when the news came of her romantic escape from Loch Leven. An army immediately rose for her support, but it was not sufficiently strong or sufficiently well led to resist the forces of the dominant faction, and after the Battle of Langside, May 13, 1568, she fled to England.

Mary landed at Workington on May 16, 1568, a penniless, forsaken woman, and was again in the hands of enemies who, if less cruel, were not less resolute than the rebels of Scotland. But even as her first fall from power, when her husband Francis died, was the prelude, the necessary prelude, to her influence in England, so this second fall proved the occasion for a revival of influence, a restoration, which was in its way more remarkable still.

[1] For these and other kindred papers, see *Papal Negotiations*, p. cxxviii, also the *Month*, June 1898, p. 587. The evidence of Father Hay, of Roche Mamerot, the Queen's confessor, and others, is there examined in detail.

CHAPTER IV

THE RISING OF THE NORTH (1568–1569)

A TRAIT of the time, which this chapter covers, and one not easy to describe, is the under-feeling of unrest in English politics. Great changes were taking place, but every one expected greater changes still.

The ultimate reason for this was that there were now two parties in the realm, between whom the balance was not settled. Protestantism was still evidently unsafe, and this because of the strength of Queen Mary's party in Scotland. Hitherto Cecil's great revolution in Church and State had been supreme all over these islands, for even Mary had governed through the ministers and on the lines laid down by England at the Treaty of Edinburgh. Now that Mary was kept prisoner by violence, the whole Conservative party both north and south of Tweed were restive, and as long as they had the means of defending themselves they disdained to submit. But the Tudor side was the strongest, and gradually bore down all opposition. Edinburgh surrendered to them in 1573, and therewith all organised resistance was overcome.

After that, so long as the stern Morton kept down rivals in Scotland, the security of the Reformation remained assured. But no sooner did he fall, in 1581, than, as we shall see, it was again found that a very large party in the State, having only submitted to force, still wished for their freedom. This, however, will occupy us again later. Until a new generation had been educated to hate the ancient ideals, the traditions of so many previous generations continued to exercise their attraction, and the new order was not in stable equilibrium. All through the period covered by this chapter it was in some danger.

§ 1. *Queen Mary's Friends*

There were from the first two reasons for keeping Mary a prisoner; she was the next heir to the throne, and she was a Catholic. It was on the score of religion, broadly speaking, that the Cecil party were resolved to bury her alive, if not to murder her, while it was on the score of the throne that Elizabeth desired to keep her under restraint, on the same selfish principle that led her not only to keep the question of the succession permanently closed, but also to strike down any serious candidate, as, for instance, her cousin, Catherine Grey. On the other hand, Elizabeth was in the abstract not averse to Mary's return to Scotland. She did not of herself approve of revolution against royal authority anywhere. But, as we have seen, she had a habit of adopting her ministers' views and making them her own, even when her inclinations tended in a different direction. Never did she act this part more characteristically than now. The French ambassador, de Forest, wrote that Elizabeth was at first warmly in favour of helping her cousin, but her trusted councillors pressed a different policy upon her, with which she gradually fell in.[1] On the 12th of June he asked for a decision in Mary's business, but could get no answer or reassurance. On the 11th of July he found the Queen prolific of promises, but when he wrote to Mary, it was to tell her that patience was now her only remedy.

No wonder that contradictory statements as to Elizabeth's intentions went current. Those who ardently desired to see Mary back relied upon indications which Elizabeth had given of her personal preference for sending the fugitive home with honour, though no clear promise had been given. The Reformers, on the other hand, who were resolved that she should be kept in perpetual durance because of her religion, had no difficulty in finding signs that her return would never be permitted. On the whole this

[1] Teulet, *Relations*, ii. 369, 373, 374.

latter was the common opinion, as all the ambassadors' dispatches show.[1]

On the 20th of June there was a session of the Privy Council "touching the Queen of Scots," in which Lord Arundel and the Duke of Norfolk represented the Conservative peers. No strong measures against Mary were advised, such as were frequently recommended in the private correspondence of Cecil's party. Nevertheless, the last resolution passed declared that Mary's restoration was "too dangerous," especially "considering the comforts and aids from her kindred [i. e. the Guises], which shall be also coloured from Rome, to make her, with the pretence of Title, the vanquisher of all those, both in Scotland and in England, that do dissent from the Church of Rome; upon which foundation also is laid the whole strength of her title." [2]

On the score, therefore, of her Catholicism and of her legitimate claim to the succession, her restoration was denied; and as there was no middle course, her perpetual imprisonment was thus early decided upon.

In this the Cecil party had its way; nevertheless the Conservative peers were so far from giving up the struggle, that a letter found its way to Rome this same summer to say that they were resolved to upset the existing Government, to restore Mary, and to bring back Catholicism to England.[3]

[1] According to Mr. Froude, " To the French ambassador, to de Silva and Lord Herries, Elizabeth distinctly and repeatedly said. that at all events, and whatever came of the investigation, Mary Queen of Scots should be restored. She made this positive declaration because without it the Queen of Scots would not have consented that the investigation (at York) should take place " (*History*, viii. 382). This seems overstated. It is true that Lord Herries reported Elizabeth to have said as much (*Scottish Calendar*, ii. 465); but his report is surely not sufficient evidence of Elizabeth's precise words. It is also true that to de Forest Elizabeth repeated: " Plusieurs fois, et par serment et parolles bien expresses et pleines d'affection, qu'elle n'avoit aultre intention que de remectre la dicte dame d'Escosse en son royaulme," and that she would not allow anything contrary to Mary's honour to be proposed at York; but this is not quite the same thing as saying that Mary should be restored, whatever the revelations made at York. The ambassador, moreover, discerned clearly that Elizabeth's Government did not intend to restore Mary for the present (Teulet, *Relations*, ii. 388, 389). De Silva from the first saw that she was doomed to perpetual imprisonment (*Spanish Calendar*, 1568, p. 85).

[2] *Scottish Calendar*, ii. 439, J. Anderson, *Collections*, IV. i. 102.

[3] Ridolfi's first letter to the Pope in " the summer of " 1568 is lost, but next spring we hear that its proposals still held, and we learn what they then were. See below.

If it was Elizabeth's first intention " qu'elle voulloit honorer et recevoir la Royne d'Escosse, ainsi qu'il estoit convenable à sa dignité et première grandeur, et non à sa fortune présente," [1] much more was this the predominant feeling among the people of the North. The Council of the North itself sent letters to the Earl of Northumberland, a member of their board, to see that she was honourably used. He at once came to Carlisle and claimed by Border custom the custody of the fugitive princess, who had landed within his liberties. But Elizabeth's official, Lowther, the sub-warden of the Northern Marches, refused to surrender her without an order from his official chiefs.[2]

Meantime " many gentlemen of diverse shires . . . came to welcome her Grace . . . and heard her daily defences and excuses of her innocency, with great accusations of her enemies, very eloquently told." [3]

But the orders from London soon put a new face on the welcome accorded to the refugee. Sir Francis Knollys, Mary's first gaoler, wrote to the Earl of Northumberland and told him plainly " not to meddle any further "; and the Council, taking the same line, summoned him to leave the town. In the same spirit, Knollys gave " a plain rebuke " to the Council of the North for having written as they had without the Queen's commission; and Christopher Lascelles, a Yorkshire Catholic, who asked for an interview with the Queen, was unceremoniously sent out of the place, while Francis Dacre, son of Lord Dacre of Gillesland, seems to have been treated with similar scant courtesy.[4]

After this no further signs of respect were shown, but the spontaneity with which the demonstrations of respect had begun so alarmed Sir Francis Knollys that, in his first letter on taking over his charge, he professes he can see nothing but trouble if she remains in England, and suggests that she should be allowed to go back to Scotland, after " a former inkling " had been given to her enemies of what was intended. What Mary's lot would have been if that had been done, there is no need to say.

[1] Teulet, *Relations*, ii. 369.
[2] *Scottish Calendar* (Bain), ii. 410, 412.   [3] *Ibid.*, p. 417.
[4] *Ibid.*, ii. 413, 457, 480.

But ere long the courtier's confidence returned. His first alarm, he says, was "a scruple"; the measures of repression already taken have "calmed and quieted very well the swelling minds of the hot-disposed papists, and I trust it will be good lesson to all subjects hereafter to attend wholly and dutifully upon her Majesty's (*i. e.* Elizabeth's) pleasure. Also I do think that Nottingham and Fotheringay be in counties nothing so much given to papistry as those more hitherwards. Wherefore, if her Highness will bridle the papists shorter, I see no danger in transporting the Scottish Queen thither." [1]

To prevent her escaping, therefore, she was brought further inland, first to Bolton Castle, in Wensleydale, and later on to Tutbury, in Staffordshire—a tacit testimony to her popularity, which, as the Spanish ambassador wrote (July 3, 1568), was steadily increasing :—

"The Queen of Scots has certainly many friends, and they will increase in numbers hourly, as the accusations of complicity in the murder of her husband are being forgotten, and her marriage with Bothwell is now being attributed to compulsion and fear. This view is being spread, and friends easily persuade themselves of the truth of what they wish to believe, especially in this island." [2]

The Catholics, however, were now troubled by new rumours, which threw doubt on her religious constancy, and not without some cause on her side. Her representative, Lord Herries, a Protestant, had been treating with Elizabeth for conditions, which were eventually granted (unfortunately for Mary, not in writing) in better terms than were ever offered again, and amongst these conditions, which Herries accepted, was the introduction of the Book of Common Prayer into Scotland. This was in due time proposed to Mary, and her answer, though not preserved in any definite form, was understood both by Herries and by Knollys to be affirmative, but with an important differ-

[1] *Scottish Calendar* (Bain), p. 421.
[2] *Spanish Calendar*, 1568–1579, p. 48.

ence : Herries does not say that she would become an
Anglican herself, Knollys does say so.[1] It is clear that the
latter misunderstood her, for his subsequent explanations
do not at all bear out his previous statements.

She went too far, certainly, if Knollys' words are strictly
true—that she listened to sermons against popery " with
contented ears and gentle weak replies." But the bitter
Calvinist, who invariably misrepresents her religion, also
exaggerates here. He probably could not imagine any
religion that was gentle and still sincere.

Yet there can be no doubt that Mary did go too far,
and that, in a suspicious age, both friend and foe put too
much emphasis on her mistakes, such as they were. She
then had no Catholic advisers at all. She had asked Lord
Scrope for a chaplain, and he answered, with official
brusqueness, that there were no Catholic priests now left
in England.[2] Her councillors now were Lords Fleming and
Herries, faithful subjects indeed, but men who, being
Protestants, were likely to mislead her in the delicate
circumstances of that time. It was certainly right for her
to show that she was tolerant, and there was certainly
nothing at all intrinsically wrong in preferring the Anglican
to the Scottish kirk for the Protestants of her kingdom.
But it was not right for her to listen to Protestant sermons,
or to be present at Protestant services, which were intended
to undermine her faith, which led to popular misinterpreta-
tion, and had been repeatedly condemned by the Popes.
Of these prohibitions, however, she was probably unaware,
for in Scotland there had been even greater slackness among

---

[1] Herries wrote to Cecil : " *I* wish religion in Scotland to be as here "
(*Scottish Calendar*, p. 462) ; and to Huntly : " These heads be *in a manner
condescended upon, viz.* for religion according to the manner as it is in
England," etc., etc. (*ibid.*, p. 470). Knollys, however, wrote : " This
Queen should abandon the Mass in Scotland and receive Common Prayer
after the form of England " (*ibid.*, p. 465). Mary gave instructions to
the Bishop of Ross on this project in June 1569 (*ibid.*, p. 651), but we
do not know the details.

[2] It has been erroneously said by Leader (*Mary Queen of Scots in
Captivity*, p. 39) that she then had a chaplain, Sir John Morton. But far
from this, when Mary was believed to be dying in 1570, and inquiries were
secretly made in the country for a priest, none could be found (Bishop
Leslie to Archbishop Beaton, Hosack, ii. 506). The Bishop of Ross therefore
procured Ninian Winzet to come to her, under the disguise of a perfumer
(*Scottish Calendar*, iii. 530), but he was soon (May 4, 1571, *ibid.*, p. 566)
sent back by Shrewsbury, who had divined his real character.

Catholics about " church-going " than in England.[1] Thus, though she was faithful in substance, she was making mistakes in matters which, if not essential, were much more liable to cause scandal than she realised. On the 24th of July the Spanish ambassador writes to say that he hears through the French ambassador from her agent, Lord Fleming, that she had actually become a Protestant ! This rumour had a considerable effect on Mary's fortunes at this time.[2]

Mary herself, by her prompt answers, prevented the report ruining her cause. She wrote warmly to de Silva on the 31st of July repudiating the idea.[3] But, as she did not give up attending the prayer meetings, the rumours did not cease. When Bishop Leslie came to see her in September, in preparation for the pleadings at York, he seems to have spoken to better effect, for she then made a new series of protests, the most effective of which was spoken out frankly during one of the English services in the great hall at Bolton Castle.[4]

For the English, Catholics as well as Protestants, the matter was more or less settled now,[5] but the Catholics abroad were naturally slower to be convinced. The Spanish ambassador at Paris was twice pressed by Archbishop Beaton, Mary's ambassador there, to write in her favour to King Philip, and in the second letter the ambassador says that it was the Archbishop who really did most " to maintain her in the Faith." [6] Philip, however, had already written in September expressing belief in her sincerity,

[1] W. Forbes Leith, *Memoirs of Scottish Catholics*, 1909, i. 17, 18.

[2] *Spanish Calendar*, 1568, p. 62.

[3] Froude, *History*, viii. 374. This letter is not in the *Spanish Calendar*, and according to Froude, Mary represented herself as a victim of Elizabeth.

[4] *Scottish Calendar*, p. 510. Knollys was especially vexed at this, because some " Papists " whom he had admitted or coerced into coming, doubtless in hopes of their profiting by the sight of her conformity, would now be moved in the opposite direction.

[5] Not wholly, however, for Mary continued to attend the English service in 1569 (Leader, *Mary Queen of Scots in Captivity*, 1880, pp. 40, 117), and in June of that year she again agreed to introduce Anglicanism into Scotland. She wrote (April 18, 1570) to some correspondent, whose name is not mentioned, that she might " be forced to embrace [the English] religion " (Labanoff, iii. 35. See also *Scottish Calendar*, iii. 163).

[6] Teulet, v. 42, 44; cf. 38. The miserable want of principle shown by Catherine de Medici and the French Court at this time probably had a bad effect on Mary; and Beaton feared that Fénelon, the French ambassador, would advise Mary to turn Protestant (*ibid*).

but also desiring that she should have support and encouragement.

Pope Pius V was slower to declare himself satisfied. His nuncios at Paris and Madrid had, soon after Mary's flight to England, asked their Courts to intercede that she might come to France, " for then," said Mgr. Ceneda, somewhat ominously, " we shall at least be sure that she will remain Catholic." When, however, Pope Pius eventually took notice of the negotiation, it was in order to put a stop to it altogether, and the reason given is remarkable : " His Holiness's mind is still undecided which of the two Queens is the best " (August 18, 1568).[1]

One would not have expected that from Pius V, and it is impossible to understand the words, unless we advert to his negotiations with Ridolfi, then in progress, to which we shall return. It will be sufficient to say here that Ridolfi's first plan was for Elizabeth's conversion, not, as has been erroneously imagined, for her assassination.[2]

To return to Queen Mary. On November 30, 1568, she wrote to the Pope asking pardon for having attended some English services since she had come to England,

---

[1] *Papal Negotiations*, p. cxxxiii n.

[2] The latter thesis was maintained by the late Lord Acton in a series of letters to *The Times* (November 9 to December 12, 1874), which letters *The Times* itself, in an obituary notice of Lord Acton (June 20, 1902), summed up in the following terms :—

" Pius V, who had been the only Pope proclaimed a Saint for centuries, commissioned an assassin [*i. e.* Ridolfi] to murder Elizabeth, and the confirmation is found in the official life of Pius in the *Acta Sanctorum*."

The reference here is to *AA.SS.*, May 1, § 173 (ed. 1866, p. 661) : " Pius cogitabat . . . illam malorum omnium sentinam, seu (ut appellabat ipse) flagitiorum servam, de medio tollere." These words, if they had stood quite by themselves, might no doubt have been interpreted as meaning assassination, *e. g.* " Pius thought of *making away with her, who was the cesspool of all evils*, or, as he called her, the slave of crime," and therefore he sent Ridolfi. If we look into the context, however, we soon find reason to pause, and all doubt is at an end if we consult the original Italian, from which the Latin is translated. The Italian sentence is very long and laboriously balanced ; the essential clauses are these : " Pensando Pio, da una parte di soccorer la Reina di Scotia . . . dall'altra . . . *di levare a un tempo la sentina di tanti mali* (nodrendo Elizabetta dissentioni . . .) deputó alcuni homini .. . . de'gli cattolici gliene dessero contezza." " Pius, thinking on the one hand of helping the Queen of Scotland, and on the other of *clearing the cesspool of so many evils* (for Elizabeth nourishing dissensions, etc., etc.), deputed certain persons among the Catholics to give him information " (Girolamo Catena, *Vita del Glorioso Papa Pio V*, Mantua, 1587).

The clause, which might, apart from its context, bear a sinister meaning, is perfectly innocuous in the original language. The passages are quoted in full in *C.R.S.*, xxi. 335.

which she thought (being in strict confinement, and the use of her own religion being forbidden her) was not wrong If it was, she begs pardon for it and for any other fault of which she has been guilty, and will make such *amende* and do such penance as the Pope and other Catholic princes may remain satisfied.[1] She will live and die a Catholic.

Letters sent by secret means over long distances always take a long time. Mary's communications with Rome were frequently three or four months *en route.* We may, there-fore, regard the letter of May 9, 1569, to Archbishop Beaton as the official answer to the above letter of the Scottish Queen; and now at last it is declared that the Pope " believes her to be truly constant, and that her troubles are due to her fidelity. He is as warm in her cause as could be desired, and will commend it to Christian princes." [2]

We now return to the English Catholics. The Spanish ambassador's forecast, that many would rally to her as time went on, was verified in a remarkable way before the end of the year.

Cecil, who had also observed the tendency in her favour, both in England and in Scotland, arranged the conferences at York and Westminster nominally in order to arbitrate between the Queen and her rebels, but really in order to make the quarrel between them irreconcilable. For this purpose all the foulest accusations and the most damaging evidence against the Queen were brought out and circu-lated, while her advocates thought it the only dignified course to make no formal defence. And yet the confer-ences certainly told in Mary's favour.

It is not easy to explain precisely why this result

[1] Labanoff, vii. 16. This would have crossed the letter from Rome, of December 14, to Archbishop Beaton (Arch. Vat., Arm. xliv. vol. iii. f. 194), which exhorted the Archbishop to go on comforting and strengthen-ing Mary, as " the Pope fears lest, amid such disturbance in the Church, such calamities in her own fortunes, she may be forced to remit something of her persevering reverence for this Holy See."

[2] Cardinal Rusticucci to Archbishop of Glasgow, Arch. Vat., Arm. xliv. vol. iii. f. 217. The advice is added, to urge her to ever greater constancy. The first letter addressed directly to Mary was January 9, 1570 (printed in Laderchi's *Annales*), and is said to be in answer to hers of October 15, 1569 (? lost). Mary answered April 30, 1570 (? lost, carried by Henry Kerr), and this was answered July 13 (Arch. Vat., Arm. xliv. vol. xii. f. 283). These briefs are all exhortations to constancy.

followed. No doubt many were shocked at first, and some were probably estranged permanently. But looking to the past, the English Conservatives would consider that the party of violence in Scotland (with which it was Mary's alleged crime to have once connived) was in effect the very same (except for a few changes of *personnel*) which had so often revolted in the past, and had now deposed her, and strove to overwhelm her with accusations. As to Mary's peccadilloes, they were long past, very obscure, and the harm they had worked was very limited. The revolutions of Cecil and his Scottish allies, on the other hand, had brought thousands to ruin, and still weighed heavily on the necks of the majority. The whole device of the conferences was part of a general policy, which every one knew to be purely selfish and remorselessly hostile to the Scottish Queen. It was of a piece with the persecution at home, the cruel chicanery of which was notorious. While Elizabeth was promising honour and protection to the fugitive, Cecil had brought about grievous obloquy, the extermination of her friends, the support of her enemies, the imprisonment of her person.

Finally, the conferences, considered as a judicial inquiry, were disgracefully partial. They were conducted in the absence of the accused, to whom neither the charges nor the evidence were, in fact, communicated, while the crimes of the accusers passed without inquiry or comment.

Yet, after all, there was no formal pronouncement against Mary. On the contrary, on the 10th of January Moray was informed that, while nothing had been proved to his discredit, no evidence had been proposed "whereby the Queen of England should conceive or take any evil opinion against the Queen, her good sister."

The interpretation which men of that day would put upon such a conclusion was, that Mary's fault was one which subjects should let pass into oblivion. It could not be repeated, and left no obligations of justice to be rectified.

The proceedings as a whole, taken in connection with Cecil's endeavours to get Queen Mary to resign her rights as queen, were such as would easily lead men of conservative ideas to think that she had been gravely injured, and that the time for curbing such unjust practices had arrived.

This feeling was much strengthened at this very time (December 1568) by the seizure of half a million ducats of Spanish treasure on board some Spanish ships which had put in to Plymouth and Southampton. Though the money was not taken without a certain formal excuse, it was a proceeding of unparalleled high-handedness, and we cannot wonder at the Duke of Alva proceeding immediately to retaliations by seizing English shipping in the Low Countries. The rupture of friendly intercourse spread from Flanders to Spain and to Portugal, and to some extent even to France. But having the command of the sea, the position of England was very strong.[1] Not only was Spanish and Flemish property seized in England, but piracy in the Channel increased by leaps and bounds. Still there was also much discontent at home. There were risings in Suffolk, and the mercantile community were sorely vexed at the loss to trade and merchandise, which for them altogether outweighed the gain in booty taken by piracy, though much of this went into the pockets of Cecil's party. No wonder that the Conservative Lords were inclined to make capital out of so gross a political crime, committed by political opponents.

Thus the year 1569 found the equilibrium in England in a very unstable condition, and besides the troubles with Mary and with the Catholic Powers already mentioned, the Protestant party were restless and angry at the ill success of their fellow-reformers abroad. As has been said before, foreign influence was at this time a most potent factor in English politics.

The French Huguenots were badly beaten this year at Jarnac and Moncoutour, and Alva was regularly victorious in the Low Countries, and his victories, even more than his cruel repressive measures, moved the English Reformers to injure the Catholic cause wherever they were able to do so. At home the war of extermination against the English Catholics was carried on more and more fiercely, while

[1] The Spaniards were now for the first time driven to think of protecting themselves at sea; but Alva was unable to make up his mind how to act (*Spanish Calendar*, 1568, p. 196).

ships, money and harbourage were freely granted to the
Huguenot and Gueux rovers.   It was this desire for revenge
which was the predominant motive for the seizure of the
Spanish treasure, with all its far-reaching consequences.

On the other hand, the revival of the Conservatives and
Catholics was also growing, for the reasons above explained,
and so there gradually arose what we should now call an
" opposition," though in those days of absolutism it might
also have been called, and eventually was called, a conspiracy.

The nominal leader of the whole party was the young
Duke of Norfolk, an easy-going nobleman, on whom the
danger of resisting the Tudors had been early and vividly
impressed by the cruel execution of his father, when he
was but eleven years old.   His grandfather also then lay
under sentence of death, and many others of his family
as well had fallen victims to the tyranny.   A good, kind
father, and pliant to every change of religion at Court, he
was not strong, nor a born leader, nor was he clear about
principles.   For the moment, however, he was deeply moved
by the aversion of the *ancienne noblesse* to the upstart
courtiers who ruled in Elizabeth's name.   By birth and
position at least, as well as by his popularity, kindliness,
and good-fellowship, he was the acknowledged head of the
English nobility, and among the commons, too, he had a
strong following, in London as well as in his own parts
of the country.   He had, indeed, received the Elizabethan
Settlement of Religion without demur, and had accepted
the command of the army that was sent to Scotland in
1560 to establish Protestantism there, and had not shown
hitherto any predilection for the old Faith.   Anglicanism
predominated in his household, but the ancient Creed also
lasted on there, and it was believed that he might be
recovered to Catholicism without great difficulty.

Of his supporters the ablest was perhaps the Earl of
Arundel (the father of his first wife), and the most sincere
was Thomas Percy, Earl of Northumberland, both Catholics,
and the second known to practise as well as to profess
Catholicism.   Besides these there were a considerable
number of peers and politicians, who for various reasons
were opposed to the Cecil faction.   The most important of

K

the latter was Sir Nicholas Throckmorton, once amongst the most advanced of the anti-Catholic party; but now, since his journey to Scotland on behalf of Mary Stuart, he had joined the opposition. He died, however, too soon for that side to derive any notable advantage from his great diplomatic talents. With these forces we must also take account of the representatives of the foreign Catholic Powers : Despes for Spain, Fénelon for France, the Bishop of Ross for Mary Stuart, and Ridolfi, the factor for the Pope.

Despes had very difficult cards to play. King Philip wanted him to encourage the Catholics, but to do so under the orders of the Duke of Alva, and Alva was still intent on peace at any price with England. Now it is impossible to encourage drowning men to continue to struggle, and at the same time to say, " Hands off ! " You must either pull them into the boat or hit them over the head with the oar. Despes tried hard to affect neutrality; but he aroused Elizabeth's fiercest anger by exclaiming against her seizure of the Spanish treasure. Some of the later trans-actions of Ridolfi eventually gave a handle for his virtual expulsion. De la Mothe Fénelon was acting at the present moment with a policy far more Catholic than was usual with French ambassadors of that day, and, wonderful to say, actually co-operated with Spain until the proposition of the Anjou match at the end of 1570.

John Leslie, Bishop-Designate of Ross,[1] was in some ways a valuable friend to the Catholic cause, for at a moment of obscurity and uncertainty he declared sincerely against any compromise by his mistress in the matter of religion. But not being a trained diplomatist, he ran risks and made mistakes which a more experienced man would probably have avoided. The fortunes of his mistress were, in truth, at so low an ebb that there was inclination on his part, as on hers, to grasp at any remedy, however desperate, however little adapted to the interests of the English Catholic body at large. Still, he was sincere, loyal, unselfish, though not strong, as the sequel showed. Mary, too, though

[1] That is to say, he was so far only appointed by Queen Mary. This was not confirmed by the Pope till 1575 (Maziere Brady, i. 147). After that he would probably have been consecrated.

so inspiriting and so chivalrous, was not a good judge of men. She declared herself ready to give her life for the cause, and she expected no less from others. If the English Catholics and Conservatives were generally over-cautious, Mary and her minister were proportionately reckless, with what result it is not difficult to foresee.

Of Ridolfi, the papal factor or agent, we must speak more fully than is strictly necessary, considering the subordinate part he at present plays, partly because he becomes of greater importance later, partly because so many erroneous and exaggerated statements have been made current against him, though it will not be necessary to return to the allegation, mentioned above, that he was an assassin.

Roberto di Pagnozzo Ridolfi belonged to a well-known merchant family at Florence.[1] He had been trading in England since 1560,[2] and had become head of the Guild of the Florentine Traders of London. In later life he was made a Senator (in 1600), and was sent as ambassador to Portugal. In 1569 he was the most influential, perhaps the only, Catholic banker in London, for all the other Italian bankers had to some extent taken sides with the English Government. This gives us a measure by which to judge the man. He did not owe his position to any remarkable personal gifts or to long experience. His fortunes depended partly on circumstances of birth, which had provided him with useful connections in Florence and elsewhere (his brother, for instance, was a banker in Rome), and partly on the circumstances of England, where the Catholics had no one else to trust but him. He was sanguine, pushful, honest, quite sure that his own judgments were right—and in times of great stress self-confidence often avails much. He was also dexterous in managing business affairs on a considerable scale with men of rank and power. But he had little training beyond that of the counting-house —no experience of the administration of great States. His ideas on the balance of European power, on the politics of

[1] See Guido Carocci, *La famiglia dei Ridolfi* (Firenze, 1889), and Tiribelli-Giuliani, *Famiglie celebre Toscane*, vol. ii. *s.v.* Ridolfi.
[2] In his MS. memoir (Florence, *Archivio di Stato*, Fil. 4185), Ridolfi says that he was nine years in England, and this must outweigh Camden, who says he was here for fifteen years.

his day, were quite superficial, little better than those of an ordinary Italian *cittadino*, in whose eyes the decisive power in European politics was the union between France and Spain under the hegemony of Rome—a mere dream, so far as practical politics were concerned. And hence it was that all the plans which Ridolfi took up were bound to fail.

And here the question presents itself, whether one may go so far as, with Lingard, for instance, to attribute these plans entirely to Ridolfi. The problem, though it can hardly now be solved satisfactorily, is the more important seeing that Ridolfi sometimes described himself as a papal agent or even ambassador, and also professed to be the deputy of various English nobles, though he had no testimonials from them to define his authority.

Upon the whole, there is no doubt that Ridolfi was trusted by all the Catholic parties, and that many did allow him to speak in their names. They must bear the responsibility, therefore, for what he negotiated for them, and in this there is no reason to question his general honesty. On the other hand, he had every opportunity for managing the transactions that passed through his hands in his own way. The leaders could not control him in the least. To the Pope he seems to have written once or twice a year only, and as the post time was about four months each way, it is clear that Rome could not direct or check him to any purpose. Neither could the parties in England. He was often their only intermediary. Despes, for instance, after important negotiations for a year, first with Lord Arundel, then with the Duke of Norfolk, casually remarks that " he does not know and has never seen " either of them.[1] All had been done through Ridolfi. Add to this that all was arranged by word of mouth (without the check of letters, which were too dangerous), and that the negotiations were carried on in Italian, a tongue foreign to all but himself, and we shall realise how very unlikely it was that Ridolfi could help giving a distinct turn of his own to business left so long and so completely in his hands. In later negotiations it becomes abundantly clear that his

[1] *Spanish Calendar*, p. 164.

personal influence was most considerable. The inference can hardly be avoided that it was powerful at a much earlier date.[1]

§ 2. *The Catholic Plans*

Such, then, were the very disparate political forces which were now endeavouring to check the policy of the omnipotent Cecil, and we now turn to the consideration of their plans. Originally these were necessarily very vague and varying. We at first only discern a sort of haze of hopes, expectations, ideas, without being able to say with what tenacity each plan was held, or by whom it was proposed. There were three predominant ideas : the first, that Mary should be declared heir to the throne of England, and treated as such; the second, that Cecil should be deposed ; the third, that Elizabeth should be converted.

(1) As we look back this third point may seem to us extravagant, and it was no doubt the first idea to be discarded when it came to practical politics. Still, though we cannot tell where it originated, it certainly held its ground till the end of 1568. Irresponsible people had held it before, and would hold it again. In any case it is clearly involved in the statement we have already heard from Pope Pius that " he did not know which of the two Queens was the best." It is confirmed by the presence among the Spanish ambassador's papers of a tract on the reasons for her conversion, which was sent in draft to Philip on the 12th of December, 1568.[2] It is also confirmed by the account given by Fénelon of the first plans negotiated by Ridolfi with the Catholic and Conservative Earls.

(2) The first mention of freeing Mary, if necessary by force of arms, seems to have occurred at the advent of the Bishop of Ross. After his coming to see her at Bolton (September 1568), she wrote to her ambassador at Paris of offers to set her free ;[3] and when the Bishop reached

---

[1] A summary of the earliest documents about Ridolfi's plans will be found at the end of this chapter.

[2] Printed in English in *Spanish Calendar*, 1568, p. 86; in Spanish by Lettenhove, v. 733.

[3] Quoted in Alva to Philip, October 30, 1568. Teulet, *Relations*, v. 44

London, the Spanish ambassador wrote (November 6) to his master with very similar news.[1]   From this time onwards this object was never long forgotten.

(3) The deposition of Cecil was necessarily a preliminary to any constitutional reform of the present situation, and all, even the Protestants, agreed in this.   As the opposition grew stronger, this part of the project became more urgent, and by the 12th of March both the French and the Spanish ambassadors knew it had been decided upon by the Duke of Norfolk and his allies, though in effect the attempt to do so was never made.   More than once during April Norfolk and Arundel were ready, but Leicester " softened." [2]

At the end of May Norfolk came openly to words with the great minister, and at another time, when Cecil wanted the Council to support him unanimously in approving the seizure of the treasure, the Duke and his followers stayed away.   In June a compact was actually concluded between the new confederates, and the articles of agreement were drawn up by Leicester, and signed by him as well as by Norfolk, Arundel and Pembroke.   The engagement was that Mary Stuart should marry Norfolk and be restored to Scotland, into which she should introduce Anglicanism, and promise that she should never impugn the rights of Elizabeth.   To these terms Mary consented, and they may be regarded as the programme of the opposition of that time.[3]

But these trivial successes, so very slight and so hard to win, did not bode well for the eventual triumph of the cause.   Cecil, of course, soon found out the plans of his

[1] *Spanish Calendar*, 1568, p. 83.   Lord Montague's brother-in-law, *i.e.* Leonard Dacre, is here said to have made the offer to liberate her.   On January 8, 1569 (*ibid.*, p. 97), an oral message was received from Mary which must have got much improved *en route*, for she is said to assure Philip that if only he would help, she will be Queen of England in three months !   No such hopes were ever expressed in sober ink.

[2] Information from the Bishop of Ross, conveyed to Despes in June 1569 (*Spanish Calendar*, p. 166).

[3] See Camden, *Annals* (1635), p. 109; Leader, p. 76; Lingard, vi. 198; *Scottish Calendar*, ii. 651, etc.; *Hatfield Calendar*, i. 412.   The negotiations, needless to add, were extremely complex and extremely insincere. Everywhere one finds quarrels too deep to heal, faith too often broken for confidence to be restored.   Very little light is thrown on the aspirations of the Catholics as a party, though one does see them occasionally, through Spanish spectacles, in the dispatches of Despes, especially that of June 15 (*Spanish Calendar*, p. 166).   The views of the dominant parties in England and Scotland are fairly clear, and may be conveniently followed in the *Hatfield*, *Scottish*, *Domestic Addenda*, and other *Calendars*.

opponents, at least in general; but he did not at first
dare to meet them directly. So long as Leicester was
against him he was insecure. He therefore affected to be
coming round to the Duke's side, and suggested that his
Grace should be sent to Spain to arrange a complete settlement of all difficulties. Then the confederates were troubled
by a domestic quarrel. The young Earl Dacre of the
North died, and the succession to his immense property
occasioned a considerable split between the Duke and his
Catholic followers.[1]

Still, the kingdom at large was growing more and more
discontented with Cecil's policy. There were riots in Suffolk
in July, and the state of Ireland was causing great anxiety.
Cecil himself never lost heart; on the contrary, he sometimes made Despes quite angry by his refusal to see any
cause for fear. No less than 10,000 crowns were offered
him as a bribe in July to settle the matter of the confiscated
treasure, which showed that the Flemings at least thought
him still supreme, and Despes frankly owned that he then
had the upper hand.[2] By the beginning of August, however, there were fresh rumours of a crisis, and a conflict
was practically certain, when the Regent Moray wrote to
the Queen warmly denouncing Norfolk's policy. All now
depended on whether Leicester could draw Elizabeth to
Norfolk's side. Instead of this, he himself swung round,
denounced Norfolk to Elizabeth, and confirmed her in
favour of Cecil. The confederacy had utterly broken
down.

Then came the question, whether the Duke would fight
or surrender. For a while he refused obedience, and his
friends, especially the Catholics of the North, prepared for
active measures. But at the end of the month Norfolk,
after having told his confederates to disarm, submitted,
and was sent to the Tower, together with many of his
friends.

[1] The property now fell to three young daughters, and the Duke,
who was their guardian, espoused them to his three sons. The Catholic
Lords wanted Leonard Dacre, their uncle, to succeed, and so to preserve
the title and the estate in the family. Mary Stuart herself was asked
to intervene, and supported this latter side. But the Duke, who had
the English law in his favour, adhered to his plan and carried it through.

[2] *Spanish Calendar*, p. 177.

For the Catholic North it was hard to go back. They had begun to think of force sooner : they had shown their hand more freely. They knew that, being Catholics, they could expect no mercy. When the summons came to surrender, they refused obedience, but it was not until the 14th of November that the Rising of the North began.

§ 3. *The Rising*

The final resolution was taken very reluctantly, and it was only the feeling that they had their backs to the wall which eventually caused them to draw the sword. Once that step was taken, other motives came into evidence, especially that of religion, which was deep and sincere. But the reason why the struggle should be begun at this particular juncture was not so obvious.[1] The only clear cause for immediate action was loyalty to feudal chiefs, who were threatened by the new men; and this was all through put forward as the primary motive for action. The restoration of religion, however, was not glossed over, and if fortune had taken a different turn it would have been heard of much more. The liberation of Mary Stuart, too, could not be published as a motive until she was actually freed, or she might have been immediately murdered. It resulted, therefore, in the rising being chiefly fought on the mediæval ground of fidelity to the over-lord.

This may be further illustrated by considering the course which the rising followed. Durham was occupied successfully on the 14th of November, and Mass was restored, with evident popular satisfaction. Then with a comparatively small force, chiefly of horse, the Earl of Northumberland began to march southward, and as it seemed with excellent results, for in the course of a week he had advanced sixty miles, under the banner of the five wounds, restored Catholic service wherever he went, and the Queen's forces at York had not dared to meet him.[2]

---

[1] There was, indeed, some recrudescence of persecution at this juncture, as the *Domestic Calendars* show a great increase in prosecutions under the Uniformity Act.

[2] This is the more remarkable because Elizabeth wrote (November 18) to urge Sussex to fight, being unable to believe in her unpopularity. It

In one sense that was an unexpected success, and
Chiappino Vitelli, one of the great Italian generals of his
day, and then, as it happened, in London, declared that if
they continued to advance they were fairly sure to win.[1]
But on reflection we can see that the results were not as
remarkable as they appeared. In reality all that they had
done was to march through the lands where the names of
Percy and Neville had been all-powerful for centuries.
Durham, a short distance from Brancepeth, was under the
immediate influence of the Earl of Westmorland, while the
most southerly point reached was only a morning's ride
beyond Percy's castle of Topcliffe. Though they had
hitherto met with some support, there was no appearance
of a general rising. If they could have set Queen Mary
free, and put her at their head, their chances would have
been good. But they knew, by previous inspection, that
Tutbury Castle could not be surprised or carried by a
coup de main,[2] and they had not men enough to send out
a strong flying column for her relief. As they marched
gradually southwards, the Queen was carried by her guards
to Coventry, whence the Northern horsemen could not
possibly free her.

A change of plan was now decided upon (November 22).
They would strengthen their base in South Durham by
carrying Barnard Castle, which commanded the southern
road, and by taking Hartlepool, through which they hoped
to draw assistance from the Catholics abroad. Both objects
were accomplished without serious difficulty. The garrison
of Barnard Castle mutinied, and went over to them—a
significant fact—and the town surrendered in a fortnight.
But in the meantime Elizabeth's army had been mobilised,
and a force of 14,000 men was launched against them,
which they had no chance of resisting. The footmen were

---

would be curious to know whether this arose from Elizabeth's ignorance or Cecil's; probably from the latter, as the draft is at Hatfield.
The letter also contains a protest against the Earls' proclamation, that
they are in favour of religion : their only object is to introduce a foreign
enemy (*Hatfield Calendar*, i. 442; Haynes, pp. 555–8; cf. Sharp, p. 54).
Elizabeth afterwards told Fénelon : " Jamais subjets n'eurent moins
occasions que les siens de mouvoir choses semblables contre leur prince " (!).
Purton Cooper, *Dépêches de Fénelon*, iii. 4.

[1] *Spanish Calendar*, p. 213.   [2] Sharp, p. 193.

disbanded (December 16), while the Earls and their gentle-men fled northwards on horseback, and crossed the Scottish border (December 21, 1569), where Percy and his companions were for the moment in safety.

Though the insurgents were punished with exemplary cruelty, not a village in the country-side being without its gibbet and corpse or corpses swinging in chains, yet this did not prevent a repetition of the Rising a fortnight after the executions had taken place. Leonard Dacre rose at Naworth, in Cumberland, with exactly the same result as before, being forced to fly into Scotland after the first conflict with Elizabeth's troops.

From all this we see that the feeling evoked by the Rising corresponded with the motive to which the Earls in their proclamations primarily appealed. The Queen, they said, was surrounded by " new-set-up nobles, who not only go about to overthrow the ancient nobility, but have misused the Queen's Majesty's own person, and have also set up and maintained a new-found religion and heresy, contrary to God's Word." [1] Feudal loyalty to the " ancient nobility " threatened by " new-set-up " men is put first; that must open the way. This was what Norfolk and the rest had agreed to do in the summer. Now this was openly pro-claimed together with loyalty to the Catholic religion and respect for the Queen.

In effect the appeal to feudal loyalty succeeded wonder-fully when the feudal over-lord was at hand to excite it. But where he hung back, or did not, for whatever reason, take the field, no result followed. Where the over-lord marched his men under the royal banner, they seem to have obeyed with mechanical fidelity. The rising was, in fact, put down by an army which was largely or predomi-nantly composed of Catholics, whose reliability was at first suspected by Elizabeth's officers.[2] Such men might fairly

---

[1] For the proclamations of November 15, 1569, see Sharp, *Memorials of the Rebellion of* 1569, pp. 41, 42 n.; quoted above from B. M., Harleian 6990, f. 44; *Additional Calendar*, p. 111; Strype, *Annals*, I. ii. 313 and 314. For their " Protestation," addressed to the Earl of Derby, etc., see *Hatfield Calendar*, pp. 445, 446. The proclamation was multiplied by hand, and the wording varies a little. All except the Harleian read " abused her Majesty " for the outspoken words quoted above.

[2] This is evident from the long inaction of the royal forces at York, and from the course of the siege of Barnard Castle. It is also distinctly

defend their action by the argument that it was not clear that this affair of nobles, not all of whom were Catholics, was really in the best interests of the Church.

Thus, as things fell out, the appeal to the nation on the religious motive was not definitely made, the preliminary appeal to feudal loyalty having missed fire. The rising was, indeed, led by men who might justly be considered representative Catholics, and they intended to restore Catholicism if they were successful. Yet they did not represent the whole party, or get effectively into touch with it.

It would be idle to affect surprise at the men of the old *régime* making one attempt to regain by force the liberty they had lost through tyranny, especially when risings were frequent all over Europe, and were cordially supported in England by the Protestant party, if in favour of their own co-religionists. This, however, is not enough to justify an insurrection entered into without preparation, against much good advice,[1] and on a scale that never promised success. It was disowned and regretted by nearly all the leaders themselves when too late. They were not under the impression that Elizabeth had been, or (perhaps) was even about to be excommunicated.[2]

While we cannot pretend that the Catholic insurgents

---

affirmed by Sir Ralph Sadler : " There are not in all this country ten gentlemen that do favour and allow of her Majesty's proceedings in the cause of religion." After the rising was over Cecil owned that Elizabeth " had the service of all sorts, without respect of religion " (*Cabala*, p. 159), and Sir Ralph Sadler had earlier " found the gentlemen of this country, though the most part of them be well affected to the cause, which the rebels make the colour of their rebellion, yet in outward show, well affected to serve your Majesty truly against them." Sadler, *State Papers*, ii. 313.

[1] The Duke of Norfolk no doubt dissuaded it, so did Mary Stuart, so did the Spanish ambassador. Alva's orders on this point to Despes were peremptory (*Spanish Calendar*, pp. 171, 172, 175). Though, as we shall see below, Spain was never averse to an insurrection which should be strong enough to succeed without her aid, no such thing was expected, and a weak insurrection was sure to be contrary to their interests, and to every one's except that of the dominant faction (cf. Sharp, p. 190).

[2] *See* Northumberland's confession, June 13, 1572; Sharp, p. 204; *Additional Calendar*, p. 407. The same conclusion follows from Morton's *Memorial* (quoted below), which attributes the failure of the rising to the excommunication having been withheld. There were some, no doubt, who hoped that the excommunication might come. But all the public acts of the Earls appealed to the sentiment of *respect* for the Queen.

showed any sound generalship, or any of that reckless daring which would, in their circumstances, perhaps have been their most prudent course, they at least avoided the reproach of being mean or cowardly, revengeful, selfish or unchivalrous. The commoners rose primarily to protect their lords, and practically forced the Earls to draw the sword for the common cause. The noble side of the Earl of Northumberland's character came out later, after his betrayal, in the dark hour when he was questioned by his foes, and faced a violent death. In all these vicissitudes he acted with a moral courage worthy of the highest Percy traditions.

Note on Ridolfi's First Plans

The following are abbreviations of the earliest documents which speak most fully of Ridolfi's plans :—

(i) Fénelon's dispatch gives perhaps the earliest recorded form of the project in March 13, 1569 (*Dépêches*, ed. Purton Cooper, 1838, i. p. 258). He writes to Catherine de Medici that Ridolfi, who is treating de la restitution de la religion catholique en Angleterre, had an understanding with Lords Arundel and Lumley, and then with the Duke of Norfolk, who is now very earnest in the business. Lords Derby, Shrewsbury, Pembroke, Northumberland, who are not yet confirmed in the new religion, have consented to follow the Duke.

But, pour ne donner desplaisir à leur Royne, laquelle ils honnorent et révèrent grandement, et to avoid bloodshed, they think that before making public their plan qu'ils prétandoient pour la religion catholique, it will be necessary de retirer des mains du secrétaire Cecil et de ceux de son party (qui sont touts passionnés pour la nouvelle religion) le maniement de l'estat, which they have seized : affin que l'ayant eulx en leur mains, ilz puyssent par après, de leur seule authorité et sans contredict, bien conduire le faict de la religion catholique. There are also other private reasons for desiring Cecil's fall, and as for his party, they are presque touts gens noveaulx, mal appuyés. As to Elizabeth, encore qu'ils veuillent mener doulcement, they perceive that she is timide et en crainte d'estre abandonnée. So they will conduct her sans grand peyne, au poinct qu'ils desirent.

The co-operation of France and Spain is much desired. Ere long Ridolfi will go to Rome, and bring back ung brief du pape pour ceste Royne, lequel ces seigneurs, estantz lors en authorité luy presenterent hardiment, et par ceste ordre commanceront de besoigner au restablissement de la religion catholique.

No details are given about the brief. It would, of course, not have been an excommunication. That would have required a Bull, and would have been opposed to all that went before. Briefs were later on (in 1583), as we shall see, prepared for James I, when his conversion was hoped for. One was called "excusatoria" for previous heresy; another was "hortatoria ad fidem." The brief here contemplated might have been something similar.

(ii) With the dispatch of Fénelon should be compared the letter from Ridolfi to the Pope himself of April 18 following. Unfortunately the points on which we feel the greatest interest are here referred to as already known since "last summer." Whence it follows that a plan similar in general outline to that communicated by Fénelon was sent to Rome by Ridolfi in the summer of 1568. That letter is, unfortunately, not forthcoming now. But we remember a session of Privy Council held at midsummer, when Cecil forced assent to his ultra-Protestant policy from the very noblemen mentioned by Fénelon above. It cannot cause wonder if Ridolfi should soon after have written of " propositions " from some of those nobles which aimed at the reversion of that violent policy.

The following is an analysis of the letter of April 18 (Arch. Vat., *Miscel.*, Arm. i. xvii. 99) :—

" I think your Holiness will remember the proposition made to you last summer." Now you will see that many are well affected to the cause. The one thing needful is co-operation between Spain and France. We have already begun to arrange this between the ambassadors here. They should agree to suspend commerce until full satisfaction is made for all recent robberies. This, however, cannot be actually done, because the money taken has been squandered; and as most of the revenue comes from the customs, if they fail, all must fail. The ministers who do all the harm would then fall. The Pope should therefore keep the two powers united, and without jealousy of each other's preparations for war. He should also deposit a small sum here, the administration of which might be supervised through the Spanish and French ambassadors. The writer will correspond either through the Duke of Alva or else through the French Court.

(iii) No Spanish version of Ridolfi's early schemes has yet been published, but there are various stray references to them in *Spanish Calendar*, pp. 83, 85, 109, 111.

CHAPTER V

THE EXCOMMUNICATION (1570–1573)

§ 1. *The Bull* (1570–1571)

MICHELE GHISLIERI, Pope St. Pius V, was beyond question the greatest Pope of the Counter-Reformation period. He had very considerable powers as an organiser and legislator, and, what was more important still, he had the gift of spiritual leadership in a very high degree. No one came into contact with him without being inspired with new courage and ardour. A man of unflinching adherence to principle, he never failed to exhort and encourage others to great deeds in the cause of the Church. Whereas the Roman Pontiffs are, as a rule, notable for sagacious temperance and compromise which does not give up principle, he was so intent on great achievements that he did not fear risks. He had sent Bishop Laureo to help Mary, and it is impossible not to think regretfully of what might have been if some one with Pius's high principles had gained her confidence before the Bothwell clique won its fatal ascendancy in her counsels. Again, the Pope's strong character was shown, after the harm was done, by a condemnation more clear and outspoken by far than that of any other Catholic contemporary,[1] and he was the last to let bygones be bygones.

In regard to England, Pius's chief work was the excommunication, a stroke of incomparably greater importance than any made before. Its results, however, were only in part successful, and many have been the differences of opinion, as to whether it was justified or not, by its chance of bringing about the triumph of the cause; or, again, whether the partial successes won balanced great losses which cannot be denied. These are questions which can, of course, never be decided finally; and before pronouncing

[1] See *Papal Negotiations*, pp. cxxviii–cxxxiii.

POPE ST. PIUS V, MICHELE GHISLIERI, O.P.

From the portrait by Zucharelli, Stonyhurst College

on them we must go as far as we can into the history of the Bull, about which we unfortunately still know only very little.[1]

Though Pius V went eventually so far in hostility to Elizabeth, he began, like his predecessor, with readiness to be conciliatory. This is shown by an exchange of letters at his accession with one Bernard Ferrario, a gentleman of Pavia. He had lived in England, and was friendly to Elizabeth, and still held a pension from her, though persecution had driven him back home. He now offered to return and work there for her conversion and for the good of the Church. Pius answered, with his usual fervour, that he would " spend half the blood in his body " to advance these objects, if they could be accomplished. Though nothing seems to have resulted from the correspondence, we see from it and kindred documents that Pius was not at first without hope of Elizabeth's conversion, and that gentle measures might be effective.[2]

Early in 1567, or thereabouts, Pius received a series of petitions from Sir Richard Shelley on the conversion of England by gentle means.[3] We do not possess the answers, but the inference is that the petitioner knew, to some extent, what sort of projects would have been welcome to the Pontiff. After the excommunication Sir Richard's adherence to Elizabeth was openly attested again.[4]

As to Ridolfi's early plans—if any deduction is permissible from our slender evidence, it is that he did not at first go any further than other English Conservatives or Moderates. That the Pope approved, is a probable assumption. But at this time he can have understood very little of the problem, and was not likely to strike out any definite policy.

We now turn to one who certainly did much to give Pius's policy towards England a new turn. Nicholas Morton, D.D., preacher at Canterbury under Pole, had found his

---

[1] Pius, among other signs of strength, showed a remarkable capacity for keeping secrets: A news writer of May 13, 1570 (Vat. *Urbino*, 1041, f. 274), speaks feelingly of " la impenetrabil mente del Papa " in regard to the excommunication, etc.

[2] Arch. Vat., Arm. lxiv. n. 28, correspondence of the Protector Moroni, ff. 111 to 117, March to May, 1566. Ferrario had also written to Cecil March, 1565, *Foreign Calendar*, n. 1027.

[3] Arch. Vat., *Varia Politicorum*, lxvi. 280–86. *Rome Calendar*, 70, 185.

[4] See *D.N.B.* under " Shelley."

way to Rome, and had become English Penitentiary at St. Peter's, and in the last year of Pope Pius IV he made a proposal to the Pontiff for the "reduction" of England to the ancient Faith, but the petition was not acted upon.[1] Next year the same petition was presented to Pius V, who answered (as he had answered Ferrario) that he would be glad to shed his blood in so good a cause, but that the revolutionary movement in the Netherlands made the project impracticable just then. When Alva's strong arm had restored order there to some extent, Morton returned to his project

Now Pius had in the meantime conceived no little admiration for Alva's vigour and military skill, and he was simultaneously getting worse ideas of Elizabeth. He there-fore received Morton's proposals with much greater favour than before, and resolved to let him go to England. Never-theless, the opinion of the Pope's advisers was against giving Morton any definite political mission. His own account is, that at first he was to have had some formal permission from the Pontiff "to sound (*tentare*) the inclination of the English, especially of the nobles, for the reduction of the kingdom." In Morton's mind that would, no doubt, have signified some declaration from the Pope that the Queen was, or would be, excommunicated, and that she should be deprived. The Pope, however, refused him this power, though Morton was under the impression that he would have preferred to give it. The truth probably was that Pius knew from Ridolfi and others that milder measures were being essayed, and did not wish to impede them. A brief, dated February 13, 1569, was given to Morton for Alva, to whom he was to explain his projects. These, says the Pope, are "religious and dutiful (*sancta et pia*), and for their execution he relies chiefly on the aid of Heaven. We have thought best neither to warn him off (*deterrere*) nor to let him act without your knowledge."[2]

How Morton got on with Alva, and what answer he received, we have no information. It is difficult to think

---

[1] For Morton's transactions I rely on his memorial presented to Cardinal Alessandrino after 1575. MS. Parma. Bib. Palatina, 651, n. 2.

[2] Laderchi, continuation of Baronius's *Annales*, 1569, § 270.

that Alva was encouraging, for his letters of this period to Despes enjoin the greatest caution. Still, he did not stop the mission, and Morton went on. He occupied himself chiefly (it would seem) in the work of a penitentiary, reconciling those who, yielding to pressure, had lapsed or gone to Protestant services.

The Earl of Northumberland mentions in his Confessions that he had an hour's conversation with him " at my house " (? Topcliffe). Morton did not speak about any Bull or aid from the Pope, but discoursed of the want of priests and other missionary topics. On the other hand, Thomas Markenfield, one of the chief advocates of the Rising, reported later on, that he had questioned the papal agent whether the Queen were excommunicated or not. Morton did not say that she actually was, but alleged that she was " lawfully," because she had prevented the Pope's nuncios from coming to England, which was an offence which *per se* entailed excommunication, so that it was " lawful to take arms against her." But the Earl, and many others, thought that Markenfield was not a sufficient witness on this point.[1]

Morton would seem to have been in England during the summer, when plans for a reversal of Cecil's policy were most warmly discussed. He visited many, making his way into the Marshalsea prison in order to interview Bishop Bonner, and going to the North to see Northumberland and Markenfield. The latter seems to have been one of the most advanced advocates of an appeal to arms. Morton was much impressed by that party, and having agreed with them that no step should be taken before the Pope had been consulted, he returned to Rome, apparently before the crisis of September. On his arrival he informed the Pope fully of the readiness to rise which he had observed ; and Pope Pius, much consoled, promised, with his usual generosity, to accord all their demands, which we may suppose were chiefly a grant of money, intercession with Spain for aid and co-operation, and the excommunication of the Queen.

An opportunity for writing to Alva was offered by the

---

[1] Sharp, *Memorials of the Rebellion of the North*, p. 204. It is an error, due to the Bishop of Ross, to say that he reconciled the Earl. *Ibid.*

L

news of a rising in Suffolk, which took place in July, and
probably became known in Rome at the end of October.
On the 3rd of November, therefore, the Pope wrote to Alva,
earnestly urging him to make the most of the opportunity.
This, however, was bad diplomacy. Alva was put on his
guard by the Pope's earnestness, and, as usual under such
circumstances, dread of the French at once suggested itself.
What if Pius prevailed on the French to interfere and to
restore Mary? In that case Spain would have to ally herself
openly with England and to attack France, and to this
move Pius would perhaps answer by excommunicating
Spain.   So Alva, held up by this difficulty of his own
creation, sent the letter on to Philip, December 11, 1569,
to ask for advice, saying ironically of the Pope that he was
" so zealous that he thought everything could be accomplished without using ordinary human means." [1]

On the 5th of December Alva also wrote to Zuñiga,[2] the
Spanish ambassador at Rome, a long explanation to be
set before the Pope, similar in sense to the above, and again
full of irony at the Pope's disregard of human prudence.
In this letter, however, he omits those strong phrases about
defending England against France under all circumstances,
which let us see how utterly different were the objects of
Spanish and of papal politics at this time.

This answer, which may have reached the Pope in the
middle of January, would have shown Pius that, if anything was to be done against Elizabeth, he must take the
initiative. Moreover, at the same time the first vague
rumours began to come in that the projected rising had
unexpectedly taken place. Pius, undismayed by Alva's
coldness, wrote to him, on the 4th of February,[3] yet another
pressing exhortation to action, and, suiting his acts to his
words, opened the process for the Queen's excommunication
the very next day.

---

[1] Alva's letter is printed in Navarette, *Documentos Inéditos*, iv. 519.
Pius's letter of November 3 may have been occasioned by news sent to
Rome *by Alva himself* (see *Venetian Calendar* under November 5). Philip
was approached at the same time, but warned the Pope of the great danger
that might ensue by premature action, dispatches from the nuncio at
Madrid, *Nunz. di Spagna*, iv. 112.   Philip was also vexed at the Pope
approaching Alva, as if he were an independent sovereign. *Ibid.*, 116.
[2] Mignet, ii. 419; *Documentos Inéditos*, iv. 516. It is here dated
December 4.   [3] Laderchi, § 383.

On the 5th of February Alexander Riario, Uditore Generale of Causes in the Pontifical Court, and afterwards a Cardinal, opened a commission "in the Bedchamber room of his Palace of Justice" [? in the Capitol] on an indictment against the Queen of England for notorious heresy, to the following effect:—

WHEREAS some years back the Kingdom of England was infested by heretics, schismatics and infidels, and whereas Queen Mary had entirely extirpated the said heresies, and brought back the said realm to due obedience to the Holy See; she, the said Queen Mary, dying, and Elizabeth her sister succeeding: the latter, where she ought to have followed her sister's footsteps, and to have exhorted the said people to live Christianlike and Catholicly, NEVERTHE-LESS this same Elizabeth, instigated by the devil, as is notorious, inexcusable, and of public fame, erecting her horns against the apostolic authority, HAS forced and com-pelled the peoples of that kingdom, and in particular Bishops, Archbishops, and other ecclesiastical persons, to take a wicked oath against Church liberty, not to recognise any other supreme governess, whether in ecclesiastical or in temporal causes, except herself, the asserted Queen, and this under grave, afflictive and even corporal pains. ALSO she has visited the said Bishops and others with her pre-tended commissaries, and deprived, despoiled some of them for refusing the said oath, and bestowed the bishoprics, benefices, etc., on heretics, married men, and non-clerics. ALSO she has consigned to prison all who hear divine offices and the Mass according to the order of our Holy Mother the Church, and leaves them to perish and to die. WHAT is still more detestable, scandalous and of the worst example, she makes laws, prints heretical books on the administration of the Sacraments and the divine offices, and commands them to be observed. ALSO she does not fear to live and to allow sermons to be preached in the heretical and Calvinistic manner, and to tolerate condemned and manifest heresy, and to hear ecclesiastical causes; she forbids priests to celebrate *more Catholico ;* she is present at heretical sermons; she allows meat on forbidden days; she has the Lord's

Supper celebrated *more hæretico;* and commits other enormous crimes. These things are public to the whole world, inexcusable, notorious, and redound to the contempt of the Apostolic See.

This charge was subdivided into seventeen articles, which were proposed to twelve witnesses, whom the process describes as " viri docti et promoti in facultatibus suis." The first day (Sunday) was taken up with the evidence of Sir Richard Shelley. He had been ambassador several times for Henry VIII and Mary, and was now Grand Prior of the English Tongue of the Knights of St. John (late Turcopolier). He deposed to the truth of the articles described, mentioned his leaving England rather than take the appointed oaths, and he read an interesting letter from his cousin, Thomas Copley, describing his flight abroad, which had taken place only two months before. Next day, February 6, the witnesses were Thomas Goldwell, the Bishop of St. Asaph, Maurice Clenog, Bishop Elect of Bangor, and Nicholas Morton, of whom we have just heard. On the 7th appeared Henry Henshaw, late Rector of Lincoln College, Oxford, Edmund Daniel, late Dean of Hereford, and Edward Bromburgh, fellow of New College, and priest of Winchester, and (probably on this day) William Gyblet, Bromburgh's companion throughout life. This group form an interesting link between the pre-Reformation and post-Reformation Church of England. Daniel having died, the rest returned as missionaries; and Henshaw lived long enough to be nominated one of Blackwell's " assistants " in 1598. No names are mentioned for the 8th; and on the 9th the witnesses were William Allot and Richard Hall, D.D. The former had been a chaplain of Lord Morley and Sir Thomas Wharton; the latter, who was of Pembroke College, Cambridge, was afterwards a professor at Douay. On the 10th and last day, Richard Shelley the younger was heard, and the two Kyrtons, Thomas, a priest of the diocese of Salisbury, and Henry, a bachelor of laws.[1]

---

[1] *D.N.B.* has biographies of Clenog, Goldwell, Hall, Morton and Shelley. Bromburgh and Gyblet reappear in the life of Campion, whom they accompanied to England. For the signatures and further notes on Goldwell, Clenog, Henshaw, Thomas Kyrton, Daniel, Morton, see *C.R.S.,*

The witnesses were certainly good representatives of the English Catholics, and even what remains of their evidence is of great importance. Not every one could depose to the truth of every count, but all have special information or experience on one point or other. After the advice of the Cardinals had been heard, sentence was pronounced by the Pope in person on the 12th of February, and it is given in full by Laderchi. But there is no need to go into it here, as the Bull of Excommunication went over the same ground immediately afterwards. On the 16th, within a day or two of the completion of the process, the letter of the Northern Earls, which they had sent off before the Rising began, came in, after the usual three months' post, and it probably consoled the Pontiff. He answered it on the 20th with a strong exhortation to fervour and courage, and encouragement to face death boldly in so good a cause.[1]

On the 25th he issued the Bull of Excommunication, of which the following is a condensed translation :—

" The Lord who reigns on high (*Regnans in Excelsis*) instituted a Church which should be one, and gave its government to Peter and his successors. This one he placed above all nations and kingdoms, ' to root up and destroy, to scatter and waste, to plant and build,'[2] in order that He may maintain a faithful people in the unity of the Spirit. In the discharge of this duty we labour with all our might

---

ii. 3, 4. The original record of the process is unfortunately lost, as also the office copy of it, which Laderchi, the continuator of Baronius, had in his hands. Fortunately he copied out considerable extracts (his MS. is at Rome, Bib. Vallicelliana, MS. S. 50, ff. 492–519). He then translated into Latin the evidence, which was given in Italian, and printed it under 1570, §§ 322–344 (ed. 1883, pp. 153–63). He cancelled the Italian copy in his MS.; but, owing to his having used for this a new ink of a slightly different tint, the original Italian can still be read under the cancellation, and offers several useful corrections of the printed edition.

[1] We learn the date of the Earls' letter, November 8, 1569, from the Pope's answer, printed in Laderchi, 1570, § 384. Drafts are in Arch. Vat., Arm. xliv., t. xv., f. 13 b., also *Brevia Pii V.* xix. 132. On the 22nd he wrote to Philip (Arm. xliv., t. xv., f. 17 b., also *Epistolæ*, ii. 47, and *Brevia*, xix. 123) asking him to credit what his nuncio would tell him about the Rising (Laderchi, *ibid.*). Further correspondence on the subject will be found in the *Nunz. di Spagna*, vol. iv., etc., January to August, 1570. But the views there expressed, though very interesting in themselves, fell so far behind the march of events, that it is not worth while following them further here. See the *Rome Calendar*.

[2] Biblical quotations in the introduction are frequent, *e. g.* Jeremias i. 10; xxiv. 6; xlii. 10; xlv. 4; also Zach. ix. 10.

to preserve that unity, now assailed by so many adversaries. Amongst others is that servant of infamy, Elizabeth, who styles herself Queen of England, the refuge of wicked men.[1]

" Having taken possession of the kingdom,[2] she monstrously usurps the chief authority in the Church, and has undone Queen Mary's reform, and filled the Royal Council with obscure heretics. (*Then follow the counts of the indictment given above.*)

" All this being notorious and confirmed by very many grave witnesses,[3] sin being added to sin, and the ruin of religion growing daily worse, under the direction of the said Elizabeth, whose heart is so hardened that she has set at naught not only the charitable prayers and counsels of Christian princes,[4] but also our own, by her refusal to allow nuncios of the Holy See to enter the realm,[5] we are of necessity compelled to have recourse to the weapons of justice, unable to control our grief[6] that we must proceed against one whose predecessors have rendered signal services to Christendom.

" Relying, therefore, on His authority, Who has placed us on this supreme Seat of Justice, in the fulness of Apostolic power, we declare the said Elizabeth a heretic, and a fautor of heretics, and that all who adhere to her in the aforesaid

[1] *Servant of infamy* (flagitiorum serva), *the refuge of wicked men.* Probably such men as the Cardinal of Châtillon, the Prince of Orange, and other great apostate leaders are meant. The custom of those who excused Elizabeth at the expense of her ministers is also rebuked, and there is an allusion to the alleged improprieties with Leicester and others, which the Northern Earls mentioned so bluntly (p. 138 above), and which never ceased to rankle in the minds of Catholics, as will be seen below.

[2] *Having taken possession of the kingdom.* Elizabeth's illegitimacy is nowhere mentioned; but there is a reference here to the Bull which declared the issue of Anne Boleyn unable to succeed.

[3] *Many grave witnesses*, i. e. those called during the process.

[4] *The charitable prayers and counsels of Christian princes.* One thinks of Despes's paper, *Spanish Calendar*, December 1568, p. 85. It is likely, too, that, when her marriage with foreign Catholic princes was being discussed, the Pope should have been told that attempts to convert her had been made.

[5] *Refusal to allow entrance to papal nuncios*, i. e. Parpaglia and Martinengo.

[6] *Unable to control our grief.* This clause has its legal importance. Judgments of this class are to be interpreted, not as acts of hostility to do the utmost harm, but as acts of fatherly authority, necessary for the eternal salvation of the person condemned, and for others also of the Church at large. They are to be interpreted in the most loving sense. The bearing of this principle will appear later.

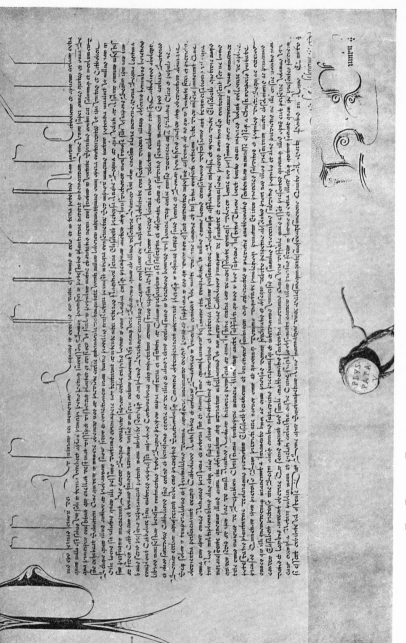

The Bull of Excommunication against Queen Elizabeth, February 25, 1570

From the original membrane in the Vatican Archives

incur the sentence of anathema, and are cut off from the unity of the Body of Christ. Moreover, that she has forfeited her pretenced title to the aforesaid kingdom, and is deprived of all dominion, dignity and privilege. We declare that nobles, subjects and peoples are free from any oath to her, and we interdict obedience to her monitions, mandates and laws. Those who do otherwise we involve in the same anathema.[1] At Rome, the fifth of the Kalends of March, 1569, the fifth of our Pontificate." [2]

The main scope and object of the Bull are expressed with a force and directness that makes comment upon them unnecessary. Excommunication from the unity of the Church for gross heresy and other offences, and deprivation of the rights of sovereignty—these points cannot be overlooked by any one; and the impression produced is that the Pope has acted under motives of such strength that they have left him no alternative, no room to do otherwise.

But besides the main issues, there are certain omissions worthy of notice. Thus nothing, or next to nothing, is said on Elizabeth's illegitimacy, on her rights as the accepted sovereign, on the duty of rising against her, on the rights of Mary Stuart. It is true that the crisis in England could not end in the conclusion which the Pope desired, without decisions being taken on those subjects, but they are not settled here. We can see that the Pope was fully alive to them, and we can presage the determination which he would give when necessary. But in his mind they are of secondary importance, and can only become practical matters for him when the excommunication has taken full effect.

Thus at last completed, the Bull was to have been conveyed to England by Dr. Morton, when the news arrived that the Rising had taken place and had altogether collapsed. Being bad news, it had come a good deal faster than usual, that is, in about two months instead of three.[3]

Nevertheless, every one knew in general that the Catholic

---

[1] *Those who do otherwise we involve in the same anathema.* A comparison of this clause with the parallel section in the excommunication of Henry VIII, shows that the possible extensions of the sentence to the subjects of the monarch are here very much reduced.

[2] For further information about the date &c., see end of the chapter.

[3] Morton's Memoir, *ut supra.*

party was not exterminated, and Pius may have had letters on this point of which we do not know.[1] At all events, he resolved not to give up the policy which he had initiated. He had already sent Ridolfi 12,000 scudi, and had, perhaps, promised up to 100,000.[2] And he soon sent Ridolfi a copy of the Bull in cipher through the nuncio at Paris, and Ridolfi communicated it to Despes, who sent copies to Alva on the 10th of May and to Philip on the 13th.

Meantime the Pontiff had sent a copy to Alva direct, on the 30th of March, asking him to publish it in Flanders. This Alva was very far indeed from consenting to do; but he wrote, May 9, a forcible letter to Zuñiga at Rome pointing out the moral impossibility of the English Catholics obeying such orders, the conflict of conscience that would thereupon ensue, to the great detriment of religion. Later on (May 23), he answered Despes in the same sense, deeply regretting the step taken, and cautioning the ambassador not to let any one know that he had so much as heard of the matter. King Philip also wrote (June 30) sincerely regretting the Pope's action, " which will embitter feelings there, and drive the Queen and her friends to oppress and persecute the few good Catholics who still remain in England." His instructions to Despes, however, did not exactly correspond with those of Alva. Instead of telling him to stand off, he was to discover all he could from Ridolfi about the Pope's plans, about which Philip was very anxious. These conservative Spaniards had evidently no hand at all in the excommunication, and disliked the Pope's new policy.[3]

We must now return to Ridolfi, who received first one copy by cipher from the nuncio in Paris, then (according to his later memoir) about eighty copies, some printed,

---

[1] Despes on the 18th of January, 1570, writes that the excommunication is desired in England (*Spanish Calendar*, p. 229).

[2] *Spanish Calendar,* p. 245. This is also alluded to in the letter of February 20. Laderchi, following Gabuzio, says, § 385, that the Pope actually sent 150,000 scudi, whereas from Despes (Lettenhove, *Relations*, v. 652) it seems he never meant to give more than another 12,000. Philip was reported to have sent Alva 200,000, and 10,000 to the Earls, but only in January (*Nunz. di Spagna.* iv. 118. *Rome Calendar*, p. 323).

[3] For Alva's correspondence with Zuñiga, see Mignet, *Marie Stuart,* ii. 420; with Despes, see Lettenhove, *Relations*, v. 652–73. For Despes's correspondence with Philip, *Spanish Calendar*, pp. 245–54. Philip also showed the nuncio at Madrid that he was angry (*Nunz. di Spagna*, v. 140, July 17. *Rome Calendar*, p. 339).

some in MS.,[1] and one of these was affixed to the door of the Bishop of London's palace in St. Paul's Churchyard on Corpus Christi day, the 25th of May. Elizabeth's Government soon found out that this had been done by Mr. John Felton, a Catholic gentleman of good means, who was arrested and sent to the Tower to be examined under torture on the 25th of June, and confessed on the 27th that he had put it up with the aid of an Irish priest named Cornelius.[2]

Felton behaved himself throughout with the greatest courage. Condemned as a matter of course to the death of a traitor, he denied to the last that he had intended or done the Queen any harm—that is, he believed the Bull was for the salvation both of herself and of the kingdom, and he sent her from the scaffold his great diamond ring,[3] though he refused to acknowledge her as Queen (August 8, 1570).

[1] Ridolfi's Petition, Florence, *A.S.* 4185, as above.

[2] There are many apparent discrepancies in the different accounts of this transaction. 1. Ridolfi, in his Petition, speaks as though *he* had done everything himself, without any one's aid; but this is in his manner, and must not be urged. 2. Felton's confessions have perished, but the indictment, which was presumably constructed from them, gives the above details, that he was aided by an *Irish priest, Cornelius*. 3. But the earliest Catholic reports speak of *the chaplain of the Spanish ambassador*. 4. So with Fénelon, who wrote, July 25 (*Dépêches*, iii. 254–5), and Sander, who wrote to Cardinal Hosius (6 kal., Sep. 1570, in S. Rescius, *De Atheismis et Phalarismis Evangelicorum*, 1596, p. 497). 5. This is repeated by Pollini, *Istoria della rivoluzion d'Inghilterra*, 1594, who adds that his name was Peter Berga, of Catalonia, and chaplain of the church of Tarragona. There was an intrigue, perhaps a scandalous one, to arrest a Spanish chaplain, by means of a Catholic woman. " Mr. Cobham " was to have been the agent, and Sir Henry Neville, an officer in the Tower, was its promoter. (*Hatfield Calendar*, July 11–21, pp. 473–6.) 6. We have also the tradition of the Felton family (written in 1627 by a priest, Mr. Ferrar, from the relation of Felton's daughter, Mrs. Salisbury), printed *Acts of English Martyrs*, pp. 209–12, and according to which Felton went to Calais himself, and brought over the Bull, and was assisted in putting it up by Lawrence Webb, *D.U.I.*, afterwards a professor at Douay.

On the whole the indictment is the best evidence. The Spanish ambassador says nothing in his dispatches about his chaplain. It is true that Alva's strict prohibition of interference (May 23) would have prevented the ambassador from allowing any of his staff to take part in the publication; but then this cannot have arrived in time to have its effect, and the chaplain *might* have acted without telling his master. While we cannot reconcile all the above evidence, we must remember that there was no intrinsic difficulty in Felton having had several assistants.

[3] This, however, was partly due to a sporting desire to dish the jackals of the law (and in particular the Lord Chief Justice), who, according to the odd precedents of that time, were claiming it as their prey. The record of Felton's indictment and trial are preserved in the *Baga de Secretis*, see *Fourth Report of Dep. Keeper*, 1843, p. 265; for Felton's Life, see Camm, *Lives of English Martyrs*, 1905, I. ii., pp. xx, 1–13.

Even before Felton suffered, another victim was being prepared for the Puritan blood-lust. This was the lawyer, John Storey, late Member of Parliament, and Chancellor to Bishop Bonner. He was living at Antwerp, employed in the Spanish Custom House, a post of trust indeed, but an invidious one when heretical books and letters were under embargo and war was threatening. One day he was lured on to a smack in the harbour, the hatches were closed down, and he was secretly carried to England. He was there condemned to the cruel death of quartering, nominally for having befriended some of the exiled Northern men, but in reality, of course, to pay off old scores from Queen Mary's time. The whole incident—the elaborate fraud, official and legal, of his capture and condemnation—affords a striking proof of the advance which savagery was making, not merely with the mob, but also in official and clerical circles. Cecil and the chief Ministers of the Crown gathered round the gallows to grace his quartering, which was conducted with appalling brutality (June 1, 1571); and, more horrible still, popular writers, and preachers like Fulke, recall his agonised cries of pain with smug satisfaction, as showing their victim was " manifestly void of patience, and no martyr, as the Papists did mightily boast of him."

It is true that from the first Catholics of all countries regarded both these sufferers as martyrs; nor can there be any question, when one considers the whole evidence, that they were executed not so much for any danger they had caused the State, but rather as victims of anti-Catholic prejudice. But, of course, their cases are not on a par with those of the later martyrs, against whom nothing offensive of any sort could be alleged, except disregarding the law which made priesthood treason.[1]

---

[1] Bishop Challoner in the eighteenth century, when Catholics were most intent on showing their inoffensiveness, was rather ostentatious in omitting James Leyburn, who alone among the sufferers after 1581 denied Elizabeth's sovereignty because of the Bull. We do not know Challoner's position towards Felton, as he only professed to treat of *Missionary (i. e.* Seminary) *priests*, who came into England later. No doubt some of those Catholics (and they have been many) who have admired Gallican ideals would have refused to admit Felton's claim to martyrdom; and though his name and Percy's occur in Leo XIII's decree of 1886, it must be remembered that this is so far only permissive. For the Life of Storey, see Camm, *Lives of the English Martyrs*, 1905, ii. 14–110.

To return to the period of Felton's death (August 8, 1570). By this time it seemed clear that the Bull would lead, not to Elizabeth's fall, but rather to the notable injury of the Catholics,[1] and an account of a speech made by the Pope in a Consistory of August 3, records that Pius spoke amid tears (*deplorans*) of the bad prospects,[2] and added that the Cardinals Santa Croce and Buoncompagno, the future Gregory XIII, had been of his mind for the publication of the Bull.

Nevertheless, when the Emperor Maximilian asked him to withdraw the Bull, he refused. Maximilian had begun by being a "compromise-Catholic," not very dissimilar from Elizabeth at her accession; but time had made him much more orthodox. At present, however, he was at odds with Pope Pius, who wished him to depose the Protestant Electors, which Maximilian altogether refused to do. Lord Cobham, who was sent to him as ambassador in the summer, encouraged this resentment, and the Emperor, who was quite out of sympathy with the Bull, declared he would get it changed. It had, in fact, already been disregarded, both by Spain and France, and the English Catholics concluded that what the great Powers might do, they also were allowed. A good case could certainly be made out for withdrawing the Bull.

But Pius was probably right to refuse. A change might have led to still worse complications. His letter to Maximilian, however (January 5, 1571), is not very felicitous, for it does not touch the real difficulty—the increased trouble caused to the English Catholics. "Why does the Queen make so much to do, if she does not mind?" he asks rhetorically. Here the Pontiff was not very well informed. Though personally much annoyed, Elizabeth's Government was not perceptibly endangered, and such anxiety as the Bull caused arose from a mistaken and hurtful inference. Cecil and his party assumed that no such Bull as this would have been launched unless there had been a league of

---

[1] When Campion went to Rome in 1573, the Cardinal of Sta. Cecilia questioned him about the effects of the Bull. " I said it procured much severity in England, and the heavy hand of her Majesty against the Catholics."— Campion's Trial, *apud* Simpson, p. 291.

[2] Maziere Brady, *Episcopal Succession*, ii. 337.

Catholic princes against the Protestants,[1] an idea which, albeit absurd to those who knew the mutual relations between France and Spain, was wont to arouse the sectaries to frenzy all over Europe; and these outbursts of fanaticism were always harmful to the English Catholics, and sometimes (as on the present occasion) led to the passing of barbarous laws which endured for centuries.

But while the Bull was a failure from so many points of view, that does not prove that its effect was entirely, or even predominantly, injurious. Alva and Philip were, no doubt, right in saying that harm would ensue—loss of prestige to the Pope, grievous troubles of conscience to the faithful, and the final loss of many who were previously holding on, though weakly, to the old cause. Against this must be set the inestimable advantage of making it evident to all the world that Elizabeth and her followers were cut off from the Catholic Church, that to accept and submit to her was to reject that Church. The Bull made clear the iniquity of attending Protestant churches at her command, which nothing had hitherto been able to bring home to the Tudor Catholics, with their miserable proclivity to give up religious liberty at the sovereign's whim. Now at last those who refused to attend grew into a body, and won a special name, that of the Recusants.

There had, indeed, been refusals before, and at first the Government had neither an army of officials sufficient to demand obedience nor stability sufficient to exact it. But as their power grew, their tyranny became more and more extensive in application, and the resistance of the Catholics more and more weak, irregular, inconstant. Now the officials could affect to believe that *every one* was compromised, that none would refuse when the royal authority was sufficiently insistent. It is hard to see what else could have roused the Catholics from their fatal lethargy but a great thunderstroke like this Bull.

Whether it might not have been issued earlier with advantage, can hardly be settled now. It would have

---

[1] *Rome Calendar*, p. 375. Fénelon, *Dépêches*, iii. 196, 225, etc. Previous references to fear of this bogey, *ibid*. i. 229, 323; ii. 23, 47, 106, etc. See also Walsingham's and Cecil's letters, *Domestic Calendar*, 1558–1580, 324, 334.

depended on the extent to which the clergy would have backed it up. Even in 1570 they were not in a position to do so immediately—they were not, in fact, ready till after six or eight years, when the young men educated at Douay and elsewhere had completed their training. So that even the good that did come from the Bull was slow and tardy. On the other hand, this delay was accidental to some extent, so far as the English Catholics were concerned We have seen that the revival of the English Catholic clergy really began between 1564 and 1567, when they were beginning to show very great activity and vigour in controversy. They were making what would probably have turned out to be permanent settlements at Louvain, and were even beginning to send missionaries into England—like Laurence Vaux and Thomas King, S.J.—when the outbreak of the wars of religion in Flanders threw everything back again for another ten years.

We cannot, therefore, conjecture what would have been the result if the Bull had been launched earlier, or kept back till later. As to the harm which ensued through inquisitorial questions sometimes based upon it, it may be asserted with perfect confidence that an enemy so astute and relentless as Cecil would always have found other matters on which to ensnare his victims. The " bloody question," of which we shall hear so much later, was often asked on other topics besides the Bull.

That Pope Pius acted under a misapprehension cannot be questioned ; and no valid excuse has yet been proposed for his having taken a step so important in matters which, though religious, were also secular and political, without consulting with, and deferring to, those who understood the whole situation from within. On the other hand, the excuse due to his great distance from the scene has hardly yet been appreciated. It then took three or four months for confidential letters to reach him from England, and the consequences of so tardy a post are to us now hardly realisable. It seems extraordinary to see him, in order to help the Rising, begin the process of excommunication a month and a half after the Rising was over, and sign the Bull before news of the failure reached him. But so it was all through.

Owing to difficulties on the Continent, the initiative had to be taken in Rome, to which (owing to the deliberate interception of all correspondence) reliable news came with the greatest difficulty. If Pius had been near, if he had had the ordinary facilities for correspondence, his action would have been differently planned and differently timed, and its results would doubtless have been far more often successful.

One circumstance must not be overlooked in our retrospect over this great drama, and that was the Pope's high character. Intense as was the hatred borne by the fanatics to all that was papal, even they did not, as a rule, doubt the high principle and pure intention which animated St. Pius. Bacon not so long after wrote of "that excellent Pius Quintus, whom I wonder his successors have not declared a Saint." [1]

Finally, it is a remarkable coincidence that the Parliament which Elizabeth summoned in her thirteenth year to take measures against the Bull should have been the first to resist the Tudor dictation. It began those Puritan victories over the Crown which were to culminate in the subversion of monarchy itself in the next reign but one.

It may be remembered that one count of the indictment on which Elizabeth was condemned was, that she allowed "sermons in the Calvinistic manner." That was correctly worded. Elizabeth at heart preferred the old doctrine, but having decided to break with the ancient Church, she could obtain little effective assistance except from the Calvinists. Hitherto, though using Calvinists freely, she had managed to keep her Settlement of Religion to some extent free from their doctrine. But now, as her Government (which controlled the elections) [2] were only able to count on Puritans for support, a strong Puritan majority had been returned, which insisted, in spite of Elizabeth's vehement resistance, on imposing the Thirty-Nine Articles permanently upon the country. She had sown the wind, and now reaped the storm.

[1] Bacon, "Of a Holy War," *Works*, ed. 1838, ii. 523. The words, however, are spoken by Bacon not *in propria persona*, but are given to a speaker in a dialogue. St. Pius was canonised in 1712.

[2] Despes writes, September 2, 1570: "Cecil is making lists of those whom he wishes elected, all of whom are strong Protestants."—*Spanish Calendar*, p. 273.

FURTHER NOTE ON THE BULL

(a) *The Date.*—On the original Bull is " Anno Incarnationis dominicæ Millesimo quingentesimo sexagisimo nono Quinto Kal. Mart. Pontificatus nostri Anno Quinto."

Owing to a variety of reasons the date of this Bull has been cited with extraordinary want of accuracy. In the first place, it seemed (*a priori*) most probable that it would have been issued *before*, not *after* the Rising, and this was, in fact, reported freely by contemporaries. I find it so in a letter of a Jesuit father written this very year, 1570. It is so set forth in Adriani, *Istoria dei suoi tempi*, Firenze, 1583, the most popular memoir writer of the day. This false chronology found its way into the lives of St. Pius, and the Annalist Laderchi was so bewitched by it that he actually declared the process was held a year after the issue of the Bull, in order to justify its previous issue ! And when he printed the Bull he calmly altered both the year of the Christian era and the year of the pontificate ! No wonder after such blunders that both Catholic (even Dr. Lingard) and Protestant writers (also the Record Office, *Dom. Eliz.*, xlix. 53) should have gone astray on this point. But see *Rome Calendar*, p. 328.

Bulls are generally dated, as is here clearly expressed, by the era of the *Incarnation*, which was reckoned to have begun on March 25; or, in other words, according to " Old Style." " New Style " had, in fact, not yet been introduced. The date of this Bull is thus February 25, 1570, according to our reckoning. And as Pius succeeded on Christmas Day, 1565, this was his fifth February.

(b) *Text.*—As the original membrane was never sent away, it is still preserved in the Vatican (*Castello*, Arm. ii., caps. vi. n. 5) in excellent preservation, Bulla still attached. It is reproduced in this volume. Original printed copies are also fairly frequent. There is one in the Record Office, *Dom. Eliz.*, xlix. 53, British Museum, *Fragmenta Antiqua*, c. 18. e. 2. n. 114. This is countersigned, for purposes of authentication, by Francesco Gratiano. It is also printed in Sander, *De Schismate* (Rishton's continuation, ed. D. Lewis, p. 301), in the *Bullarium*, in Laderchi's *Annales*, *Venetian Calendar*, 1570, pp. 449, etc., etc.

(c) *Answers.*—A special proclamation against the Bull was issued July 1, 1570. A copy R. O., *Dom. Eliz.*, lxxi. 34.

Though the Bull has been attacked and defended so often—and inevitably so, considering its vital importance—there was, nevertheless, not so much literary controversy about it as might have been imagined; far less, for instance, than about Campion's *Ten Reasons*. Bullinger's *Refutatio*, 1571, was the official answer, translated into English by Golding. There was also a tract by Norton, and later on, in 1582, a " View taken " by Jewell, and a Latin tract by Renniger, a Court chaplain. All things considered, this was very little. The truth was that Elizabeth did not care that an indictment of such terrific vigour should be much spoken of, even by her defenders. Catholics, too, had many reasons for not bringing it too much forward. It was a sore irritant to the Protestants; while its very chequered success prevented even the faithful from being proud of it. Leaders like Allen rather apologised for than defended it (*Defence of English Catholics*, Chap. iv., pp. 59, etc.; Latin translation in *Concertatio*, pp. 323, etc.), and the outspoken Nicholas Sander, having written in its defence, was persuaded by his friends not to publish (Allen, *ibid.*, p. 65, reprint of 1913, p. 83).

§ 2. *Ridolfi's Mission* (1571–1573)

We now approach an obscure and inglorious incident, about which the sober truth will never be quite as interesting as the romantic stories which have too often passed current as history. The villain of the piece has been displayed as a stage assassin, from whom foul play should be every moment expected. In reality Ridolfi was not without a certain honesty and piety, and it needs some attention to see how he sank to the lax morality of which we must pronounce him guilty.

When relief of grievances is impossible, when complaint is made criminal, and every attempt at obtaining redress is suppressed with cruelty, conspiracy unfortunately becomes inevitable, when large bodies of men are affected. The insular position of England enabled the Government to cut off such of its inhabitants as it proscribed, from foreign aid and even from flight. No remedy met the eye but prostration before the tyrant, and the bitter feelings of the Conservatives, after the collapse of the Rising and the distribution of the property of the insurgents among the new men, can be better imagined than described. But long schooled in subservience, they kept their peace, and if two foreigners had not exerted themselves to bring the secret trouble to a head, we should have heard no more about it.

These two were Roberto Ridolfi, the Florentine banker, and John Leslie, Bishop-Designate of Ross. Both are known to us already, but it is necessary to study them more closely still, for their characters have been obscured by excessive praise and blame. They were, in fact, both average good men for their stations and circumstances. But both were thrown into new surroundings, and in these they were called upon to play very difficult parts, the honourable discharge of which required special gifts of character and a previous training, which they did not possess. The Churchman, in days when violence was chronic in Scotland, saw nothing exceptional in making plans for insurrections while he was an ambassador in

peaceful England. The banker, used to hearing of the
assassinations and other signs of debased political morality
in Florence under the Medici, saw no insuperable incon-
venience, after he had turned politician over here, in
adapting himself to similar low principles.

Both represented foreign interests which Elizabeth's
Government had treated with monstrous injustice. For
she was keeping Leslie's sovereign, the Queen of Scots, a
captive, and destroying all loyalty to her in Scotland, while
the native and foreign pirates who used England as their
base had captured and disposed of booty to the value of
4,000,000 crowns from those who were Ridolfi's friends
or compatriots. Both men, therefore, had good reason
for striving against Lord Burghley and his party. But
when the Churchman launched into political intrigues
and the banker dreamt of alliances and planned campaigns,
they were dealing with matters they did not understand,
though they had by birth a casual acquaintance with them,
and thereby they managed to deceive both themselves and
their friends egregiously.

Ridolfi had been imprisoned in Walsingham's house on
suspicion at the time of the Northern Rising in October
1569. But nothing transpired against him. He came out
with greater credit than before, and Pius V apparently
gave him some sort of appointment as " factor " or correspondent, and, as we have heard, sent him over money for
the Earls, and eighty [1] copies of the Bull of Excommunication to get published. It appears that he wrote to Rome
on June 6 and July 1, 1570,[2] urging that all Catholic countries should publish the Bull of Excommunication. On the
1st of September he reported that the old understanding
of 1569 between the Conservative Lords still held good,
mutatis mutandis. It will be well to give an abstract of
this message, for, slight though it is, it forms perhaps the
most complete and most authentic account we have of
Ridolfi's ideas and ambitions.

---

[1] On the other hand, Ross says Ridolfi received six printed copies and
gave him one (Murdin, p. 35).
[2] The letter of the 1st of July, in which the letter of June is referred
to, is preserved, Arch Vat., *Varia Politicorum*, ic. 175; *Rome Calendar*,
p. 338.

M

Ridolfi to the Pope

September 1, 1570.

" Certain Signori have asked Alva to help by sending them arms. They will then, with the aid of all Catholics, free Mary and restore religion. To-day Despes writes that if ·Alva consents (and I feel sure he will) Mary's followers in Scotland will attack from that side also. So that all will succeed, especially if your Holiness sends a subsidy to Flanders. Success will be further ensured if the exclusion of English commerce is maintained in Flanders, France, and Portugal, and the Bull is published, for the greater part of the inhabitants are Catholic. With Lord [Guglie] are Sir Thomas Stanley and Sir Thomas Gerard. They will be assisted by the followers of Lord Derby (Gauci), and of all Lancashire, in all about 12,000 men. Not far off them are Sir Thomas [? Fitzherbert] and friends in the county de Bester [Derbyshire], with about 6000 men. In the counties of Surrey, Sussex, Hampshire, there are Lord Southampton, Lord Montague, the Earl of Arundel, Lord Lumley, and Lord Windsor, who will rise with 15,000 men and master (*impatronirse*) the Court. Elsewhere, towards Cornwall and Wales, are Sir de Lunai [Sir John Arundel] and the Earl of Worcester, each of whom will raise 6000 men, all Catholics. From Norfolk and Suffolk a good number would come, were it not that a premature rising was unfortunately discovered there just lately, and that seven gentlemen, all Catholics, are under sentence of death, and one to perpetual imprisonment. Luckily there are many more not detected. Unless some project like the above is favoured, the Protestants will become unconquerable, and with their leagues will endanger all their neighbours. Still Elizabeth is now in fear, because of the evident divisions in the realm, and King Philip might even now bring back Catholicism by demonstrations in favour of his friends there." [1]

In view of what followed, it may be as well to say that the important point in the new plans turned out to be, that

---

[1] Arch. Vat., *Var. Pol.*, ic. 171; *Rome Calendar* in full, p. 346. The corrupt forms of the names are probably due to the ciphering.

the English were to take the first step.   In this first plan,
in fact, the English, it is said, would do all, if only they
received weapons and money from abroad; in the later
plans foreign auxiliaries from 10,000 to 20,000 men were
postulated.   Next we note the assurance of triumph
throughout—the tens of thousands of insurgents, the Court
" mastered "—and in the end Mary is happily seated on the
throne.   Nothing is said about the Duke of Norfolk, nor
are there any vouchers or witnesses, or any military opinions
of the feasibility of the plan of campaign.

At the same time that this was sent off Despes wrote to
his master his account of the enterprise, perhaps made up
from information supplied by the Bishop of Ross.[1]   Here
the ideas are more moderate.   He speaks of 12,000 men
in the Lancashire contingent, but he leaves all the rest in
the vague.   The Duke of Norfolk is here actually excluded
because he is a Protestant.

In later versions of his scheme [2] Ridolfi gave more and
more prominence to Spanish auxiliaries.   This was reasonable,
but it makes it incumbent on us to read here the following
severe censure by the Spanish generalissimo, though it was
written later (on the 29th of August), after the receipt of
Ridolfi's final plans :—

" I have seen the discourse which Ridolfi has given on
what may be done in England.   When the man that makes
the discourse has no one to criticise the suppositions on
which he argues, he will draw his conclusions most happily.
It is like a judge passing sentence after hearing one side
only.   And a man like this, who is no soldier, and has never
seen war in his life, thinks one can pour armies out of the
air, or keep them up one's sleeve, and effect with them what
his fancy depicts.   For to talk as though one might have
one army to take the Queen of England, another to free
the Queen of Scots, and at the same time to seize the Tower
of London and capture the ships in the river—really I

---

[1] *Spanish Calendar*, p. 274.   Dispatch of 2nd of September.   The
Spanish text is in Lettenhove, v. 705.

[2] I identify as one of these later plans the document preserved in the
Vatican, *Nunziatura di Spagna*, II. (olim xiii.) ff. 399–408, about July
1571.

think that even if your Majesty had agreed with the Queen of England to do these things, you would not have enough to do it in an instant, as he proposes that it should be done. Wherefore, Sir, in the case of men of such little balance as those who treat these topics, and have such little comprehension of what is practicable, nothing at all should be risked upon their words; but only on their deeds, when their part is actually executed." [1]

If there had only been more men like Alva this chapter would have been considerably shorter. This, however, represents Alva's final views. He did not at first see his way so clearly. But to return to our story.

Ridolfi's plans may have reached Rome at the end of October, and it is to be feared that the Pope was at once captivated by them; for he wrote to Mary exhorting her to make the venture. His letter seems to be lost, but some indistinct recollections of it were given later by Barker: " He would embrace her, and all them that took her part, *sicut gallina pullos suos*, and that he did dispense with all them that would rebel against Elizabeth." There was also a covering letter from the nuncio in France, which spoke of money and other aids, and that " his well-beloved factor Ridolfi" had already 12,000 crowns to relieve those who had suffered in the Northern Rising. [2]

Pius's letters reached Mary early in February 1571, [3] and they were accompanied by a letter from Ridolfi, in which he urged that Mary should give over treating with

---

[1] Alva to Philip, or Zayas, August 29, 1571.—Gonzalez, *Apuntamientos MS.*, pp. 198–209.

[2] Murdin, *State Papers*, 1759, p. 126. Barker's confessions, November 7, 1571.

Great difficulty was found in conveying this aid to the places where it was needed. Ridolfi had recourse to Despes in order to get it distributed through Alva to the refugees in Scotland. But Alva, in his extreme caution, refused to undertake the office of intermediary, and hence many complications and misunderstandings, on which see Lettenhove, *Relations Politiques*, v. 652, 669, and Fénelon, iii. 256. Many references to the transmission of this money or of that sent by Philip are found in the examinations of the Duke of Norfolk's servants in Murdin. These difficulties of transport, in fact, proved eventually the occasion for the discovery of the whole negotiation.

[3] A summary of Ridolfi's message to Mary, sent back, probably, by Raulet to Archbishop Beaton, February 6, 1571, is printed in Hosack, ii. 503. John Beaton brought over letters in January (Murdin, p. 24, § 9).

Elizabeth for a restoration by her aid, and should throw herself into what was really his own plan, viz. that a messenger (*i. e.* himself) should go to the Pope and obtain from him full sanction for the revolution sketched above, and a commendation to King Philip so warm that Philip would be sure to accept it; and if he did so, the enterprise was certain to be successful.

When Mary received these communications she was in more than usual trouble, owing to the failure of all previous attempts in her favour, and to the fear that France might now abandon her. Desperate as the plan might be, in her position she was prone to catch at any straw. On the 8th of February, therefore, she wrote a letter to the Bishop of Ross, which is extant,[1] surveying her present policy. She balances the bad faith of England, and the inutility and possible hostility of France, with the warm offers of the Pope, the strong probability of Philip's aid, the proffers of marriage with Don John or the Duke of Norfolk, and the chances of Ridolfi bringing his negotiations to a happy conclusion, and she finally decides to accept Ridolfi's offer. It is a well-thought-out, clearly-conceived plan, and, considering the agony she was undergoing because of the injuries done to her cause, we can hardly wonder at her choice. Moreover, by giving a man like the Duke of Norfolk, who was anything but an adventurer, a last word in the settlement, she may have thought that she was taking a precaution quite sufficient for the occasion. But unfortunately, in spite of her many statesmanlike powers, Mary was ever a bad judge of men, and so it proved in the present case.

The Duke, on whom the responsibility for the decision was now thrust, was a good-natured man, with little power of initiative or strength of character. Whether it was that his spirit was broken young, by King Henry's murder of his father, the Earl of Surrey, or whether it was merely the subservience of the age, he had done nothing but drift all his life, from one religion and from one policy to another, with every turn of the Tudor will. And yet for him all had, till lately, fallen out fortunately. All

[1] Labanoff, *Lettres de Marie Stuart*, iii. 180–7.

around him the old nobles had gone under, while he had prospered, and popularity had come without his seeking it. On the other hand, as the head of the English nobility he was looked up to by all the Conservative peers. Closely connected with many by marriage, he could not but be strongly influenced by their views. Many had offered to draw the sword for him two years earlier, if he would speak the word. Instead of this, he had yielded, and gone to prison; yet, with his usual good luck, he had escaped ruin, and, though not yet altogether free, was in hopes that he might be so ere long.

Towards Queen Mary his normal attitude was that of indulgence, good nature, hope. He dreamt that his happy star might dispel the shadow of her constant ill fortune. To Elizabeth, on the other hand, he used the subservient, even cringing language and bearing of the day, and declared himself an unbending Protestant, and without any ambition to alter the established order. When the two influences came into immediate contrast, his fear of the Tudors dominated all else. " I will not cast away myself, my children and my friends for none of them all." [1] Even so he could not bring himself to turn a deaf ear to the appeals of the imprisoned Queen. " If I can comfort and quiet her I am content [to do as she wishes]; otherwise not." His answers to Mary were generally in the form of kindly ejaculations : " Time will remedy "; " She must have patience "; " God speed it well." Told of the Pope's promises he answered, " Well ! " and said no more.

But the time was now come when he must make his choice between the two sides. He had been changed from the Tower to the easier custody of his own house, on condition that he should think no more of marrying the Queen of Scots.[2] Nevertheless, she continued to appeal to him, and to ask his advice, as if he remained her fiancé. But to do this in the present state of affairs brought the whole matter again to a crisis, for his marriage with her was, in fact, part of the policy on which she asked advice. The appeal " put him into a marvelous strait," as the Bishop of Ross noted.[2] On the one hand were his good nature

[1] Murdin, p. 105.   [2] *Hatfield Calendar*, i. 473.   [3] Murdin, p. 26.

and the dictates of chivalry towards a princess in distress,
who was also heiress to the throne, whom he would also
have been happy to marry; on the other hand, how could
this be done without appealing to the Catholic Powers for
aid? That, in turn, meant that he must become Catholic
himself, and break entirely with the present tyranny, with
which no compromise could be expected. That was
indeed " a marvelous strait " for one who had never done
'anything but drift. Eventually, as so often happens with
irresolute men, his course was decided by the traditions of
his party and the prevalent sentiment in his immediate
environment. His subordinates, especially his secretaries,
Barker, Bannister and Higford, all assumed that he would
take Mary's part. We have already seen, in the case of
the Northern Earls, the mutual influence of the feudal
chief on his retainers and of the retainers on their chief.
The same influences were at work here. The Duke, being in
confinement, could not deal in person with the Bishop of
Ross and Ridolfi, but his subordinates acted in his name.
They had an unlimited confidence in his fortunes, and pushed
forward without scruple.

From all this it will be seen that Norfolk's character
afforded no safeguard to Mary's cause. He acted the part
rather of a follower than of a leader. Nor, again, was
Bishop Leslie a reliable guide. Though faithful, clever
and energetic, he had not the courage to cross his mistress
when he knew she was going too far,[1] nor the high principle to keep clear of exaggerations, sharp practices and
risky projects in her service.

The only person who shows both resolution and ability
is Ridolfi, the least reliable of all Mary's allies. Not that
he was a stage villain, as has too often been supposed, but
because his methods, standards, and ambitions were not those

---

[1] This, for instance, is the account he gave to Barker of his reasons
for favouring Ridolfi's mission, which he affected to consider as a mere
jump in the dark : " He [the Bishop] had none other shift but to send
Ridolfi, partly because his mistress thought him the fittest man, and
partly to stay her vehement passions expressed in her letters, that by his
cold dealing he had nothing done for her. Wherefore, said he, if Ridolfi
be once gone, she can no more make such an ado with me, because she
hath such trust in him. If he can do her good, then hath she her desire;
if he cannot, then she must be content, for there is none other help to be
had."—Barker's examination in Murdin, p. 116, § 4.

of a statesman, but of the stockbroker and cosmopolitan trader, in short, those of his fellow-citizens the Medici. Though a respectable man in his way, he could not help addressing every one who dealt with him as he would his customers, assuring them of the great success that would attend leaving their fortunes in his hands. His promises were cleverly adapted to the taste of each. He was also strong and resolute enough to use another tone when circumstances advised. He would then, as we shall see, be pushful, insistent, imperative, and even endeavour to carry his point by scorn, anger and reproach.[1] Then the circumstances of the persecution gave him a remarkable power. He was often the only go-between at liberty, while Norfolk, Despes, Leslie and the rest were for long periods under suspicion or arrest. How far his statements may be trusted is a question that will frequently present itself, and we may say at once that they should be received with great caution.

Mary having agreed to Ridolfi's mission by her letter of the 8th of February, the Duke's consent was obtained, we know not how, and his secretary, William Barker, was appointed to consult with Ross and Ridolfi. These three were now constantly together, and arranged the plans, which are now known as the Ridolfi conspiracy. Ridolfi no doubt took the chief part in making the arrangements.

Ridolfi's *modus operandi* appears to have been this. Out of the instruction (now lost) which Mary had sent, he proceeded to draw up by himself " other instructions for his journey." [2] These are the two well-known papers— one representing Mary's, the other the Duke of Norfolk's, commission to him—which have long since been found in the Vatican and at Simancas, and have been printed both in Italian and Spanish.[3] Though Ridolfi was unquestion-

---

[1] Barker says: " Indeed Ridolfi was quarrelous . . . a bitter man, and would burst out into speeches of [the Duke] . . . saying he was too dastardly and soft."—Murdin, pp. 92, 93. Cf. p. 126 for his method of egging on the Duke: " Always he was in hand of seditious matter."

[2] Murdin, pp. 36, 47.

[3] The Instructions are printed from the Vatican in Labanoff, *Lettres*, iii. 221–250. From Simancas, in Gonzalez, *Apuntamientos*, Nos. 23, 24, p. 215 (abbreviated), and dated July 17; *Memorias*, vii. 360. In MS. in Froude's MSS. in full, B.M. 26,056 b., 240; *Rome Calendar*, pp. 393, 401.

ably the *rédacteur* of these papers (in itself a very irregular
proceeding), we cannot doubt that the principals eventually
authorised them. Very, very confident as Ridolfi showed
himself that every one would act the parts he allotted
them, he was not the man to have started off on so serious
a negotiation without making sure that the promises he
received should lack no essential formality. The reason
for doubt would be the Duke of Norfolk's frequent assertions in his subsequent examinations that he had refused
consent to this or that point in Ridolfi's proposals. It is
not possible to explain all these denials now; but one cannot
help suspecting that after such refusals Ridolfi returned
again with the passages rearranged in such a way that
the Duke in his easy-going fashion then let them pass—
perhaps as formalities on which foreigners would insist,
though of little real importance—and afterwards forgot
that he had admitted them. The question will recur, in
connection with Ridolfi's credentials.

There is little or nothing in the commission from Mary
which one would not have expected. In that from the
Duke an interesting point is his promise to embrace Catholicism openly when he can do so without detriment to the
cause. Ridolfi went to the Duke by stealth after dark
(for he was still under restraint) to interview him on the
subject, and returned " satisfied by the Duke of Norfolk
in all things, as well touching religion as otherwise." Moreover, Barker spoke strongly to the Spanish ambassador
as to the Duke's sincerity in this matter. It is true that
Ridolfi in this case, too, suggested the words used, but the
Duke's secretary would never have uttered them unless
he had had the Duke's permission to do so.[1]

The Duke's consent to the main points of Ridolfi's
mission was probably given at this personal interview,
which presumably took place about the 10th of March.[2]
The most important outstanding matter was the form of
the letters of credit, and here for the first time the Duke
of Norfolk made difficulties. When Ridolfi broached the
subject at their meeting he had cut him short. Then he

---

[1] Murdin, pp. 35, § 4, and 128, § 7.
[2] This is the chronology adopted in the Duke's indictment. *Reports
of the D. Keeper of Public Records*, iv. 268.

stoutly refused to sign. Draft letters having been sent from the Bishop of Ross, he threw them on the ground, and swore : " God's Blood ! Would he have me commit treason ? If I should write any such letter as he hath desired, I should enter into treason, and therefore I will not do it." [1] And according to his own account he never did.

But Ridolfi would not give up his quest. Barker was disgusted, and said to the Bishop : " Ridolfi will mar all with his curiosity " (*i. e.* pertinacity). But the Bishop answered : " There is no remedy ; these Italians stand upon their honour." [2]

The final plan was that the Bishop of Ross should take a draft of the credentials to the Spanish ambassador, and depose, with Barker as witness, that the Duke would abide by them. The ambassador should send copies to Brussels and Madrid in his own cipher. Barker and Ross did so, and seem to have thought that this settled the matter. But now that we can consult the Vatican and Simancas Archives we find what purports to be an actual *signed* credential in each, as well as a letter from the Duke of Alva, stating that when Ridolfi came to Brussels he had " cartas de creencias de la Reina y del Duque." [3]

At first sight this seems suspicious. There may certainly have been double dealing, but it does not follow that there must have been. What Norfolk denied was *signing* the credentials. The credentials presented by Ridolfi probably came in cipher from the Spanish ambassador, without autograph signature, but with the name indicated either by the number " 40," which generally stood for " Norfolk," or by other signs. The Vatican credential, which I have seen, is on *foreign* paper, and headed " copia " ; the Simancas copy is exactly similar. [4]

---

[1] Murdin, pp. 143, 144. The statement is repeated.
[2] *Ibid.*, p. 120.   [3] Teulet, v. 78.
[4] " Copia," that is, " fair copy," or " duplicate." This word does not affirm that the signature was autograph in the original cipher. Mr. Froude found the " credit " from the Duke to Philip at Simancas, and has printed it, ix. 408. It has also been referred to in *Memorias*, vii. 357, and printed by Lettenhove, *Relations*, vi. 91, from Simancas. *Estado*, 823, fol. 81, of which I have a copy by the Archivist. Sr. Montero. The latter agrees exactly, except for a few necessary modifications in the form of

Both interest and importance attaches to the lists of English nobility which Ridolfi took with him to Rome and Madrid, which have now come to light, together with his other papers. Out of sixty-four nobles, forty are declared to be friendly, eighteen neutral, only six hostile. This classification, regarded as the conclusion arrived at by a shrewd man, who perhaps knew more about Mary's friends than any one else at the time, is remarkable, and it seems most likely that the unexpectedly high figures really corresponded with a genuine inclination on the part of the English nobility to recognise Mary, and to treat her as a queen.

But then these lists pretend to be, not a guesswork reading of hearts, but a summary of ascertained facts, and as such we must look upon them in a very different light. We cannot possibly believe that the opinions of the peers, which they represent as known, were definitely ascertained. On their face values, therefore, these lists are not only incredible, but plainly meant to deceive; that is, to produce by unusually bold assertion an un-warranted sense of security in the strength of Mary's party. No one would have dared to ask all the questions which these papers assume to have been asked, each of which would have been a capital offence. Ridolfi, indeed, told Barker that " he had spoken with his friends, who all (!) did only desire to know what course the Duke would take. They would join him with their [friends]." But the Duke, when Barker told him, was quietly satirical : " Full little doth Ridolfi know our opinions ! " Then, after stating that Ridolfi was mistaken, even about Lords Arundel, Lumley and Montague, Ridolfi's chief Catholic friends, he concluded by saying : " But if the other two were as

---

address, with the Vatican copy, *Miscell. S. Angelo*, Arm. xiv., caps. iii., no. 4. watermark A.R.

Lingard did not know the credentials, and mistakenly spoke of the *Instructions* as if they were credentials—and therefore described them as " never signed " by the Duke—vi. 257. Mr. Froude is, therefore, quite right in printing the credential with the Duke's name attached ; but then he falls into the contrary error (p. 393, text and notes) of considering the signature as autograph. On p. 394, however, he himself says the letter was sent " in cipher " ; and if he had reflected he would have seen that this must have been *without* an autograph signature. His strong condemnation of the Duke here is a mistake.

mighty as Ridolfi would make them, and the third as
trusty as he takes him, I will not cast away myself, my
children and my friends, for none of them all." [1]

What a speech this for one whom Ridolfi (though he
well knew his disposition) was representing as straining
at the leash to join with his fellow nobles in a fight for
freedom ! The Duke was not, indeed, always in doubt, but,
whatever we allow for the influence of mood, we can at
all events see that he, the proposed leader, regarded Ridolfi's
statements of the dispositions of the nobility as based on
pure ignorance or false reasoning. It is hardly necessary
to labour the matter further, but if any one will carry the
inquiry from the general to the particular, and investigate
(let us say) the allegations that the Earl of Shrewsbury
was on the side of Mary and Norfolk, he will find himself
inclined to go almost as far as Dr. Lingard, who roundly
described Ridolfi's lists as made " undoubtedly for the
purposes of deception." [2]

The alleged letters of credit for Ridolfi bear date the
20th of March. This is also the date assigned to them in
the indictment, and may be taken as marking the conclusion of Ridolfi's preparations. With characteristic boldness he had procured from Elizabeth's Government some
sort of commission to treat with the Duke of Alva about
terminating the mercantile complications which had been
caused by the violent confiscations on both sides after
the seizure of the Spanish treasure. And now, to give
more effect to this part of his plan, he solicited, and, with his
usual forcefulness, obtained, a special audience with Queen
Elizabeth, which she granted him on Lady Day, a Sunday
in that year. This favour probably secured him and his
papers from all molestations from spies and searchers
while leaving England, which he did next day, never
to return.

How far the conspiracy which he left behind him was an
objective reality, how far a creature of his own imperious

---

[1] Murdin, p. 105.
[2] Lingard, *History*, vi. 256 n. He is here following Gonzalez, who
naturally took the side of Alva against the Italian. *Vice versa* we shall
find the Tuscan chronicler Adriani (followed by Laderchi and other
Italians) taking Ridolfi's side against the Spaniards.

imagination, we shall never exactly know. It is clear that there was a good deal of plotting, as well as a good deal of fancy. Much as he mistook the disposition of Norfolk and his friends, this was not his fundamental error, which was the idea that the Pope could combine France and Spain against England,[1] or at least that Spain and Rome in alliance would be able to conquer in the coming struggle. Confident in this, he does not seem to have considered, being neither a soldier nor a diplomatist, that accuracy of detail made much difference, when once the appeal to arms was made.

As to the Duke, it would, of course, be absurd to extenuate his weak, insincere toying with a vast counter-revolution without foreseeing the means, or intending to face the risks, necessary to bring his project to an honourable conclusion. So far as one can understand his drifting, hesitating mind, he wished to see what offers he could get from abroad, and thought that the negotiations of Ridolfi were, broadly speaking, only inquiries, which would not commit him very far. As to the forms of such inquiry, he knew that Ridolfi would go to any lengths in pledging his, that is, the Duke's, credit; and yet, with indefensible folly, he allowed him to go forward. In excuse for this trust-fulness, however, it should be remembered that Ridolfi's first plans were conservative and loyal to Elizabeth. There is reason for suspecting that the Duke had not fully realised how greatly the Italian had changed, or, when he got abroad, would change, his original ground.

The Duke of Alva, to whom Ridolfi immediately betook himself, was a very different man from the easy-going, inexperienced English nobleman. Firm, wary, unwavering in his religion, Alva was much too serious to play fast and loose with the grave issues now put before him. He had always been steadfastly on the side of peace with England.

---

[1] Though the alliance of France with Spain did not figure in Ridolfi's present scheme, it had been commended in all its earlier versions, and he had even pressed it on Mary in his preliminary proposals; it was she who cut it out (Hosack, ii. 502; Labanoff, iii. 187).   Yet we have heard Alva tell Philip that they would have gone to war with France if she had undertaken to execute the sentence of excommunication; and *vice versa* France agreed to help England in case Spain undertook to execute it (Lingard, vi. 252).   Much likelihood of co-operation between such a pair !

Not, indeed, that England had given him the least reason for friendship, but, in the face of France, Spain's unvarying and reckless rival, England was too useful an ally to be trifled with. He had tried to overawe her Government two years before, by the seizure of English commerce, but as soon as he found that this policy did not succeed, he at once changed, and was now steadily soliciting a renewal of trade. He was in no mood for a policy of pin-pricks, or for any reckless aggression, the result of which might be dangerous.

But the plan which Ridolfi set before him had in it certain elements which appealed to him forcibly, which supplied exactly what had seemed to his military mind to be wanting in previous speculations. The difficulty, as he described it to his master, Philip II, was not insular but European. If he were to make any attack on England, he would at once be hard pressed by France in his rear, and by the German Protestants on his flank, as well as by the revolution in his front. But if, instead of Spain attacking, the English Catholics were to rise, and Spain were only to intervene later, in order to lead Mary Stuart to a throne which France at least acknowledged, even claimed, to be hers, the whole situation was changed, and there was not only no difficulty in Spain doing what she was asked—it was altogether to her advantage. So much so, that if the rising did occur, and the favourable situation were created, he should act immediately, without waiting for express orders from Spain.

Another immense advantage which the new scheme seemed to offer was an escape from the Anjou match. The bare possibility of Elizabeth marrying a Frenchman acted, of course, like a nightmare on Alva. This, or any escape from such a consummation, would be welcome.

Still he had one grave doubt, and that regarded Ridolfi himself, whom he described, and with evident truth, as " very liberal of speech," [1] a person with whom to be guarded, and he sent both to Rome and to Madrid a note of warning,

---

[1] " Muy liberal en el hablar " (Teulet, v. 85). In Gonzalez's *Apuntamientos*, p. 111, Alva calls him *gran parlaquina*, a great chatterbox, but I do not find this term in the original letter, though it is no doubt perfectly correct.

with which King Philip was so impressed that he passed on the hint to Despes in England.[1]

Alva strongly warned Ridolfi to keep silence, but the " chatterbox " could not resist the temptation of writing post-haste back to his friends in England to give them an account of his success. His messenger, Charles Bailly, with dispatches that would have betrayed the whole conspiracy if they had at once been read, was in Lord Burghley's power a fortnight after Ridolfi had bade him farewell. But though the ciphers could not at first be read in their entirety, Lord Burghley was effectively apprised of the dangerous character of Ridolfi's negotiations,[2] and this warning was emphasised by the capture about the same time of papers and prisoners at Dumbarton, by which several of Queen Mary's English Catholic friends were betrayed in the course of the summer.

It is important to notice here the changes which took place in the plan of campaign as it passed through Alva's brain. The initiative to be taken by the English is very much enhanced. In the Instructions the plan contemplated is for the two movements to be co-ordinated. The foreign contingent will land, and Norfolk's forces will rise to protect the landing. But in Alva's conception the blow is to be struck in England some little time beforehand, and the Duke engages to keep the field from twenty-five to forty days, if necessary, before aid arrives.[3] Here, again, we surely see Ridolfi, as usual, suiting his plans, not to the actualities of the case, but to what will interest his expected allies, to what will draw them into action.

Still more clearly is this seen in the plan for the capture of Queen Elizabeth. What the Instructions say is : " I am resolved to try the hazard of battle, and to attempt to free Queen Mary by force, and at the same moment to seize the person of the Queen of England, in order to assure myself of the Queen of Scots." [4] In Alva's letter the

---

[1] Alva to Philip, May 7, 1571, Teulet, v. 74–87; Philip to Despes, June 20, 1571, *Spanish Calendar*, p. 319.

[2] Bailly's examinations are in Murdin, and more briefly in the *Hatfield Calendar*. Lord Lumley, on receiving Ridolfi's letter, begged the Bishop of Ross to prevent his writing again (Murdin, 49, § 2).

[3] Labanoff, p. 242, compared with Teulet, v. 81.

[4] " Insignorirmi a un tempo della propria persona della Regina d'Inghilterra per assicurarmi di quella della Regina di Scotia " (Labanoff, p. 245).

thought appears twice over in this form. " In case the Queen of England were dead, whether a natural death or not, or if they seized upon her person, without our having anything to do with it—then all would change." [1] In the first case the idea is to preserve Elizabeth's life as a pledge for Mary's; in the second Elizabeth's death enters the discussion, and it does so for the first time, and is given in the first place. There is no underlining or emphasis on the alternative, and it is unfair of some historians to print the phrase in italics. There is no suggestion that death will be the simplest alternative, or that she is to be executed when captured. The " enterprise of the person " (empresa de la persona) is that she should be captured as Mary had been, or as James was so often afterwards. When the Regent Lennox, however, was taken, and a rescue was attempted, he was wounded and died. Alva had something of that sort in his mind ; not assassination pure and simple, and even so, it was clearly going beyond and against Norfolk's instructions. Whether these advances were due to Alva, to Ridolfi, or to both, we cannot now say, but once introduced they do not soon recede into the background.[2]

Ridolfi reached Rome about the end of April, where the Pope, who had already supported him so heartily, now received him warmly, and is said to have approved of all his plans. It does not, however, appear that Ridolfi

---

[1] This is repeated twice on p. 86 of Teulet. But on p. 79 he gives apoderarse, " to get into his power," without alternative.

[2] When the matter came up for discussion at Madrid, we find in the report that the empresa is mentioned nine times, and in very different terms : p. 429, matar ò prender ; dispachar ; p. 430, aprehension y muerte ; la muerte ; prenderla (twice over); conservarla sera difficoltoso ; p. 431, la empresa della persona ; muerta (page numbers refer to Mignet, vol. ii.). In the shorthand report of the questioning of Ridolfi, the vague word effecto is used almost all through, dispachar also once (B.M. 26,056 B. fol. 221 b.). These being hasty shorthand reports, we must not pay so much attention to their wording as we should to Philip's formal letter on the subject afterwards, to Alva, July 14 (Simancas MS. Estado, leg. 547, fol. 161). Here we read : matar o prender, and also coger o dispachar. In Alva's final answer to this of August 29 (Apuntamientos, p. 198), he uses the word prender alone. So far as the documents go, therefore, the form is never simply "kill," but either " take " or " kill-or-take," in all those in which precision might be expected. In the hastily scribbled reports of speeches every variety of form is found. No serious importance attaches to the latter point, but the inference might be that the speakers, too, were treating the subject as one of alternatives.

communicated other papers besides the instructions before mentioned, with letters of credit, that from Mary bearing her autograph signature and royal signet, while the similar letter from the Duke is marked *Copia*. Then, with ample letters in his favour,[1] he continued his journey to Madrid, where he arrived on the 28th of June.

Philip, as we have heard, was previously ill disposed towards him; but now, laying aside his usual caution, he embraced the cause of Ridolfi with the same fatal facility with which he had lately let himself be imposed upon by Hawkins and by Stukely. The irritation caused by the constant losses to the pirates and rebels was intense, and we can appreciate it better, when we recollect our own feelings while the U-boats were sinking our ships. Here annoyance was impairing a judgment which used once to be at least cautious.

King Philip was not alone in this. The matter was discussed at his Council table on the 7th of July, and some disjointed but very interesting notes of the session remain[2]

---

[1] The speech to Pius V, attributed to Ridolfi in Agatio di Somma's *Vita di Pio V.*, MS. Arch. Vat., Misc. Arm. xi. 60, cannot be authentic as it stands, it evidently belongs to an earlier period. But it might be a letter of Ridolfi's before the Northern Rising.

Besides the brief to Philip of May 5, printed in Teulet, v. 73 (also by Mignet and Laderchi, 1571, § 6, who adds other letters of the 15th and 16th), there are in the Vatican minutes of letters sent to Mary, Norfolk, the Bishop of Ross (for Lords Arundel, Derby, Montague, Lumley) of May 8, Arm. xliv. n. 3, ff. 107, etc. Ridolfi himself wrote to Mary. This, with other letters mentioned above, is printed in Brognoli, *Studi Storici sul regno di Pio V*, Roma, 1881. See *Rome Calendar*, pp. 407–26.

[2] Simancas, leg. 823. The archivist's endorsement is: "Copia de minuta en varios papeles sueltos, que tienan por carpeta lo que se platico en consejo sobre las cosas de Inglaterra en Madrid, Sabado 7 de Julio, 1571." It is altogether in the hand of Secretary Zayas. This has been printed by Mignet (*Marie Stuart*, ii., pp. 428–31). See also his text pp. 145–7), and it has also been copied by Froude from the original MS. B.M. *Add.* 26,056, ff. 216–21 b. Mr. Froude has added considerably to the text. Mignet does not give a speech by Cardinal Spinosa, Froude gives two speeches by him. Whether this is right or wrong, one cannot tell, but they seem to fit into the places given them. They are very much more incoherent than the rest, and range over much more ground. This I interpret as indicating that he (or the Secretary) was reading various papers by Ridolfi, Vitelli, the nuncio, etc. Mr. Froude, however, assumes that these opinions were not read, but spoken by the persons in question. This assumption I cannot grant, partly because I find no precedent for such procedure among many Council minutes of a similar nature; partly because some of the speakers suggest that such secrecy should be kept that not even Ridolfi or the nuncio should be informed. But how could that possibly have been said in their presence?

A summary of the minutes by the Spanish archivist Gonzalez is given to show that all his wise men were as destitute of penetration as himself. We do not detect in any of them an endeavour to look beneath the surface, and to probe the likelihood of Ridolfi's proposal turning out practicable. Indeed the second speaker, Don Hernando de Toledo, both began and ended with the words : " In the presupposition that this should be done " (*Sobre presupuesto que conviene hacerlo*, etc.), and the fourth says : " It is presupposed that the apprehension and death of the Queen is all." They regard the undertaking as in two distinct parts. " The enterprise of the person of Elizabeth " and the re-establishment of religion and order. The former they consider as England's business, the latter as that of Spain, and on that alone do they offer advice. There were five councillors present, the Duke of Feria, Don Hernando (Ferdinand) de Toledo (then Prior of the Knights of St. John in Castile), Ruy Gomez (afterwards Prince of Eboli), Doctor Martin Velasco, and Cardinal Spinosa (Archbishop of Seville, and grand Inquisitor), who acted more or less as chairman. Proceedings opened, it would seem, by the reading of a summary of the project in the form to which Alva had reduced it. The Duke, Don Hernando, Ruy Gomez and Doctor Velasco all spoke of the urgent necessity of action, that " there was less risk in making the venture than in declining it," and gave their views as to the military preparations, commander, money, etc., the two latter dwelling more particularly on the dangers, and on the great need of secrecy : no letters should be written, no answer returned to Ridolfi; money alone should be given, " which will be the truest of arguments and testimonies." The Cardinal summed up, suggesting that not even the Pope nor Alva's Council should be informed of the resolution taken.

Then he went on, it seems, reading various papers and quoting opinions of the nuncio, of the King and of Chiappino Vitelli on the best means of carrying out the " enterprise

---

in his *Apuntamientos*, 1832, pp. 360–3. But he starts with the very serious mistake of saying that the debate was on the capture and putting to death of Elizabeth, whereas the " enterprise of the person " in all the precise documents is *an alternative*, capture *or* putting to death. This mistake has had wide results, having misled Lingard, and all our earlier historians. Mr. Froude has done well in restoring the alternative.

of the person." Then opinions were offered again, probably on the new information just given. Again the necessity of the undertaking was dwelt upon, and an interesting point was raised by an opinion of the nuncio which had been quoted, viz. that the execution of the Bull against Elizabeth would afford a good title for Spain's interference. All the speakers, including the Cardinal, spoke *against* this. It would excite all the neighbouring Protestant peoples, as well as France, whereas the support of the just title of Queen Mary, " *la verdadera successor, Princessa opresa y captiva,*" would be intelligible, if not welcome to all, and exclude the idea of foreign conquest. Indeed, it is remarkable that the Bull is never alluded to by the Spanish councillors in justification of any part of their plans; but only here, in order to waive its applicability.

As to the " enterprise of the person," which interests us so much, though often alluded to, there was very little said,[1] and that little of no great importance. The speakers are all preoccupied with other objects; their stray remarks on assassination, which occur here and there in long pages of memoranda, are of very uncertain application, though the general impression produced is that the speakers approved.

In reflecting on the morality of this debate, we must not go beyond our text. It cannot indeed be denied that the subject of Elizabeth's assassination, as a possible alternative to her capture, was proposed at the Council board of King Philip, and that, far from any protest, the matter was generally regarded as being helpful to the King's affairs. But we must remember that there was no question of sanctioning, encouraging, undertaking or rewarding the murder. The Council's business was to advise whether

---

[1] Mr. Froude, in his theatrical way, has put long speeches on this " enterprise " into the mouths of Ridolfi and Vitelli (p. 503); but this cannot be justified historically. The words of Ridolfi (except for Mr. Froude's hit at Lord Montague) represent the answers which he made to the Count of Feria, but not on this occasion. The speech of Vitelli is made up of snatches taken from five or six different places and persons in the report of the debate. As has been said, the evidence *against* the presence of either in the Council Chamber seems conclusive. The notes of the conversation between Ridolfi and the Count de Feria at S. Geronimo, July 7, are in Froude's MS., 26,056 B., f. 221, cf. Mignet, ii. 145; but they are very rough, incoherent and vague.

the national policy of non-interference should continue, or be changed, in view of the proposed *coup*. Ten years before, the answer would have been an unqualified rejection of the whole proposal, but in the present state of affairs, especially with the Anjou match looming in the foreground, what wonder if the vote was unanimously in favour of action? It was not edifying, but, all things considered, we cannot call it very astonishing.

On Ridolfi, however, our sentence must be very severe, for it is clear that he, aided by the Bishop of Ross, was the architect of the whole of this odious " Castle in Spain," though, if he had once been frank with any one, it would all have fallen of itself, without involving as it did the lives and fortunes of so many and reflecting on the honour of so many more. If he had told Norfolk and his friends that foreign aid was not to be expected until he had first taken strong and decisive measures, that cautious conspirator would have laid aside the dream of insurrection. If he had told Alva of the weakness of Norfolk's character, there would have been no further debates on the project.

But it was Ridolfi's way to talk a man like the Duke into the mood in which he would pledge himself (at least virtually) to action, and then to think that action was sure to follow. As banker he knew that, if Norfolk pledged himself to a money payment under similar circumstances, the debt would certainly have been paid, and with his counting-house education, he imagined that a promise of audacity would as surely be followed by some deeds of daring. Similarly with the Spaniards. If he could persuade them into action, they would, he thought, carry all before them, and the need of help from Norfolk would be reduced to a minimum. So he goes on deceiving every one, himself included, and remained in the end convinced that the failure of his plans was due solely to the favourable moment having been let slip through the rivalry between Alva and Vitelli for the command of the invading army ! [1]

---

[1] So Ridolfi's memoir, already quoted, Florence, *Arch. di Stato*, filza 4185. Ridolfi's fellow-citizen, J. B. Adriani, *Istoria dei suoi tempi* (Firenze, 1583), ff. 877, 898, tells the same story, having perhaps heard it from Ridolfi himself. This ensured Ridolfi's version of the affair a wide vogue in Italy. Even Laderchi repeats it, and lays all the blame for failure upon Alva (*Annales*, 1571, § 14).

Did he exaggerate about " the enterprise of the person " ?
We are unfortunately in the dark as to what Ridolfi did
exactly say, but we cannot help noticing that the further
he gets from England, the more impression his words make.
The suspicion is obvious that this may have been due to
the improvements he went on introducing into his description of the plot. This, however, is only conjecture.

That illusory speeches were sometimes used deliberately
in this intrigue was frankly owned by the Bishop of Ross.
He regarded it as his duty, he said, to use inflammatory
discourses, in order " to assaie what the Duke would do for
the relief of my mistress," and he declared that Ridolfi
was his leader in this, instancing his " tale about Castruccio,
who attempted a suchlike desperate enterprise [*i. e.* schemes
like that of seizing the Queen's person], and brought it to
pass . . .[1] and changed whole estates by such enterprises
suddenly executed." [2] Both intriguers, then, urged (but
vainly) Castruccio's exploit on the Duke as an example to
follow ! A wild and impracticable scheme, we see, was
urged, confessedly on no better pretext than that a similar
adventure proved successful in the quite dissimilar circumstances of an Italian revolution two hundred years
before. It is not pretended that the proposal would of
itself help Mary's cause. The defence is, that by dis-
coursing on such matters one might discover those who will
run risks for Mary's sake ! No attention is paid to the
danger of provoking comment on such reckless projects,
comment which, in effect, did ensue, and did lead to the
discovery of the proposal. The confession, naïvely made
here, that discourses of this sort were set afoot in order to
attain an ulterior object, may not improbably be applicable
to other discourses of this conspiracy. Ridolfi may have
been a satisfactory banker, but he was anything but a
reliable politician. Though we cannot *prove* that he
romanced on a large scale, it is not doubtful that he did
so sometimes.

[1] Murdin, p. 43. Barker, moreover, says that the Bishop " did abuse
my Lord's name always to serve his purpose " (*ibid.*, p. 106). The Duke,
too, sometimes showed suspicion and irritation at the liberties Ridolfi was
taking (*ibid.*).

[2] Anderson, *Collections*, iii., 210, 212. The person meant appears to
be Castruccio Castracani, tyrant of Lucca, who died 1328.

If we wonder at cautious Philip being imposed upon by such a talker, we must remember that Philip's ambassador in England had been reporting for some time in terms that must have done a good deal to prepare the King's mind for the banker's proposals. In reality, however, as has been indicated, Don Gereau was not an independent witness here. He had for months, even for years, drawn his information from Ridolfi himself, often from Ridolfi alone. Thus he was not really confirming, he was only reiterating, Ridolfi's words. The accident of position had given the Florentine an extraordinary power of imposing himself on the leaders of Catholicism abroad and on its friends at home. False principles did the rest. As an assassin he may not have been very dangerous or very criminal—the evidence is not conclusive—but as a deceiver it would clearly be hard to overstate his guilt.

The end of the negotiation was now very near. On the 14th of July Philip wrote [1] to inform Alva that he would take his part in the enterprise with alacrity, and ordered money and arms to be prepared at once. But at the close of his letter he mentions that Ridolfi could not return, because some parts of the plan were already known. As we have heard, Burghley, without knowing details, had discovered from Ridolfi's messenger that he was carrying on secret negotiations with Alva and the Pope, and in June he found out plans for the escape of Queen Mary. The Government, therefore, was very much on the alert, and Ridolfi's party at first feared that all was known. Then, when they saw this was not so, and were beginning to breathe again, there came the arrest of Norfolk's servants in August, who were found passing money to Mary's followers in Scotland. Terrified by torture and fear of torture, these men gradually unfolded all they knew, and this evidence was strengthened by the discovery of some compromising correspondence of the Duke of Norfolk, so that by September all the principal parts of the plot were known—not, however, the proceedings of Ridolfi abroad, which have only come to light since " the opening of the archives " in the last century.

---

[1] Simancas, *Estado*, leg. 547, f. 161, unpublished.

This gradual unfolding of details enabled Lord Burghley to proceed to the destruction of Mary Stuart's party with the utmost thoroughness. Elizabeth, as usual, surrendered to his guidance during the whole crisis, and he thus was able to secure a complete victory for his party.

The Duke of Norfolk was tried and condemned to death in January 1572, but Elizabeth resisted for several months the pressure which Lord Burghley brought to bear upon her in order to secure his execution. But her ministers, backed by the Puritan Parliament, were eventually too strong for her, and Norfolk was executed in June. In August a similar fate overtook the Earl of Northumberland, whom the Government had bought for £2000 from the Scotch, with whom he had taken refuge. On the same day the French King and his mother, Catherine de Medici, perpetrated a still graver crime in the massacre of St. Bartholomew, after a period of intimacy with Protestants so close that the Catholic party had spoken openly of them as apostates.[1]

This horrible atrocity set the fire of hatred burning at white heat in the breasts of all the fanatics of England and Scotland. Again there were cries for Mary Stuart's blood, and she was saved only by Elizabeth's respect for royalty. But her party in Scotland was finally marked for destruction, and at last, in June, Edinburgh Castle was breached by English cannon, and Kirkcaldy of Grange was hanged at the cross on August 3, 1573. Lord Burghley and his ally, the Earl of Morton, now held the whole island in a firm, unrelenting grasp. No political combination for the relief of Catholics in either country was thinkable, until the fall of Morton in 1579 again reopened the whole question.

Thus closed the only period in which the two sides in the Reformation Settlement came into open conflict. No doubt it was inevitable that a counterstroke should come some day, especially as the Catholic reaction was now making notable progress in neighbouring lands. In England, however, the occasion had arisen quite unexpectedly,

[1] So it was reported from Rome to Mgr. di Bramante, December 14, 1570, *Nunziatura di Francia*, iv., 103. For further information about the Duke of Norfolk, and his last *Apologia*, see *Catholic Record Society*, xxi. p. 10.

and without any reference to continental movements. The Catholic Queen of Scotland, who was also heiress to England, expelled by her Protestant subjects, had taken refuge in this country, and hereby that entire subjection to the Crown which had hitherto held the Catholics motionless was modified. Respect for regality told against, as well as for, subjection. The equilibrium was unsteady. A rising might have been foretold.

But Mary, though so potent to arouse high enthusiasm, was a bad judge of men, and over-anxious to throw herself upon the pikes. She was greatly mistaken in Ridolfi, Ross and Norfolk; and, believing that all had the same readiness as herself to die in the cause, she ran risks which hazarded the very existence of her small and weak party. She did not, indeed, call upon the Northern Earls to rise, but one feels that this was one of those chivalrous but imprudent adventures which was to be expected under her inspiration.

Then, too, Pope Pius strikes in—another great leader, admirable for exciting enthusiasm, but again not the shrewdest judge of men or of politics. He, too, raises the war-cry at an inopportune moment, with consequences that are at first unfortunate.

But better to fight and lose, than never to resist at all. Though none of them were victorious, these attempts at the defence of religion and of country (the cause of Mary resolved itself into that of the throne, and, as we should now say, of the Conservative cause) led to the gradual formation among Catholics of a love of liberty, of courage, and independence (as understood at those times), the first results of which would soon be visible. It will be more convenient, however, to pursue our account of the conflict with foreign Catholics before turning to the revival of Catholicism in England.

CHAPTER VI

CONFLICTS WITH FOREIGN CATHOLICS

(1572–1579)

§ 1. *A New Generation of Leaders* (1572, 1573)

THE foreign policy of Queen Elizabeth throughout her reign remained true to the principle laid down from the first in *The Device for the Alteration of Religion* : " If controversy of religions there be, to help to kindle it." This was the guiding principle now as ever, but in application this period shows one very notable variation. In the year 1577 Queen Elizabeth advised the Estates (we might say the Parliament) of Flanders " to maintain the Roman religion in which they were born and bred," and she offered (under conditions) to aid Spain in coercing them, if they endeavoured to change.[1] The reasons for this will appear as we proceed. But in brief it may be said at once that the explanation lay in the Queen's anxiety lest the Spaniards should fail altogether, and leave the Netherlands a prey to the French. To out-and-out Protestants (modern as well as ancient) this was a matter of indifference, so long as Spain, a zealous Catholic Power, was ousted. But Elizabeth, with all her selfishness, had a deeper insight into the consequences of such a change on the balance of power. But to see how the situation developed we must go back a little.

On the whole Elizabeth had nothing much to dread either from France or Spain at this period. With Catherine de Medici at the head of affairs in France, England not only had nothing to fear, but she acquired an influence in French domestic policy which she has never had since.

---

[1] The matter is frequently mentioned in December 1577, *Foreign Calendar*, 1577–1578, pp. 371 (§§ 8, 13, 15, 20), 382, 390, etc. Froude adds that the envoy of the Estates, the Marquis of Havrech, was advised that there should be " no liberty of conscience, and no separate chapels or conventicles to divide the union " (x. 420 n., but no authority is cited).

Catherine and Elizabeth were similar in character, and thoroughly understood each other's objects. The Queen-Mother of France, without scruple on the religious side, raised up the Huguenots to counteract the Catholics, and so to enable her to hold the balance between them. This led to the recognition of Elizabeth as a party to the peace with the Protestants, signed at Blois in April 1572, which made her patron of her French co-religionists. It must be confessed that however selfish and unprincipled the English Queen showed herself in the use she made of her position, her faults are indeed venial compared with those of the French rulers.[1]

If after the massacre of St. Bartholomew (August 1572) the English Queen lent aid to those who were in arms against their sovereign, the Treaty of Blois had given her some ground for doing so, and the French Government, with its hands full and its exchequer empty, did not dare to proceed to open measures against her. Finally, when Catherine wanted a settlement, she arranged one, the *Paix Monsieur* (1575), in which whole fiefs and provinces were handed over to the Huguenots. This led to the Catholic people establishing in self-defence *La Sainte Ligue* (1576). Though its excesses must be regretted, this League eventually saved the Faith in France by making its defence a popular movement; whereas before sides had been taken on the feudal principle that one had to follow one's chief, whatever part he took. This abuse the new religionists had exalted into an article of the creed : " Cuius regio, eius religio." [2]

The French Queen, then, was on the whole playing into

---

[1] But it is only fair to the French rulers to say that their compatriots take a diametrically opposite view. Thus H. de la Ferrière, editor of the *Lettres de Catherine de Médicis*, 1880, though he ardently admires the French Protestants (and quotes approvingly Michelet's phrase about Coligny, " ce Christ des guerres civiles ! "), considers England and Elizabeth as utterly perfidious, Throckmorton as the originator of all French troubles (vol. i.). English bad faith is *traditionelle* (iv. l.), and he speaks of England *à la double face* (p. xlix), and of *leur péché originel, comme dit Michelet* (p. l.), etc., etc.

[2] *La Sainte Ligue*, the popular confederation of the French Catholics, must, of course, be distinguished from " The Great Papal League " of Catholic princes to exterminate the Protestants. The latter, as we shall see at the end of this chapter, was a mere bogey invented by Protestant politicians to keep their followers in line.

the hands of the Protestant party and their English patroness, and helping forward the policy of the *Device.* Elizabeth was exerting great influence in favour of French Protestantism, but Catherine was doing nothing for English Catholicism.

The twice projected marriage of Elizabeth with a royal French prince, first with Henri and then with François, Dukes of Anjou and of, Alençon, might, if it had been seriously entertained, have had a very great effect indeed upon the progress of religious toleration in England. But the negotiations in both cases were far from being inspired with that sincerity which could alone have made success possible. The French Court would have been glad to obtain an English crown for one of their princes, and it was chiefly honour for which they sought. On the English side, Elizabeth's ministers were always determined to frustrate, if they could, a match which would have seriously interfered with their monopoly of power; while Elizabeth herself, always undecided, was not very likely to be resolute in this case, especially as it was the courtship which she enjoyed most. The prolonged negotiations, which were revived from time to time all through this decade, never advanced beyond preliminaries; some of these, however, were interesting and instructive.

The first suitor, Henri de Valois, then Duke of Anjou, and afterwards King Henri III of France, was by far the finer fellow, and he extricated himself from the intrigues by insisting that he and his suite must have liberty of worship. Elizabeth had been ready to concede him Mass in private, but this he considered incompatible with his honour.[1]

To François de Valois, the next Duke of Anjou, afterwards Duke of Alençon, and *par excellence* " Monsieur " (*i. e.* heir presumptive to the Crown), who was put forward by Catherine de Medici after Henri had withdrawn, less favourable terms were offered. He was considered to be likely to turn Huguenot himself, so there was less need of meeting him half-way. He was told, indeed, that he should

[1] Anjou's demands, January 7, 1572 (*Foreign Calendar,* 1572–1574, n. 21, etc.).

have all that had previously been granted, with but one exception, which, however, was all-important. He was not to be allowed Mass, but was assured that " the English service differs in most part from that of Rome only in the language." [1] Catherine de Medici was naturally somewhat nettled at this, and declared it would not be " honourable " for her son to abandon his religion or to live without it.[2] But she could not at the time get any better terms, and the negotiations were gradually relaxed, though never broken off, and were revived again with greater appearance of warmth during the years 1578 to 1581.

As with France, so with Spain—Elizabeth had no reason for alarm on that side. True, under Ridolfi's deceptive promises, Philip did think of war, but the plan was abandoned as soon as made; not a soldier was moved, nor the least actual preparation made. Philip had always been, and would always be, on the side of peace with England, whenever that was possible. Nature inclined him to it, and his ill-knit empire required it. He was destined to remain of that mind for another fifteen years, until Drake at Cadiz burnt into his soul the lesson that fight he must, if his empire was to last.

But though pacific, he was not afraid of war, nor unaware that some fighting was inevitable, nor did he doubt that he had the means to wage it. When nuncios and others urged him to war, he did not show any settled aversion to the subject in general. But he knew his own limitations far better than those who were urging him to action. He understood the extreme intricacy of the Flemish problem, the hostility of France, and the difficulty of organising a fleet. His administration—based as it was on the radically unsound theory that paternal tyranny is the ideal form of government—became continually more and more inadequate, in proportion as his difficulties multiplied. In practice, therefore, peace was necessary, and he had to ignore, with such dignity as he could put on, the insults and injuries offered to him, and to persevere in an external profession of amity.

---

[1] Answer given to De la Mothe Fénelon, March 18, 1573 (*Foreign Calendar*, 1572–1574, p. 283).   [2] *Ibid.*, p. 298.

Yet Elizabeth and her ministers could not feel at their ease. Their aggressive policy was detested by the great Catholic populations,[1] who would have flown to the counter-attack if their Courts had not been rotten or incapable. Hence a constant dread of reaction. " Our policy is not good," wrote Secretary Wilson, " because it is not perpetual." The whole passage is worth consideration :—

" Surely if we think that by our own political wisdom in England we have hitherto had quietness, we deceive ourselves greatly. It is the weakness of our neighbours, who, being hitherto troubled, would never have power to deal against us, although they never wanted will and courage. And, if we have been the cause of this trouble abroad, and fed the factions (as the world giveth it out)— the policy is not good because it is not perpetual. In the end the harm will wholly fall upon us, that are the suspected maintainers, covertly and underhand, of all these foreign broils and troubles. Better not deal, than not go roundly to work ! "—Brussels, May 18, 1577.[2]

That is, the work of revolution and Protestantising must be carried to its ultimate conclusion. It is true that, writing to Leicester, he only puts the trouble caused by Elizabeth hypothetically : " If it be true . . . as the world giveth out." But, far from denying the truth of the charge, his urgent conclusion is that the breach must be made final.

Not long after this Sir Amias Paulet writes (January 24, 1578) from Paris in commendation of the same policy : " As long as our neighbours are occupied abroad, there is no doubt of our quietness at home. But if they be quiet in France and Flanders, our trouble is no less assured,

---

[1] The complaints of the Catholics may be divined from the grumblings of the Calvinist pirates from Flushing, when Elizabeth proceeded coldly, in spite of her ministers' favour : " They say these unworthy proceedings with foreign nations make the English the most hated men in the world, and to be contemned for mere abusers, (and as men) who put on religion, piety and justice for a cloak to serve humours withal and please the time, while policy alone is made both justice, religion and God with them " (Herle to Burghley, March 14, 1575, *Foreign Calendar*, p. 270).

[2] *Hatfield Calendar*, ii. 153.

unless our bargain be so well made that who troubles us may be troubled at home by those of his own nation." [1]

One might continue indefinitely quoting such passages, but these statements from the two principal ambassadors will suffice. Without question, the policy of the *Device* has been, and will be, carried out faithfully.

Though for very different reasons both Philip and Catherine tolerated England's policy, there were sure to be others, great and small, who would urge a different course, and we must now turn our attention to them. First amongst the leaders of this class we must reckon the Pope. Pope Gregory XIII, the successor of Pius V, though not in truth so vigorous or decided as his predecessor, was a man of the same school. He was courageous, and perfectly confident that the best solution for the troubles of the day was recourse to mediæval ideas and methods, which had been so helpful in the distant past. This courageous policy was attended with brilliant success. Everywhere about him he saw the Catholic Counter-Reformation growing stronger and taking deeper and deeper root. Towards England he was especially attracted, and it may be questioned whether any Pope of his age conferred greater benefits on our Church. When he came to the throne in 1572 it lay desolate, in appearance moribund. The signs of life were, as we have already seen, so slight that they can only be recognised by careful comparison with earlier and later stages of the movement. When he died, in 1585, the English Catholics were the talk of the world. If their difficulties were still extraordinary, their organisation was complete (so far as the acute persecution would permit), their missionary zeal was heroic, and the tide of conversions was marvellous. Gregory may well claim the honour of having been the foster-father of all this good. He was generous of support, as never Pope before nor since. He was generous, too, of encouragement, as we shall see repeatedly later.

Nevertheless, he was not a great politician, especially in regard to England. His simplicity, his legal training, his optimism, led him along lines very different from those

---

[1] *Foreign Calendar*, 1578, p. 469.

followed by Catherine de Medici and by Philip of Spain, and as his English policy had to depend almost entirely upon the latter, his calculations were too often quite at fault. His Secretary of State, too, Tolomeo Galli, Cardinal of Como (though he deserves the eternal gratitude of historical students for the admirable order he introduced into the archives), was a shallow, imprudent man, with little of that traditional caution for which the papal diplomacy is generally distinguished.

When Gregory began his pontificate, the Roman diplomatists were still under the spell cast over them by Ridolfi. They seriously believed his statement that the English nobility was still ready to rise in the Catholic cause,[1] and that the previous opportunity had been lost by Spain's delays. From the first, therefore, the nuncio at Madrid, Niccolò Ormanetto, who had once been a secretary of Cardinal Pole, and was now Bishop of Padua, kept plying Philip with plans for the *Empresa*, which the King listened to with his usual grave politeness, but nothing at all was done.

In the autumn, towards the close of this year, 1572, the English in Flanders write to beg that the Pope would take council with Dr. Sander, whom they have sent, with Dr. Morton and Bishop Goldwell, who were already in Rome. They do not urge any definite objects, but they seem to wish for a sort of standing committee in Rome. which might speak and act as the occasion arose. Sander went early in 1572, and while there wrote his celebrated tract *De Schismate Anglicano*. Eventually he was sent on by the Pope to Madrid, where he had his first audience, November the 26th, 1573. It is not likely that the papal diplomatists had at that moment any serious plans for the "Enterprise." The immediate object was rather to urge Philip to continue his pensions and alms to the exiles, which were threatened by the conventions entered into by Alva, and afterwards by Requesens, the latter agreeing to send away those exiles who had taken part in the

---

[1] " Li altre complici non si sono mai scoperti, et si stanno e staran fermi, finche à V.S. et al Rè Cattolico paria tempo che si debbino muovere : Di questo ne son certissimo." Ridolfi's memorial to Gregory XIII, Florence, Archivio di Stato, filza 4185, p. 7.

Northern Rising. But they eventually only retired to the neighbouring province of Liège, close by, where they received their pensions as before, when there was money to pay them.

Late in 1573 the rebellion of Gerald Fitzgerald, fifteenth Earl of Desmond, began to attract attention at Madrid. The parallel between his rising, looked at from a Catholic point of view, and that of the Prince of Orange's, seen through Protestant spectacles, was striking; and to the Catholics it would seem to be favourable to the Irishman. We cannot wonder if from this time forwards the idea was entertained of paralysing Elizabeth, as she had paralysed Spain, by fomenting troubles in her realm. Nor can we be surprised that the papal negotiators, ignorant—like so many others of that day—of the nature of sea-power, could hardly understand why Philip, who was aware of his weakness at sea, found so many reasons for hesitating. Still, the guerrilla warfare in Munster went on, and in 1575 several envoys were sent abroad to ask for help. Friar Patrick O'Hely and the Bishop of Meath made representations on Desmond's behalf, and later in the year, Desmond's cousin, James Fitzmaurice Fitzgerald. The latter, a man of remarkable courage and perseverance, and full of genuine devotion to his country, betook himself first to Paris, where he made a good impression, and even obtained, it is said, a pension. Thence he went to Rome, where he found amongst others the English adventurer Thomas Stukely, who is now destined to play a considerable part in our story.

§ 2. *Sir Thomas Stukely* (1570–1576)

Thomas, generally called Sir Thomas, Stukely (or Stucley), was the third son of a Devonshire knight, Sir Hugh Stukely of Affeton, near Ilfracombe. He was forty years of age, and his life had been spent in a ceaseless round of war, adventure, and travel in every land. He had fought in the armies of England, of France, of the

Empire, and of Spain, and had everywhere won a reputation for courage. But his changes from one camp to another had not brought him unsullied renown. He had pursued the then fashionable career of a pirate, he was a spendthrift, his word could not be relied upon. Though he afterwards professed to have been throughout a Catholic at heart, he had changed his creed with every Tudor sovereign, and he had enriched himself with the plunder of churches and monasteries.

At first Elizabeth had favoured him and encouraged his piracy, but when he lost his money and got into trouble she took a strong dislike to him, and prevented his acquiring lucrative appointments in Ireland. It appears that he got on with the Irish better than most English captains did, and seemed to be likely to rise to high office in that country. Elizabeth thwarted these ambitions and summoned him to England; but Stukely, on leaving Ireland, shaped his course for Spain, and reached the harbour of Vivero on the 24th of April, 1570.

On arrival he found that circumstances were preparing him a favourable reception at the Court of Philip. The King was smarting under the insult and injury which Elizabeth had recently inflicted by seizing his treasure-ships (December 1569). So he gave Stukely's blustering proposals for an invasion of Ireland just so much attention as might show that he could retaliate in kind if he would.[1]

But the effect of these measures did not bring about the result which he desired. Stukely's brags were caught up by the English spies at Madrid, exaggerated according to their wont, and forwarded to their mistress. She was irritated and finally alarmed, but not inclined to conciliation. She complained (February 1571) to the Spanish ambassador, Gerau Despes, that her sworn enemy, Stukely, was receiving the large pension of 500 reals a day, and men to invade Ireland, which kingdom (she heard) had

[1] The principal authority for Stukely is Richard Simpson's *School of Shakspere*, 1878, and Mr. Pollard's article in *D.N.B.* The partiality of the latter writer for Elizabeth's Government is evident. Both were ignorant of the Vatican Papers, and give credence to spies. An example of the errors which this led to is given in the next note.

o

been conferred on Philip by the Pope. She meant, however, to defend herself, and had called out her fleet.[1]

This was more than suited the interests of Spain. The Spanish ambassador, with Philip's approval, sought to assure her that her fears were ill-founded, and on the 22nd of April, 1571, Secretary Zayas sent an official explanation. There had once been "the intention of helping Stukely secretly in order to encourage the Irish Catholics, but it had become evident that he had but a small store of capacity, forces, and knowledge of the business." He would, therefore, be now sent away "to accompany the Princes in search of adventure." That is to say, he was to join Don John of Austria, who was about to start on the great naval campaign which culminated at Lepanto.[2]

Zayas's story—that Stukely, though treated better than he deserved, was still not trusted—is confirmed by documents in the Vatican Archives, which fully show that he was not yet reconciled from heresy; indeed, that the Pope had refused absolution (October 31, 1570). But the favour was no doubt granted next year, in response to his renewed and more serious petitions of February 4, 1571.[3] Stukely's reputation also suffered from a violent quarrel with the Archbishop of Cashel, who was then also at the Spanish Court. Eventually they both had to leave.[4]

[1] *Spanish Calendar*, 1571, pp. 293, 297, 298. The complaints of Elizabeth are founded on the reports of the informer Robert Huggins (or Hogan) (*Foreign Calendar*, 1569–1571, p. 394), who has deceived both Mr. Simpson and Mr. Pollard. For instance, the money said to be given for the expedition to Ireland (*ibid.*) was in reality given to pay off the ship at Vivero (Vatican Archives, *Varia Politicorum*, xcix. 189, etc.). Mr. Simpson expatiates on Stukely's receiving at Philip's hands the knighthood of the Order of Calatrava on January 22, 1571 (*loc. cit.*, i. 78. *D.N.B.*, lxv. 125, gives January 21), but no authority is quoted. King Philip, on the contrary (January 31), calls him "Knight of England" (Galba, c. i. fol. 5), and Stukely had styled himself "illustris eques" in the previous September (*Varia Politicorum*, xcix. 165).

[2] *Documentos Inéditos*, xc. 451; *Spanish Calendar*, p. 305. Don John eventually started in June.

[3] The Nuncio Castagna wrote from Madrid on his behalf (*Nunziatura di Spagna*, iv. 147) on September 24. Stukely's petition is presumably that preserved in *Varia Politicorum*, xcix. 165. The answer of the Holy Office, approved by the Pope (October 31, 1570)—*Non se debbe concederla altramente*—is in *Nunziatura di Spagna*, xiii. 242, cf. 206, but what the conditions here alluded to were is not stated. The second series of applications was made by Stukely, February 5, 1571 (*Nunziatura di Spagna*, iv. 168).

[4] Some details will be found in Simpson, pp. 74–92. The spy Huggins had promised beforehand to kindle this quarrel (*Foreign Calendar*, 1569–1571, p. 316).

Away from the Court, Stukely was seen to greater advantage. He joined the Christian fleet against the Turks, and fought with honour and success at the Battle of Lepanto (October 7, 1571). It would have been well for him if he could always have lived under arms, but in those days armaments were rarely kept together for more than a single campaign. The fleet was soon disbanded. We then find him at Rome, blustering and intriguing as before. Every one was encouraged and excited by the recent victory, and Stukely, with his credit now entirely repaired, seems to have acquired an ascendancy over the officials of the Roman Curia which, as will appear in the sequel, eventually led to very serious mischief, and even now caused Pope Pius V to make an offer to King Philip which marked a new stage in the hostility of Rome to Queen Elizabeth.

On December 1, 1571, the Cardinal Secretary wrote to his chief representative in Spain, the Legate Cardinal Alessandrino, saying that the Pope had heard with pleasure of Stukely's plans, and that if the King did not wish to involve his own name in supporting these plans, the Pope would allow them to be started in his, always recognising that the responsibility for action must rest entirely (*in tutto et per tutto*) with the King.[1] It might have been supposed that Philip would have welcomed the offer, for during Stukely's absence Ridolfi had contrived his plot, and had shown how in England itself Elizabeth's Government was weaker and more unpopular than had previously been supposed. The Pope's suggestion about Stukely, however, was firmly declined. On the 11th of January, 1572, the Nuncio Castagna wrote in the following sense :—

" Philip knows the plans of Stukely, but considers them too vast, too serious, too dangerous (*grandi, gravi, periculose*). Ridolfi's schemes were *importante e di sostanzia*. Stukely's, even if they could be successfully executed, would not lead to much more than to the excitement of feelings (*humori*), to war, to the slaughter of prisoners, etc. If there were another enterprise directed against the root of the matter

---

[1] Vatican Archives, *Varia Politicorum*, xcix. n. 194. There are supplementary letters (*Nunziatura di Spagna*, iii. n. 69, n. 67) of December 6 and 15. *Rome Calendar*, p. 472.

(*i. e.* the Government itself), Stukely might be useful to distract attention from it. But "to declare war against that kingdom, and to assault it directly, without the insurrection of the principal lords within the realm—for that these times are not ripe, and the King would not so much as think it over at present."[1]

So Philip held his hand, and nothing was done for the next three years. Stukely, however, continued to maintain his position at Rome, especially with Pope Gregory XIII and the Cardinal of Como. This favour was in great part due to Stukely's friendship with the representatives of the English clergy then in Rome, of whom the ablest, Dr. Owen Lewis and Dr. Maurice Clenog, were Welshmen. The former became Stukely's confidential agent and advocate; the latter, who was the Provost of the English Hospice at Rome, assured the Pope, in a still extant memorial, that Stukely was a man "sent from heaven" (*divinitus*) for the English enterprise.[2]

Early in 1574 the Nuncio Ormanetto made a fresh effort to stir the King into action, first in regard to the Turks, from whom the Italians suffered most and had most to fear, then in regard to England and Flanders. Philip answered that lack of money was his chief difficulty. He had spent, he said, twenty-four million crowns to protect Europe against the Turks; if the Pope expected him to continue his efforts, the contributions from Church property must be very greatly increased. The proposals of the nuncio were, however, formally debated in Council on the 4th of February, and declined.[3]

Still, the news from Ireland made Philip think that something might, after all, be done there. On the 22nd of May following, the nuncio reported that Philip had sent a military man to report on the situation, and that he meant to give assistance. But by the 10th of October he had got no further than the resolution of sending money;

---

[1] Vatican, *Borghese*, i. n. 607, f. 493.

[2] Vatican Archives, Arm. lxiv. tom. xxviii. 353. The date would have been about 1573 to 1575.

[3] Arch. Vat., *Nunziatura di Spagna*, viii. ff. 22, 28, 67; Mignet, *Marie Stuart*, ii. 199; Stirling Maxwell, ii. 21, 22, quoting Simancas, leg. 924, f. 4.

the complications of Flanders prevented him from doing more.[1]

Throughout 1575 the idea of interference by force in Ireland was growing, especially in Rome, where Patrick O'Hely, a Franciscan (appointed Bishop of Mayo July 4, 1576),[2] had arrived about June from Madrid, and gave out that Philip had approved of the plan of making Don John king of that island. This was so evidently an exaggeration that Zuñiga, the Spanish ambassador at Rome, ordered him to keep silence. And here it may not be amiss to quote the ambassador's words, as summarised by Don John's biographer, for the investiture of Ireland will come up again later on, and in a much corrupted form :—

" Zuñiga advised the suppression of Don John's name, because he had observed that the Pope, in talking of the affairs of England, never failed to say that no Spanish or French claimant of the Crown must be put forward, but that they must support the claims of some native-born Catholic; and that his Holiness insisted on this point so strongly as to render it probable that he did so, not merely because he believed an English candidate would have the fairest chance of success, but also because ' he was very much resolved your Majesty should not acquire more territory than you now have; and it might be that if Don John were to obtain the Kingdom of Ireland, [your Majesty] might think it as much [your] property as any of the realms God had already given you.' "[3]

Stukely, who had clearly heard Friar O'Hely's report, in spite of Zuñiga, sped to Naples, where Don John was, and gave him an account of the plans discussed in Rome, which, as he represented them, were simply fantastic. Their sum was that he (Stukely) was to conquer England with 3000 men, to set Mary free, and call in Don John, who would ascend the throne and reign happily ever after. Don John, needless to say, perceived at once that these were the plans of one who " made light of difficulties, as is the way with

[1] *Nunziatura di Spagna*, viii. ff. 205, 294.
[2] Mazière Brady, *Episcopal Succession*, ii. 155.
[3] Stirling Maxwell, *Don John*, ii. 106, 107.   June 24, 1575.

men driven from home and longing to return to it." Still, he promised to refer to Philip, which he did, adding that a raid on England might, after all, be of good service in the Flemish troubles. Though Stukely was an incredible blusterer, I daresay that his primary object here was only to obtain from Don John some general approbation of the idea of a "raid," not to ask his approbation of the vague scheme which he adumbrated.

Philip answered Zuñiga on the 8th of September, and Don John on the 22nd. To the latter he said, with a secretiveness which is to be noted, that schemes like those of Stukely were both impossible intrinsically and dangerous, seeing that discussions of that sort were easily talked about, and often came round to Elizabeth's ears. To the ambassador he was more communicative. He denied that O'Hely had the least authority to use his name, and he protested that the Pope's alleged anxiety lest Spain should acquire new crowns was hardly consistent with the urgency with which the enterprise had been commended to him on any terms. Still, he was not averse to the project of a raid, and he offered to provide in secret pay for 2000 men for six months, as well as the cost of transport, if the Pope would undertake before the world the whole responsibility, management and credit of the expedition.[1]

Zuñiga communicated Philip's ideas to Gregory in October, but found the Pontiff cooler and slow to commit himself. The Cardinal of Como, however, spoke more freely. The plan, he said, had originated with "two or three persons of zeal," and their idea was that 5000 men landing near Mary's prison should raise the country. The expedition might sail from Civita Vecchia, and Philip, as he would reap so much of the profit, should contribute in effect the whole of the expenses, which would be about 100,000 crowns. The Pope believed Mary to be the rightful heir to the throne; if she placed herself in his hands, he would agree to her marrying Don John, or any other whom

[1] Stirling Maxwell, ii. 107. It is with regret that we read that Philip concluded by asking whether they knew in Rome of any project (*tratado*) against the Queen's person (p. 108). This presumably refers to Ridolfi's plot. Philip had heard of it from Rome, and Ridolfi was saying, as we have just seen, that the majority of those who were pledged to him were still undiscovered, and would still stand by their word.

Philip wished. Zuñiga broke off, and told Philip that he thought the expedition had no sound foundation, and would cost far more than the estimate. Nevertheless he, too, thought the raid might do good, for even if it failed, Elizabeth could do no more harm than she was already doing.

Thus we see a general consensus on this point, that a raid, even if it fails, will not make matters worse than they were, and might relieve the pressure. Of course, it was a short-sighted policy. Philip's true defence lay in being strong at sea, at least sufficiently so to defend his home waters and his chief trade routes. But this was an idea of the future; we must not be surprised that no one suggested it in those days.

But while this policy of a raid, in spite of its defects, might have been a useful one for Philip, this was not sufficient to justify the action of the pontifical Government. If they had appreciated the risk to which they were expos- ing the English Catholics, we may be sure that they would never have acted as they did. Elizabeth's Government, however, succeeded all too well in isolating both themselves and their victims from the observation of those abroad, so that erroneous impressions about England could not be corrected, especially by sanguine people like Pope Gregory and his Cardinal Secretary. Don John, daring as he was, even to recklessness, saw more clearly than they that the plans they were entertaining were the projects of men " driven from home, and who, longing to return to it, make light of difficulties." He, however, was basing his opinion on Stukely only, the most irresponsible of the exiles; the papal officials, on the other hand, were relying mostly on men like Drs. Maurice Clenog and Owen Lewis, who were described as " persons of zeal." It was thought that they would not be greatly deceived in what regarded the interests of their own friends. But this, too, was a false inference. The *mirage* due to home-sickness in exiles produces in minds that are generous and high-principled illusions which are fallacious in the extreme. Of this our history offers but too many examples.

An agreement on the new raid policy was arrived at in

the course of the winter 1575–1576.   The deliberations were leisurely enough.   Spain's offer of September was answered in October [1] by the proposal, quite reasonable in itself, that Allen and Englefield should be called from Flanders to give their advice.   But Allen, for some unknown reason, wrote to excuse himself, and a second letter was sent on Christmas Eve by Dr. Owen Lewis, who had, no doubt, been a party to the negotiations all through, to explain the case and to bring Allen to Rome.[2]   In the meantime the Pope caused a careful search to be made for the records of the old papal rights in these islands regarding taxation and the like. Though this might be interpreted in a bad sense as counting spoils before they were won, in reality the procedure was quite justifiable.   Its object was to see how the debts for the war of liberation (as he considered it) should be assessed, and to avoid granting to Spain an undefined or exaggerated right of claiming reprisals.[3]

On the 20th of February, 1576, the Cardinal of Como announced that the two Englishmen had already arrived and got to work; and their reports were probably ready before very long, as they reached Madrid by the end of March.   It would be interesting to know their opinions, but their memorials have not yet seen the light.   There can, however, be no question that both would have been in favour of the expedition.   We have, in fact, a subsequent letter of Allen's to Dr. Owen Lewis, written in this sense.[4]

By the 17th of April the King, having considered the subject, came to the conclusion that he would support the expedition, and offered the Pope 100,000 crowns for its expenses; but it was to sail under the Pope's banner, and he was to take all the responsibility; the time of departure

---

[1] *Nunziatura di Spagna*, ix. 29.   Dispatches of October.

[2] I have not found this letter of the Cardinal of Como, nor Allen's answer of the ides of November (referred to in the next letter).   Another letter was then sent (December 24, 1575), which commended his labours for the Seminary of Douay, and said that Dr. Owen Lewis would explain more fully.   Arch. Vat., Arm. xliv., xxviii., no. 106, Como's Register.

[3] *Nunziatura di Spagna*, ix. 40, November 10, 1575.

[4] Printed *C.R.S.*, ix. 45, cf. Arch. Vat.; *Nunziatura di Spagna*, ix. 90.   Como to Ormanetto, February 20, 1576.   The enclosures of the dispatches to Madrid of February 28, which probably included Allen's memorials, are missing.   Ormanetto's acknowledgment of their receipt, March 29, in *Nunziatura di Spagna*, x. 74.

was to be the February following, 1577.[1]   This was accepted
by the Cardinal of Como on the 17th of May, 1576, but
the question of the commander was left uncertain.[2]   Allen
and Englefield were now sent home, with orders to dispose
men's minds for the coming enterprise, as the occasion
might serve.   Maffei, in his *Annals of Gregory XIII*,[3] gives
several particulars of this convention, but as he does not
quote the exact words, there may be some inexactitude
here and there.   He tells us, amongst other things, that
Don John was to be in supreme command, that the Bull
of Excommunication should be renewed,[4] that if the scheme
of putting Mary on the throne failed, the brother of the
Earl of Huntingdon should be proclaimed.[5]   It was finally
also suggested that to screen the Pope's warlike preparations
they should be described as being against the Turks, or to
help King Sebastian of Portugal.   This last idea led to
further developments later.

What a comment upon these deliberations and consultations to find that the man intended as successor to
the throne was perhaps a baron without either money or
power, who had been dead for three years ![6]

In order to keep Philip up to the mark, the nuncio

---

[1] *Nunziatura di Spagna*, x. 103.

[2] *Ibid.*, ix. 164 (Como's autograph).

[3] G.-P. Maffei, S.J., *Degli Annali di Gregorio XIII*, 1742, p. 241.

[4] But Maffei does not say, as Becchetti represents, that the Bull
already had been renewed (*Istoria*, 1798, xii. 312).

[5] This name appears first in the summary of the Spanish dispatch
sent by Ormanetto, April 17, 1576 (*Nunziatura di Spagna*, x. 103–9),
and reads " Untinton," and this is set down in Ormanetto's comment
as " Utioton."   Maffei prints " Vrincton."   Becchetti evidently considers
this as " Winton," and prints " Winchester."

Having regard to these authorities according to priority, we must,
of course, adopt Untinton, or Huntingdon ; and, as we shall often hear,
the Hastings family, which bore that title, was one of the representatives
of the House of York.   Nevertheless, the difficulty in deciding what
individual of that house is intended is considerable.   The then Earl had
three brothers, but all were (apparently) strong Puritans.   Their names
are never mentioned among the lists of Catholics, such as those prepared
by Ridolfi or those printed *C.R.S.*, xiii. 89–141, but amongst them Sir
George is the least unlikely.   More probably Sir Edward, Lord Hastings
of Loughborough, is intended, brother of the previous Earl.   He was a
good Catholic, and it is likely that Philip knew him during Mary's reign.
He has a biography in *D.N.B.*, but from this we learn that his death had
taken place long before, March 5, 1573.

The Marquis of Winchester had a brother, Lord Chideock Paulet,
who was probably a Catholic (*C.R.S.*, xiii. 89), but he had no sort of
claim to the throne.

[6] See the preceding note.

now kept begging that the expedition should take place immediately; but in vain. It was August before he heard, on what seemed excellent authority, that the first instalment of Philip's subsidy had been paid, in order that preparations might begin. Then " he could hardly believe his ears " when he was assured from Rome that this was not so. The money had been appropriated to some other urgent need ! In September 1576, however, five months after the offer had been formulated, the first payment was really made. In the meantime, however, the state of affairs had changed very considerably for the worse.

§ 3. *Don John and the Crisis in Flanders* (1576–1578)

During the years 1576-1577 the strong but cumbrous and badly organised Government of the Spaniards in Flanders passed through an extraordinary crisis, during which many parts were temporarily reversed. Elizabeth, whose soldiers were serving under the Prince of Orange, advised the Flemings to remain Romanists and true to Spain, while Don John, who came meaning to free the Queen of Scots, received offers from her rival of England.

The confusion is so great that it will be well, before we come to details, to map out the principal points we have to keep in view. (1) The central fact for us is that Don John meant war with England, and thought for a time that he had the means of waging it. (2) Moreover, Philip consented to war for the second time. This, however, he only did under certain conditions, and we shall have to inquire (3) whether those conditions were ever fulfilled, and whether Don John's hopes and plans could ever have been realised. (4) Finally, there is a tragic by-play, the murder of Don John's secretary, Escovedo, ostensibly the sequel to the dangerous suggestions in regard to England proposed by himself and his master.

The breakdown of Spanish government began with the unexpected death of the Governor, Don Luis de Requesens, followed immediately by that of their most skilful general, Chiappino Vitelli, Marquis of Cetona. Requesens had governed fairly well, and had made some progress towards repairing Alva's errors, but on the 5th of March, 1576, he was gone, and no successor came for eight months. Philip was not wholly to blame for this, for he appointed Don John to succeed within a week or so after receiving the news. Don John, again, was not wholly to blame, for Philip insisted on retrenchments, which (however necessary as a general policy, considering the bankruptcy which seemed imminent) Don John was sure to think ruinous.[1] The King also withheld information of primary importance, as, for instance, on the English enterprise. Now Don John was an excitable man, who would have been paralysed if that sort of thing had continued; so he sent Escovedo to ask further aid and instruction.[2] But Philip, who had not yet made up his own mind, again gave no answer, but peremptorily ordered Don John to betake himself to his new post.[3]

Don John still demurred, and came himself to Madrid early in September to arrive at an understanding with his brother, and when he left again for Flanders, in the last week of October, the King, says Antonio Perez, " communicated to him [his permission for the English enterprise] in confidence, for himself alone, and authorised him, for various reasons, and especially because of the Pope's manifest desire, to execute the enterprise in case the Spanish

[1] The need of the moment was to restore discipline among the Spanish troops, who had mutinied for want of pay. To meet that want (if the nuncio at Madrid reported aright) Don John " claimed to have so much money as would satisfy the arrears, and some money in hand for the future." But the nuncio adds, this " exceeds by far the sum they proposed to give him " (Dispatch of September 4, 1576, Arch. Vat., *Nunziatura di Spagna*, x. 282).

Philip's theory was that pay for troops in Flanders should come from thence. He never gave the money, which was eventually supplied by a loan from Elizabeth to the States. On the other hand, he much wanted to discharge all foreign troops in Flanders.

[2] Don John wrote, May 27, 1576 : " The true remedy for the evil condition of the Netherlands, in the opinion of all men, is that England should be in the power of a person well-affected to your Majesty's service. At Rome and elsewhere the rumour prevails that in this belief your Majesty and his Holiness have thought of me, as the best instrument you could choose for the execution of your designs " (Stirling Maxwell, ii. 119, following Gachard, *Correspondance de Philippe II*, etc., iv. 161).

[3] Maxwell, ii. 122, following Simancas, MSS. Estado (el. 569), f. 141. It is conceivable that Escovedo was given some further explanations by word of mouth, but there is no probability that these explanations were such as Don John might legitimately have expected.

soldiers should have to return by sea."[1] These words, penned by Perez himself before the trouble about Escovedo had become serious, seem to be fully reliable.[2] They set before us clearly the first point we have to keep in mind— that Philip did give his consent to the enterprise. The leave is, indeed, only given very tardily and under important conditions, which were later worked out more precisely in a long dispatch of the 11th of November, and sent after the new commander, who by hard riding had reached Luxemburg about the 4th, to find that the rising against Spain had spread so fast that at first sight Flanders might have seemed entirely lost.

To understand this we must go back to Requesens' death, which left the Netherlands rulerless, though seething with civil war, religious unrest, and dislike of Spanish rule. Discipline and finance, never very efficient, soon lapsed almost altogether. In June the unpaid troops had begun to mutiny, and to pay themselves by looting; and early in November, while Don John was still on his way, a terrible outbreak took place. The Spanish soldiery again sacked Antwerp (November 4, 1576) with a ruthless barbarity as disastrous as " the Spanish Fury " of 1567. This second enormity, crowning as it did a long series of other gross outrages, made the Catholics themselves rise in horror against the Spanish soldiery, and their Estates (Parliament, as we might say) now become the chief enemy of Spain. They made common cause with the northern provinces under the Prince of Orange, though he had turned Protestant, and though the north was overrun with Calvinism, and was in rebellion against the Spanish governors; as yet, however, they had not formally rejected Philip's title. A compromise on the religious division having been arranged, the Flemings arrived at a national agreement (as we might call it) that the country must be pacified by the dismissal of the Spanish soldiers. This resolution, embodied in the " Pacification of Ghent," was proclaimed by sound of trumpet at Brussels

---

[1] Note by Perez, written eight months later, in June 1577. Printed by Gachard, *Correspondance de Philippe II*, v. n., 2006 n.

[2] If, however, this is so, then the more romantic account given by Vanderhammen and Stirling Maxwell (ii. 123), " Into the scheme for the invasion of England and the marriage with Mary Stuart Philip appears to have entered with real or affected warmth," must be abandoned.

on the 8th of November, 1576, just after Don John had reached Luxemburg. The rebellion, however, had not yet spread to that distant province, and there the young general was received. All else seemed for the moment lost.

But Don John was a fighting man, who had led the Spanish soldiers a hundred times to victory, and was now thoroughly confident in their prowess and in his power of command. From a military point of view the situation gave him little alarm. What caused him care, and sometimes even anguish, was the knowledge that Philip would (as in fact he did) insist on a settlement by peaceful means.

Philip was right. True though it was that Don John and his men would probably have gone through any force the Flemings could oppose to them, yet the most brilliant victory would have been more costly than peace, and a protracted war would be ruinous. The economic danger was as bad as, or worse than the military *impasse*. Philip realised that Flanders could only be kept permanently by a policy of peace and economy. On peace, therefore, he insisted, and with decided success up to a certain point. The fiery soldier was turned into a diplomatist and a constitutional ruler for several months, and for a time he was triumphant, notably at his entry into Brussels on the 1st of May, 1577.

But all the while, as we now know from his private letters, he was chafing at the yoke put upon him, and burning with desire to have recourse to arms. Eventually the irreconcilable hostility of Orange and his party prevailed over Don John's laboured effort to be pacific. For though he meant it sincerely, so far as obedience to superior orders was concerned, it was not connatural to him, and he could not persevere when the trial became too strong, however much Philip might desire him to do so. Late in July he seized the citadel of Namur, in the belief, which, whether quite justified or not, was not unreasonable, that his life was not safe any longer at Brussels from the plots of the Prince of Orange. From that moment the chances of peace rapidly dwindled, and the chronic war began once more to loom in the foreground. Philip's attempt to stop the financial drain, and to secure peace, through Don John, had failed.

As to these public matters a reasonable certainty is not hard to obtain, for records concerning them are numerous. With regard to Don John's own intentions there is more difficulty. Documents, indeed, are not wanting, and there is no little allurement in the Prince's picturesque and chivalrous character. The matter, too, concerns us nearly, for his dreams were of rescuing Mary Stuart, and he was the first great captain who considered the subject of invading this country. But there are also considerable obscurities. The interior mind is always hard to estimate, and Don John's character is especially difficult to measure. The illegitimate son of Charles V was ever sighing with somewhat unbalanced earnestness for glory and a crown, which he, as the hero of Lepanto, had done something to deserve. But for all his disordered dreams he was a loyal and (usually) an obedient soldier, though more of a fighting man than a great general or ruler.

Always remembering, therefore, that retrenchment and the peace of Flanders were to be the primary objects of Don John's mission, we proceed to inquire what limits this imposed on his secondary object—the upsetting of Elizabeth's mischief-making Government, which was deemed to be the occasion and promoter of all the troubles of Flanders; after which he would free Mary Stuart, wed her, and mount the English throne.[1] Philip himself had not suggested this enterprise, and it was only slowly and somewhat reluctantly that he consented when pressed. For while to the papal negotiators and others it seemed that the English and Flemish questions were inseparable, and that the best policy was to solve the English question first, Philip takes the other view. The English enterprise is to him " most

---

[1] Don John had been named as a match for Mary (*Foreign Calendar*, 1564, n. 10) even before Darnley had come on the scene in 1565, and we may assume that it was quite inevitable that people should talk of their marrying, so long as they were both marriageable. It does not seem that either side did any courting, nor yet that they ever interfered with those who described the match as sure to take place.

As soon as ever Don John arrived in Flanders, the lot of the unfortunate captive was aggravated, and new intrigues were woven around her by Leicester, Walsingham and Lord Burghley. See her letters to the Archbishop of Glasgow (Labanoff, iv. 344–404, especially 364, 365).

desirable for the service of God," and most useful for Flanders; yet not as something fundamental to its happiness, but as a crown to its prosperity. Hence his insistence that Flanders must be attended to first. And not only must peace be re-established—a sufficient force must also be left to thwart a French attack on the base during the proposed invasion. For by the terms of the Treaty of Blois, France was bound to attack any country which first attacked England.

This resolution of Philip's, having been intimated orally to Don John before he left, was debated and embodied in a memorandum of the 11th of November,[1] before Philip had received news of the sudden spread of defection and trouble in Flanders, which had taken place a few days before. No doubt ordinary people would think that such a revolution would fulfil the condition which Philip had laid down in his memorandum as making the English expedition inadvisable. Philip himself was, of course, of that opinion, and as soon as the full extent of the new Flemish troubles were known, he again sent word to the Nuncio Ormanetto that in the present circumstances nothing could be done until it was seen how Don John would maintain himself in Flanders.[2] And, indeed, this would seem to have been an obvious counsel of common sense.

On the other hand, Don John was not an ordinary person. An ambitious soldier, confident in his men and in his star, his predilection was certainly for trusting to the arbitrament of war. We know that he will obey the orders and work for peace, but our interest is roused by his inclination for the opposite policy. If only he had entered into details and explained his plans the value of

---

[1] The memorandum (Simancas, leg. 570) is printed by Lettenhove, *Relations*, ix. 15–21. Cf. Stirling Maxwell, pp. 125–9. The Simancas Paper is not dated, and Stirling Maxwell conjectures that it was not sent because of the danger, but explained to Escovedo, who left Madrid for Flanders about this time.

[2] Arch. Vat., *Nunziatura di Spagna*, x. 412, dispatch of December 17, 1576. Philip had not as yet told Ormanetto of Don John's secret instructions, and was here referring to the expedition that was to start from Rome. But the argument from the one to the other is obvious. If nothing should be done even in distant Rome, how much less in Flanders. The same policy, " Flanders before England," was often laid down both before this and afterwards. See Ormanetto's dispatches of September 26 and November 10, 1576, and May 31, 1577.

his letters would have been doubled ! But he never gets to details; we cannot find out whether he thought of dealing first with the Estates, or with Orange, or with England. His dispatches are frank and vehement in their protests, here and there almost rude in his complaints against the unendurable position in which he finds himself. But they confine themselves to the general question of peace and war. They tell nothing of the disposition and marshalling of troops; indeed, he had then none to move, for the Spaniards, on whom he built such high hopes, were for the moment locked up in various garrisons. They were in numbers few, only 7000 foot and 2000 horse,[1] but their discipline, experience and courage made them the finest troops in the world.

But however good the soldiers were, we ask ourselves, could Don John have ever thought seriously of invading so great a country as England with so small a force? The answer would seem to be that he did so, but in his dashing, unreflective way.[2] He never had time or means to make working plans.[3] If he had, he would presumably have seen

[1] Gachard, v. 20, 139. Don John wanted them augmented to 8000 foot and 3000 horse (p. 54).

Though our document always speaks of " Spanish troops," it is possible, even likely, that the Italian troops were included under them. This would bring up the totals from 10,000 men to 20,000 men. If the German *reiters* were thought of, then there might have been 30,000 or 35,000 men. The total Spanish army in the Netherlands was, before the mutinies, estimated at 60,000 (including all garrisons, Walloons, militia, etc.). But Don John on his arrival found this a great exaggeration. Gachard, v. 54.

[2] In a letter to Perez he says (May 2, 1577. Gachard, *Correspondance de Philippe II*, v. 365 n.), in his abrupt military style : " People will say—there is neither money, nor fleet, nor men. Yes (*lit.* and), all this is necessary, and that one should have it (ready) : and it is a mistake to think that without it States can be preserved. And (still) believe me, that with a medium force this matter would be put right."

I understand him to mean that if Philip is pressed hard enough, he will provide what is needful, and he must do it, rather than see the country go.

[3] Some, of course, there were who made suggestions at this time. Elizabeth's spies, or intelligencers, sent word that Don John was informed that the freeing of Mary Stuart by means of a small number of horsemen would be very easy ! (*Foreign Calendar*, 1576–1577, n. 1288, February 20, 1577; Lettenhove, ix. 213). But such reports about political enemies are almost always inaccurate.

In May (after Don John had given up the Enterprise) his secretary, Escovedo, gave the Nuncio Sega the following vague account of a plan which he (Escovedo) would advise, and which we may perhaps assume to represent Don John's mind. There were to be three landings : a

the need for many more troops.   He probably never realised
England's power at sea, or the way in which the landing
of a purely Spanish force would have united all parties in
England against them.   He seems to have rested simply on
the great probability that if his army was once in England
it would have cut up any such bands as Elizabeth had yet
set in the field, the greatest of them being the 14,000 men
which she had sent against the northern Earls.   But even
if this hypothesis were true, an invasion which had no
other chance of success than that, would surely have failed
completely.   Neither Mary Stuart nor the English Catholics
had cause to regret that his attempt to aid them was never
made.

Turning to Don John's correspondence, we do not at
first (during November and December 1576) see any trace
of preparations for, or even of thought about, the enterprise.[1]   He is evidently so occupied with the immediate
present that he can think of nothing else.   But when, in
January, the Estates begin to insist that his troops must
return by land, not by sea—which would make his plan of
invasion impossible for the future—he awakes to the situation, resists violently, and writes strong letters to Philip,[2]
to persuade him to renew hostilities.[3]   It is clear that, as
soon at least as the opportunity begins to pass away, Don
John becomes desperately keen to avail himself of it.

---

small force from the north of Spain was to land in the north-west, to
distract attention; a second was to aim at Sheffield and free Mary;
while the main force landed in the south to attack London (Arch. Vat.,
Inghilterra Fiandra, vol. i. f. 369).   If Don John had led the expedition,
he would no doubt have headed the southern force.

[1] Gachard, *Correspondance de Philippe II*, v. 54–127.   The application to the Pope, and perhaps the mission of Gastel, show that the idea
was not really given up.

[2] Gachard, *ibid.*, pp. 131 *et sqq.*   Don John's letters to Perez are
always more strong than those to the King.   But the earliest of these
on this subject which I can find is dated February 16, 1577.   Martin
Hume, *Españoles é Ingleses*, p. 187.

[3] If it should seem strange that Philip's mind was not better known
after the instructions of November 11, it should be remembered that
these instructions perhaps did not come in writing, but only by word
of mouth through Escovedo.   He, being an advocate of warlike measures,
would be liable to give a freer scope to war policy than the King intended,
especially as Philip's conditions (having been laid down before he knew
how serious the case really was) were not as clear as they would have
been if written later.

P

Perhaps the earliest clear sign [1] that he desired war is offered by his application to the Pope for assistance. While in Italy he had come to know a good deal about Pope Gregory's desire for the *Empresa*, and his readiness to assist it.[2] So he wrote about the end of the year,[3] but unfortunately the letter is not yet forthcoming; and this is to be regretted, not only because it would be of great interest in itself, but also because the application had, as we shall see, a long train of consequences, which we should understand much better if we knew precisely how they had begun.

[1] M. de Gastel's mission to Elizabeth is not a *clear* sign of intended invasion, but still it must not be overlooked.

Almost immediately on Escovedo's arrival Don John sent this Burgundian gentleman to Elizabeth, primarily for innocent reasons, to announce his arrival, to beg her not to aid the rebels, etc. But incidentally there was one commission liable to excite suspicion. He was to ask Elizabeth for the hospitality of her harbours, in case the Spanish soldiers returning to Spain should be constrained by storm or otherwise to run in. As there was a plan in the air for these soldiers to invade England on their journey, this request may awaken a sinister interpretation. Philip himself saw this, and he wrote to deprecate any plan of turning hospitality received into an occasion for surprise and invasion. Gastel's *Instructions* are in Lettenhove, *Relations Politiques*, ix. 79; Philip's comment in Gachard, v. 158.

It may, indeed, be that Don John was prepared to act thus. He was both unscrupulous and "slim" when it came to war, as were other soldiers of his day. In this case, however, as there is no certainty that Don John was then resolved on the Enterprise, our verdict against him must be quite conjectural.

Another reason for doubting is, that the request was liable to frustrate the object which it is supposed that Don John intended, and would put the English on their guard. They did, in fact, remember Ridolfi's idea of pretending to send the Spanish soldiers in Flanders back to Spain by sea, and as soon as the plan was suggested again they were at once alarmed, and complained to Don John (December 28) through the envoy Edward Horsey. Don John asked him whether the idea of invasion at that moment was not *une chose pour rire*, and Horsey did not deny it (Gachard, v. 131). But that is, of course, not a complete statement of this intricate matter.

[2] The Venetian ambassador, Tiepolo, wrote, June 2, 1576, indicating the Pope's desire that Don John should go to Flanders (M. Brosch, *Juan d'Austria in den Niederlanden*, Institut für Oesterreichische Geschichtsforschungen, xxi., Innsbrück, 1900, p. 460). On the 15th of June, 1577, he wrote sending some news of the papal loan, which, though not far wrong, is everywhere a little inaccurate (*ibid.*).

[3] The date is conjectured first by a letter of Cardinal di Como to Spain of January 15, which says that no news at all from Don John had yet arrived (*Nunziatura di Spagna*, ix. 325). Allowing three weeks or so for the post, we infer that the application was not before Christmas. Again, as Sega's briefs were dated February 11, 1577 (*Foreign Calendar*, 1577, p. 550), and a fortnight or so must have passed before he could have been chosen, brought to Rome and got ready, the letter cannot have been later than the second week of January.

If Don John had followed Philip's *Instructions* exactly, he would not have written at all. The course marked out was that he should not inform the Pope until after the expedition had started. Then he might request a nuncio and other aids, in order to bring about a happy termination for the undertaking.[1] We must suppose that the soldier thought his deviation from orders was justifiable under the circumstances. On the other hand, he did not tell Philip, which shows that he knew he was on dangerous ground. How great the danger was, the sequel will show.

The letters to the King during the first half of January indicate that Don John would have been glad to attack England at once and at whatever risk. Something like this is hinted in his letter of January 6, and in February he claimed credit for not having made some such venture, " as many others would have done." [2]

But in the latter half of the month there is a change. For, although he continued till the end of the month to resist the States about the departure of the Spanish soldiers (which was then, and is still generally, interpreted as showing that he still desired to lead them either against Orange or against Elizabeth), on the 17th of January he sent back Stukely to Rome, with the message that there was no chance of his being able to employ him in the English expedition.[3] From this date, therefore, the English *Empresa* is no longer a practical matter. On the 21st he tells Philip he will now endeavour to settle the troubles by means that are suave and conciliatory.[4] So by degrees, and not uniformly with every one, the cherished plan is laid aside, to be taken up again, however, at the end of May   But it is now the subject of a grievance. Everything has gone wrong because this has been neglected ; even now it ought to be taken in hand. This frame of mind continued till

---

[1] Lettenhove, *Relations Politiques*, ix. 21.

[2] Gachard, v. 137, 182.

[3] Arch. Vat., *Nunziatura di Spagna*, xiv. (1577, n. 6), Don John to the Pope, January 17, 1577. *Ibid.*, ix. 364, same date, Don John to Philip. On the 13th of March, Stukely wrote to Philip from Genoa (*ibid.*, 386). When the Cardinal of Como had seen Stukely he wrote to Don John, saying he now at last understood that there would be no escape from the terms agreed to (*Nunziatura di Spagna*, xviii. 119, April 2, 1577).

[4] Gachard, v. 149.

the end of the year 1577. It was not until early in 1578 that Don John, treating with the Dukes of Guise through Alonso Sotomayor, told them that until better times should come, when the King of Spain's forces by land and sea would be free to co-operate, all hope of action must be laid aside.[1]

Don John, we see, was not a man whose mind worked steadily by method and calculation. His resolutions were formed by impulse, sometimes on the inspiration of the moment, sometimes they were awakened by the stimulus of opposition, and his complaints are not always to be taken at the foot of the letter. But he was frank, courageous and vigorous, and one cannot but regret that circumstances made it from the first impossible for his many fine qualities to find their proper scope amid the great difficulties that surrounded him.

§ 4. *The Papal Subsidy* (1577–1578)

We now return to Don John's application for papal assistance in his projected Enterprise. Pope Gregory at once entered into his plan, and sent as nuncio Mgr. Philippo Sega, Bishop of Ripa and Governor of Ancona, whom we shall often meet with again. In order to avert suspicions, however, he was formally directed not to Don John, but to the Estates, and his first duty was to promote peace, and to prevent the Estates arriving at any conclusion dangerous to the Faith, now that they were in league with the Prince of Orange. But his secret instructions (not yet found) ordered him to assist Don John in the Enterprise, and bills for 50,000 crowns (£12,500) were given him, to be paid over as soon as the expedition had started.

When Mgr. Sega reached Flanders, on the 12th of March, the idea of launching the English expedition immediately had been laid aside, and the foreign troops were already marching off by land towards Italy. The nuncio, therefore, had nothing to attend to, except to watch over the interests

---

[1] Stirling Maxwell, ii. 286, but the exact terms of the message are not given.

of Catholicism in Flanders, and to report to Rome. But in the meantime news of his mission reached King Philip in a form calculated to excite his suspicions.

The news came through the nuncio at Madrid, who asked Perez to arrange for him an interview with the King, as the Pope wished to express his pleasure that the English expedition was now going to take place. Perez, who had repeatedly told Mgr. Ormanetto that this Enterprise would not be taken in hand until Flemish affairs were better settled, was somewhat surprised. But without betraying this, he learnt from the nuncio for the first time the fact of Don John's application for " a nuncio, Bulls, briefs, and money," and that accordingly a nuncio had been sent with all these things.[1]

The audience was arranged, and Philip—who also kept a discreet silence, both as to Don John's having acted without orders, as well as to his not reporting what he had done—declared himself gratified with the Pope's action and with the secret instructions given to Sega. Ormanetto reported this to Rome in his dispatch of the 25th of March, evidently pleased with his interview.[2] Nevertheless, when Perez sent his next dispatch to the Netherlands (April 7) he informed Escovedo that Philip, while sincerely desiring the execution of the Enterprise, " by the Pope or otherwise," was " astonished to hear of the courier sent to Rome by Don John, without information sent to us," and added that a justification would be expected.[3]

Before going further, it is necessary to explain that we have now arrived at that mysterious intrigue in which Perez was the protagonist, and which culminated so tragically next year in the murder of Escovedo. Much has been written on this obscure subject, and it is, of course, no business of ours to follow out anew the practices of both parties, or to pass judgment again on a grave but very interesting crime, except in so far as the story of the papal subsidy is mixed up with those darker problems. For our present purposes it will perhaps be sufficient for us here

---

[1] A. Perez, *Relaciones*, Paris, 1598, p. 277.
[2] Vatican Archives, *Nunz. di Spagna*, x. 547.
[3] Gachard, v. 297, from Perez's draft at The Hague; *Cartas de Antonio Perez*, pp. 27–32.

to regard it as the besetting fault or misfortune of both Perez and Escovedo that (as secretaries often do) they carried their master's peculiarities and failings to extremes. If Don John was none too obedient in act, and in his complaints both impetuous and unrestrained, Escovedo would both write and act as if he were on the very point of rebellion. If Philip loved silent deliberation and rigidly official methods tempered with the exercise of absolute power, Perez, whose papers were always irreproachable in form, knew how to carry on his intrigues while drafting his master's letters, speaking his language, and inducing him to act autocratically. It is now generally acknowledged that he could ruin his adversaries in Philip's estimation merely by suggesting glosses, by manipulating phrases and misapplying words. This, no doubt, he did in the case of Don John and Escovedo.

The text of the letter of April 7 just quoted gives us some idea of the man's astuteness. It contains various remarks uncomplimentary to Philip. He is called "that man," and is described as hard, unsympathetic, selfish, etc. This, however, is really only a snare, to make Escovedo think that this correspondence must be unknown to the King, and that Perez was on his side against Philip. By this means Perez would lure him on to state his grievances and his proposals more frankly. But the original draft, which is now at The Hague (*Cartas de Antonio Perez*, pp. 27–32), still bears in the margin the notes of King Philip, approving of his secretary's ruse ! That being so, can we really trust the straightforwardness of so insidious a strategist anywhere? [1] It is not, however, our business to pass sentence against him, but we may be well upon our guard against accepting unconfirmed evidence drawn from his *Relaciones*.

Escovedo answered Perez's letter of the 7th of April on

[1] See Mignet, *Antonio Perez et Philippe II*, Paris, 1845, 32 : "Perez a dénaturé, dans ses *Relaciones* et dans son *Memorial* la correspondance de Vargas à l'endroit de don Juan," etc. M. Hume, *Españoles é Ingleses nel siglo xvi.*, 1903, p. 185, says : "Perez . . . enveneno al Rey contra su hermano, torciendo y glosando sus palabres, y las de Escovedo." Similar sentiments in E. Gossart, *Espagnols et Flamands au xvie Siècle*, Bruxelles, 1906. Similar opinions may be found in Stirling Maxwell, ii. 308, Andrew Lang, etc. But the older non-Catholic writers before Mignet defended Perez, especially Von Ranke.

the 29th of May, saying that the application to Rome had
been made, " in order to obtain from the Pope both money
and the Bulls necessary for the enterprise of England while
there was hope that the Spanish troops would depart by
sea." [1] These words, it will be noted, confirm exactly
what the nuncio had already said respecting Don John's
application, and Perez might well have accepted the evidence
of two concordant and independent witnesses. But *more
suo*, after quoting the nuncio's words, that Don John had
asked for " Bulls, briefs and money," he goes on to add
this comment in the margin : " It was understood afterwards (that among the things asked for and sent) was also
the investiture of the kingdom, for the person of Don John." [2]

The glosses which Perez added later in the margins of
his *Relaciones* no doubt accord with the sort of comment
which he would have suggested at the time to the King, and
it is hardly necessary to explain how seriously a suggestion
like this would distort the matter in Philip's eyes.   To
ask for " Bulls and briefs " would have seemed a sensible
precaution to the Spanish monarch.   To ask for and obtain
the investiture of the kingdom seemed to mean that Don
John was aiming at a crown independent of Spain, to
which it might also often be hostile, and this with the
Pope's assistance.[3]

We are fortunately able in this case to trace Perez's
mischief-making gloss back to its source.   Vargas, Spanish
ambassador at Paris, had sent in the report that, among
the papers taken on the Irish Franciscan Bishop, Friar

---

[1] Gachard, v. 375, from original MS. at The Hague.   What Bulls
were " necessary " is not specified.   Presumably what is meant will be
a Bull, such as was afterwards discussed at the Armada time, justifying the
war, also a renewal of the Bull of Excommunication, indulgences for those
who gave aid, briefs of exhortation to peers, prelates, etc.   Philip had
said that the Bull of Excommunication ought to be renewed with an
additional clause on the Deprivation from Ireland, *Nunz. di Spagna*,
viii. 339, October 25, 1574, and Becchetti, *Istoria degli ultimi quatro secoli*
(1798), xii. 312, says that this was done.   But I question if this is accurate.

[2] Y aun con la investidura del Reyno en la persona de Don Juan,
como se entendió despues (*Relaciones*, 1598, p. 277).

[3] In reality there was little likelihood that Gregory would have granted
such an investiture.   He had already practically refused it (pp. 197, 221);
and it would have involved an injury to Mary Stuart's claim, which
was to have been one of the chief supports of the invading force.   On
the other hand, Gregory undoubtedly wished Don John to get the
throne, and if that time had ever come, would have helped him.

Patrick O'Hely (whom we have met before), and sent to Elizabeth, there was found "una investidura del Regno de Inglaterra, hecha en persona del Señor don Juan en Roma."[1]

The intelligence is here set out in its true light. It is a rumour current in Paris, and professing to derive authority from other reports published in England or Ireland, and as this English rumour is known to us from other sources,[2] we are able to apply at once an important correction. The investiture was not for England, but for Ireland. Thus modified the story (even though presumably not true) has some *vraisemblance*, for the Pope did claim a right of investiture over that country, which, as we have lately heard, had been talked about at Rome by O'Hely himself. This would make the origin of some such rumour intelligible enough, even though the Pope himself had never issued any such instrument, and indeed there is neither proof nor likelihood of his having done so.

Now let us notice the way in which Perez manipulated the report as sent by Vargas. We must not, of course, blame him for the mistaken substitution of the name of England for Ireland, for which he was not responsible, but we must blame severely his other modifications of the news. Vargas does not suggest that Don John applied for the investiture, Perez does. Vargas gives the pedigree of the rumour, which every one accustomed to weighing evidence will recognise at once as radically affecting its reliability. Perez not only suppresses it, but appears to give it exactly the same authority as the letter of the nuncio. In effect all those who have followed him [3] tell the story precisely as he desired, putting the grant of investiture exactly on a par with the reception of the subsidy. This is a clear case of a deceptive gloss.

One more instance of Perez's unreliability may be given. It is not a serious one, but it further illustrates the story

---

[1] Mignet, *Antonio Perez et Philippe II*, Paris, 1845, 29, quoting Arch. Nat., fonds Simancas, ser. B. liasse 44, n. 84. He unfortunately gives no date, and calls O'Hely Patronio. He was arrested near Limerick in the summer of 1578, as we shall see below.

[2] *Foreign Calendar*, 1578, n. 611, January 25, 1578.

[3] E. G. Vanderhammen, p. 318; Geddes, p. 251; Stirling Maxwell, ii. 287.

of the English subsidy. Mgr. Ormanetto, it may be remembered, had reported favourably, on the 25th of March, of
the audience he had just had with the King. Perez gives
an opposite turn to the story. The King is represented as
" very angry," and as having " dismissed the nuncio " [1]
with a sharp answer. This already shows inaccuracy, and
this in turn may be due to duplicity; for what Perez says
of the interview in March about the subsidy was true of
a later interview in May about the raid policy, which
Ormanetto was then pressing again.[2] To this Philip did
give a decided negative, which might perhaps be described
as Perez described the answer of March. In that colloca-
tion it seemed to tell against Don John and Escovedo,
whereas in reality it did not.

Enough has now been said to show that Perez's *Relaciones*
should be regarded with caution, unless they can be confirmed from elsewhere; and again it is clear how injurious it
was to the Catholic cause of that day, to have an intriguer
like this at the very centre of affairs. Yet we certainly
ought not to lay all the blame upon him. Under the strain
of war and bankruptcy, of misfortune and revolt, the friction
between the various parts of Philip's clumsy political
machinery was becoming insufferable. No wonder if
Escovedo and Don John were restive and troublesome.
Burning to be up and doing, they managed (not without
Perez's perfidious advice) to adopt exactly that line of
bluster which most effectively awoke Philip's suspicions and
inclined him to leave them unsupported.

It was a well-known aphorism among Philip's courtiers
that to obtain any favour one had to pretend the most
extreme urgency.[3] Don John and his secretary carried

---

[1] I am here quoting the version of Dr. Michael Geddes, Chancellor of
Salisbury, *The sad catastrophe of Antonio Perez*, in his *Tracts*, 1714,
p. 252. Geddes, to be sure, is very prejudiced against Philip; but Perez
published his *Relaciones* expressly for people of that sort. Geddes does
not reproduce Perez's *finesse*, but he shows forth bluntly what Perez
conveys by insinuation.

[2] Como's order to Ormanetto is April 12, 1577 (*Nunz. di Spagna* ix. 410).
He was to ask that the plan of last spring should now be carried out, and that
Philip should contribute the rest of the 100,000 crowns, which he had
promised. Ormanetto's report of his unsuccessful audience was written
May 31 (*Nunz. di Spagna*, x. 588). Perez's account in *Relaciones*, 1598,
p. 27.

[3] Thus even the dignified nuncio from Rome had to act a part. " Truth
it is," he remarks one day, " one has to show fire in this, and in every other

this principle to all lengths. They demanded leave to resign, to leave the country, to die on the battlefield, to bathe in the blood of their enemies.[1]   Even nowadays we know that our officers will gird at the War Office with a vehemence that would surprise an outsider.   In those days speech that was free was very frank indeed.   Don John, considering himself a prince, would write to the King with an incisiveness which that dignified monarch might well resent, while to Perez both Don John and his secretary (believing him their friend, though he really showed everything to Philip) spoke angrily of the King himself, and they even went so far as to say that they would like to come back to Madrid in order to put some life into the administration. It is unnecessary to explain how extremely dangerous such speech (especially if couched in cryptic language, as here) was in those days of absolutism, and with the subtle Perez to put sinister interpretations on their turbulent effusions.

If Philip bore all this for a long time, we must remember that he was a patient man, and that all governors of Flanders had made much the same complaints, though in less objectionable terms.   He prepared, however, to send Don John a successor, though the outbreak of hostilities made it inexpedient to change generals at that time.   The English enterprise, too, slipped further and further, amid all this dissension, from the sphere of practical politics.

Towards the end of June Mgr. Sega perceived that a crisis was coming in Flanders, and might arrive at any moment.   Under the circumstances he thought himself justified in advancing to Don John (with all due promises for repayment) the 50,000 crowns which he had received for the English Enterprise, in order that the Spanish commander, left unsupported by his own Government, might take measures to defend the country against (what he conceived to be) the Protestant revolution.[2]

---

matter of importance : and to keep the embers alive, one has—both with the King's ministers abroad, and with his Majesty at Court, and in my own home—to make show, as much as ever one can, of the greatest ardour in everything " (*Nunz. di Spagna*, x. f. 29, January 27, 1576).

[1] Gachard, *ibid.*, v. 136, 182, " Este ynfierno," p. 363.

[2] The undertakings entered into by Don John at Malines are preserved in the Vatican Archives, *Inghilterra Fiandra*, i. 351–357, and they bear date June 24 to July 4.   The repayment of this loan was solicited by the Roman diplomatists for years, but in vain.

This was the end of the papal subsidy for the English Enterprise. Pope Gregory did not blame Sega for his act; but looking back on its consequences, we see some reason for thinking that Philip's close-fistedness was, after all, the more prudent policy; for Don John, soon after receiving this money, besieged the citadel of Namur (against the nuncio's judgment),[1] which precipitated the renewal of the war. Nor was Sega's parting advice more felicitous than his loan. He was called off in July to be nuncio in Spain, *vice* Mgr. Ormanetto, who had died, and in the last dispatch before he went (July 1) we find him still urging the English Enterprise, and begging that Escovedo might be sent to Spain to press the matter on the King's notice. It is true that these formal recommendations rather marked the drift, that affairs were taking than exercised a decisive influence over their course. But that course was not tending towards success.

Escovedo was the first to go under. Philip now regarded him as Don John's evil genius, the man on the Spanish side who was chiefly responsible for the failure to keep peace, and whose turbulent mind might embroil Spain in still further troubles. To be pressed by such a man was exasperating. What followed is still partially veiled in mystery. Two attempts to poison him were made in Perez's house, and the unfortunate man was finally stabbed to death on Good Friday night in the streets of Madrid by Perez's bravos, not without Philip's connivance, as is almost certain, though his motive has never yet been fully accounted for.[2] Escovedo might have been removed from Don John's side by much simpler means. It remained true, however, that, so far as we know, Philip had no serious reason to dislike or dread Escovedo, except such as grew out of his blustering ways[3] of dealing with the Anglo-Flemish problem.

[1] Vatican Archives, *Inghilterra Fiandra*, i. fol. 347, July 1, 1577.

[2] The suggestion, now accepted by many writers, is that Perez had some intrigue with the Princess of Eboli, of which Escovedo acquired knowledge. Perez certainly had the means of getting Philip to order Escovedo's assassination, and did so, to prevent his telling tales. But the evidence is very slender.

[3] Escovedo's bluster was a cause of trouble with the Flemish Estates and with Elizabeth, as well as with Philip II. Eight letters from him (March, April, 1577) were intercepted, and are now in the British Museum (Vesp. C. vii. 96–98, mostly in cipher). They were the cause of strong protests from the Estates, and were eventually published by them as

On the 1st of October following Don John sank prematurely to his grave. As we look back over the unfortunate story of his aspirations to liberate the Queen of Scots and to free Spain from the perennial troubles caused by Elizabeth's Government, we cannot, while recognising his many fine and kindly qualities, wonder at the ultimate result. His plans were always (so far as we can see) impossible of execution, and perhaps felicitous in never being attempted at all; and again, there was never a time when he really grasped the problem before him, or even addressed himself seriously to it. The peace policy, imposed by Philip, was far more successful than the soldier thought it would be, and his misconceptions led him to fatal mistakes. That his misfortunes were primarily due to the inadequacy of the Government he served, must be allowed; but one sees very little to indicate that he could ever have been the man to bring freedom and repose to the English Catholics.

§ 5. *The Irish Expedition of* 1579, 1580

The extraordinary pertinacity of Pope Gregory and his ministers in urging Spain (and later on, France, when the opportunity served) to the Enterprise of England, and their eventually undertaking it themselves with utterly inadequate forces, shows a phase in the Pope's mind which needs more explanation than can be drawn from the immediate context of the papal dispatches we shall now quote.

In the first place they consider it as a religious duty, a crusade, not a conquest or offensive war. They always call it the *Empresa;* they regard it as a war of liberation. They conceived England as held under by tyranny, and they thought that the majority would welcome the religious freedom which they wanted to introduce. They looked forward to the Government remaining English, and they are always decidedly on their guard against Spanish aggrandise-

---

proving the bad faith of the Spaniards, and their plans against England. Mgr. Sega confessed that their evidence on that point was strong (*Nunz. di Spagna*, January 10, 1578, xi. 128).

ment.[1]   In their attitude towards Mary Stuart, too, the religious and constitutional ideas predominated. The sentimental feeling, so common later, for a beautiful lady in distress, is never alluded to. What is always foremost is that she is the rightful heir, in durance because of her fidelity to the ancient laws and the old religion.

Moreover the Italian and Roman mind inevitably adorned the idea of such an Enterprise with all the characteristics of a crusade; for nowhere was the crusading idea (that is, the duty of defending religion by the sword against those who attacked it with the sword) more in vogue than in Rome. To begin with the lowest motive, nowhere else was the need of preaching and pressing that idea so urgent. The tide of devastation from the East kept ever and anon approaching, surging westwards up the Mediterranean, bringing danger to the very shores of Italy, and deeply impressing every one : Rome knew that but for the Crusades she would have been submerged. Though Lepanto had been fought, there was no certainty yet that Turkish power was on the wane, the Mohammedan armies were gaining on the Christians among the Balkans, and the prospect was still dark.

Then, too, as the Crusades had sometimes brought a period of peace to Europe, by acting as a vent for the war-lust so common in those ages, so Gregory hoped that the Enterprise might possibly unite France and Spain. For if they were at one, the Reformation, which had grown strong between the rivalries of Charles and Francis, might yet be driven out of Christendom.

If we could limit ourselves to these points of view, we might consider Gregory's insistence as not only blameless, but perhaps even as laudable. But it is not possible to stop there. We must confess that his zeal was not according to knowledge, nor practical, nor quite free from a suspicion of affectation. That he should have been ignorant of the

[1] Cardinal Moran, *Spicilegium Ossoriense*, pp. 59–64, publishes a letter from the Archbishop of Cashel, offering to recognise Philip as King of Ireland, if he will free the country. This draws a letter from Cardinal Alciati, the Cardinal Protector. Ireland, he says, is a fief of the Holy See, and must not be offered to Spain. The Archbishop answers, If we cannot turn to Philip in our miseries to whom shall we go? June to August, 1570, following B. Museum, MS. Additional, 26,056.

principles of English sea-power was not wonderful at that day, but it is not to his credit that he should have ignored its effects, which were so very evident. More careful observers like Alva and Philip of Spain discerned far more clearly the sources of power which controlled the situation, though they could not organise well enough to counteract the advantages of Elizabeth's insular position. But Gregory, not seeing the reason of her influence, unwisely concluded that her power was contemptible.

What we cannot at all excuse is the want of straight-forwardness with which the papal diplomatists suppressed all serious objections to their pet idea. They spoke as though it was rather impious to entertain doubts as to its final success. We shall hear immediately the nuncio Sega at Madrid dissuading it and proposing difficulties; which warnings, if attended to at Rome, would have saved immense losses. Instead of this, he is so answered that he never raises another difficulty again. This was not mere time service; Sega was not so clear in his mind that he could not alter it by attending at command to another aspect of the subject. The Cardinal of Como's letter had the effect of such a command, and so deprived his informations of their chief value.

Another indication of this determination to see things in their own way is afforded in a letter from Ormanetto of June 29, 1577, who mentions that O'Hely, Bishop of Mayo, and Dr. Sander are at Court, and " urge the resolution [about the Enterprise] as much as they can, and *they help by describing the Enterprise as most easy.*" [1] Here the point is not so much that earnest advocates, like these clerics, should use such a misleading superlative, but that the nuncio should send back this news, as likely to awaken the interest of the Pope.

Another instance might be the winning over by Mgr. Sega of the Chief Inquisitor, Quiroga, from being an opponent of the Enterprise to becoming its supporter. The end of it was that both men had changed from a position of cautious aloofness, to which their unbiassed judgments had led them, to the support of an obviously risky measure on the fatalistic

[1] *Nunz. di Spagna,* x. 627.

assumption that God must bless and prosper what was undertaken for a good purpose. All this is again reported to Rome as a matter of some importance.[1]

It is unnecessary to add more of these small but tell-tale incidents. Gregory and his subordinates, in spite of their good motives, were drifting out of their proper course. They thought they were giving an example of zeal, which did not hesitate at trifles. But they were in reality provoking instant destruction for the men they were trusting, and a fearful retaliation on their own friends.[2]

Stukely's return to Rome, early in April 1577, at last convinced the Cardinal of Como that the great plans which he had made for the overthrow of Elizabeth through Don John had entirely failed; and it is evident that this disappointment made the Cardinal lose his temper. He wrote to the nuncio in Spain, calling the Queen a she-devil (*diavolessa*), and begging Philip to crush her to powder (*rendergli farina per pane*, to make her flour for bread). What was more foolish still, he contemplated sending Stukely to attack Ireland. This unwise resolution he announced in a tone quite unworthy of his high position. " We cannot keep him back," he wrote on the 24th of May, " inspired as he is by ardour and hard driven by want." And again, on the 8th of October, he says that Stukely " will go desperate unless he is employed." It would be a good thing, he thought, to imitate Elizabeth's policy of pin-pricking, and " to plant a thorn in her side such as Orange is in ours. Stukely will be the man for this." On the 27th of October, 1577, he writes that the Pope has resolved to employ both him and Fitzgerald against Elizabeth, and hoped (fond

[1] *Nunz. di Spagna*, xi. 15, etc., September 13, 1577.
[2] Another Crusade characteristic may be noticed, which possibly explains an otherwise obscure corner in Gregory's mind. The plans of the crusaders were almost entirely devoid of strategy—so were those of Gregory. In mediæval times men had gone to the East, as they had gone to Border warfare—sometimes only by ones and twos, to help to guard some wall or castle, to relieve some city, to attack some invading force. War was always in progress : no fresh provocation was given by a newcomer. There was always good work to be done by willing arms, and every valiant blow told. Gregory preached the Enterprise in the same spirit, with hardly any regard for the actual military conditions of the problem before him. To us, with our knowledge of Elizabeth's power, this seems inexplicable. The precedent of the crusaders, however, though it does not excuse him, helps at least to explain his mind.

illusion !) that they would be ready to start in a few days.[1]

The levity with which the Cardinal (and, of course, Pope Gregory must bear his part of the blame) rushed into preparations for war is the less excusable when we remember that he had been warned of Stukely's unreliability, and does not seem to have been under any great delusion (as others were) concerning the worth of the man. The Nuncio Sega had written thrice on this subject [2] from Flanders, the third letter being especially interesting, as it was sent off after an interview with Elizabeth's agent, Dr. Thomas Wilson,[3] who had denounced Stukely as " a braggart and a bankrupt " (*un fallito frappatore*). The Cardinal's answer betrays the narrow-minded spirit by which his policy was now shaped. He wrote (July 1, 1577) :—

" The Pope was pleased with your answer to Wilson on the subject of Stukely. But if the man is not worse than the English ambassador has made out, I do not see why we may not hope for some good service from him. If he is poor and a bankrupt, the reason is that he has been driven away from home. If he is a swashbuckler (the Cardinal plays on the martial meaning of the word *frappatore*), he is so because he desires to return." [4]

It seems that the Cardinal did not really think Stukely a hero, and risked the Pope's good name by employing a man of doubtful reputation in an enterprise which could not be brought to a creditable termination unless it was entrusted to a leader whose honour and integrity were above suspicion. Stukely was not such a man, but James Fitzgerald was, and the different issues of the expeditions which they commanded exactly corresponded to their respective characters.

---

[1] *Nunz. di Spagna*, ix. 437; xx. 69, 77, 87.

[2] Later on (January 5, 1578), he added : " Neither the King nor the Archbishop of Toledo, nor Perez, nor Escovedo, think much of him (Stukely). Doctor Sander also is reticent about him " (*Nunz. di Spagna*, xi. f. 108).

[3] This interview is of importance as an index to Wilson's honesty. Some very grave accusations against Mary Stuart rest on Wilson's word (D. Hay Fleming, *Mary Stuart*, p. 225, n. 54). But here his animus and deceitfulness are amply proved by comparing the account which he wrote home of the interview with that sent to Rome by Sega (*Calendar of Hatfield Papers*, ii. 152; with Vatican, *Inghilterra*, i. 367).

[4] *Nunz. di Spagna*, xx. f. 3.

Stukely's part was the first to be played out. The Pope having created him Marquess of Leinster, he left Civita-vecchia in January 1578, and reached Cadiz on the 5th of April. But he was not allowed by King Philip to refit there, so he went on to Cascares. There he met Sebastian, King of Portugal, who at once attempted to induce the papal commander to take service in the expedition he was about to lead into Africa. Stukely, with characteristic love of novelty, not only agreed, but wrung from the Cardinal of Como an unwilling consent.[1] He went, he fought, and fell at the disastrous Battle of Alcazar, on the 4th of August, 1578, a cannon-ball having cut off both his legs early in the fight.[2]

The merits or demerits of characters such as Stukely's cannot be summed up in any one word of praise or blame, any more than those of Hawkins or Raleigh or Drake, or even of Elizabeth herself. Courageous and persevering, he was full of vaunting ambition and great aims, and had an astonishing power of impressing other men with respect for his capacities. But though he could make friends, he could not keep them. He changed sides more often than most of the unstable politicians of that age, and after death his memory was execrated by the men who a few months earlier had based extravagant hopes upon his valour and prowess.[3] On the other hand, while his popularity failed abroad, it rose at home, and he eventually came to enjoy, as the ballad-writers and playwrights of the time prove, a certain kind of debased popularity, such as was once extended to Dick Turpin or Colonel Blood. Stukely was, in fact, a man of his age, an age in which adventurers and

---

[1] *Nunz. di Spagna*, xx. 219, May 30, 1578.

[2] Such was the account which San Joseffe (San Gioseppe), the next in command, sent to Rome, *Inghilterra*, ii. 118. It is needless to add that the disappointment caused by the defeat, and the revulsion of feelings in regard to Stukely, occasioned other less pleasant accounts of his last adventures. Some said he was shot in the back by his own men, others said he was leaving his own company to rally the Spaniards, or to get help from them. But it is at least certain that he died a soldier's death in the front rank of the battle.

[3] Maffei, *Annali di Gregorio XIII*, 1742, i. 355–60, gives a valuable account of Stukely which is based in great measure on the nuncio's dispatches. He is naturally rather apologetic for Gregory's Government, and accepts suspicions against the Englishman too easily; *e. g.* that he was already in treaty with Elizabeth, etc.

Q

new men were in the ascendant. They recognised their own, and liked his pluck, even though he was a prodigal who had turned against them and perished in a quarrel with which they had no sympathy.

We now turn to the adventures of the brave James Fitzgerald,[1] an Irishman who possessed a full portion of the chivalrous fighting spirit for which his countrymen are so famous. He started in November 1577 in a small Breton ship, but soon captured another, which he declared to be an English pirate. Hereupon he put into the nearest port and marched off in triumph with his soldiers to church (it was the feast of the Epiphany, 1578) to return thanks. The Breton ship, however, used the opportunity to weigh anchor, and sailed off with most of his munitions of war. Fitzgerald followed, and, after numerous other adventures, discovered the runaway in a French port, where, through the friendship and favour of the French Court, his property was restored to him.

But by this time all his stores and money were exhausted, and he returned towards Madrid (August 1578), but secretly, for fear of English spies, to beg for fresh aid, and he obtained it from a somewhat unexpected quarter. His cause was taken up by Dr. Nicholas Sander, a really great Churchman, learned, convinced, fearless, honourable. But he was also an extremist, or at least the " forward " man of his party. He was pining for active employment, and weary to death of trying to get Philip to act, and now he volunteered to join the expedition in person. At first the King would not allow this for fear of offending Elizabeth. But the nuncio, Sega, who had rightly conceived the highest idea of Sander's abilities and determination, at length induced Philip to let him go. At Lisbon a ship was by degrees fitted out underhand for Ireland, in which he was to sail, not, indeed, as legate or nuncio, but still as an accredited agent of the Pope.[2] Sega, delighted with this success,

---

[1] James Fitzmaurice Fitzgerald signs himself Jacobus Desmonde de Geraldine, and is generally called Il Geraldino by the Italians. A biography, but a prejudiced one, in *D.N.B.*

[2] No Brief or Bull giving him faculties has yet appeared. Official letters to him are addressed simply to " Doctor " Sander. He uses no other title in his own missives.

wrote to Rome, " I trust more in the prudence, foresight and religious convictions of that man than I should (as I might say) in a whole army " (November 22, 1578).[1]

All was at last ready for departure, when one of San Joseffe's soldiers was brought before a magistrate of the town for some unimportant offence against civil discipline. He surprised his judge by claiming exemption from jurisdiction because he was a papal soldier. So the whole story of the expedition became public, and was soon the talk of the town. The King of Portugal ordered the disbandment of the force, and Fitzgerald again seemed as far as ever from attaining the object he had in view (April to June 1579).

Half desperate, but not despairing, Fitzgerald and Sander now chartered first one small coasting vessel and then another, and so finally started from Spain in June and reached Dingle Bay in safety on the 17th of July, 1579. The Desmonds soon rose, and Munster was overrun by rebels, but the brave man who had thus successfully, after so many disappointments, enkindled the fire of war, was also its first victim. Fitzgerald fell at the moment of victory in a skirmish fought not long after he had landed.

This is not the place to enter into the details of the guerrilla warfare which ensued. If the Cardinal of Como had really desired nothing more than to irritate Elizabeth at any cost, he might have been satisfied. The war was as alarming, as annoying, as vexatious to Elizabeth as it could be,[2] short of causing her Government a disaster or any really grave danger (except, perhaps, after the defeat at Glendalough, August 25, 1580), or of straining her finances to the breaking-point, or of preventing her supporting the rebels of France and Flanders. But against this is to be set an enormous waste of papal treasure, a lamentable loss of life and property in Ireland, and, besides, the further conse-

---

[1] *Nunz. di Spagna*, xi. 499.

[2] " This rebellion is the most dangerous that has yet been, owing to foreign aid " (Waterhouse to Walsingham, August 3) ; " The most dangerous thing that has fallen out since the Conquest " (Chancellor Gerard to Secretary Wilson, September 17, *Irish Calendar*, pp. 178, 187). The alarm was greatly increased by the simultaneous return to Scotland of Esmé Stuart, September 1579, who, as we shall see later, was morally sure to raise an anti-English party in Scotland—a grave danger for the Protestant domination. Mendoza thought the Government would now compromise.

quences, to which we shall return, and the great disaster of Smerwick, of which we must now speak.

The succours which the nuncio in Spain was to have sent to Smerwick in the spring of 1580 did not start till the end of August. The delay was not due to their magnitude, for they consisted of about 600 men (of whom only about 400 eventually landed), under the command of Bastian San Joseffe, with arms for 2000 Irish. It was caused by the incredible pettiness and lack of business capacity in the officials with whom the nuncio had to deal. " They make me doubt whether there is a sun in heaven," he wrote on the 25th of May, 1580.[1] These striking words are worth notice, for they bring us back to the fundamental reason of Spain's want of success in its great mission as premier Catholic nation—its officials were not educated up to what was required of them; hence ruinous delays, and the slow but sure failure of the enterprises, which depended on their energy.

The evil omen of the bad start made by the relief expedition was soon followed by a crushing disaster. They were smartly attacked by the English, and bombarded in the small fort at Smerwick, in which they had entrenched themselves. Their courage failed, and they surrendered after only three days' fighting. The English, to their everlasting shame, after reserving about fifteen officers for ransom, slaughtered all the rest of their prisoners, putting some of them to death with atrocious tortures and throwing the rest over the cliffs on to the rocks and surf below (November 10, 1580).[2]

The guerrilla warfare, however, still dragged on. It was supported in 1580 by James Eustace, Lord Baltinglas, and the Earl of Desmond escaped slaughter till 1583, though the direct effects of the expedition had worked themselves out by the end of 1581.

---

[1] *Nunz. di Spagna*, xxv. 299. San Joseffe's force consisted to some extent of the residue of Stukely's contingent, which had now found its way back from Africa. It is sometimes estimated at 800 fighting men in five vessels. Sega's *Relatione*, in Kretschmar's *Invasionsprojecte*, p. 207.

[2] Many details, some very gruesome, will be found in A. Bellesheim, *Geschichte der Katholischen Kirche in Irland*, Mainz, 1890, ii. 161–180. But in his account of Stukely, too much credence is given to Bagwell, who trusted the reports of the English spies.

But by that time, as all students of English Catholic history know, the Elizabethan persecution had acquired most of those hateful features which it so long retained. The Royal Proclamations of 1580, the Parliamentary laws of 1581, gave the legal sanction to severities so cruel that the legislation of 1585, which marked the culmination of the persecuting movement, could do little more than ensure the summary execution of the measures which had come into use during this period. It has never been doubted that the Irish expedition was in part responsible for this access of angry feeling.

I may quote two sentences from the Spanish ambassador's dispatches. On the 21st of August, 1580, Mendoza wrote :—[1]

" This Queen has ordered (four earls) five barons and three hundred gentlemen to be imprisoned . . . in fear of the rising of Catholics here as well as in Ireland."

On October 16, after describing minor successes of the rebellion in Ireland, he adds :—

" With the aim of preventing disturbance here, they are continuing the imprisonment of Catholics, who suffer with great patience, and give no signs of a desire to resent it; saying publicly that they are powerless to move, except with the certainty of strong support and the co-operation of foreign troops."

These extracts will suffice to illustrate the close connection between the Irish Rising and the increase of persecution, and to indicate how unfair to the English Catholics that connection was. The Irish expedition was the occasion, but certainly not the cause, of the Elizabethan atrocities. They were due in the first instance to the fanatical hatred of the zealots for the new religion against the adherents of the old, a rage which had been proved by numerous acts of cruelty extending back for many years.

But this does not acquit Gregory and his Cardinal Secretary of having acted with very great imprudence in this unfortunate affair.

[1] *Spanish Calendar*, pp. 50, 53. The nuncio in Spain reports much the same news, November 14, 1580 (*Nunz. di Spagna*, xxv. 530).

When it had failed, Gregory adopted the policy of denying responsibility. It was not a very generous course, but there was no other escape. The Spanish nuncio was asked to beg Philip to ransom the imprisoned officers,[1] because in reality the attempt had been made more in his than in the Pope's interests.[2] The money, as we have seen, had really come from Spain, though Philip, on his side, might still refuse to acknowledge responsibility, on the ground that the money was raised by papal taxation on Church goods. But against this it could be justly alleged that this was not done without Philip's express permission.

It was an ambiguous position, corresponding to the difficulties that pressed Philip on every side. He would have liked to take a more vigorous part against Elizabeth, but for the prospect of serious complications over the succession to the Portuguese throne. To enforce his rights to it, such as they were, he would need all his fleet, and a very considerable army as well, not merely to overawe the Portuguese opposition, but also to keep off what he feared much more, the interposition of France and England. The Pope, who was very much opposed to the seizure of Portugal,[3] made every endeavour to turn Philip from his purpose, begging him, through his nuncio, and a special legate, Cardinal Riario, to direct his arms against England instead, and so to free himself from the never-ending com-

---

[1] There were six Spaniards, three Genoese, five Italian prisoners, and the ransom asked was 12,360 scudi (£3000). Nothing was paid by King or Pope (though the Pope did not refuse to contribute a little), but Mendoza assisted Bastian and some others to escape. There are many papers on this subject in the Vatican (*Inghilterra*, i. and ii.), including Mendoza's passport for Bastian, under the name of Carlos Sintron, dated February 3, 1583 (*ibid.*, ii. 294).

[2] " Sua Santità vuole che V. S. (Sega) l'aiuti appresso S. Maiestà (Philip) à la qual tocca senza paragone più, che à S. Stà di haver cura della loro liberatione. Poiche, se ben il negotio in nome et apparenza era de S. Stà, si sa peró che in effetto era della Mtà sua " (Como to Sega, March 6, 1581; Bib. Vat., *Ottoboni*, 2417, i. 256).

[3] The King of Portugal died on the 31st of January, 1580, without any direct heir. The Duchess of Braganza was the nearest relative, and subsequent generations have vindicated her right to the throne. But Philip claimed as nearest direct male heir, and according to Spanish jurists his claim was valid. Philip settled the matter by invasion. The frontier was crossed June 12, and Lisbon was occupied on the 25th of August, after some resistance by Don Antonio, the illegitimate son of the penultimate King, had been overcome. On the 24th of October Oporto was occupied, and the conquest completed.

plications of Flanders. As a last chance the Pope even went so far, on the 20th of September, 1579, as to offer to the King not only greatly increased power of taxing the Spanish Church, which he had hitherto strongly resisted, but even offered to give him 300,000 crowns from his own treasury.[1] But Philip would not be turned from his object.

During the preparations for the Portuguese expedition, and during its actual course (February to September 1580), nothing else could be thought of, and this pre-occupation accounts in part for the delay in the dispatch of San Joseffe, who did not sail till August. But when the Spanish arms were at last victorious, Philip was more ready (October 1580) to entertain the plan of sending aid to Ireland.[2] But while he was negotiating, news came in of the destruction of San Joseffe's force, and then a French fleet began to menace Portugal. This made Philip withdraw his offer, though the Pope continued to urge him to action so long as the Desmonds maintained their resistance in Ireland.[3]

Broadly speaking, and keeping in mind the documents already quoted, the initiative was from first to last almost entirely papal. Nevertheless, Philip being so very much more powerful a sovereign, his responsibility in the eyes of the world outweighed Gregory's. This was the line taken

---

[1] The offer is conveyed in the Cardinal de Como's long letter of September 28 (*Nunz. di Spagna*, xx. 651–64). This had been laid before Philip by October 17 (*Nunz. di Spagna*, xxii. 470). Many subsequent letters treat of its discussion in a half-hearted fashion, first by one minister, then by a council of war, etc. It suited Spanish diplomacy to make no formal answer, but to leave events to speak for themselves (see next Note).

[2] Sega announces, October 10, 1580 (*Nunz. di Spagna*, xxv. 484), that Philip was thinking of sending 5000 men to Ireland *after Don Antonio had been captured*. This was supposed to be the formal answer to the Pope's offer of September 1579. See also Philippson, *Ein Ministerium unter Philipp II*, pp. 199, etc. On December 5 and 22, 1580, Sega forwarded " the correspondence which had passed, believing, however, that the Pope will not fall in with the plans " (Arch. Vat., *Inghilterra*, i. ff. 180–88).

[3] When the Bishop of Lodi was sent as nuncio to Spain he was instructed not to urge the English *Empresa*, as things then stood (*Ottoboniana*, 2417, i. 280, end of 1581). But January 8, 1582, he was commissioned to ask aid for Ireland, where the Catholics still held out, and if this served to keep Elizabeth " travagliata, saria molto ben pagata la spesa " (*ibid.*, f. 289). On the 30th of April and 9th of July (*Nunz. di Spagna*, xxx. ff. 53, 74) the same orders were repeated. Next year Philip did give a shipful of arms to the Bishop of Killaloe, who wrote, July 5, 1583, to say that he was sailing (*Inghilterra*, i. f. 253). Whether they ever reached Ireland I have not found. But the Earl of Desmond continued to fight on till the 11th of November, 1583.

by Elizabeth, though for interested motives. She spoke *honorablement* of the Pope to the French ambassador, Castelnau de Mauvissière (the Anjou match being then in view), but adding ironically that " she wished no harm to the *pauvre bon-homme, qui estoit si liberal de donner les royaumes, qui n'estoient pas en sa puissance* " (November 6, 1580).[1]

Another unfortunate consequence of this belated expedition, to which we shall recur, was that it eventually (in 1580) coincided with the great efforts of Allen and the English clergy for the spiritual revival of their fellow-Catholics at home. When the Irish expedition was first planned and decided upon (1575, 1576) no one could have foreseen that great missionary undertaking. The decision was taken under the impression that there was nothing else to be done; and, indeed, but for Philip's endless delays, the attempt might have been made, and the flame of revolt might have flared up and died down again long before the religious expedition was talked of. As things fell out, however, no sooner had Campion and Persons landed, and proclaimed that they had no political ends in view, than Bastian San Joseffe sailed for Ireland at the head of a Papal-Spanish force. Every one will see what misconceptions this would cause in regard to the missionaries' professions. Though we may to some extent excuse the prime movers of the expedition, on the score that these evil consequences could hardly in their circumstances have been foreseen by them, we must also confess that their action contributed powerfully to give colour to the belief, which Walsingham and others were striving to impress on Elizabeth and the English Protestants, that a great papal league among the Catholic Powers had been formed for their extirpation, and that the Jesuit missionaries had their share in it. They had none, though Dr. Sander, their friend but a man of different traditions, played a not inconsiderable part in the expedition. To this we shall return in Chapter VIII.

---

[1] R. O., *French Transcripts*, Baschet, 28 (under date). The allusion is to the unofficial reprinting of the Bull of Excommunication in France early in 1580, which Elizabeth feared was equivalent to a renewal of the censure.

§ 6. *The alleged Papal League of* 1580

As the Irish expedition proved a nemesis for the romantic, crusading ideas of Pope Gregory, so in turn does the fiction of the Papal League reflect a sinister light on the Pontiff's adversaries.

In times of peace we scarcely remember how rash and headlong a people may be in catching up and crediting the lightest rumours when the passions of war are loosed. In particular, the report of secret combinations between possible rivals arouses instant suspicion, and too often immediate and indiscriminating credence. Something similar is often observed at other times of popular excitement—during party or labour warfare and the like. To omit other examples, we all remember how seriously the English people at the beginning of the late war in South Africa took the " Bond League " between all men of Dutch origin, though it was afterwards proved to be a pure imagination.

During the Reformation period unfounded reports of this sort were common, and many of them took the form of some alleged Papal League among Catholic princes for the conquest or extirpation of Protestants. Though never frequent in England, such rumours were early current in Germany, where the Reformers found them very effective as a means of inducing their followers to concerted action against the Catholics.[1] In 1567 we find the Emperor Maximilian deprecating the harm done by these malicious rumours, which he quaintly calls, " the exploded, poisonous figment of a Papal League." [2]

---

[1] A sample may be quoted from Mr. Pollard in the Cambridge *Modern History*, ii. 201 (slightly condensed). " In 1527, Otto von Pack forged a document purporting to be an authentic copy of an offensive league between the King of the Romans and the Catholic princes against the Protestants and Luther. For this the Landgrave paid Pack 4000 crowns, and it was agreed by the Lutherans to anticipate the attack of the Catholics, and the Landgrave at once began to mobilise his forces.   But all the Catholic parties denied the alleged conspiracy, and eventually Philip of Hesse himself admitted that he had been deceived.   Illogically [!], however, he demanded that the Bishops should pay the cost of his mobilisation, and as they had no force to resist, they were compelled to find 100,000 crowns between them."

[2] " Das ausgesprengten giftigen figment aïner bäpstlichen pündnuss." Hopfen, *Maximilian II und der Kompromiss-Katholicismus*, München, 1895, p. 252.

As the Reformation spread westwards, so did the sphere of the league rumour. In 1559, 1565, 1566, Scotland itself was not exempt from its disturbing force.[1] In 1572 Morton, in the name of King James, published one such bogus league to the whole nation in a Royal Proclamation.[2] After this, amid the troubles of Flanders and the wars of religion in France, one finds in France and Belgium that the repetition of the great Papal League rumour was very frequent.[3]

In general, we may say that the times were so suspicious that it was impossible for Catholic sovereigns to meet without its being affirmed as most certain that all Protestants were straightway to have their throats cut. The rumours noted in the last paragraph were consequences first of the Treaty of Cateau-Cambrésis in 1558, 1559, then of the conferences at Bayonne in 1565, and then of the complicated negotiations of 1576–1579, when, on the one hand, Spain had to exert herself greatly to find soldiers for Flanders and the expedition to Portugal, while the Pope fitted out Stukely and Fitzgerald for their raid, and the French were forming their popular *Ligue*. No Papal League between princes was, in fact, concluded during those two decades; but the rumours of them gave Walsingham and other zealous Protestants an occasion to negotiate for a General Protestant League in 1577, 1578, which, however, in its turn, also never came into being.

The only one of these multifarious rumours with which the historian of the English Catholics need concern himself is that which was current during the year 1580. The prolonged, though really trivial, preparations for the Irish expedition were a public secret which must have proved a veritable godsend to the English spies abroad. It enabled them to earn their stipends with ease, by sending home the chatter at the Courts of Rome and Madrid, and the talk in

---

[1] Pollen, *Papal Negotiations with Mary Queen of Scots*, 1901, pp. xxxviii, etc.

[2] *Ane advertissement to the faithful, that euery ane may vnderstand the bludie and Tressonable Interprises of the Papists*. Imprintit at Sanctandrois be Robert Lekpreuik. A.D. M.D.lxxii. Copy in the British Museum. C. 18, e2, 112 : reproduced opposite.

[3] In the *Foreign Calendars* from 1572 to 1579 thirty-four references to the Holy *League* will be found in the indexes.

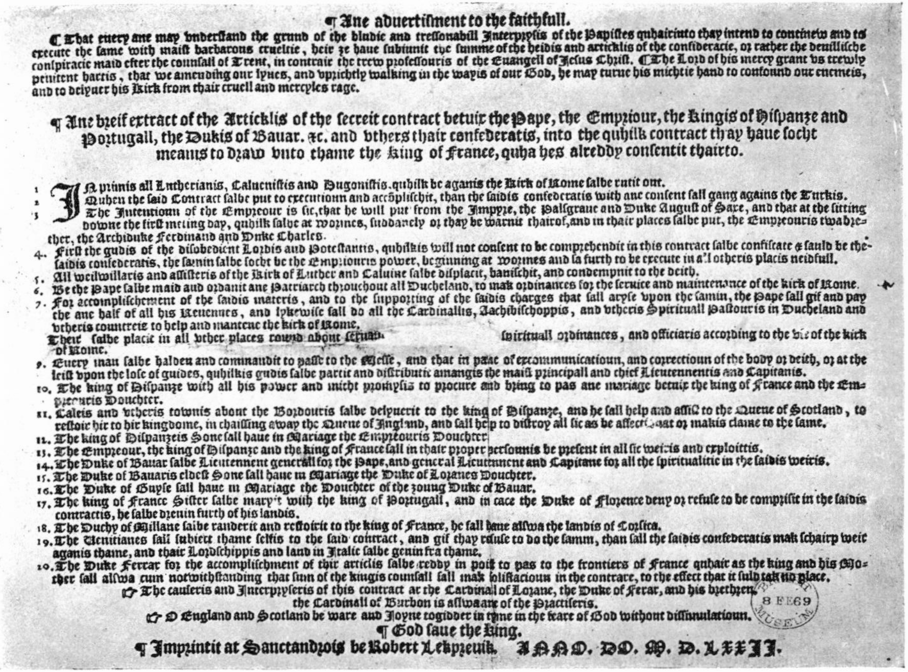

¶ Ane aduertisment to the faithfull.

¶ That euery ane may vnderstand the grund of the bludie and tressonabill Interprysis of the Papistes quhairinto thay intend to continew and to execute the same with maist barbarous crueltie, heir ze haue subiunit the summe of the heidis and articklis of the consideracie, or rather the deuillische conspiracie maid efter the counsall of Trent, in contrair the trew professouris of the Euangell of Iesus Christ. ¶ The Lord of his mercy grant vs trewly penitent hartis, that we amending our lyues, and vprichtly walking in the wayis of our God, he may turne his michtie hand to confound our enemeis, and to deliuer his Kirk from thair cruell and mercyles rage.

¶ Ane breif extract of the Articklis of the secreit contract betuix the Pape, the Empriour, the Kingis of Hispanze and Portugall, the Dukis of Bauar. &c. and vthers thair confederatis, into the quhilk contract thay haue socht meanis to draw vnto thame the King of France, quha hes alreddy consentit thairto.

1 In primis all Lutherianis, Caluenistis and Hugonistis, quhilk be aganis the Kirk of Rome salbe rutit out.
2 Quhen the said Contract salbe put to executioun and accomplischit, than the saidis confederatis with ane consent sall gang agains the Turkis.
3 The Intentioun of the Emprour is sic, that he will put from the Impyre, the Palsgraue and Duke August of Saxe, and that at the sitting downe the first meting day, quhilk salbe at Wormes, suddanely or thay be warnit thairof, and in thair places salbe put, the Emprouris twa brether, the Archiduke Ferdinand and Duke Charles.
4. First the gudis of the disobedient Lordis and Potestatis, quhilkis will not consent to be comprehendit in this contract salbe confiscate & sauld be the saidis confederatis, the samin salbe socht be the Emprouris power, beginning at Wormes and sa furth to be execute in all otheris placis neidfull.
5. All weilwillaris and assisteris of the Kirk of Luther and Caluine salbe displacit, banischit, and condempnit to the deith.
6. Be the Pape salbe maid and ordanit ane Patriarch throuchout all Duchland, to mak ordinances for the seruice and maintenance of the kirk of Rome.
7. For accomplischement of the saidis materis, and to the supporting of the saidis charges that sall aryse vpon the samin, the Pape sall gif and pay the ane half of all his Reuennes, and lykewise sall do all the Cardinallis, Archibischoppis, and vtheris Spirituall Pastouris in Duchland and vtheris countreis to help and mantene the kirk of Rome.
Thair salbe placit in all vther places round about [illegible] spirituall ordinances, and officiaris according to the vse of the kirk of Rome.
9. Euery man salbe halden and commandit to passe to the Messe, and that in paine of excommunicatioun, and correctioun of the body or deith, or at the leist vpon the lose of guides, quhilkis gudis salbe partit and distributit amangis the maist principall and chief Lieutennentis and Capitanis.
10. The king of Hispanze with all his power and micht promysis to procure and bring to pas ane mariage betuix the king of France and the Emprouris Douchter.
11. Caleis and vtheris townis about the Bordouris salbe deliuerit to the king of Hispanze, and he sall help and assist to the Queue of Scotland, to restoir hir to hir kingdome, in chassing away the Queue of England, and sall help to distroy all sic as be affect[illegible]at or makis claime to the same.
12. The king of Hispanzeis Sone sall haue in Mariage the Emprouris Douchter.
13. The Emprour, the king of Hispanze and the king of France sall in thair proper persounis be present in all sic weiris and exploittis.
14. The Duke of Bauar salbe Lieutennent generall for the Pape, and general Lieutennent and Capitane for all the spiritualitie in the saidis weiris.
15. The Duke of Bauaris eldest Sone sall haue in Mariage the Duke of Loranes Douchter.
16. The Duke of Guyse sall haue in Mariage the Douchter of the zoung Duke of Bauar.
17. The king of France Sister salbe mary't with the king of Portugall, and in cace the Duke of Florence deny or refuse to be comprisit in the saidis contractis, he salbe drenin furth of his landis.
18. The Duchy of Millane salbe randerit and ressoirit to the king of France, he sall haue alswa the landis of Corsica.
19. The Venitianes sall subiect thame selfis to the said contract, and gif thay refuse to do the samin, than sall the saidis confederatis mak schairp weir aganis thame, and thair Lordschippis and land in Italie salbe geuin fra thame.
20. The Duke Ferrar for the accomplischment of thir articlis salbe reddy in poist to pas to the frontiers of France quhair as the king and his Mother sall alswa cum notwithstanding that sum of the kingis counsall sall mak solistacioun in the contrare, to the effect that it suld tak na place.

☞ The causeris and Interpryseris of this contract ar the Cardinall of Lorane, the Duke of Ferar, and his brethren, the Cardinall of Burbon is alswaa ane of the Practiseris.

☞ O England and Scotland be ware and Ioyne togidder in tyme in the feare of God without dissimulatioun.

¶ God saue the King.

¶ Imprintit at Sanctandrois be Robert Lekpreuik. ANNO. DO. M. D. LXXII.

Royal Proclamation of Scotland, 1572, announcing a fictitious Papal League

British Museum

the Spanish harbours, all of which was naturally very hostile
to Elizabeth's Government. Mr. Simpson says with truth:
" Warnings poured in from Italy, Spain and France. Mariners
returning from the Mediterranean or from Spain gave information of vast preparations, all appointed for England," [1]
etc. No doubt there were such preparations (though
not for England), and there were such rumours, and the
recent publication of the *Foreign Calendars* would make
it easy to multiply Mr. Simpson's quotations by ten. But
we are fortunately no longer under the necessity of surren-
dering to numbers, as Mr. Simpson did. Access to the
archives of the Catholic Powers now enables us to tell with
certainty what their intentions really were; the mere multitude of informants, with the same prejudices and the same
limits to obtaining authoritative information, must not make
us false to the modern historian's first principle, to trust
to first-hand authorities. We have already told the story
from those authorities, and it is quite easy for us now to
see how much was true in these rumours (and, of course,
much was true), how much false. Sometimes they miss the
mark by very little, sometimes by very much. But in no
case can one tell, till one has first learned the truth from
safe sources. At present we confine our attention to the
Grand Papal League of 1580.[2]

The first inkling of this " Papal League " rumour probably came to the Government by a letter of January 12, 1580,

---

[1] R. Simpson, *Edmund Campion*, 1867, p. 231.

[2] A rumour, modern in origin, but very frequently referred to, may
well be noticed here.   Prince Labanoff, *Recueil des Lettres de Marie Stuart*,
vii. 152–61, has printed two intercepted letters between Paris and Rome
(October 31 and November 8, 1580).   There is no name of writer or ad-
dressee, but the Paris correspondent is with great probability conjectured
to be the Archbishop of Glasgow, as the letters certainly refer to his negotiations.   The name of the Roman correspondent is printed by Labanoff
as " The General of the Jesuits," without alleging any reason, or even
using square brackets.   (His reason may have been the mention of a message about " Father Saunders," whom Labanoff probably mistook for
a Jesuit).   This mistake has been widely copied, by Simpson, Law, Philippson, etc., who have inferred that the Jesuits were deeply concerned in the
preparations for war made by the Catholic Powers at this period.   But the
inference has no other foundation than Labanoff's error.   The Government
calendarers have been more accurate and kept clear of it.   Thorpe's
Scottish Calendars (1858, i. 415, and ii. 928), and Boyd's, v. 533, describe
the document and its contents—Mr. Boyd does so in detail—and make no
reference to the Jesuits.   Boyd refers to two more copies in the British
Museum, also without name of writer.

when Cobham, English ambassador at Paris, reported that
" a league is discovered between King Philip, the Pope and
the Duke of Tuscany." On the 23rd of February he writes
again : " I hear daily of confederacies, and seek to discover
what I may." [1] As the object of these alleged leagues and
confederacies is not specified, Cobham probably did not
expect that they would refer to England.

Our next news comes from Catholic sources. On the
10th of April Sir Francis Englefield, then in Flanders,
wrote to Mgr. Sega at Madrid that his Paris correspondent
had sent him ten articles of a league " said to have been "
concluded at Rome between Rome, Spain and Tuscany on
the 18th of February, and begged for information about
their authenticity. Mgr. Sega, unable to answer offhand,
sent an Italian translation of the articles to Rome, and
made the same request. The Cardinal of Como answered
at once that the articles were " dreams of newsmongers
(*sogne di novellanti*) who can never be restrained from
reporting what they like." [2]

Returning now to Cobham at Paris, whom should we
find coming to him on this subject but Mary Stuart's former
advocate and ambassador, John Leslie, Bishop of Ross? In
May he had made the somewhat strange request that the
English ambassador should help him in his endeavours to
recover the arrears of the Queen's dowry. [3] Now (July 2),
with protests that he desired to serve Elizabeth, he delivered
to Cobham the ten articles, supposed to have been agreed
to by the three confederates, and he asserted that Bishop
Goldwell, Dr. Morton, and others lately sent from Rome,
were agents for carrying out these proposals. He bargained
that his name should not appear, though the fact of the

---

[1] *Foreign Calendar,* 1580, pp. 128, 178.

[2] Sega's letter (*Nunz. di Spagna,* xxv., ff. 240–43; R. O., Bliss,
Roman Transcripts, 77, May 2, 1580) gives the substance of Englefield's
letter. The articles agree with those printed in *Venetian Calendar,* 1580,
pp. 650–51, and Carew MSS., *Calendar,* ii. 288, under July 30, 1580. Como's
letter, May 30, 1580, is in Bib. Vat., *Ottoboniana,* 2417, i. 250. Englefield's
Paris newsagent is thus the first publisher of the rumour. He alleged it
had been published by the nuncio in Paris. If this is true, we must suppose
that the nuncio treated the matter as a joke. But it is more likely that
the newsagent was victimised or mistaken; for I can find no reference
whatever to this league in Mgr. Dandino's dispatches.

[3] *Foreign Calendar,* p. 257.

confederacy and its objects might be published, and this, he hoped, might " save the Scottish Queen harmless." [1]

What the Bishop's object was in making this statement, it is not possible to tell. If he had reflected, he must have realised that in making these depositions before the representative of Elizabeth, he was giving evidence sufficient for the execution of Bishop Goldwell and his companions, evidence which in effect did play a considerable part in aggravating the persecution, and in securing the death-sentence upon more than one. Cobham cynically suggests that his motive was merely mercenary, but it is more likely that the true explanation lay in the factious feeling which as a Scot he entertained even for the Catholic English. This had been recently accentuated by a quarrel with the English at Rome,[2] and, on the other hand, sections 3 and 7 of these so-called articles did less than justice to his mistress's claim to the English Crown, and exaggerated the alleged rights of the Pope to dispose of the throne. That was just what one might have expected in a counterfeit document, and cannot possibly excuse his irresponsible action. This is the first instance which we have met of gross factiousness within the ranks of the Catholics themselves, one side coming to believe so much evil against the other that they deliberately invoke the common enemy against their rivals.

The articles may be summarised as follows :—

Elizabeth was to be declared illegitimate by the Pope, and a usurper; and the Bull of Excommunication should be published in all countries (§§ 4, 9), and the Pope should keep France from interfering (§ 8). The allies, Rome, Spain and Florence, should invade England with a force of 50,000 men (§ 1), and should be joined by the English Catholics (§ 10). On the success of the enterprise, the reconversion of the Protestants should be taken in hand (§ 2),

---

[1] *Foreign Calendar*, p. 355, dispatch of July 12. The articles had been sent by his " last dispatch," apparently July 7, but they are not in the *Calendar*. They may, however, be supplied from the copy given by Cobham to the Venetian ambassador at Paris, and now summarised in the *Venetian Calendar*, pp. 649, etc., December 2, 1580. The Carew copy (see last note) purports to emanate from Rome, February 23, 1580, and to have been sent to Elizabeth by the Prince of Condé.

[2] *C.R.S.*, ii. 162–76. Further details will appear in the next chapter.

the Church lands re-claimed (§ 5), and a new king elected, who should hold the country as a fief of the Holy See (§ 3). Mary Stuart should receive aid to recover Scotland (§ 7); and the King of Spain might arrange a marriage for the new King, and also for a treaty, but was not to receive other advantages (§ 6).

The process of abbreviation of itself inevitably impairs the *vraisemblance* which the composer of this document has not unsuccessfully imparted to his original. A certain and immediate detection of its fictitious character would not be easy.[1] In effect both Englefield and Sega, though their suspicions were aroused, did not at once scout the possibility of the articles being true. Even though Sega knew nothing about them, there was, he knew, the chance that something of the sort might have been concluded recently, through the sole agency of the Spanish ambassador at Rome, though it had not yet been sent on to him. We, too, must not abruptly dismiss the paper on internal evidence only, or be too strong in our condemnation of Leslie, Cobham, and now of Walsingham for having failed to do so. It was a case that called for further inquiry. Their fault, their very great fault, lay in acting without investigation.

To prove a negative is almost always a long and difficult task. The most satisfactory proof of the inadmissibility

[1] Though the articles were well enough contrived to avoid immediate detection, yet when their fictitious character is otherwise established it is not difficult to note improbabilities in the articles themselves. Thus, the army to be sent to England was supposed to be over 50,000 men, a force far beyond the capability of the allies. One has only to remember the difficulties Gregory had in sending 700 men to Ireland, and that the great Armada itself only carried 30,900 men.

Some of the other articles were not very likely to be mentioned in a real treaty of this nature, but were well calculated to excite Protestant odium against the Catholics. For instance, (§ 5) that Church lands should be taken back from present owners, and (§ 9) that Elizabeth's excommunication should be published throughout Europe, etc. There is, perhaps, an attempt to divide the Catholics in the §§ 3, 7 : that Mary Stuart should be sent back to Scotland, and a new King elected for England, who should acknowledge England as a fief of the Holy See. The Duke of Florence is given a place in the confederation, because he had armed soldiers for Philip in 1578, and sent them to Spain under the command of his brother Pietro.

The place of origin is presumably Paris. The forger seems to have aimed primarily at interesting the Protestants in Flanders and in England, but there were also many things in this paper which would go down well with Catholics. The proviso that Spain was not to control England, or to receive increase of territory is noteworthy.

of this paper lies in a careful consideration of the line of politics then followed by the Catholic diplomatists in regard to England.   If their policy is clear, then we cannot admit the authenticity of a paper which claims to give the key to that policy, but does not fit in with it at all.   Now the line of the negotiations about England has been indicated in the previous chapters, and at the alleged date the League plan nowhere fits in with the actual circumstances.[1]

The answer of the Cardinal of Como is again a complete proof, for it is impossible to conceive any diplomatic reason why he should have wished to deceive his own representative.   Strongest of all single arguments is that to be derived from the course of the subsequent negotiations.   The Holy See kept on, as before, urging and pressing Spain to undertake the English Enterprise.   Yet it never added, " as you have already agreed to do on a larger scale than we now propose." Again Philip's constant answer was, " In that case you must greatly increase your contribution "—yet he never adds, " And you are already bound under treaty to do a great deal more." [2]   If this treaty had been a reality, such omissions would have been impossible.

---

[1] Besides this palmary argument from the purpose and connection of the actual negotiations, there is also the argument from archive study. Its outline would be more or less as follows : Though the Roman, Spanish and Tuscan archives have now been open for many years, have been arranged by competent archivists, and investigated by capable scholars in search for matters of this sort,—yet nothing about our league has transpired.   I have myself investigated the subject at Rome and Florence (esp. Arch. di Stato, *Carteggio Medici*, filza 3294, which contains negotiations with Rome for this period), and arrived at the same conclusions.   At Simancas I could again find nothing.   But, intent on other subjects, I made no prolonged inquiries on this; so that my negative here is not so strong in itself, though it coincides with that of other searchers.

A negative conclusion would have been of little value, if it had only been the question of finding one particular document.   But that is not the contention.   The point is that a compact, such as this professes to be, could never have come into existence by the sudden simultaneous freak of the representatives of three great Powers.   It presumes previous and subsequent correspondence, instructions, powers, drafts, cautions, ratifications, on a very large scale.   The archive argument turns on the inexplicable absence, from three large and well-preserved national archives, of an inter-correspondence which ought to have been copious in each.

[2] Here, for instance, is a summary by Philippson of an attempt to move Philip, made in November 1580. " Nuncio and Legate began again to urge the 'Holy Enterprise' (against England). Whereupon Philip declared roundly that the matter could not be discussed until Flanders, from which the expedition must start, had been entirely recovered, and until the Pope gave a greatly increased subsidy " (Philippson, *Ein Ministerium unter Philipp II*, p. 202) ; exactly the same position as ten years before.

Now that the Papal League rumour was subscribed with Bishop Leslie's name, and appeared to refer to England, Elizabeth's ministers were ready to make use of it. Yet there were serious difficulties in the way of actually publishing it. Elizabeth did not at all relish the idea of her illegitimacy· or her excommunication being noised abroad. For this or some similar reason, no serious inquiries were made, that I can discover, into the verisimilitude of the League from those who might have been able to give reliable information, with the following quasi-exceptions.

An attempt was made to probe Mendoza, and that immediately. On the 10th of July a set of complaints was drawn up, on which the Queen was to confer with him, and they commence with a reference which we at once recognise as applying to this League. The conference took place, and from Mendoza's reports home, on the 16th and 23rd of July,[1] we gather that he did not even understand the allusion to the Papal League, which is what most concerns us; and it may be that his frank answers showed Elizabeth that there was little gain to be expected from discussing this rumour in diplomatic circles, and she does not seem to have done so again.

More than four months later (November 28), Cobham inquired whether he might not make some investigations in the French Court, and the phrase he then used for the articles—" the paper which I sent you some months ago "[2]—leaves one under the impression that there had been no serious correspondence about them since. Nor was there any now. The silence of our archives seems to show that Elizabeth was undecided either in regard to the utility of the inquiry, or perhaps even as to the authenticity of the articles.

Nevertheless, Cobham, without it would seem mentioning it in his dispatches,[3] did seek an interview on the

[1] *Foreign Calendar*, p. 350; *Spanish Calendar*, 1580–1586, pp. 41–43. With his second letter Mendoza sent what seems to have been the above set of complaints, which had been supplied to him. Philip's answer was much delayed. It was on the 26th of November (*Calendar*, pp. 67, 68) that the message came back: " An answer could easily be given (to the complaints), but yours did perfectly well." Though we might have wished for the fuller answer, it was then, in practice, too late to matter.

[2] *Foreign Calendar*, p. 502.

[3] No reference to this is found in our Record Office *Foreign Calendar*,

subject of the articles with Lorenzo Priuli, the Venetian ambassador, from which, however, he obtained no advantage. The answers he received were somewhat sceptical, but Priuli accepted the paper with thanks, and sent it home (December 2, 1580) with the comment, " I will contrive to ascertain whether I have been told the truth, for these English are so artful in their negotiations that I cannot be sure that this story may not have been their invention, or if not entirely so, at least to some extent."

After this the rumour began gradually to take new shape. Thus, on the 9th of January, 1581, Mendoza reports, " The heretics constantly assert that your Majesty, the Pope and the King of France have a league against them." [1] This, it will be noticed, brings in a new idea. Before we had the Duke of Florence, because he was helping Philip in Portugal. Now the King of France is introduced, probably because the Alençon match was unpopular with the Puritan party.

On the other hand, the Prince of Orange, on the 10th of February, wrote solemnly to warn Elizabeth again about the treaty of Spain, Rome " and certain Italian potentates," [2] which must be our League. He was an old hand at spreading stories of this sort, and in his *Apology*, which he had just published, he refers to several.

But though Elizabeth's Government could make no effective use of the League in foreign politics, it was mean enough to employ it as an incentive to further persecution at home. Since the spring of 1580 that persecution had been on the increase, and a further step downwards was now taken. By a well-known proclamation of July 15, 1580, " against rebels and traitors in foreign parts," all England was warned that the English Catholics abroad had invited the invasion of the Pope, the King of Spain and some other princes,[3] and under the religious excitement which this

---

but a full report is given in the *Venetian Calendar*, pp. 649–51, December 2, 1580, from Venetian sources.

[1] *Spanish Calendar*, p. 71.   [2] *Foreign Calendar*, 1581, p. 58.
[3] A copy of the original proclamation is in the British Museum, *Grenville Library*, 6463, n. 207. Two drafts of this, with many variations and corrections, are in the Record Office, *Dom. Eliz.*, cxl., nn. 18, 19.

caused the severities against the English Catholics, which had already been commenced in response to the Catholic revival, and in retaliation for the Irish expedition, were continued.

Mendoza, in his dispatch of the 23rd of July, gives a vivid picture of the sequel :—

" A few days ago orders were given to publish the proclamation, which I send to your Majesty herewith. As will be seen by its tenor, it is inspired by fear lest the Catholics should rise. You will also see that all the Catholics, not only here, but throughout the kingdom, who had been imprisoned and released on bail, or on giving sureties to appear in court whenever summoned, are now ordered to present themselves within twenty days in the prison of this place under pain of death. Great numbers have already entered, insomuch that in my judgment we ought to give God infinite thanks to see the joy with which they bear trouble and persecution, such as they have never been afflicted with before." [1]

More than a year later, November 16 and 17, 1581, during the trials of Campion and his companions for the bogus " plot contrived at Rheims and Rome," we find the Papal League rumour repeatedly brought in as evidence. Thus Elliott asserted that Campion had exhorted his hearers to remember the coming of a day of change. Whereupon the Queen's Counsel at once exclaimed, " Lo, what would you wish more manifest ? The great day is threatened : comfortable to them and terrible to us. And what day should that be, but that wherein the Pope, the King of Spain, and the Duke of Florence have appointed to invade this realm ? " It is not necessary to quote Campion's indignant and powerful vindication of what he had really said. This is sufficient to show that this fictitious League had already been accepted and enshrined among the stock Protestant prejudices, which the Queen's Counsel can awaken in the jury at will.

[1] Fuensanta and Navarette, etc., *Documentos Inéditos*, xci. pp. 501, 502; *Spanish Calendar*, p. 43. The imprisonment was simultaneous with the proclamation, though due to other causes.

In the same trial Father James Bosgrave, S.J., and the martyr Luke Kirby were both condemned, on no other ground than that of having heard talk about the League abroad without denouncing it when they returned to the realm. Bosgrave afterwards faltered, and was exiled; but Kirby underwent with heroism the martyr's death.

CHAPTER VII

THE BEGINNING OF THE CATHOLIC REVIVAL
(1568–1579)

§ 1. *The Exiles and the Foundation of the English College, Douay* (1568–1573)

THE English Catholic revival, which began among the English Catholic exiles at Louvain between 1564 and 1567, failed, as we have seen, through the religious revolution which broke out at that place in 1568. But the Michaelmas of that same year (1568) saw the commencement of the Seminary movement, which, from very humble beginnings, grew to be the source of a powerful and permanent Catholic renaissance.

Dr. William Allen, the founder of the first Seminary, had, as we have already heard, after a distinguished University career, been driven from Oxford by the adherents of the new religion. Nevertheless, as an influential teacher or tutor in several Catholic families, including that of the Duke of Norfolk and among the gentry of Lancashire, he maintained the struggle strenuously against the party of violence, until he was forced to fly to Flanders about 1566. There, besides printing several books which he had already composed against the heresy of the day, he studied for the priesthood and was ordained at Malines. After this he went to Rome (1567); partly for health; partly because that pilgrimage was especially dear to all English Catholics; partly because a friend, Dr. Vendeville,[1] one of the most enlightened Catholics of Belgium, was making the same journey; partly because, as there was no opening

---

[1] Jean Vendeville, then a married man, and a Regius Professor at Douay, afterwards (1588) Bishop of Tournai.

for him elsewhere, he would have been glad to obtain the post of a chaplain at the English Hospice at Rome.[1]

Though the results of this pilgrimage were not exactly what Allen had expected, we may be sure that it contributed powerfully to bring him more intimately than ever into sympathy with the Counter-Reformation, which, under Pius V, was so potent at Rome. Vendeville, with Allen presumably at his side, had pressed the Pope to undertake a great missionary scheme of Vendeville's own devising.[2] As is always done in such cases, the promoters of the plan would have gone round to all those persons of similar aspirations who might be able to help; and in this way Allen would probably have met, as early as 1568, many of those leaders of the Catholic reaction with whom he was afterwards so familiar.[3] St. Pius, however, did not eventually accept Vendeville's plan, and the confraternity at the English Hospice did not elect Allen to a chaplaincy; so the friends returned again to Flanders.[4] On their way Allen proposed to Vendeville an amended scheme, in which we clearly recognise the conception of the future Douay Seminary. The aim now was to found an institution for England and Flanders conjointly, in which students might live, ready to set to work as soon as the day of peace should dawn.[5]

[1] So Father Persons' *Memoirs*, C.R.S., ii. 62. See Fitzherbert, *Vita Alani*, in Knox, *Letters of Cardinal Allen*, p. 7.

[2] According to Fitzherbert, *ibid*., he contemplated a scheme for the conversion of all infidels.

[3] I have found in a Jesuit archive abroad (*Anglia Hist*., i. 59–69) a plan of about this date for the conversion of the world: *Ad insigniter propagandam religionem*. It is anonymous, but may well be Vendeville's scheme itself.

[4] During part of this journey they had the future Cardinal Bellarmine in their company (*Selbstbiographie*, ed. Döllinger und Reusch, 1887, p. 56). It would be interesting to know, were that possible, whether Allen discussed his plans with this great upholder of Seminary education, who was also always full of interest in England.

[5] Though Douay was not at first a *missionary* college in exactly the same sense as later, the difference may be exaggerated. Writing to Vendeville in 1578, Allen said, " We thought it would be an excellent thing to have men of learning always ready outside the realm to restore religion, when the proper moment should arrive, although it seemed hopeless to attempt anything while the heretics were masters there " (*Letters*, p. 54). But Vendeville had at first taken a more hopeful view, and had assured Viglius that Allen's scholars would " in two years be ready to aid the Church in England, even at the risk of their lives. If God helps, they would restore orthodox religion with great and rapid success, and gain

With Vendeville's cordial co-operation, Allen opened a small hall or college at Douay on the above lines for the Michaelmas term of 1568. He had at first four English and two Belgian scholars, but the latter soon found better berths, and the English in slowly growing numbers devoted themselves to study, tutoring, and to the religious instruction of English exiles and travellers who passed that way, many of whom were very ready to learn. In this quiet way did the institution continue for the first five or six years of its existence.

Though we know nothing of Allen's political creed at this period, he was clearly, like all others, living in hopes of a change for the better. But no such change came. The rising in the North collapsed; the Queen was excommunicated, but went on in appearance unaffected; the hopes that Mary's friends and the Conservatives would turn Burghley out of office remained unfulfilled; and Norfolk, Allen's protector and patron, was beheaded. The day of religious liberty was much further off than ever.

We have already examined the steady deterioration of the fortunes of the Catholics in England from a political point of view in consequence of these misfortunes; and a word must be added here to illustrate the hard conditions under which they lived in Flanders. Of this we have some evidence in a short series of begging letters sent from the English at Louvain to Gregory XIII at the beginning of his pontificate.[1] They begin July 17, 1572, with a petition

---

very many souls " (*ibid.*, p. 22). It was no wonder that different people should take slightly different views on such a matter, nor that prospect and retrospect should have been the one rather sanguine, the other sober. Father Persons slightly overstates the facts when he says, " There was no intention at all (as I have often heard Mr. Dr. Allen affirm) of the end of returning again into their country to teach and to preach " (*Memoirs, C.R.S.*, ii. 190). The words " at all " are too strong. But there was not the same studious preparation for immediate return that came after 1579, nor the missionary promise, nor the quasi-festival of departure. The high-water mark of missionary zeal, as we shall see, came later, when Father Holt could write to Father Agazario of " the fervour of the students, whose feet itch to run to racks " (Persons' *Memoirs, C.R.S.*, iv. 95). That was in 1583.

[1] These papers are all contained in the correspondence of the Cardinal Protector Moroni, Arch. Vat., Arm. lxii. vol. 33 and Arm. lxiv. vol. 28. The letters are generally in pairs—one to the Pope, couched in more general terms, the other to the Cardinal Protector, in which some explanatory details are usually added. They are all dated from Louvain, but some of the signatories certainly lived at Antwerp or elsewhere.

from Gilbert Burnford, Chancellor of Wells, Giles Capel, Canon of Wells, and John Martial, the second master of Winchester School, and now a well-known writer, for alms, as persecution at home has cut off all supplies from thence.[1] On the 10th of August comes a more important paper, signed by thirteen of the better known clerical leaders.[2] Our bishops, they begin, should be our spokesmen; but all have been killed off, except two, who are now in close confinement. The state of England is very sad, and the Faith is in danger of dying out, though an infinite number are forced into conformity against their better wills. They then beg the Pope not to cease doing all he can for them, though they will not suggest any definite measures. To Moroni, however, they add that Bishop Goldwell, Dr. Morton, and Dr. Sander are fitting men to advise him.

On the 23rd of August another little gathering of Englishmen at Louvain, calling themselves "The College of Preachers," explain that there are many English scattered through Belgium, "at Mechlin, Antwerp, Bruges (?), Dunkirk, and Brussels, who desire English preachers and catechists." They beg that the Pope would add to the annual alms he already bestowed on the exiles some support for this very good work; and they end by saying that, if the college is founded, it will at once send preachers to England.[3] The petitioners ask that Englefield might be their almoner, and, in effect, we find that he gave out to them twenty crowns each next year. But this was, of course, insufficient to relieve the distress permanently, and

[1] Arch. Vat., Arm. lxii. 33, ff. 130, 131. They state that they have been in exile for thirteen years.

[2] *Ibid.*, Arm. lxii. 33, ff. 134-6. The signatories are Thomas Harding (*D.N.B.*, xxiv. 339); Charles Parker (D.D., residing generally at Brussels); William Allen (no mention of his presidency of the Douay Seminary, which was then little known); Richard Hall (D.D., and afterwards Professor at the English College); Thomas Stapleton, D.D. (*D.N.B.*, liv. 101); Henry Jolliffe, late Dean of Bristol; Giles Capel and Gilbert Burnford (as above); William Taylor, late Master of Christ's College, Cambridge; Thomas Hide, late Canon of Winchester; Thomas Bailey (afterwards Vice-President of the English College); Laurence Webbe (D.U.J., afterwards Professor there), and Edmund Hargate; the document is drawn up in his hand.

[3] Arm. lxiv. 28, ff. 72-7. Signed by Taylor and Hide (as above), Thomas Metham (who did return to England, and eventually became a Jesuit, see Foley, vii. 503), John Fenn (of New College, Oxford, see Gillow, ii. 244).

in the following March we find Capel, Burnford and Martial begging for a continuation of the grant,[1] while John Oliver requests a share in the papal bounty.[2]

" The College of Preachers " did not eventually survive, and a word or two must be added about other settlements, which also failed sooner or later. Amongst these were " Oxford House " and " Cambridge House," commenced by English University men at Louvain.[3] The Bridgettine nuns of Syon, then under Abbess Catherine Palmer, were the only religious who have continued till the present day, though the English Carthusians under Dom Maurice Chauncey at Bruges were destined to survive for more than two centuries. The considerable body of English sisters under Margaret Clement who entered among the Flemish Augustinianesses at St. Ursula's, Louvain, survive still, through a later English filiation called St. Monica's. But the Franciscans, who migrated from Greenwich, soon got lost entirely among their foreign convents, never having existed as a separate English community. Sander in 1561 remembered the migration very clearly, and Father Persons in 1600[4] recollected the report of it. It was presumably the religious troubles in the Netherlands, 1576–1585, which obliterated the records of their achievements. A similar fate overtook the Dominican nuns, who were originally under Mother Elizabeth Cresner, and included a half-sister of the martyred Bishop Fisher. In his report of the distribution of papal alms in 1571 Englefield says that they were " almost worn out with old age." [5]

The subject of papal support to the exiles itself requires some notice, though a connected account is not yet possible. It began with the distribution through Parpaglia of five

---

[1] Arch. Vat., Arm. lxii. 33, f. 1.

[2] *Ibid.*, Arm. lxiv. 28, f. 73.

[3] Persons' *Memoirs, C.R.S.*, ii. 62.

[4] *C.R.S.*, i. 43; ii. 62. It is odd that Friar Bourchier, who is believed to have belonged to the convent, should have made no mention of the migration.

[5] Parpaglia describes them in 1560 as living in Zeeland in great want (Bayne, *Anglo-Roman Relations*, p. 257). Englefield's letter of May 26, 1571, from Louvain to Moroni, is Arch. Vat., Arm. lxiv. 28, f. 58. Sander to Moroni (*C.R.S.*, i. 43) adds that one of the sisters was eighty at the time of the migration from England, which was conducted by " the excellent Father Richard [Hargrave], the Dominican."

hundred crowns at the close of his mission in October 1560.[1] On December 20, 1564, an appeal was made to Pius IV by some Oxonian who had lately been ordained in Rome, and the Pope answered : " We will provide for you and for others, both in Rome and in Flanders. For the heretics God will provide in His own time." Evidently this kindly Pope was anxious to be generous, but what he was able to achieve we cannot yet say.[2] A petition to Pope St. Pius V was sent up from Louvain March 8, 1568, with a note begging Father Polanco, S.J., to lend his aid. This letter was signed by Maurice Chauncey, Nicholas Sander, and John Rastall, and it stated that among the exiles then at Louvain there were sixty-eight priests, forty religious men, twenty-five nuns, thirty-seven students, seven families, amounting to thirty persons, besides thirteen others.[3] After this Sir Francis Englefield appears as distributor of an annual grant of five hundred scudi in 1571, and a little later (? 1575) the distributor was Dr. Thomas Clements.[4] Whether it was continued after the great troubles of 1576, etc., does not yet appear.

The Spanish almsgiving was on a somewhat larger scale, but it was very irregularly paid. Almost all the important

[1] The money-note, sent off September 3, reached Parpaglia October 13 (see Parpaglia to Moroni, October 13, 1560, printed in Bayne, *Anglo-Roman Relations*, p. 257). Rumours of this grant were picked up by Cecil's correspondents for Italy, Giannetti and Sheres, and sent to England (*Foreign Calendar*, September 7, 1560, nn. 494, 496) ; but, as usual, they exaggerated the amount to be given, which they state at "certain thousands of crowns." A list of seventeen exiles to be benefited is in Arch. Vat., Arm. lxiv. 28, f. 281.

[2] Stonyhurst MSS., *Angl.*, ii. 2, originally, no doubt, in the archive of the English Hospice. Persons has endorsed the speech, which is in Latin, " Vel Sanderi, vel alterius cuiusdam eiusdem generis " ; the hand is not that of Sander. The writer describes the trials of his college (evidently New College, Oxford) in detail ; but says little about himself. He might be Kyrton, or Bromborough, or Gyblet ; see Wainewright, *Ushaw Magazine*, December 1911, pp. 257, etc.

[3] Arch. Vat., Arm. lxiv. 28, ff. 337, 338. The figures have already been quoted.

[4] Dr. Thomas Clements gives an account of his distribution to Cardinal Sirleto in an undated letter (Vat. Lib., *Regina*, 2020, f. 446), viz. to the Bridgettines of Syon, 200 crowns; to the Carthusians, 50 ; to the College of English Preachers in Brabant, 50 ; to Thomas Freeman, 20 ; to the following 5 crowns each : George Tyrrell, Gilbert Burnford, Edward Taylor, Thomas Parker, the younger Wotton, Nicholas Fox, Andrew Wagge, Henry Holland, John Askew (? Ashewus), William Smith, Mrs. John Story, D. Latam and Hugh Charnock. The rest was kept to distribute as need arose. Printed, *Recueil des travaux . . . d'histoire*, vol. xli., *Mélanges d'Histoire Moderne*, No. 67, Louvain, 1914.

political exiles, the Countess of Northumberland, the Earl of Westmorland, etc., received small allowances, as well as the exiled nuns.[1] On January 3, 1575, Elizabeth made proposals to the Spanish Governor Requesens that thirty-one of these exiles should be banished and their pensions stopped.[2] Philip, however, while sanctioning their banishment from Brabant, allowed their pensions to be paid (*i. e.* when money was in hand) at Liège.

The little glimpses we get of the lives of the exiles, from these and similar passing notices, show how sad and heavy the outlook must have been, without prospect of amelioration, while death, sickness and want thinned out their ranks year after year. Though there was no lack of zeal anywhere, and distant or conditional plans for action were not uncommon, no method of helping themselves under present circumstances had been evolved. The cause of this paralysis lay ultimately in the extreme rigour used against Catholics at home. This both cut off the flow of alms abroad, and made the return of missionaries seem inopportune, because of the grave danger it would bring upon their hosts. To explain this we must again turn our eyes to England.

§ 2. *English Catholicism at its Lowest*

It will be remembered that the rise of hopes shown by the Catholics at Mary Stuart's arrival in England in 1568 had been met by an increase of severity, and that one of the exciting causes of the Northern Rising was the more rigorous enforcement of the Statute of Uniformity in the

[1] Vendeville, in 1568, begged for a pension of 300 crowns for the Douay Seminary; but it appears not to have been paid after 1570. Compare *Letters of Cardinal Allen*, p. 23, with p. 246.

[2] Twenty-six of these (the Earl of Westmorland, Countess of Northumberland, etc.) were concerned in the Northern Rising, five others (Sir Francis Englefield, etc.) in alleged conspiracies abroad. Their names are given in Elizabeth's letter, printed in Lettenhove's *Relations Politiques*, vii. 402, from Simancas, leg. 2579, f. 99. There is a *List of Fugitives certified to the Exchequer*, December 26, 1576, in R.O., *Dom Eliz.*, cx. 9. Several lists of exiles have been printed by Father Birt in the *Downside Review* for 1915. See also R. Lechat, *Les Réfugiés Anglais dans les Pays-Bas*, Louvain, 1914 ; and for convents and other foundations, P. Guilday, *English Catholic Refugees on the Continent*, London, 1914.

latter half of 1569. One new feature of that date was the order to stir up both the Sheriffs and the Justices of the Peace all through the kingdom. Without their aid very little could be done, and it was generally believed that they had hitherto been very slack in supporting the new laws. But pressure having been put upon them, they conformed after the fashion of their contemporaries, and almost to a man swore and protested their readiness to enforce the statutes.[1]

Then followed the disaster of the Northern Rising, which involved Catholics all over England in searches (one of the worst afflictions of the persecution), fines, and very often in imprisonment; and on the top of this came the untimely excommunication, a heavy trial to those of weak faith. Then, again, Ridolfi's and Leslie's reckless bid for Spanish succour almost resulted in a death-blow to the Catholic nobility, and by 1573, as we have seen, Queen Mary's friends, both in England and Scotland, had been well-nigh annihilated as a political party, and as a religious party, too, their forces were never lower. Lord Burghley had his opportunity for putting constraint on the consciences of his victims, and he availed himself fully of his chance. The probability is that no political prisoner was offered liberty, except on condition of conformity; and, as we have so often seen, the subjects of the Tudors, Catholic and Puritan alike,[2] had very rarely, at this period, the power of resisting pressure from the Crown.[3]

Another proof of the settled severity of the persecution is the advent of the spy, and his engagement as a Government official. After the Ridolfi conspiracy we find Burghley's man, William Herle, confined in the Marshalsea and in the Tower for the special purpose of undoing the Catholic prisoners there, and Davy Jones sent " informations "

[1] R.O., *Dom. Eliz.*, lix., November 1569, contains many such declarations, nn. 21, 22, 25, etc.

[2] It was only after 1572 that the Puritans began to be nonconformists.

[3] The common formula which one sees is, that the prisoner was freed " on submission to her Majesty," or " on obeying the laws." It is to be feared that this " submission " included submission to the Oath of Supremacy. We have clear instances of this in the case of prisoners for Mass in 1564. R.O., *Dom. Eliz.*, xviii. nn. 7, 8, and especially n. 19. The " submission of Mr. Roper," however, July 8, 1568 (*ibid.*, xlvii. 7), does not explicitly include the oath.

from the same and other prisons to Walsingham's secretary. The rack, too, was brought into use, and no one could hold out against it; the great majority gave in as soon as it was threatened.

Of special importance for this period of our history (1568–1580) was the great severity exercised upon Catholics at Oxford. Some persecution, indeed, there had always been;[1] but the highly conservative character of the University had preserved it to some extent as a place of refuge for Catholics; and so it would continue for another decade, though in an ever-diminishing degree. The Earl of Leicester, its unworthy chancellor, had at first been favourable to Catholics; but after he had gone over to the Calvinists, his vindictiveness towards the ancient faith was signalised, as Anthony à Wood notes, by the increase of Commissioners for Religion, who " ever and anon summoned those that smelt of Popery, or were Popishly affected, suspending, imprisoning and expelling them." [2]   In 1568 Bishop Horne of Winchester " visited " Merton College, and Father Persons in retrospect attributes much importance to the proceedings of the Commissioners at Balliol in 1570, which ended, after many delays, in the removal of Richard Garnet from his fellowship.[3]

Edmund Campion, who had been at Oxford since Mary's reign, may be considered a typical case of a Catholic scholar living on while all around him changed.   As to heresy, he declared later, on entering the Society, " I never at any time defended it pertinaciously "; and Persons calls him " animo catholicus."   He had yielded, however, occasionally and to some extent, his worst lapse being the taking of deacon's orders from Cheney, according to the reformed

[1] For the earlier history of the Catholics at the universities, see N. Birt, *Elizabethan Religious Settlement*, 1907, pp. 253–96.   To his authorities may be added that of the Spanish ambassador on the imprisonment of students in 1560, 1561 (*Spanish Calendar*, pp. 156, 218).   In 1563 a student on his way to Louvain (but it is not stated where he came from) was thrown into prison, and died of the effects.   News of this reached Trent, and interesting letters about it passed between the legates there and St. Charles; Baluze-Mansi, *Miscellanea*, iii. 511, n. xxv.; Šusta, *Römische Curie und Concil von Trient*.

[2] Wood, *Historia et Antiquitates Universitatis Oxoniensis* (Oxford, 1674), i. 290.   The Spanish ambassador interceded for the Catholics in 1567, and was promised redress (*Spanish Calendar*, 1558–67, p. 656), but without effect.   [3] *C.R.S.*, ii. 16.

formulary, in order to receive the benefice of Sherborne in Gloucester.[1] About the same time Persons, his junior, being about to take his degree, dealt with him, for he was then proctor, to pass over the Oath of Supremacy in the ceremony. Campion was ready to do so, but the presence of another official, who was a zealous Protestant, prevented the execution of his plan, and Persons, according to the fashion of the day, took the oath against his convictions. The incident is not unimportant, as indicating how tests which would seem to us sufficient to have excluded every single Catholic from the University might occasionally be eluded.

Another sidelight on the life of Catholic students at Oxford at this period may be found in the autobiography of Father Thomas Fitzherbert of Swynnerton. Born about 1552, he must have had a truly pious upbringing, could remember praying in boyhood for the grace of martyrdom, and made his first Communion at ten, being carefully prepared by his mother. If such a one was sent to Oxford at an early age, we may conclude that his parents considered the place as adapted (so far as the time would permit) for Catholic education, and on arrival he was put into communication with a Catholic confessor, "an aged and not very learned priest." Hitherto he had never heard a Protestant sermon, but now curiosity tempted him to go. He asked his confessor for advice, and was told that he might if he went to listen only, not to pray or participate. He went and took his place, but at the very first word of the Protestant preacher his old aversion was roused; he fled, becoming more determined than ever to bear himself as a Catholic, and to encourage others to do the same. This brought him into difficulties, which are not clearly described; but he was driven, amongst other shifts, to hide for long periods, which must have brought his University life to an end, and he was finally confined to prison.[2]

From scattered information of this sort we gather that among many circles of young men who came from Catholic

---

[1] He compounded for the first-fruits of this, March 3, 1568–1569. R.O., *Composition Books*, 1560–1566, Series iii.

[2] Foley, *Records of Society of Jesus*, ii. 210, 211.

homes the old religion was still held in honour, and that, in spite of the earlier visitations, there was also a considerable leavening of Catholics among the dons, who protected Catholicism in their *entourage*, so far as they dared. Wood, for instance, tells of William Wyott, sub-rector of Exeter College, who, merely for refusing to accuse his subordinates (against whom no evidence was forthcoming), was confined first in the Castle, then in Bocardo, from January to March 1570, "to the great impoverishing of his health," as the chronicler dryly remarks, saying nothing of the gross injustice, and of the violation of University rights, which such treatment involved.[1]

One result of all this harshness was to drive out a considerable number of those who were Catholicly minded, and of these many had the courage to go over and throw in their lot with Allen, whose high aims and hospitality, in spite of his poverty, were well known at the University. The *Douay Diaries* begin to record the arrival of these non-priests in 1570, until, in 1574, mention is made of twelve having come over in one ship. It was only constant want of funds which prevented Allen from enlarging his college to considerable dimensions. As it was, the Seminary began with many names that were to be afterwards famous in the mission-field as martyrs or writers—Campion, Mayne, Ford and Martin, Holt, Hart, Turner, Morton, Colleton and others. The advantage to be derived from their zeal and talents was, however, still a matter for the future; for the moment their presence seemed only to add to the pressure of Allen's poverty, and to multiply witnesses to the thoroughness of the Tudor oppression. What accounts they would have given of the state of Catholics at home may be learnt from a contemporary tract by an unknown Catholic exile, which appeared in January 1573.[2]

---

[1] Wood, *Antiquitates*, 1674, p. 291. Cf. *Lives of the Martyrs*, Ven. James Fenn.

[2] *A Treatise of Treasons against Queen Elizabeth*, 1572, f. 162 b. This work gives a full and valuable picture of the political feelings of the English Catholic party. All the blame for their misfortunes is laid on Cecil and Bacon; Elizabeth and the nobility are excused; the excommunication is not mentioned. Cecil made many efforts to discover the author's name, but in vain. It is an answer to a pamphlet by "R. G.," issued October 13, 1571, which supported the execution of the Duke of Norfolk. This pamphlet I have not been able to identify.

" For, besides the late extreme executions in the North, in Norfolk, and about London (above the measures of the delicts, because most of them were Catholics), and besides all your prisons pestered with Noblemen and Gentlemen, no man almost wotteth why—besides this (I say), where few, or none to speake of, can pass from town to town unsearched : where no letter almost goeth from friend to friend unopened : where no man's talk with other scant scapeth unexamined : where it is accounted treason, rebellion and sedition to have or to see, to send or to receive, to keep or to hear any letter, book or speech, that might show you any part, either of this conjuration, or of the crafts and falsehoods used to bring it to pass :—yea, when the just commendation of any Nobleman among ourselves (whom these base fellows do envy or malign) is accounted a crime and derogation to your Queen : and where any man that justly imputeth any of these disorders unto those Catalines is taken and punished, as an attributor of the governance from your Queen to a subject—can any man, that hath will or judgement, see other therein than thraldom and slavery ?   Yea, what servitude can be greater ?   What governance can be further from clemency or mercy ? "

It is clear on all sides that the Catholics were extremely depressed during those heavy years 1572 and 1573.   Considering their lack of resisting power (such as was afterwards developed under the new religious influences), it may be thought that their fortunes were never at a lower ebb. But this very abasement occasioned a slight relief.   Cecil and the Protestants became less anxious about a seemingly moribund political reaction ; and before the end of 1573 most of the Catholic prisoners who had been immured in consequence of the Northern Rising and Ridolfi's plots were allowed their liberty.   At the same time a prison was begun for the detention of constant Catholics.   On the 11th of March, 1572, the half-ruined castle of Wisbech was commandeered from the Bishop of Ely for that purpose ; but we have no early prison list to show who were sent there, if, indeed, any were consigned there in this year.   Perhaps this policy of internment did not for the time seem necessary. On the 1st of July, 1574, Bishop Watson, half blind and half crippled, the only Catholic bishop who survived, was allowed to go to his brother John, where, however, he was to remain close, and under some sort of pledge "not to meddle with any person in matters of religion." [1]

§ 3. *Return of the Seminarists* (1574–1579)

All through these depressing years the problem at Douay had been growing graver and graver. What should be done with the scholars who had gathered round Allen? Many had completed their studies, but no future opened out before them, while promising younger men could not be received for want of room.

At last one of them, "named Mr. Barlow (and sure it ought to be remembered to his perpetual praise), offered to go into England, and to prove [*i. e.* probe, find out] what spiritual good might be done there, and if he found hope of profit to call for more. And so he did, and hath showed himself since a most constant confessor of Christ, suffering imprisonment many years for the truth of His Catholic cause." [2]

This happened in the year 1574, and we now see that Mr. Louis Barlow's return coincided with the period of greatest depression among the Catholics taken as a whole, but also with the appearance of certain better signs. The Government were slightly relaxing their cruelties, and the reaction consequent on the excommunication was slowly kindling new warmth in the minds of the more fervent.

No sooner had the new priests returned, than the wisdom and advantage of the step became clear. The year 1575, for which a Jubilee was proclaimed by Pope Gregory XIII, was in many ways a year of awakening for Catholic England. The Rev. Henry Shaw, one of the first to return, told Allen in December of this year, that—

[1] T. E. Bridgett, *The Catholic Hierarchy deposed by Queen Elizabeth*, 1889, pp. 174, 186.
[2] Persons' *Memoirs*, *C.R.S.*, ii. 190; Knox, *Douay Diaries*, p. 24.

" So many men came to him to be reconciled from all sides, and with such earnestness, that he really had no time to think of anything else. They welcome him cordially, they take him in so gladly everywhere, and treat him so kindly, that he, having expected something very different when he started hence for England, now praises their piety, and is full of gratitude. At first he had thought of moving on immediately, but cannot bring himself to do so, in view of their gracious prayers.

" He also stated that the numbers of Catholics are increasing daily so abundantly that even (Lord Burghley), who chiefly, indeed almost alone, bears rule in the State, is looking decidedly askance (*plurimum suspicatur*) at the wonderful and constant growth. In secret he has confessed to a certain noble, that for one staunch and constant Catholic at the opening of Elizabeth's reign, he was sure there were now ten. He sees that he makes no progress by depriving them of honours and dignities, nor by confiscation of goods, bonds, prisons, or exile—not even death can terrify them. People think, therefore, that he is now inclined to welcome the coming Catholic movement, if he can see his way to ensure his own safety. Many of the nobility, too, wish us well, and desire to be commended in our prayers.

" He further writes that the condition of our people is very sad and miserable. It is now some time since, blinded by the snares and lies of the heretics, they have indulged in vices of every sort; so that (when) recalled to the unity of the Catholic Faith, they recognise their previous state, they are deeply grieved, and vehemently detest heresy and all its iniquities." [1]

" Hope springs eternal in the human breast," and the hopes of Mr. Shaw, we see, were very human. But that does not diminish the value of his evidence in regard to what was passing before his eyes. The Catholic revival had begun. On the other hand, Lord Burghley was very far indeed from welcoming the new movement. On the contrary, the Privy Council, in which he had so much influence, was constantly more and more active in urging

[1] Knox, *Douay Diaries*, pp. 98, 99.

S

on the persecution.   Walsingham, too, since the end of 1573,
had his place on the Council; and to him perhaps, even
more than to Cecil, should be ascribed the increased barbarity which now ensued.   The first outbreak took place
before the return of the Seminarists.   On Palm Sunday,
April 4, 1574, a carefully planned attack was made simultaneously on various Catholic houses in London; and to
say nothing of the sufferings of the lesser folk, three ladies,
Lady Guilford, Lady Morley and Lady Browne, were consigned to the Tower, and four Marian priests to close
custody.[1]

In 1575, as soon as the seminarists had begun their
mission, measures of even greater severity and on a large
scale were resorted to.   In the summer the recusants of the
Midlands were attacked in a body.   Representatives were
summoned to the Star Chamber, and determined efforts
were made to enforce conformity, with what degree of
success is not recorded.

Nevertheless the revival was spreading rapidly.   Letters
received at Douay at the end of 1576 declared that the
number of converts "almost exceeded belief," that one
priest had reconciled as many as eighty on a single day, and
that the young men whom Allen was now sending in,
though at first they had been regarded with some suspicion,
were doing extremely well.   George Blackwell, the future
arch-priest, was especially commended, so was Mr. Licentiate
Wright.   They were both in prison ere long, but even there
Wright effected so much that he wrote to ask Allen for
priests to help him.   Looking at the same movement, but
from an opposite point of view, the Bishop of Chichester
wrote to Cecil that "those backward in religion grow worse
and worse." [2]

A paper is extant,[3] written by Allen himself at this
period, on the work in progress for the conversion of

---

[1] Dasent, *Acts of Privy Council*, viii. 218.   Lady Browne seems to
have been the most courageous, as she held out for four years; her servant,
Mrs. Barham, remained constant till the end of 1578 (*ibid.*, x. 204, 438).

[2] *Douay Diaries*, pp. 114, 143.   Bishop Coortesse to Walsingham
(*Domestic Calendar*, p. 539), March 24, 1577.

[3] *C.R.S.*, ix. 62–69.   As it is evidently written in order to be explained
orally, perhaps by himself, to the then General of the Jesuits, the form of
the paper is that of an abstract.

England, from which we learn his views and hopes in some detail.   First he speaks of the country : There are large tracts, especially in the north and west, and a considerable number of towns (including Lincoln and Winchester), where priests might effect much good.   There was no county where they had not some place of refuge, and resident missionaries had been sent to many likely and some less promising stations, including Cambridge.   " Even in the most heretical districts occasions are not wanting for helping on the cause." " Indeed, there is no town in which a prudent, devoted man may not reap a rich harvest for the Catholic faith."   In London, especially among the students of the Inns of Court, " our men have, these last years, made wonderful headway, both by personal intercourse—for nowhere do men lie hid more safely than in London—and still more by books in the vulgar tongue, written in Belgium and imported. Even at Court Catholics have their patrons."   Allen does not enumerate his friends, as Ridolfi did, by copying out half the peerage, but he names fourteen great families, omitting their titles, and adds that there are more, in every county some.   For the future his hopes are chiefly founded on his College of Douay, with its good commencement, its excellent reputation, traditions, and teaching.   With its present pension from the Pope, it may turn out about ten priests a year : " If only funds were sufficient, almost every one in England would offer themselves.   As it is, we have to turn half of them back."   Finally he touches on the subject of the Jesuits joining in the work, and mentions, as likely men, the two Rastalls (connections of Blessed Thomas More), Gaspar Heywood (son of the epigrammatist), and especially Edmund Campion, " whom his countrymen consider a most brilliant orator, of very ready wit."

In matters of Church government the Popes began from 1576 onwards to deal with Allen as the ecclesiastical leader of the English Catholics.   It has already been pointed out that when government through the ancient hierarchy became impossible, the Holy See began to grant faculties at first directly to individuals, then to little groups of clergy, who had powers of sub-delegation (Chap. III, § 2).   Allen was not included in the earliest of these groups (1564 and 1567), but he was included by Pius V in a later group of three before 1572.[1]

During the first years of Gregory XIII, while the College of Douay was still in its minority and undertaking no active work for England, nothing is heard of its president.[2] About 1573 he is grouped second with Owen Lewis and Dr. Stapleton.[3] On the 30th of August, 1575, the work of the college being now well known, faculties are conveyed to " the Rector of the English Seminary," and to him alone, by formal brief; and after this we do not find any other Englishman in those parts entrusted with these powers, while Allen is gradually given all the faculties usually entrusted to Archbishops and heads of churches.

In April 1575 the generous Pope Gregory XIII made a grant of one hundred crowns (increased in 1581 to one hundred and fifty crowns) per month to the Seminary. This foundation enabled the college to tide over many a trial which amid the ever-growing bankruptcy in England would otherwise have been fatal.

From 1575 onwards, therefore, the English Catholics were no longer the same shepherdless flock which they had been for so many years. They had a head and an organisation, very informal, it is true, but respected and efficient; and the new priests, though so few in number, had a spirit which made itself, before long, felt by friends and foes

---

[1] No grant by Pius V to Allen has been preserved integrally; but a seventeenth-century summary of " All the faculties granted to Cardinal Allen, both before and after his promotion " to the cardinalate (*Letters of Cardinal Allen*, p. 361) mentions the above grant under Section A. Section B, however, appears to go too far. It states that Allen " was placed over all these missions, with all the power, spiritual and ministerial, necessary in such a case." But the first missionary, Barlow, did not start for England till 1574, *i. e.* after St. Pius's death. The Pope could not have placed Allen over missions not yet begun. The seventeenth-century *rédacteur* has probably placed some undated paper too early in the series.

[2] In the petition of 1572, mentioned above, Allen signs third out of thirteen. In an undated petition for faculties, probably about 1573, he is mentioned sixth out of ten, and only as " Doctor of Theology and Professor." This petition dwells on the dearth of parish priests, which is such that Catholics in need of the sacraments will get confused and confess to any priest, even to those without faculties, *ignaris aliquando et falsis fratribus* (Arch. Vat., *F. Castello*, xiv. 2, 25).

[3] We do not know the exact date, but the older form is reproduced in the extended faculties of 1578 (*Letters of Cardinal Allen*, p. 70). There was another, still inedited, paper of faculties for him, August 5, 1579, see *Index Brevium*, Arch. Vat., Arm. li. 24, n. 477.

alike.   The response made by the latter was a sharp increase
in severity.

In June 1577 John Aylmer, now Bishop of London,
wrote to Walsingham on the need of greater severity:
" The Papists increase in number and obstinacy."   Imprisonment, "by sparing their housekeeping, greatly enricheth
them."   Crushing fines, he suggests, would be more effective.
Elizabeth, however, must be carefully managed.   She should
be told that it will bring " a thousand pounds by the year
to her coffers ";   but she must also be " given to understand that it is meant to touch both sides indifferently,"
i. e. both Papists and Puritans, " or else you can guess what
will follow."   In reality this deceiver does not speak of
any except of Papists, and he cautions Walsingham that
" her Majesty must herein be made to be *animo obfirmato*, or
else nothing will be done, and all our travail will be turned
into a mockerie."   We shall come before long to the small
results which then followed on the bite-sheep's suggestion.
Perhaps this was because Elizabeth could not yet " be made
animo obfirmato " against those who still clung to the old
faith.   In any case, the *modus operandi* of the persecutors,
and the circumstances which mitigate Elizabeth's guilt,
are here clearly illustrated.[1]

The Lords of the Council, the real leaders of the persecution, held various consultations,[2] in which, according to the
ordinary promptings of cruelty, they resolved to bring
increased pressure to bear on those whom the Catholics
chiefly venerated.   So Bishop Watson, with Abbot Feckenham, and such clergy as the two Harpsfields and Dr.
Young, Weston and Smithson, " who had had a little liberty
for several months past " [3] (though even then most had
to put in periodical appearances before the Council), were
sent back to confinement under the Protestant bishops,
July 24, 1577.[4]

[1] R.O., *Dom Eliz.*, cxiv. 22.   Printed in full, *C.R.S.*, xxii. no. 1.
[2] See Bridgett, *Deposed Hierarchy*, pp. 177–9.
[3] Knox, *Douay Diaries*, p. 127 (August 1577).
[4] Dasent, *Acts of Privy Council*, viii. 371; ix. 8, 54, 123, 145, 161, 388,
etc.   In October 1579 there was a report that the gentle Abbot John
Feckenham had " broken out " against Elizabeth's " godly proceedings."
The Lords of the Council thereupon ordered the Bishop of Ely to make

News of this reached the Douay Seminary about the same time as that of the arrest of Cuthbert Mayne. He was priest in the house of Mr. Tregian at Golden, near Truro, in Cornwall, and the Council was resolved to proceed with him to extremities.[1] The priest was martyred with great cruelty (November 29, 1577), the legal charge against him being that he had a copy of the Indulgences for the Jubilee of 1575, two years before,[2] while his host was beggared and imprisoned for life.[3]

Rough measures were taken, first with the Recusants, then with their wives, then even with their children. Both men and women were called into court, and pressed by threats to conform, some of the more constant being even imprisoned, especially at York.[4] Many children were consigned to Protestant teachers for education in the new religion. This war on the weak was perhaps more degrading than any other excesses of the persecution.

Thomas Sherwood, martyred in 1578, as we should say " a boy " of twenty-seven, was pitifully racked and locked up in the dungeon with the rats, by the special order of the Privy Council.

These crimes of cruelty and violence were multiplying fast. For instance, we find orders from the Privy Council to

---

his imprisonment " close " (*i. e.* solitary), and his food, "which their Lordships wishe to be no larger than may serve his convenient sustenance," is to be brought by a special warder (*ibid.*, xi. 290).

[1] Though Mayne was a man of singularly gentle and lovable character, it was known as early as June 1576 that if caught he would be handled with savagery (*Douay Diaries*, p. 106); it would seem because of his great success in making converts, against whom " the heretics were wont to go furiously mad " (*vehementer insanire*).

[2] By a statute of 1571 (13 Elizabeth), it was high treason to bring Bulls into England. The manifold inapplicability, however, of the Act to this case is well shown by the contemporary paper, *Troubles*, i. 115–18.

[3] Morris, *Troubles*, i. 59–140. Franciscus Plunquetus, O. Cist., *De Vita Francisci Tregeon*, Lisbon, 1655 (British Museum, 867, c. 20). Camm, *Lives of the English Martyrs*, ii. 204–23. Francis Tregian (from whom there is a letter, Titus B. vii. 46) is said by his grandson, Plunkett, to have received, when young, from the Queen an invitation to illicit intercourse; and she is stated to have shown no mercy afterwards, because of his refusal. But this does not appear in the contemporary accounts. Mayne's mass-stuff appears to have been consecrated by Dr. Watson (*Troubles*, i. 85), and thus their two cases may have aggravated each other. It is interesting to find Watson actually exercising episcopal functions; later on he said, in effect, that he had not meddled with Protestants, and would not encourage " resorters " (Bridgett, p. 186).

[4] Morris, *Troubles*, iii. 248–68 : all referring to 1576–1578.

drag Recusants to church,[1] and John Tippet, son of Mr. Mark Tippet of St. Wenn, Cornwall, and a Douay student, was flogged through the city at the cart's tail, and his ear bored with a hot iron.[2]

The second martyr among the Seminarists, John Nelson, suffered on the 3rd of February, 1578.[3] At the same time (October 1577 to February 1578) the first steps were taken to realise Aylmer's suggestion of Recusant fines. Returns of recusants were sent in from the different counties.[4] The total returned was 1387. The smallness of this figure cannot, of course, be explained at this distance of time, but we must remember that the lists are primarily intended to show, not how many were Recusants, but who might be *fined* for recusancy. They do not pretend to give a religious census, as we should now understand those words. They only tell us that 1387 Catholics (mostly heads of families) have been marked out for oppression by fines; but for whatever reason, let us hope through Elizabeth's humanity, no further steps were taken for three years. An interesting census of Catholic prisoners in London was also made for this period; most of the returns, which comprise one hundred and ninety names in all, are still extant.[5]

As to the sufferings outside London, comparatively few researches have as yet been made, but the papers published by Father Morris, from the records of the Mayor's Court at York,[6] give us an only too vivid idea of the oppression which these provincial tyrants exercised when the higher powers were urging them forward. Henry Hastings, Lord Huntingdon, had become Lord President of the North in 1572, and there is a general agreement that of all Elizabeth's ministers he was the most active and remorseless, and as

---

[1] Dasent, *Acts of Privy Council*, x. 340, 342.

[2] *Douay Diaries*, p. 149, *C.R.S.*, ii. 71–80. He afterwards became Procurator-General of the Carthusians.

[3] Bede Camm, *Lives of the English Martyrs*, ii. 222.

[4] R. O., *Dom. Eliz.*, vols. cxvii. to cxx.; they are now being printed by the *C.R.S.* The general table is cxixx. 20. The inquisition is described in the *Douay Diaries*, November 14, 1577, p. 130. It had been agreed to in the Parliament of 1576 (*Spanish Calendar*, p. 526), but the matter did not pass into law.

[5] *C.R.S.*, i. 61–72, 1577–1580.

[6] Morris, *Troubles of our Catholic Forefathers*, iii. 340, etc. Lord Huntingdon's extant letters show clearly his fanatical character.

he continued in power for twenty-three years, the ruin he succeeded in accomplishing was great indeed.[1]

Lancashire, somewhat more remote from the tyranny of the Crown and the oppression of the Council of North, had preserved its ancient faith in many homes, and through the labours of Allen, Laurence Vaux and others, kept up a better struggle in the matter of church-going than any other county. It was here that the Counter-Reformation first came into evidence,[2] and that the strongest stand was made by the gentry [3] against the rising persecution.

There were some memorable proceedings at Oxford, July 4 to 6, 1578, which were often recalled by Catholics, because, on that occasion, by the judgment of God, the persecutors suffered incomparably more than their victims. A well-known Catholic book-binder at Oxford, by name Roland Jenks, was sentenced to have his ears cut, when there was a sudden outbreak of gaol-fever. Men began to fall down in court, and in a few days no less than three hundred persons had perished in Oxford, and two hundred in its environs, including the whole of the jury and of the bench of Justices.[4] Jenks escaped the fever, but not the cruel punishment. He will reappear in the history of Edmund Campion, and he eventually retired abroad, and bound books in one of the seminaries.

The chief records of the persecution are lost. They should have been preserved by the courts of the various ecclesiastical commissions, to which Elizabeth's Government entrusted the work of wearing down the constancy of the faithful. But these papers are no longer forthcoming, and they are generally supposed to have perished, together with those of the Star Chamber (except the *Privy Council Registers*), during the Puritan revolution. The *Privy Council Registers*

---

[1] See the character given of him by one who was living under his tyranny, in Morris, *Troubles*, iii. 66–102.

[2] In Lancashire the people "revolt to popery" (Bishop Barnes to Cecil, October 22, 1570, R.O., *Dom Eliz.*, lxxiv. 22; *Domestic Calendar*, p. 395).

[3] The documents relating to Lancashire Recusants are very numerous. Chetham Soc. Publications: T. E. Gibson, *Crosby Records*, N.S. 12, and J. Harland, *Lancashire under Tudors*, etc. (vols. xlix. and l.), and many unpublished papers at the Record Office.

[4] Stow, *Annales*, ed. Howe, 1631, p. 681.

are the most important collection that we have. They show orders to persecute issued on all sides. But we are not yet able to complete the picture by showing how those orders were executed. When the *Registers* of the Anglican bishops become more accessible to students, we shall probably be able to take another step forward.

The persecution was, indeed, destined to grow much worse later; and some there would be who, for controversial reasons, would imply or assert that the persecution did not begin till after the period 1575 to 1580.[1] But they either had a cause to plead, or had no personal experience of the times. Certainly it is impossible to read the records of the Privy Council without perceiving that it was as resolute in cruelty then as at any time, though their operations were not yet on the same large scale as afterwards. Again, the instruments, that is, the persecutors of lower rank, the Topcliffes, the Fleetwoods, the Youngs, were not yet very numerous, nor were the spies as multitudinous as they became later. The persecution was not so extensive; but there was hardly any savagery in subsequent years for which a precedent cannot be found in these; and there were several cases of mean cruelty practised at this early period which were happily not repeated. Among these unusual features was the Queen's visit to Norwich in the summer of 1578.

In her progress Elizabeth stayed with, or was attended by, quite a number of Catholic squires. But after she had partaken of their hospitality or given them her hand to kiss, the Lord Chamberlain in the first case (that of Edward Rookwood of Euston), stepping forward, proceeded to bully and insult his host in the presence of the assembled people, and finally bade him follow the Court as a prisoner, until he should be put into confinement at Norwich. Other victims were picked out from the gentry who came to show

---

[1] Lord Burghley, in many tracts written to prove that the persecution was due to the treasons of Catholics, not to the bigotry of the Protestants, puts the active measures of the Popes, especially the Irish expedition, *before* the repressive measures against the Seminarists (cf. *Execution of Justice in England*, 1675, pp. 38, etc.). The unreliable appellant priest, William Watson, passionate enemy of the Jesuits, improved on Lord Burghley by maintaining that persecution began after the coming of the Jesuit missionaries (*Important Considerations*, 1675, p. 65. See also p. 62).

their loyalty, and the supreme governess of English Protestantism had at last a dozen Catholic prisoners to grace her triumphant train.

Rookwood's case, of which we know many details, was especially revolting. He was newly married, and had lately come of age; but as the hour for the Queen's departure drew nigh, an excuse was made for searching his house, and in a haystack an old statue of Our Lady was found. This was dramatically brought before the Queen, who ordered it to be broken up and burnt at once, and the command was executed amid the cheers of the Puritans, though not without some manifestation of horror on the part of the Catholics.

These deliberate and repeated outrages on humanity and hospitality were doubtless made in order to impress on the Catholics of Norfolk the lesson of the victory now won by the Protestant revolution. It was the steady adherence of the men of East Anglia to the *ancien régime* at the accession of Queen Mary which had preserved the throne of England for the Tudors, and threw back the new religionists for the moment. But William Cecil, who was secretary to John Dudley, Duke of Northumberland, in 1553, and Robert Dudley, the son of the latter, were now in power; while their victims were either the very men who were then foremost to save the Tudor line or their representatives. Sir Henry Jerningham and Sir Henry Bedingfeld had then been the first to rise, and the latter still survived. But he, with other members of both families, was made to drink deep of the cup of humiliation, and so were a dozen more.[1]

One is happy to be able to add that the peculiar brutality shown on this visit to Norwich, as it had not occurred before, was also not repeated afterwards. Next year the Queen was occupied with the French match, and in her communications with the French ambassador, she repeatedly gave him to understand that cruelty to the Catholics was not to her liking, which was doubtless true. From the beginning of

---

[1] Jessopp, *One Generation of a Norfolk House*, 1878, p. 61. Lodge, *Illustrations*, 1838, ii. 220. The special vengeance on the Bedingfelds might also be connected with the selection by Mary of Sir Henry Bedingfeld as Elizabeth's warden after Wyatt's rebellion in 1554.

1579 there was a diminution in the rising flood of persecution, and at that point we may pause in our painful record of cruelty and oppression.

§ 4. *The Counter-Reformation and the Migration to Rheims*

We now come to a question of the greatest importance. Though the persecution was more grievous than ever before, the Catholics, both those at home (so far as one may generalise about so scattered a body), and especially the new priests coming from Douay, were inspired by a new and unconquerable enthusiasm. Heretofore but few had had the courage to resist the pressure of the Crown; now heroic confession of the faith was frequent, and the Catholics were clearly gaining ground. Whence had that new spirit come? The answer is, that it was due to the Counter-Reformation, which, spreading from Rome through the Council of Trent, was gradually permeating all nations in union with the Apostolic See. The spirit which was stirring in England was the same as that which was simultaneously sending missionaries to China and Japan, to America and the Indies,[1] which was rolling back the Reformation in Germany itself, and was everywhere building up a more vigorous generation of Catholics by a new system of education.

It followed, therefore, that, for the success of Allen's plans, he must infuse as much as possible of this noble enthusiasm into his followers, and keep them free from anything that might interfere with its inspirations. Such obstacles were unfortunately many, and chief among them the wars of religion, which so often broke in upon the peace of France and Flanders, and which were to prevent the full effects

[1] Young Englishmen were then becoming Jesuits in order to go to such foreign missions, and Father Persons was keen on " diverting them towards a certain Northern India " (*C.R.S.*, ii. 141); yet many demanded " other missions, seeing England is shut to them " (*ibid.*, p. 142). Thus Thomas Stevens got off to India, to work there as a missionary till death. And surely it is remarkable that of the thousands of English who have gone to India, usually to seek a fortune, the first should have gone under this noble inspiration. In a similar spirit John Yate of Lyford (who changed his name to John Vincent) sailed a few months earlier for Brazil (*Foley Records*, vii. 875).

of the Counter-Reformation movement from reaching its
maturity in northern Europe for another generation. Indeed
the very existence of the Church in those two countries
was still to be sometimes in hazard. We have already seen
the political dangers which threatened Spanish power in
Flanders between 1576 and 1578, and we must now see how
those same dangers imperilled the freedom and the very
existence of the Douay College. We shall also see that this
danger led to a new foundation in Rome, partly to supple-
ment the older college, partly also in order to secure a more
abundant influx of the Roman spirit.

The troubles of Flanders, as we have seen, rapidly increasing after the death of Requesens in March 1576, became
very grave indeed after the " Spanish Fury " at Antwerp
in the following November, which was so disastrous in the
sequel for the Spanish fortunes throughout the Netherlands.
The English College, Douay, now fell under the suspicions
of the Nationalists, partly because of the firmness of its
Catholicism, partly because of its having once enjoyed a
Spanish pension, partly because of Allen's high reputation.
He was supposed to be earnest on the side of Spain ; while
Elizabeth and her ministers, the chief patrons of the new
party, would notoriously reckon any disservice done to the
Seminary as a good turn done to them. It does not seem
that any impolitic act was alleged against the Seminarists
or their superiors; it was merely alleged that they had
shown pleasure at the misfortunes of the anti-Spanish party.
They were decried as " friends of Spain," or " traitors to
their own country and to this," [1] and in the existing ferment
nothing could be more perilous. Allen, by the advice of
his friends, left the college, November 8, 1576, and retired
to France, " both to provide for his own safety and also
to look out for a safer place for us." [2]

---

[1] Knox, *Douay Diaries*, p. 303: "Nostræ at alienæ patriæ proditores
appellamur . . . p. 305 . . . fautores Hispanorum."
[2] *Ibid.*, p. 113: Eximius Præses discessit, tum sibi a periculis
cavendi studio, tum potius ut nobis de tutiori loco provideret. There
were many examples of Spaniards and of friends of Spain being murdered
at this crisis (*ibid.*, p. 315), and Allen received a hint that plots were being
laid for him by England (cf. *C.R.S.*, xiii. 481, for plots against Catholic exiles
laid by the English ambassador, Dr. Wilson). Bourchier, *De Martirio,
Fratrum, O.S.F., in Anglia, in Belgio*, etc., 1583, gives several examples
of Franciscans killed at this time.

The concessions made by Don John then brought about a temporary improvement.   Allen was able to return on the 4th of March, 1577.   He did not stop long, however, but went in April to reside on his benefice at Cambray, returning for short visits from time to time.   In truth the peace had been very transitory, and every one foresaw a trial of strength between the two powers.   It came at Gembloux in January 1578.   But though the Spaniards won a great victory, their utter want of organisation prevented their following it up; so that ere long their enemies were stronger than ever, and the danger at Douay was ever increasing.   On March 18, 1578, new magistrates were elected; they were strongly in favour of the Prince of Orange, and the English college students received immediate notice to quit the town.

This blow had been foreseen by Allen, and he had taken the important resolution of transferring his house from the protection of the King of Spain to that of the King of France.[1] Rheims was in those days a university town; it was not so very far from Douay, and was under the protection of the Dukes of Guise, the champions of orthodox Catholicity among the feudal lords of France, who, as cousins of Mary Stuart, might be expected to exert themselves to protect the English Catholics.   Moreover, Rheims was for the moment better situated for communication with England than Douay, because the English and Dutch now controlled Antwerp and every city on the Flemish sea-coast.   So to Rheims Allen called the refugees from Douay, and he was already there to meet them.   The expense of the migration, however, and the losses it involved, prevented the work of the college being continued on the same scale as before. Allen was constrained to send away the oldest priests and the youngest newcomers, keeping only those whose clerical course was already begun.

It was a sad wrench, and the future, too, was dark. Hitherto Allen, like the other exiles, had kept entirely to the lands under Spanish protection.   The many religious wars in France, and Elizabeth's influence over Charles IX, had made that country both uninviting and unsafe to the

[1] Numbers of other Catholics did the same (*Douay Diaries*, p. 113). A long list in *Foreign Calendar*, April 27, 1580, shows three hundred in Paris.

English exiles. The generosity of the Spanish King, moreover, was incomparably greater than that of the French, and
at the same time their mutual jealousies were such that
there was every reason to fear that no Spanish help or
pension would ever be given to a college settled in France.
The migration might give considerable offence. Nevertheless Allen took the risk, writing immediately (April 4) to
Rome to ask for support, in the dire straits in which he
found himself. " I do not see in what place our men can
be placed more apt for missions to England than this is,
until Belgium recovers peace from these disturbances." [1]

Pope Gregory at once took up his cause. He wrote to
the Archbishop of Rheims, he wrote to the canons of the
Cathedral. The nuncio at Paris,[2] instructed by Allen, was
on the watch, lest the English Government should influence
the French Court to the disadvantage of the Seminary.[3]

The Pope's representations were successful. The college
met with a hospitable reception, and immediately settled
down to work again. They did not, indeed, expect to stay
long, and never took any large buildings, but lived in a series
of small houses, which still go by the name of *La Rue des
Anglais*. In point of fact, however, twenty-four years were
to run before they returned.

Yet, half a year later, they were actually being asked to
return by the very town which had ejected them. The
popularity of the magistrates, elected at Douay in the
interest of the Prince of Orange, was short-lived. By
November the men of the old party were back in power, and
invited Allen back; [4] but he neither had money for the
journey nor did he feel confident that Flanders was yet
safe.

An even more attractive invitation to go to Louvain had
come in July, Allen himself having suggested the plan. But
when the time came he had not the courage, amid the general
bankruptcy, to ask for the necessary funds. So the College
stayed on, and the Pope promised (July 1579) that he

---

[1] *Letters of Cardinal Allen*, p. 40.   [2] *Ibid.*, pp. 41–43.
[3] Such representations were, in fact, made on September 5, 1578,
though Rheims is not specified, *Foreign Calendar*, 1578–1579, p. 181.
[4] *Douay Diaries*, p. 147, November 15, 1578.

would himself decide, when the fitting moment for return should arrive, and pay the expenses.[1]

Thus it came that the English colony remained in France, though Allen would gladly, if he could, have returned to the protection of Spain,[2] and in order to retain its favour, wrote to Vendeville long and detailed accounts of the college teaching. In effect King Philip renewed the Spanish pension, which was assigned at 16,000 crowns.[3] Still, so long as the students remained on French soil, Paris rather than Brussels became the centre whence they would assimilate ideas on political and religious government, and in later years this change in the sources of inspiration would make itself deeply felt. Meantime, in view of the acute controversy that arose later between the Spanish and anti-Spanish partisans, it was in itself a noteworthy thing that Allen should not have hesitated to come to France and to remain there when circumstances made it advisable so to do.

Very real as were the trials incident to this retreat from Douay—" our second exile, with its multiplied griefs," [4] as Allen feelingly called it—they were well compensated by the establishment of the English College at Rome; for the high-water mark of Catholic missionary zeal came with the first mission sent out from that college. Its foundation, however, was accompanied by many minor difficulties, to which we must now turn.

§ 5. *The English College, Rome*, 1578–1579

When the multitude of English pilgrims, who used in the Middle Ages to be ever on the road to and from Rome, dwindled down to a few occasional wanderers, the idea must have occurred to many that the hospices founded for their benefit in Rome [5] might well be turned into a Seminary for

---

[1] *Douay Diaries*, p. 154. In May 1579 Allen wrote, " God knows what will become of these Low Countries " (*Letters*, p. 81).

[2] Allen wrote, " We should have been exceedingly glad to be in the dominions of his Catholic Majesty, since on many accounts France does not seem to be such a convenient place for us Englishmen, though we have met with the greatest kindness and affection from ecclesiastics and others in this city " (*Douay Diaries*, p. lv, July 27, 1578).

[3] *Ibid.*, p. lv, n. But how regularly it was paid we do not hear.

[4] *Cardinal Allen's Letters*, p. 50.

[5] The hospice of Holy Trinity was founded in 1351, that of St. Edmund

training priests for England. We find this mooted about 1568, probably by Dr. Maurice Clenog ;[1] and Allen must have come to some agreement about the matter during his visit to Rome in 1576, for as soon as he had returned to Douay, he began to send detachments of students thither, with Dr. Gregory Martin to look after them.[2] They appear to have lived under Dr. Maurice, then its warden, some in the hospice, some in a neighbouring house hired for the purpose.

We must now look more carefully to the characters of the leaders in the English colony; for the developments which now ensued were due very largely indeed to their personal qualities. The most illustrious of them was Dr. Owen Lewis, a Welshman of brilliant talents, which always brought him into notice wherever he might be, at Winchester or Oxford, at Douay, Rome or Milan; and he died prematurely, Bishop of Cassano, with expectations of the cardinalate. We shall meet with him repeatedly, and yet it will not be easy to make up our minds about him, for perplexing comparisons between him and the other English Catholic leaders will frequently and inevitably suggest themselves. We have already met with him as the promoter of the expeditions of Stukely and Fitzgerald, and this had so far brought him no little credit. Stukely had sailed in January 1578, and as the Pope was at first extremely sanguine of success, Lewis's star was very much in the ascendant. He was already a canon of Cambray, archdeacon of Hainault, and a referendary at the papal court. Allen was his sincere friend, and Lewis had helped the Seminary of Douay in many ways. Though he had no official superiority over the rising college, his patronage was in effect all-important, and its fate was in his hands.[3]

The most conspicuous English scholar in Rome was Dr. Gregory Martin, whom Allen had sent, possibly with a

---

in 1391. They were united in 1463. The English College is on the site of the Holy Trinity Hospice. St. Edmund's was eventually let for the college benefit. Its door still stands, Via dei Genovesi, 22.

[1] *C.R.S.*, ix. 69.

[2] *Douay Diaries*, p. liv. There are four valuable inedited contemporary papers in the Westminster Archives referring to this early period, vol. ii. pp. 31–37, and 105–10.

[3] There are biographies of Lewis in *D.N.B.* and in Gillow; and at Simancas (Estado, 959) there is a memorial by Lewis including autobiographical matter.

view to his being the rector of the new establishment.[1] But he was perhaps rather a literary man than a born ruler. Studious, retiring, amiable, he much resembled Edmund Campion, his close friend at St. John's, and still his intimate correspondent.[2] After the migration to Rheims, in April 1578, Allen at once recalled him to teach,[3] and it was at Rheims that he completed the great work of his life, the translation of the New Testament.

The return of Martin left Maurice Clenog as actual head of the college.[4] Maurice Clenog, again, was a Welshman of some mark, having been a Professor of Law at Oxford, Chancellor of the Prerogative Court at Canterbury, and Bishop-nominate of Bangor, before Elizabeth's accession led to the extinction of the ancient hierarchy. He then retired abroad, and was appointed companion to Vincent Parpaglia for his abortive mission to Elizabeth (1560); after which he went to Rome, and was warden of the English Hospice, in 1565, 1566, and again between 1576 and 1578. He presented to Gregory XIII at various times a series of schemes for the restoration of the faith in England [5] which show him to have been a man of vigour and straightforward-ness, not afraid of blows on behalf of a cause that he considered good. Unfortunately he was not an educationalist—not one to whom the sole authority over forty vigorous and excitable young Elizabethans could be safely confided.

[1] Biographies in *D.N.B.* and Gillow.

[2] Knox, *Douay Diaries*, pp. 308–20, prints seven letters from Martin to Campion. Several of Campion's answers are among his *Opuscula*. The correspondence throws a valuable light on the inner life of Catholic scholars at this period. While in Rome he wrote *Roma Sancta*, still in MS. at Ugbrooke Park, Devon, which contains a full account of the foundation of the college.

[3] In his letter of May 21, 1577 (*Douay Diaries*, p. 316), Martin says he is to depart at once. Allen thought of sending Dr. Bristow in his place after the summer (*ibid.*, also *Letters*, p. 79).

[4] The date on Maurice's patent as rector seems to have been *May* 1578, the very month that Martin left (Tierney's Dodd, ii. cccliv). For his biography, see *D.N.B.*

[5] Arch. Vat., Arm. lxiv., 28, ff. 193, 205; and nine pieces between 332 and 371. None are signed, and Clenog's hand is very like Sander's, which makes them difficult to identify. The dates would be from 1572 to 1575. Unpublished biographical material will be found Westminster Archives, ii. 108–10.

[6] " Mr. Morrice, his government, I think verily, and do partly know also, that it was insufficient for such a multitude. And how could it be other-wise, he being alone, without help, and never practised in such a manage before? " (Persons to Allen, March 30, 1579). Allen to Lewis: " Right sorry we were of the error that Mr. Maurice was made rector " (*Letters of Cardinal Allen*, pp. 74, 79).

T

When things began to go wrong, the English would be sure to say, as in fact they did, that Owen Lewis had got him the post because he was a Welshman.

Being in need of help, the Pope and the Cardinal Protector asked the Father-General of the Jesuits, May 1578, for the loan of two fathers for two months. It seemed quite a simple and obvious thing to do, for the Jesuits were " the handy men " of the time in the ecclesiastical sphere, ready for anything, especially in matters educational. Father Mercurian agreed at once, for the Pope's word was law; but he represented that the calls upon him were very numerous, and as soon as the two months were over he desired to recall his men, little realising how long the work begun was destined to continue, how much it would increase.[1]

This time it was Dr. Lewis and the scholars who called for their retention; the former because he knew that, in its present state, the college could not get on without them; the latter because they had become sincerely attached to their teachers. These scholars were a very exceptional body. They numbered over thirty English, and eight or nine Welsh. Of the English, ten were priests, whose average age was twenty-nine, and of the rest, only three were under twenty. They had all passed through the severe training of persecution, in which many had shown great heroism. Some were Oxford graduates and tutors of several years' standing; more than one of these was probably as capable of ruling the house as Dr. Maurice himself, if not more so. In the future martyr, Ralph Sherwin, they had a born leader of exceptional courage, eloquence and enthusiasm. It will be impossible to understand the course which affairs were now to take unless we advert to the influence exercised imperceptibly by such a body of vigorous and high-minded young men.

The united representations of Dr. Lewis and the scholars had their effect: Padre Giovanni Paolo Novarola, the

---

[1] Persons, *Domestical Difficulties* (1600), *C.R.S.*, ii. 85. In the confidential letter to Father Good, written at the time, some further reasons are given (*ibid.*, p. 143). As the Jesuits had come before May 21 (*Douay Diaries*, p. 316), their attempted recall would have been in July. But the chronology of recollections, whether of Persons or of others, must not be interpreted too strictly.

"Spiritual Father," and Padre Ferdinando Capecci, the "prefect of studies," or house tutor, as we might say, remained, and in October Allen sent the General a hearty letter of thanks;[1] and the college progressed in spite of difficulties. Of these the most severe was poverty. Pope Gregory had not as yet made an adequate provision for maintenance, and the funds of the hospice were quite inadequate to maintain the new developments.[2] So long as the summer lasted, living on the cheap in Rome was not unendurable. But as winter closed in, and there was no money to provide warmer clothes, or more substantial food, the young men had to contend with real hardship. Dr. Maurice, too, failed to rise to the occasion. Instead of being sympathetic and conspicuously fair in distributing his inadequate stores, he lost his temper when complaints were made to him; and in dispensing his stock of clothing, and so forth, he seemed to favour his Welsh countrymen unduly. Feeling began to run high, and unfortunately developed into a feud between the English and the Welsh, destined to be a calamity to the whole Catholic cause.

Matters came to a head in January 1579. There had been much grumbling at Christmas, when the old chaplains had been ordered to leave the hospice. It was in itself a wise measure, no doubt, but the promised compensation was delayed, and as they were all English, people said it was another case of the English being victims, while the

---

[1] *Letters of Cardinal Allen*, p. 68.

[2] Still Gregory had already granted the Roman College one hundred crowns a month, as much as he gave to Rheims (*Douay Diaries*, p. 316).

The documents for the incidents which follow are very numerous indeed, far in excess of the importance of the events. Somewhere in the Vatican Archives, but at present mislaid, is a volume entitled *De collegiis Urbis et aliis* (*olim*, Arm xi., vol. 94). Its table of contents, however, is preserved in *Concil. Trid.*, vol. 93, ff. 359–65, and shows that it probably comprehends the papers of Cardinal Moroni himself on the whole subject. At the English College, Rome, are a bundle of original drafts of the scholars' petitions (scritture, 29, 23), and a register (Lib., 304) contains corrected copies in more or less chronological order. Father Persons drew largely on this source for his full account in *Domestical Difficulties* (now printed *C.R.S.*, ii. 102, etc.). Unfortunately his chronology was defective, and to understand this one must turn to Richard Haydock's letter (printed in Tierney's Dodd, ii. Ap. 350 to 361), which gives a reliable order for the events from February 24 to March 9. The sequence of the previous events is perhaps best given in Persons' contemporary letter to Good, *C.R.S.*, ii. 142, etc. For the views of Lewis, see Tierney's Dodd, ii. Ap. pp. 361–64; for those of Dr. Maurice, *ibid.*, 372, and *Westminster Archives*, ii. 105–10; for those of Allen, *ibid.*, 365.

Welsh throve. About the 12th of January Padre Novarola was promoted to be rector of the College of Siena, and his departure occasioned the first public discussion of the present system of government. " Why should the Fathers be sent elsewhere? " it was asked; " surely it would be better to give them the entire charge of the college." It is impossible to say where the idea originated. Similar thoughts were in the minds of many, including that of Allen himself.[1]

Now followed a hot debate, lasting over two months, as to the best course to be followed. It is clear that neither the Pope nor the Cardinal Protector had clear ideas as to the right course to follow. They went, in fact, from one extreme to the other. First they threatened the scholars with expulsion; then they allowed these scholars to name a new rector; then they told them to depart in peace; at last they gave them Jesuit government, which they had so long refused. Pope and Cardinal were, on the one hand, sincerely impressed by the character and by the pleadings of the scholars; but on reflection they hesitated, knowing the danger of relaxing the discipline of a college, sympathising with Dr. Maurice's difficulties, and thinking that so clever a man as Owen Lewis, so strongly recommended by Allen,[2] ought to understand the situation better than they did. It is also clear that they were not inclined to give the college permanently to the care of the Jesuits; but we cannot tell whether this was chiefly due to a con-

---

[1] " The committing of the house to the Society was all our desires " (Allen to Lewis, May 12, 1579, *Letters*, p. 79). The petition presented on this occasion is in *Domestical Difficulties*, C.R.S., ii. 102, and Persons' erroneous chronology is there pointed out in a note. It should be added that this memorial does not contain anything about the Jesuits managing the college. That matter had evidently not yet become the chief point, as it did shortly after. But it may have been mentioned already in conversation.

[2] Allen to Pope Gregory and Cardinal Moroni, February 16, 1579, *Letters*, pp. 71–73. Though well satisfied with the issue of the debate, Allen supported Lewis all through, and with emphasis, as these letters show. St. Charles Borromeo, from Milan, did something of the same sort, through his Roman agent, Cesare Spetiano. From the first he had supported the foundation (St. Charles to Spetiano, July 24, 1577), and on January 1, 1579 (that is, just before the troubles began), he wrote again, that the Rettori (plural) of the English College were very thankful for the support received, and he tells Spetiano to continue; and this we know Spetiano did. But it is clear from the dates that the Saint did not then enter into the merits of the case.

sideration for the Society, which certainly did not wish for further engagements at that time, or to the representations of Owen Lewis, who was not less certainly opposed to the plan, or to other reasons which do not now appear.

The final stage began about the end of January, when the Cardinal Protector, in the presence of Dr. Maurice, gave the assembled scholars a very severe scolding for their insubordinate talk. When he had finished, Sherwin arose, and began with great respect to expose their case; but the Cardinal, " a stiffe man," says Persons, " in all that he once resolved or liked of," [1] sternly bade him be seated. Then John Gore, one of the younger men, jumped up and declared that this was the cause of God, and that silence was impossible. The Cardinal, more angry still, turned on the new speaker, and, at Maurice's suggestion, threatened him with summary expulsion. Hereupon Richard Haydock, one of the seniors, arose, and he was followed by the whole body, declaring that they were all of the same mind, and that if one were dismissed all would leave. At this Moroni perceived that he had gone too far, and changing his tone, began to inquire into the grievances, Maurice himself being present, and eventually told them to send in their demands in writing.[2]

This was clearly a considerable success for the scholars, and the Romans, ever ready to admire English freedom, were delighted.

" For there were at (the conference) all the family of the Cardinal, and who did wonder to see such great liberty of speech before so great a personage. And albeit I (Persons) think there must needes pass many excesses, among so much that was spoken in the place by so many youths; yet many men did imagine to see a certain company of *Laurences*, *Sebastians*, and the like intractable fellows, who brought emperors and princes to desperation to deal with them; for that they could neither with giving or taking away, neither

---

[1] *Memoirs, C.R.S.*, ii. 86.
[2] The documents then given up are printed in *Domestical Difficulties* (*C.R.S.*, ii. 104–8). The date may be about the end of January. The defects of Maurice are strongly emphasised, and the Society was asked for, for the first time, in writing. For Maurice's answer see above.

with fair words nor with foul, bring them to condescend to any one little point that they disliked. Many also strangers made this consequent : If these fellows stand thus immovable before such princes in Rome, what will they do in England before the heretics? And many said that they doubted before of things reported of English priests in England, and of their bold answers reported by letter, but now they could believe anything of them." [1]

Nevertheless, the results of this audience were not permanent. When the Archdeacon obtained the Cardinal's ear again, black looks and hard words once more became the order of the day, and Mgr. Spetiano, a prelate of great influence, was sent to offer them an oath of obedience to Dr. Maurice.

This was refused, and in the second week of February (February 8–14) the scholars took a step which was eventually to bring them success—they appealed directly to the Pope, asking him for government by the Jesuits. The Pope received them kindly, promised redress in general terms, and seemed to incline to giving the Jesuits charge over the college, while leaving Maurice over the hospice. [2]

" The next Sunday after (apparently the 15th of February) the Cardinal (Protector) having been with the Pope, called them all to him, and there, in the presence of them all, he accepted Mr. Maurice's resignation, and gave them leave to choose (an Englishman as) a new Governor." [3]

Here again the scholars had scored a great success;

---

[1] Persons, *Domestical Difficulties*, C.R.S., ii. 147.

[2] *Ibid.*, ii. 108, 109, 149.

[3] *Ibid.*, p. 149. The date appears to have been the Sunday week before St. Matthias's Day (February 24), when the second audience with the Pope took place, at Pallia. That the new Governor was to have been English appears from the scholars' answer to the Pope (Tierney's Dodd, ii., Ap. 375). In their answer to Moroni, the scholars say that Dr. Bristow was the only really fit Englishman ; but that he was so occupied at Rheims that he could not be spared (C.R.S., ii. 115).

Afterwards, on March 5, possible rectors were named again. This time the Welsh party named Bristow; the English (as they had previously excluded him) named Morton and Bavand. Tierney (as quoted above) was not aware of the first nomination.

but their pertinacious petitions [1] for government by the
Jesuits made them lose ground again.   On the Feast of
St. Matthias (February 24) four of them walked twenty-two
miles to Pallia, where the Pope had gone for a day or two's
rest, and next morning urged their request again; [2]   but
received a distinctly non-committal answer.   After they
had got back, things went from bad to worse.   Moroni
recalled his offers of the previous week, Maurice was confirmed, and the students were again offered (March 1) an
oath which involved obedience to the Welsh rector.[3]

To enforce this Dr. Maurice that day had his patent
read in the refectory.   This had been granted in the previous
May, but for some reason or other this date was altered in
the document itself to that of the current March.[4]   Arthur
Pitts, the reader, after announcing it, refused to give it back,
and showed the erasure to his companions, whereupon the
cry arose, *Falsatum est !*   An uproar immediately followed;
and the Welsh students, who were even hotter on Dr.
Maurice's side than the others against him, are said to have
grasped their knives with the point downwards, ready (so
their rivals thought) to dirk their nearest opponent.[5]
But the two Jesuit fathers who were present interfered,
and at last peace was restored.

Something had now to be done, and it was decided
(March 2) to send away four English students, in order to
intimidate the rest.[6]   But the contrary result followed :
the English went in a body to the Cardinal, and said that

[1] The Jesuits, and even the General Mercurian, tried to prevent this
insistence, but in vain (*ibid.*, p. 149).
[2] Printed *C.R.S.*, ii., 114–17.   This memorial, with others, pp. 109–
13, had been presented *mutatis mutandis* to the Protector during the
previous week.
[3] *Ibid.*, p. 150.   Another trial had been Moroni's order that each scholar
should write his opinion for himself.   Persons preserves eleven of these
(*ibid.*, pp. 118–20) interesting and evidently sincere testimonies.
[4] This was, no doubt, done quite honestly, and probably had Moroni's
approval; for he had renewed Maurice's rectorial powers.   But to rely
upon an altered date, in order to convince sharp and alert young scholars,
was the sort of blunder of which Dr. Maurice made too many (*ibid.*, p.
150; Tierney's Dodd, ii., Ap. 354).
[5] So both Richard Haydock, Allen and Persons (Tierney's Dodd, ii., Ap.
354, 367; *C.R.S.*, ii. 150).
[6] According to Dr. Lewis they were offered an alternative, " either to
be obedient *absolute et sine ulla restrictione*, and to leave all meddling and
practice in this tumult, or else to depart " (Tierney's Dodd, ii., Ap.
362).   For Haydock's version, *ibid.*, p. 355; Persons, *C.R.S.*, p. 151.

none of them could under the circumstances swear to obey Dr. Maurice. " Then depart in peace, all of you," was the cold but firm answer. Next day (Tuesday) they went to the Pope, who answered similarly, " Go, if you cannot obey." On Ash Wednesday, therefore (March 4), they all left in a body, and leaving their bundles at the house of an Englishman, John Creed, they proceeded to beg in the streets for money to take them to Rheims.

Every one was flocking to church for the feast, and the opening sermons of the Lenten courses; and in a trice the news had spread through the town. There was no lack of sympathy, and many the tear that started to the eye at the sight of these earnest young faces, as they cheerfully begged for money to return and face death for religion's sake.[1] It was at once evident that alms would not be wanting; but in the event they were not needed.

That afternoon they made their way to the Pope for a final audience, and Gregory was no more able than the rest to control his emotions. " The dearest father in Christendom," as one of them afterwards wrote, kept them for half an hour, talking most paternally with them, at first with tears and then with smiles. Finally he sent them back to the college under the protection of Mgr. Bianchetti, a pontifical Maestro di Camera, who had throughout been warmly in their favour.

It was evident that the scholars had now won. Still not even yet had Gregory promised them the government which they desired, and two weeks passed without any change following. The Welsh party now began to declare that they were surely going to succeed after all, and the English sent in a new petition,[2] when, on St. Joseph's Day, the 19th of March, they heard that the General of the Jesuits had been sent for and told that no excuse would be admitted, he must undertake the college; and therewith the struggle

---

[1] *C.R.S.*, ii. 152; Tierney's Dodd, ii., Ap. 357.

[2] On the day after their audience with Gregory, the scholars thought it best to send in the names of two Englishmen in Rome as possible rectors, and the names were Drs. Morton and Bavand (*C.R.S.*, ii. 155; Tierney's Dodd, ii. Ap. 359, 363). Dodd's copy of Haydock's letter must be wrong in reading Bernard for Bavand (Tierney's Dodd, *ut supra*), as Dr. Bernard was then Prefect of Studies at Rheims. About the 18th of March the scholars sent in a strong memorial against Lewis and Maurice, probably that in Tierney's Dodd, ii., Ap. 346 (see *C.R.S.* ii. 157).

was over.[1]   On the Feast of St. George, the 23rd of April,
Mgr. Spetiano, as Cardinal Moroni's representative, together
with the Jesuit Provincial of Rome, and Robert Bellarmine,
the popular professor and future cardinal, came to the
college, and proposed the oath of the mission to all in turn.[2]
This day was ever after considered the foundation day of
the college, and the Bull of Foundation, though it was not
finally ready till many months later, bore the date of this
happy feast of the patron of England.   The Pope, accompanied by ten cardinals, visited the new college in state on
the 22nd of July, and declared himself well satisfied with the
new arrangements.[3]

Now whatever else may be said about this whole incident
(and, of course, there were many obvious faults on both sides),
the important thing is that we here meet with an outburst
of entirely new vigour in English ecclesiastical life.   There
have been before many remarkable examples of tenacity and
steadfast perseverance; here for the first time we find so
much energy and enterprise, that it can neither be governed
nor even understood, by men of the old school.   The new
spirit bursts out, now into speeches of genuine eloquence,
now into scores of ably written papers, or, if the occasion
requires, into verse; and smaller instances of spontaneous
self-sacrifice and Christian magnanimity are too frequent
to be described here.   The genius of the Counter-Reformation has taken firm hold of the hearts of these young men.[4]

Unfortunately there have also come into existence the
makings of a deep and dangerous clerical quarrel, which has
its root in a permanent national rivalry, and is fomented
by the perennial emulation between the secular and regular clergy.   Both forms of competition are highly useful to
the body politic, when kept in due control.   In our case,
however, both Dr. Owen Lewis, and still more his nephew,
Hugh Griffin, appear to have lost that indispensable control.
They neither forgave nor forgot, and circumstances, as we

[1] Father Persons gives many details (*C.R.S.*, ii. 157, 158).
[2] The official list then taken is in *C.R.S.*, ii. 131–35.
[3] *Douay Diaries*, p. 155.
[4] Haydock to Allen, Tierney's Dodd, ii., Ap. 360 : " They (the Jesuits
see a strange difference betwixt the spirits of the young Englishmen and
of the old."

shall see, gave them but too many facilities for keeping the feud alive.[1]

§ 6. *Allen's Third Visit to Rome*

As soon as peace had been established, there was a general demand for Dr. Allen to come to Rome : " that good Dr. Allen," as Father Persons wrote, " who is all good men's hope." [2] When the summer heats were over he set out (August 21), the Pope having contributed to his expenses. He reached Rome on the 10th of October, every one, from the Pope downwards, showing him the utmost consideration. The estimation in which the English Catholics were held had evidently risen greatly, and credit for this is paid to Allen, as to their head and representative. When he told the Holy Father that he had yearned to see the Pope's

---

[1] Allen's bitter regret at the quarrel is shown in his letter to Lewis of May 12 (Tierney's Dodd, ii., Ap. 365–71). Father Persons, though his feeling is less deep, is quite clear about the great harm done (*C.R.S.*, ii. 160). For examples of English national antipathy to the Welsh, see Haydock in Tierney's Dodd, ii., Ap. 346, 347, 360, and Dr. Barrett, *Douay Diaries*, pp. 325–6. For Welsh feeling against English, see Allen's examples, Tierney's Dodd, pp. 365, 370, 371. For anti-Jesuit feelings, see Lewis and Maurice, quoted *ibid.*, pp. 362, 365, 373.

It is interesting to compare the letters of Haydock and Lewis (Tierney's Dodd, *ibid.*). They support each other exactly as to matters of fact, but differ astonishingly in attribution of motives. Haydock is far the best witness : he knows most, and is perfectly clear and orderly. But he is very much put out by having been undeservedly named for expulsion among the ringleaders, and attributes this to Lewis. But Lewis' letter shows that this was wrong. The expulsion was really due to an error of Moroni, who had misapprehended Haydock's Latin (compare p. 355 with p. 361), and thought himself insulted. Dr. Lewis' letter throws a flood of light on the proceedings of his side. Without it we could hardly have guessed how generous his intentions were, how sincere his love for the common cause. But he is incapable of seeing any mistake on his own side, is full of intrigue and love of fighting, and is much embittered against the Jesuits.

A hostile but interesting variant on the whole of this episode may be found in Anthony Munday's *English Romayne Life* (*Harleian Miscellany*, 1809, ii. 167). He was at the college during the troubles, but his evidence is in one sense worthless, for his word is quite unreliable. He swore away the lives of several of his former companions, of whose innocence he could have had no doubts, and then wrote a most bitter tract to defame them. Nevertheless, his style is lively and his memory good. In spite of the cynicism with which he mocks both sides in the college quarrel, it is an amusing story, and in many details certainly true.

[2] *C.R.S.*, ii. 160. Allen himself would have liked to go at once, and his staff urged him to do so (*Letters*, p. 81) ; but there was some previous secret understanding with the Pope that he was to stay at Rheims. Lewis knew the reason (*ibid.*), which, one may conjecture, had something to do with Sander's expedition. Father Persons urged the matter, and in June the Pope consented (*C.R.S.*, ii. 26, 135, 139, 194).

new Seminary and scholars before he died (his health was already weakening), Gregory answered, " Not my scholars, Allen, but yours." Cardinal Paleotto, Archbishop of Bologna, had not allowed his party to stay at an inn as they passed; but, having paid their bills, carried them to his palace, saying, " This house is the inn of the English." [1]

Allen's primary object in coming to Rome was to ensure the complete healing of the soreness which had been occasioned by the late controversies. True it was, that to heal an international quarrel at once and for ever was an impossible task; and, in fact, the struggle was to break out again, though in a different form, ere very long. But for the time Allen's success was considerable. He was aided by certain circumstances, especially by the migration from Rome of most of those who had taken part in the late troubles : on the one hand, Bishop Goldwell, and many of the old chaplains of the hospice, as well as the student priests from the college, and, on the other side, Dr. Owen Lewis and Maurice Clenog. The English went to the English Mission, though the seniors were eventually found to be too old to start so laborious a life. Dr. Maurice was unfortunately drowned on his way to Spain, and Dr. Lewis, at the invitation of St. Charles Borromeo, went to work under him at Milan.[2] The brilliant Welshman was for the moment under a cloud. Not only had all the costly enterprises of Stukely, Fitzgerald, and of Sander ended in failure; but the late affairs at the English College had shown that he was not a very good judge, even of the English clergy. At Milan, however, he at once came into notice, and was made by St. Charles one of his Vicars-General.

The leaders on both sides being thus for the time disposed of, there remained what Persons and Agazario

---

[1] *Douay Diaries*, p. 158; *C.R.S.*, ii. 140; Foley, *Records*, vi. 68.

[2] *C.R.S.*, ii. 162, 163. Lewis wrote to St. Charles, April 30, 1580, that " as he invited him, and the Pope persuaded his going," he would come to Milan (Milan Correspondence of St. Charles, f. 56, inf. l. 248. The letter also contains biographical matter. I am indebted for my knowledge of it to the late Père Van Ortroy, the Bollandist). Having arrived on the 16th of June, Lewis sent back a very friendly letter to Agazario on the 8th of July (*C.R.S.*, ix. 40). In his later *Memoirs* Persons says in one place that Lewis " went " to Milan, in another that he was " sent." The alternative statements probably mean that Persons had heard both stories (*C.R.S.*, ii. 162, 163).

call "the correspondence between the colleges of Rheims and Rome." By this they meant a thorough understanding between the heads of the two establishments as to what sort of men should be sent on from Rheims to Rome; what modifications of the curriculum should be introduced at Rheims; what extra studies, to meet English needs, should be added at Rome.

The discussion was, no doubt, both necessary and illuminative; every one seems to have been satisfied; but whether its results were very far-reaching we cannot say. Allen's position at Rheims was so difficult that in such matters as the choice of students for Rome, necessity too often had to be his law.

The next point, which doubtless in Allen's mind was the most important of all, was the invitation to the Jesuits to send missionaries to England. The matter had been not infrequently ventilated before: Allen himself in his paper presented to Father Mercurian in 1576 had broached it, and Father Persons had carried the matter further still during the past year.[1] The invitation was now carefully considered by the Jesuits, and Father Persons, who was called in to the discussion, has left in his *Memoirs* two brief accounts of the heads of argument used for and against. On one side, no one could question that the number of English who had been received into the Society was an argument that the Society should devote part of its labours to their country. Again, the assistance and encouragement the Jesuits had everywhere given to the English Catholic exiles—and especially to those training for the English Mission—indicated that they must consider missionary work in this country as a fit object to live for and to die for. It was time that this conclusion should take effect in action.

The only serious objection was the difficulty of maintaining the discipline of a religious order under a persecution which would render almost all external observance impossible. This was a very serious objection indeed, and what made it the more noteworthy, was that the experiment

---

[1] *C.R.S.*, ix. 69, Allen to Mercurian. Persons to Good, *C.R.S.*, ii. 141, 142.

had already to some extent been made, without success. Father David Wolfe, with three or four other Jesuits, had already worked in Ireland, where circumstances were, to some extent, more favourable than in England. Yet the results had been disappointing, and the missionaries had to be recalled for a time. But this parallel was deceptive. In Ireland the Catholics, though many, were forced to lead a comparatively wild and unsettled life. They were harried and scattered in the attempts to suppress religion by force; and communication with the rest of the Society was often impossible for years together. Now the Society is an organised body, and its efficiency comes from its being so. It may push out skirmishers and vedettes to act alone far in advance of its base; but if its men are permanently cut off from that base, if they cannot observe discipline, or correspond with their leaders and fellow-soldiers, or feel the strength and encouragement that comes with corporate action, they must lose much of their character and effectiveness, and the whole body will suffer.

Dr. Allen, however, would have been able to point out that the state of England, though in some ways worse than that of Ireland, was certainly more favourable for Jesuit mission work.[1] Men and letters could pass into England with far less risk than they did into Ireland; and the large and peaceful houses and households of English gentlemen would prove far safer hiding-grounds than the Irish castles, woods, and cabins in the time of war. Allen was even sanguine enough to expect that Bishop Goldwell might be able to cross over, and, whilst living in secret, to do much to govern the clergy. Amongst these, as they were now without any head, differences of opinion and quarrels were apt to arise, and might, so the Jesuits feared, sometimes prove not only mischievous, but even perilous.

These points settled, the general had no further objection

---

[1] A kindred topic, alluded to by Father Persons, was the question of risk to life in general. It was recognised that the risk or sacrifice of life, without some proportionate spiritual advantage, should not be entertained. But it was hoped, after what Allen had said, that the sacrifice would not be excessive (Persons, *Life of Campion*, cap. xiii.). Four years later this conclusion was questioned by the Jesuit provincial of France, Father Claude Mathieu. The cost of the mission in lives and trials had proved more severe than had been generally foreseen; but the original decision was maintained (Persons' *Memoirs*, *C.R.S.*, iv. 147).

to raise, and accepted the mission. The decision was at once carried to the Pope, who " approved of the same with his authority and benediction." It was then settled that the mission should consist of Fathers Campion and Persons, with the former as senior in command. As he was then in Prague, the general summoned him to Rome on the 4th of December, and this letter was supplemented by another letter from Allen himself, full of affection and magnanimity.

Another cause of friction at the Seminary now came into notice, and called for a remedy. This arose from the passage of students from the college to the Jesuits, a matter which eventually had to be decided by Pontifical legislation. It must be remembered that there were in those days no English novitiates for any religious order, nor were there any but ecclesiastical seminaries for Catholic youths. Young Englishmen who thought of adopting the ecclesiastical state had no choice but to enter at first collegiate establishments intended primarily for the secular clergy. Only after doing this could they appreciate the choice of vocations which the Church wished to be open to them. Whilst the abnormal circumstances of the time lasted, this would have to be recognised and reckoned with. Neither Gregory in the Bull of Foundation, nor Allen at any time, insisted on their colleges being reserved exclusively for the secular clergy; in the Foundation Bull of the German college, which came shortly after that of the English college, the presence of young religious at that college was explicitly allowed for.[1] The Pope wished the religious orders to be revived, and if his colleges assisted that good work he would be distinctly pleased, even at the cost of some of the provision made primarily, though not exclusively, for the secular clergy. One of the effects of the persecution was to give rise to a happy family spirit among all sections of Catholics, of which we shall see many indications.

On the other hand, there were morally sure to be also some men of less comprehensive minds who would not take these generous views, and these would fall into two classes. First there would be, and there were, some who exceeded in

[1] In all two hundred and sixty-seven scholars were admitted who already belonged to religious orders (Cardinal Steinhüber, *Geschichte des Collegium Germanicum*, 1895, ii. 496).

favour of the religious orders. They would think it wrong under any circumstances to hinder any one from joining, or attempting to join, the spiritually higher state. Opposed to them would be others who would insist that it was unjust to allow any one educated on funds destined for the education of secular clergy to pass to the ranks of any other clerical body. They would also insist on the necessity of stability in vocations. There would be an end to such stability (they would say) if it were once recognised as a right or a duty to forsake one's first vocation as soon as one felt an aspiration to something higher.

Both these parties go wrong, because they misapprehend the time required for making a choice of life. On the one hand, it is certain that different minds take different periods of time to make and to mature their choice. One cannot definitely limit the period for all to a few months, or to one precise period of life. It would be obviously cruel to tie every boy to his first youthful choice of a seminary, made perhaps before his experience of himself or of the world was as wide as it ought to have been. On the other hand, it would be equally fatal to regard all clerical vocations except those of the religious life as variable and liable to doubt, as soon as any prospect opened out of a new sort of spiritual life, more exalted and attractive than that professed before. The practical conclusion is that such changes of vocation, without being totally excluded, should be made difficult, and only obtainable with the sanction of a referee *omni exceptione major*.

In the present case, Allen arranged that none from the English college should join a religious order without the express permission of the Cardinal Protector, whose authority would be such as to outweigh entirely any cavils that might be made by fault-finders of lower degree.[1] It was a good move, and on the right lines. Forty years later, when organisation had been carried further, when preparatory schools had been founded, which would enable the average

---

[1] Allen to Barrett, *Letters*, p. 450. The two scholars whose entrance among the Jesuits caused friction at this time were Thomas Wright and James (or John) Barton. They entered February 3, 1580; but neither eventually persevered (N. Southwell, *Catalogus Primorum, Patrum, S.J.,* Stonyhurst MS.).

lad, before he went to an ecclesiastical seminary, to become acquainted with the various vocations open to him, and when religious orders had novitiates of their own, more elaborate legislation would be in place.

In the present case it was, of course, not the actual entrance of two English youths of which complaint was made. The cry was that others were being "enticed to enter." Definite proofs or disproofs in matters of this sort are not obtainable, and we may well satisfy ourselves here with what Allen thought sufficient to satisfy the scholars. In the letter just quoted he takes the line of assuring them that, after his long consultations with the Father General and other men in authority,[1] he is quite certain that they may be entirely trusted; and as no postulant can be received except through them, there is, to say the least, no real cause for anxiety. Thus he prudently evades the discussion of chance utterances by small, irresponsible folk, which may perhaps have been reprehensible, but which were more probably misunderstood.[2]

It was hoped that Campion might have come to Rome in time to see Allen and to concert measures with him there. But to everybody's disappointment no Campion appeared, and no explanation of his delay; so that Allen had to leave without even hearing from him. He left Rome on Ash

---

[1] Father Good records a curious incident about these conferences. Dr. Allen addressed the scholars on the whole subject before he left Rome, and even scolded them for their suspicious and narrow spirit, but the young men remained stubborn and obstinate. Not long after, it was Father Persons' turn to give a conference, and he made a most suave address (*suavissima oratio*), which carried every one away, and satisfied, for the time, all youthful objectors. Romana Historica, *Hist. Coll. Anglorum*, n. xix. Father William Good was then Spiritual Father at the college, and wrote the paper quoted above (about August 1580) in order to obtain English instead of Italian rectors—a wise measure, carried into execution later on. Some further light is thrown on these incidents by Allen's correspondence, *C.R.S.*, ix. 26 and 73.

[2] I believe these complaints to have been chiefly due to those misconceptions between Italian superiors and English subjects which were in some ways inevitable. Italian Anglomania, which dates back even to St. Gregory, with his "Angli Angeli," and was extraordinarily strong then (*C.R.S.*, ii. 142; Tierney's Dodd, Ap. 359), would sometimes suggest to a padre that this or that pious English lad must have a religious vocation; and so occasion indiscreet advances. On the other hand, English lads, always more suspicious than good Italians suspected, would too readily conceive that there was a double intention in any kind word or act, and so raise alarms about "enticement," when nothing of the sort was dreamt of.

Wednesday (February 16),[1] more than content (except for missing Campion) with all that had taken place, and especially as to the state of the new English colony in Rome. Though its troubles of the previous year had caused him grave anxiety, the connection with the centre of Christendom had from the first proved of such value as to outweigh the disadvantages (great though they were) which had come with the migration from Douay. An official report of the Rheims Seminary for 1578 'says—

" The recent overflow of his Holiness's goodness and bounty upon our scholars at Rome, the news whereof has already penetrated into England, does much daily to increase our number, and is a wonderful incentive to the English Catholics to send their sons to share in that Roman education. The consequence is, that men of all ranks are coming to us, and we are almost overwhelmed by the number of our scholars. There are many here fit to be sent to Rome, and many desire it most eagerly; but as we cannot satisfy all, many have to live upon hope for the time to come." [2]

In fact, the desire to go to Rome became a sort of rage among the scholars, and this afterwards had its disadvantages.[3]

Still, the more comprehensive the view we take of the effect produced on the English Catholics by the greatly increased intercourse with Rome, the more clearly do we see the growth of fervour and of courage which that intercourse brought about.

---

[1] So Persons, *C.R.S.*, ii. 137. He was at Siena February 29 (*C.R.S.*, ix. 19), and reached Rheims on April 2, in company with Father Darbishire, S.J., and several of the old doctors, who had been chaplains at the hospice (*Douay Diaries*, p. 162). Amongst other successes was the increase of the papal pension for Rheims by fifty crowns a month. Perhaps he also regarded it as a success, that the talk of making him a cardinal, of which Father Persons speaks (*C.R.S.*, ii. 138), had ended in nothing.

[2] *Brevissima Collectio rerum præcipuarum quæ gestæ sunt ab Anglicano Seminario Remis commorante, anno 1577–1578* (*C.R.S.*, ii. 67).

[3] Kind-hearted Mr. President, pressed as he was for room, was perhaps too easy in allowing importunate petitioners to go, though several were already too old and too formed to bear, without murmuring, the necessarily strict discipline of the place.

U

§ 7. *The Authentic Comment on the Bull of Excommunication (February to April, 1580)*

It was not until the end of Lent that Campion arrived, with the explanation that the delay had been caused by his rector at Prague, who would not let him go until his successor had arrived. And now he begged that he might not be Superior of the new mission. His brilliant talents, and his seniority, both in years and in the Society, had naturally led to his being given the precedence, but upon consideration Father Mercurian agreed to the change. In truth Campion was one of those delightful, artistic characters who are able to give the greatest scope to their talents when they have at hand a strong, circumspect friend, who will relieve them of the embarrassment which men of genius often feel in deciding on matters of everyday life. It was Campion's special gift to throw his whole soul and all his inspiring enthusiasm into every letter, speech or sermon; it was Persons' special gift to make plans, to provide means, to arrange for all contingencies. The events of the last few months had shown all this so clearly that there was no hesitation now in putting the younger man into the command.

As Persons was destined to retain this leadership till his death, it may not be uninstructive to compare him with Allen and with Owen Lewis, for it was on these three men in their different ways that the progress of the Catholic party was henceforward to depend. Of Owen Lewis we know less than of the others, but amply enough to show that the part he played was great and helpful. His special gift was facility in obtaining the confidence of the great and powerful. He was the first of the exiles who rose to office abroad. It was to his influence with Gregory XIII and the curia at Rome that we must attribute that all-important step forward by which the Pope changed the considerable alms-deeds of his predecessor into a stable revenue given to the English Seminaries at Rheims and Rome, without which those foundation-stones of the English Church could

BD. EDMUND CAMPION, S.J.

By A. Chevallier Tayler (now at Campion College, Prairie du Chien, U.S.A.), after the subcontemporary picture at Rome

not have subsisted at all. Under different circumstances
Lewis was the trusted representative of the Archbishop of
Cambray, the Vicar-General of St. Charles Borromeo, and
eventually the acting intermediary between Mary Stuart
and the Roman Pontiff. He was, moreover, always sincerely
devoted to the Catholic cause, and had he finally become
a cardinal he might have done it much good, for neither will
nor power nor opportunity would have been wanting.
Unfortunately he was not only not superior to partisanship,
he could not, as we have seen, resist the temptation to stake
everything on gaining a victory for those of his side; and
this miserable party spirit, taking root among his followers,
was the cause of many a disappointment, and of some
grave misfortunes later on.

Allen and Persons were far more magnanimous. The
Catholic cause was for them not only the chief—it was the
only affair of life; for that no sacrifices, no self-devotion
could be too great. And yet their characteristics were
again different. In Allen strength and magnanimity were
linked together by an intimate knowledge of, and most
delicate fellow-feeling with, each individual on either side.
This quality enabled him to exert a compelling and irresistible attraction on all, constraining them not only to
requite affection, but also to leave to him decisions that
are difficult. He is a ruler of hearts, a compeller of peace,
an arbiter in whose hands his followers gladly leave all
issues. There is nothing they will not do for him.

Father Persons' special characteristic is resource.
Though eloquent and clear-headed and full of deep feeling,[1]
his penetrating foresight and strong perseverance in urging
the means he sees to be necessary are even more remarkable.
He is also a born organiser and a legislator, and in these
points he makes up for certain deficiencies in Allen, who was
distinctly free and easy (for an educationalist) about rules
and customs; and even about the provision of money and
other necessaries. On the other hand, Persons has not the
many-sided sympathy of Allen. His own friends trusted him
completely, but he was not beloved by both sides (as Allen

[1] See, for mention of his tears, *C.R.S.*, ii. 132; for his *suavissima oratio*
see above, § vi. In the unsigned letter, evidently by him (R.O., *Dom.
Eliz.*, cl. 67), he breaks into verse, etc.

was), though he was really far superior to the narrow-mindedness of the party struggle.[1]

Before the two Jesuits left Rome they were given special instructions [2] by their General, and finally somewhat ample faculties by the Pope. Most of these nineteen instructions may be passed over here as pertaining to the spiritual or sacerdotal life exclusively, but some headings are of wider importance.

It is a common mistake among Protestants to suppose that the Catholic clergy in general, and the Jesuits in particular, make it their *chief* object to wage war on Protestantism. This is a caricature, because it makes an occasional duty into an entire occupation. The Instructions begin (§ 1) by laying it down that the end of the mission was to be "the preservation and augmentation of the Faith of the Catholics of England." It is only after attending to this that the missionaries should direct their attention to the sheep "who have gone astray in ignorance, or through the impulse of others." As to the heretics, properly so called, the missionaries are warned (§ 12) to avoid not only disputations with them, but even their company, when this is possible. It will doubtless always be a temptation for a new missionary, who knows his power of demolishing a dangerous enemy by argument, to rush into the war of words, where, however, the truth is more often hooted down than given a fair field. In point of fact, Campion did become involved in a disputation of this unsatisfactory sort. Suffice it, however, for the moment to say that this was not intended by those who sent him.

The eighteenth section is also important : "Let them not entangle themselves (*ne se immisceant*) in matters of State, nor should they write hither political news." Moreover, they should not start "conversations against the Queen, nor allow others to do so." The earliest form of the In-

---

[1] In later life, it is true, after the violent and prolonged attacks made upon him by the Appellants, he became somewhat too intent on self-defence, and we see traces of this in many later papers. But in the writings of this period there is no sign of this weakness.

[2] *Instructiones datæ PP. missionariis in Anglia*, 1580–1663, Stonyhurst MSS. Also in other Jesuit collections, *Instructiones*, 1577–1596, f. 322, and *Romana Hist. Coll. Angl.*, etc., No. xi. Considerable extracts will be found in Simpson's *Campion* (1867, pp. 99–100).

structions has a conclusion which was marked for omission by a later hand, and which is omitted in the Stonyhurst copy : " except perhaps in the company of those whom they hold to be exceptionally faithful, and who have been tried a long time ; and even then not without serious cause."

There will be nothing exactly novel in these clauses for those who are familiar with Jesuit legislation of the period. Warnings against talking politics are found in their rules from the first, and are frequently met with in their ascetical writers, as well as in other teachers of the time. What is noteworthy is the strictness of the wording, and the increased precautions taken in the later editions.

This stringency was doubtless due to the need of using the greatest possible prudence while on the English mission, a duty repeatedly insisted upon in these Instructions. In Catholic countries " talking politics " might be unedifying, absorbing, and the like. In England it would also be dangerous, not only to the individual, but also to the whole body. At the same time it was foreseen that persecution so grievous as that sustained by the English Catholics would make many gird bitterly against their oppressors. Such men might then appeal to the Fathers to know whether this was not justifiable, a further source of danger.

On the 14th of April the missionaries had their last audience with the Holy Father, and on this occasion they asked and obtained some extra powers in absolving, consecrating, and imparting blessings to beads and the like.[1] The ninth section of their petition requests a declaration in regard to the Bull of Excommunication, in the following terms—

" An explanation is asked of our Lord the Pope in regard to Pius the Vth's declaratory Bull against Elizabeth and those who adhere to her. The Catholics desire it to be understood in this way : that it always obliges her and the heretics ; as for the Catholics, it obliges them in no way, while affairs stand as they do ; but will only do so in future, when the public execution of the Bull can be made. . . .

[1] R.O., *Dom. Eliz.*, cxxxvii. 26–28 ; three copies, of which the first, on parchment, is probably the original. See also *ibid.*, cxliv. 64, 65.

[*Answer*] : " These graces were conceded . . . April 14, 1580, in the presence of Padre Olivier Manare."

An interesting introduction to this petition is furnished by an undated paper on the same topic, written a little earlier. It is a legal opinion of some Roman jurist, possibly Father Antonio Possevino, S.J.,[1] who puts himself the question whether the excommunication was still of force, and answers in the negative. He supports himself by various legal principles, of which the fourth, which is chiefly histori- cal, will be readily understood. The Bull, he says, was issued for a particular occasion (*i. e.* the Rising of the North). But that occasion has entirely passed, and the circumstances are changed. The Bull should not be assumed to be binding in an entirely new situation.[2]

But Elizabeth gains very little by this, for the writer holds that her war against Catholics, not in England only, but in Scotland, Ireland, France and the Netherlands also, makes it evident that she is a declared enemy of the Church. No formal excommunication, no public declaration was needed to make it clear that the penalties of a *public* enemy of the Church must necessarily be hers.[3]

Whilst answering on these lines the fourteen questions

---

[1] *Ad consolationem et instructionem quorundam Catholicorum in angustiis constitutorum quæstiones aliquot.* There is yet another copy among the MSS. of Father Possevino, S.J., in the section, *Acta cum Summo Pontifice, i. e.* Gregory XIII, with whom he was very intimate. In his *Annales* (for which see Sommervogel, *Bibliothèque de la C. de Jésus*, vi. 1092) he relates that, at Owen Lewis's suggestion, he interceded frequently for the College of Rheims, and assisted materially in obtaining its pension from the Pope. He also composed an answer to Burghley's *De Justitia Britannica*, which, though never printed, exists in MS. Two other copies of the *Quæstiones* are in the Vatican Archives: (1) *Castel S. Angelo*, xiv. cap. 2, no. 25 (cf. Theiner, *Annales*, iii. 215). This is probably the copy given in to the Pope. (2) Arm. lxiv. 28, ff. 176-9, the copy given to the Cardinal Protector Moroni. The paper has been printed by Bishop Creighton in the *English Historical Review*, vii. 81-8, from R.O., Bliss, *Roman Transcripts* (for corrections see A. O. Meyer, p. 114), no date. The first fourteen questions relate to the excommunication, the other five to communication *in sacris*.

[2] " 4° Præceptum et obligatio videntur posita pro loco et tempore duntaxat quibus spes est recuperationis illius regni ea vice et modo. Cum ergo talis occasio evanuerit, et spes sit frustrata, et ea via omnino inter- clusa, consequitur tempus illius præcepti præteriisse, et obligationem proinde cessare. Præter rationem enim videretur nunc, uti modo et ratione incommodissima ad rem fere impossibilem."

[3] " Seclusa bulla, unusquisque eam habere debet pro illegitima regina, et excommunicata " (*Ibid.*, ad 3 and more fully ad 14).

proposed to him, he adds the advice that the Pope should be asked to declare that the Bull did not at present impose any grave obligation on the English Catholics. It was this that Persons and Campion were now doing, and the short " Answer " above, which was made to their petition, is therefore in effect an authentic declaration of the extent to which the Bull was binding.

Even Mr. Simpson says of this petition and answer that it was one " for which Elizabeth's Government ought to have been thankful " to the petitioners.[1] In point of fact, however, Cecil pursued both it and them with abuse and misrepresentation, which still have their influence. The advantages of the declaration, therefore, and Cecil's characteristic perversion of it will need some further explanation.

The benefit was this, that from now onwards the Catholics in England had a clear way of making known their sentiments towards the Queen. Living in England, they knew Elizabeth's power, and they felt from the first what those abroad were too distant to appreciate—that the time would never come when the Pope would or could give any different order from that now promulgated. So from henceforth they proclaimed her without reserve their Queen in the temporal order, and this was obviously of no little advantage to Elizabeth's Government.

This change is very clearly seen in the *Lives of the English Martyrs*. The next sufferer after this date, Everard Hanse, was able to counter all the inevitable charges of treason consequent on his attitude towards the Pope by the bold declaration, repeated even at the moment of death, that he accepted Elizabeth as Queen, a statement fully sufficient to convince any man of good will. Hanse's example was followed by practically all subsequent sufferers. It is true that James Layborne, in 1583, spoke of Elizabeth as Storey and Woodhouse had done immediately after the excommunication. But in the altered circumstances his declaration was no longer regarded as a " confession of the faith," and he was from the first tacitly omitted from the Catholic martyrologies.

[1] Simpson's *Campion*, 1867, p. 100.

Before Hanse not one of the martyrs had spoken as he did. Some—those who suffered soon after the excommunication—had spoken distinctly in its support; others had avoided the subject. The youthful martyr, Sherwood, who suffered next before Hanse, had been entrapped by the Crown prosecutors because he had not got Hanse's answer ready. The poor lad had not known how to get away from the ensnaring hypothesis put to him : " If the Queen is deposed 'for matter of religion, then she is deposed." Snares of this kind, which the Catholics usually termed " bloody questions," long remained favourite weapons of the persecutors, and very deadly they were to ensure the condemnation of their victims. But the Catholics now had their answer, and after much suffering and waiting, that answer eventually prevailed.

Elizabeth, too, without a doubt benefited very greatly by the answer given to the Jesuits, which was of the greatest service in restraining the Catholics in England from attempting to obtain liberty by violence, as men so often do when under gross persecution. Though the matter is one which will need, and shall have, full discussion in its proper place, one may foresee the conclusion even now. No plot against Elizabeth's life would ever be hatched on English soil, nor would the Queen's life ever be for a minute in danger. Nothing, indeed, would prevent discontent taking dangerous forms among the exiles abroad, and these plans might, for a time, influence Catholics at home. But even in these cases, no plot could prosper without the aid of Walsingham's numerous spies or *agents provocateurs*. This immunity from conspiracy was primarily due to that atmosphere of stable, though misunderstood loyalty among the English Catholics which the answer of 1580 did so much to make permanent and to justify.

These are arguments from facts; if one is needed from the records of the time, we might turn to a later page of our history, when, the loyalty of which we speak having been carried to some extravagant conclusions by that odd character, William Watson, " the Quodlibet maker," his book was in 1602 denounced to the Inquisition as unsound. In defence it was asserted that the Jesuits themselves, and in particular Father Southwell in his *Supplication to the Queen*, had used language of similar import to Watson. The Inquisition thereupon asked for explanations from the Jesuits, and their answer, coming no doubt from Father Persons himself, consisted of a copy of the *Responsum*, which we have been discussing, with this conclusion :—

" Relying on this foundation, both the illustrious Cardinal Allen, and other Catholic writers, and many martyrs as well, addressed the Queen with the usual titles of honour in civil matters. Most important of all, Pope Gregory XIII, of happy memory, laid it down to the Fathers of the Society who were starting for England in 1580 that in all things appertaining to the civil state they should treat the Queen as legitimate, and should use her honourably in external acts and words, until the Apostolic See should legislate otherwise in this matter." [1]

We see, therefore, that in the Court of the Inquisition itself the *Responsum* of 1580 was alleged without contradiction as explaining and justifying the protests of loyalty to Elizabeth as Queen so common among Catholic writers after that answer had been given.

We next turn to Lord Burghley. Shutting his eyes to the benefit the English Catholics and their Queen would receive from the first part of the answer, he fixes his whole attention on the concluding clauses, that the answer was to hold " as things now stand," and " until the public execution of the Bull can be made." His comment, of course, was : " This only means that you are loyal while you cannot resist, and that you will rebel at the first opportunity."

How different the two conclusions drawn from the same words ! The Catholics took the document as an argument justifying their declarations of loyalty; the Protestants regarded it as proof positive of their disloyalty. This was due to two reasons : to the persecutors' prejudices, and to the different meaning each side attached to the idea of loyalty. In Cecil's sense it meant the entire surrender

[1] Edinburgh, Advocates' Library, MS. 31. 4. 15.   Another copy, Turin, Arch. di Stato, *Raccolta Mongardino*, lxi. 8; dated September 13, 1602.

of all liberty, even liberty of conscience, to the Tudor tyrant; in the Catholics' mind it meant acceptance of her as a temporal, not as a spiritual ruler.

But even this difference of ideas would not have necessitated Cecil's misconception had he been accessible to the logic of facts. He had before him overwhelming evidence of the innocent, nay, holy lives of the missionaries; but to this he would not attend; he would not draw the consequence that their declarations of innocence and loyalty were reliable. He persecuted a man like Campion to death, then justified his execution by scoffing at the document which was the charter of Campion's loyalty. If Cecil was hardened to the logic of facts, no wonder that he was inaccessible to reasoning; no wonder that he misapprehended the text he published, which in truth was not written for him.

Yet in one thing Cecil was not mistaken. The mitigation of the Bull, as we have seen before, was also a re-statement of its principle. It meant that the Church, whose members he was so cruelly persecuting, had not feared to smite him and his with her unchanging anathema.

CHAPTER VIII

BEFORE we study the advent of the Counter-Reformation in England, we must advert to some other kinds of Catholic reaction, which were affecting our country. The action of the English Reformation on neighbouring lands had been most vigorous. No sooner had it conquered here than it attacked the old order in every adjacent country, and with an energy so impetuous, that its initial success was truly astonishing. Ireland seemed to collapse at once, with a suddenness hardly less wonderful than the eventually unconquerable resistance which followed. Scotland fell next; then France was divided and crippled for a whole generation; then the Spanish Netherlands were embroiled in trouble and turmoil unspeakable. All this had been accomplished in Elizabeth's first decade, though, of course, not entirely by her. In the second, the aggression, if less vehement, had been even more widespread; the English privateers carrying on the attack far and wide over the Spanish Main.

To all this there was an inevitable and constant reaction through counter-attacks, diplomacy, literature, and the like. But the Kings of France and Spain, those chiefly affected by the English policy, would not, indeed could not, without an effort for which they were not prepared, declare war in return. They kept the peace, hoping to consolidate their power; though in the case of Spain it was clear that under continual aggression a lasting peace was impossible. By the year 1579 the reaction had reached this stage. France was endeavouring to get Elizabeth on to their own side by marrying her to the Duke of Anjou; while King Philip, as we have already heard, had got as

far as allowing a papal expedition to be fitted out for Ireland
under Dr. Sander and Fitzgerald.

If the marriage treaty with France, which was agreed
to by England and signed at Greenwich on the 24th of
November, 1579, had been accomplished, as Elizabeth then
intended it to be, an amelioration of the lot of Catholics
would almost certainly have ensued. Again, if Sander had
been more fortunate—if he had succeeded in keeping his
spark of insurrection alive longer (and there were moments,
as, for instance, after the Battle of Glendalough, August 25,
1580, when this appeared quite possible), then the opportunity of winning liberty for Catholicism would have been
distinctly favourable.

As things fell out, the chances of any permanent improvement, coming either through the Duke of Anjou or through
Sander, passed away very soon, and were quickly forgotten.
Still the doings of both men require attention; for to put
their importance at the lowest, we cannot understand the
political events which followed until we have taken the
measure of this phase in their development.

§ 1. *The Death of Dr. Sander*

The story of the expedition, in which Dr. Sander lost his
life, has already been described in so far as it concerned
the diplomacy and the arms of the Pope and the King of
Spain. We must now pay greater attention to its English
leader, partly because it was Sander's personal magnetism
which made this rising so different from ordinary tribal
risings in Ireland; partly because Sander was also one
of the chief leaders of the English Catholics; partly because
even after his death he remained, by his writings, a special
representative of the more warlike elements in the English
Catholic party.

As early as 1563 Sander enjoyed, in consequence of his
presence at the Council of Trent, where he was theologian
to Cardinal Hosius, a standing which no other of the new
generation of English clergy had yet acquired, and this
was further augmented by his various publications and his

presence at the Diet of Augsburg (1566). When Pius V, after the excommunication, but before the failure of all attempts to execute it, was thinking what Englishman to employ in case of success, Sander was the man whom the Catholic exiles commended most highly, and whom Pius had settled on for promotion. Then, when hopes of execution had passed, they still begged that Sander might be kept at Rome in some dignity, as a leader to whom the Catholics might look for guidance.[1] On the 10th of August 1572, the Catholic clergy at Louvain made a similar petition, naming Bishop Goldwell and Dr. Morton along with Sander.[2] While Sander was at Rome (1572–1573) hopes for his promotion were not easily laid aside.[3]

In reality Pope Gregory had no such intention, nor did he even see his way to grant Sander's prayers for an increased allowance to the English fugitives; [4] and eventually the English divine had to content himself with a commendatory brief addressed to Philip II of Spain, dated September 4, 1573.[5] Nevertheless, some of his ideas were destined to have an effect later on, for it is at this period that we first meet with the bold proposal that the Pope should undertake the English enterprise by himself.[6]

By the end of the year Sander was at Madrid, and there

---

[1] This appears from a fragmentary correspondence between James Brunell, a Catholic exile at Louvain, and Father Polanco at Rome (February 22, June 7, July 18, 1570, and April 6, 1572. *Epistolæ Germaniæ, S.J.*, xi. 310, etc.).

[2] Arch. Vat. Arm. lxii. 33, fol. 136. Though, according to custom, three names are mentioned, and the bishop is placed first, this is not inconsistent with a preference for Sander among the petitioners.

[3] B.M. MS. Lansd. 96, art. 40, is a petition to the King of Spain, dated Brussels, 4 id., November (November 10, 1572), asking his favour for Sander to be appointed Cardinal (Ellis, *Original Letters*, II. iii. 92). There are two other letters in favour of Sander, same volume, nn. 5, 7 (Paris, dated January 11 and 13, 1572). Another letter of commendation from the Countess of Northumberland and others to the Cardinal of Lorraine at Rome, October 20, 1572, Paris, Bib. Nat., *Fonds Français*, 15,888, 295. Also Sander to same, f. 297, now printed in Teulet, ii. 438–42.

[4] This petition, July 30, 1573, with draft answers to the effect that nothing can be done for Sander or England at present, will be found in Moroni's correspondence, Arch. Vat. Arm. lxiv. 28, but in disorder at ff. 29, 19, 20, 34, 37, 39, 40, 43, 31.

[5] The suggested draft is Arch. Vat., *Inghilterra*, i. 303, the actual draft, of September 4, is in Arm. xliv., vol. 22.

[6] This appears from a speech to the Pope (? June 1573), of which a report has strayed into a Jesuit MS., *Anglia Historica*, i. ff. 74–6. The attribution to Sander is, however, inferential, as it is not signed.

he remained for the next three years, begging Philip to help the exiles. But as he could not even get his own allowance paid him at Madrid, we can infer how little he was able to effect for his friends in Flanders.

In November 1576 he wrote to Allen a letter which is interesting because he gives in it his political creed, in that strong and trenchant style which was characteristic of the man. " The state of Christendom," he writes, " depends upon the stout assailing of England; and yet the King of Spain is as fearful of war as a child is of fire." [1]

That Philip's aversion to war was due to childish fear is, as we can see now, an exaggeration. The King was no coward; but he knew the limits of his power of organisation (though he did not know how to remedy it) better far than Sander did. It is, however, the sentiment contained in the first part of the sentence which chiefly concerns us now. " The state of Christendom depends on the stout assailing of England "—a full and frank enunciation of his belief in the need of some application of force to put right the evils of the day, and one that must be compared with a statement made later by the leader of the Counter-Reformation movement.

" This Church here," wrote Campion, after his second missionary journey, " shall never fail so long as priests and pastors be found for the sheep, rage man or devil never so much." [2] Here we see a new remedy for the ills of the world, a new confidence in its efficiency. It was not that Sander depreciated the Seminaries and the purely religious movement. This very letter contains high praise of them. Nor was it that Campion disallowed all recourse to force, but he perceives that spiritual remedies will by themselves suffice for the preservation of the Church in England, and this does not appear in Sander's formula. *Everything* there turns on " stout assailing."

Yet it must not be thought that Sander advocated force rashly, or without due constitutional limitations.

An observer and thinker no less well-informed and acute than Lord Burghley had declared that an expedition to

---

[1] Knox, *Letters of Cardinal Allen*, p. 38.
[2] Allen, *Martyrdom of F. Edmund Campion*, reprint of 1908, p. 26.

Ireland would " show great wisdom " on the part of the
Catholic Powers,[1] and he penned the words exactly at the
time when, unknown to him, Sander was preparing to sail.
This does not, of course, prove that Sander's action deserved
to be praised as prudent in every particular. But it shows
that we should be wrong to judge it exclusively by results.
The policy and the plan were not unwise, whatever the
faults of execution.

Nor, again, did the conception show any disregard for
the sanctity of law or the claims of patriotism. Under
the old traditional rule of Canon Law grievous offences
against religion were to be met by definite remedies; and
if the powers of the Crown were applied to the propagation
of heresy, the secular arm of the neighbouring Catholic
princes should be invoked.[2] Sander did not wish to go beyond
the laws that had held so long in England, and were still
in vigour through the greater part of Christendom, especially
in the land where he was living. It was not the conquest,
humiliation or the dismembering of his country of which
he was thinking, but the re-establishment of religion,
law and order, in place of regal tyranny and heretical
licence with revealed doctrines. His argument would have
been that, if one gave up endeavouring to enforce the
constitutional remedies for dangers which impaired the
foundations of national well-being, all Christendom would
be unsafe.

Sander was, of course, not at all singular in this.
Protestants as well as Catholics took the application of
physical force (on their own side *bien entendu*) quite as a
matter of course and of necessity. It could only be
those who recognised the immense power of religious
enthusiasm and of the Catholic religion, who would also

---

[1] " France, Spain and the Pope . . . would show great wisdom by
sending some part of their forces to England, Scotland and Ireland to
stir up civil wars in each of these countries " (*Hatfield Calendar*, ii. 268;
see Murdin, p. 324).

[2] As we have seen, this legislation was summarised and renewed by
Paul IV, February 15,.1559, in the Bull *cum ex apostolatus officio* (*Bullarium*,
vi. 354, Rome, 1745). The previous legislation is conveniently summarised
in the appendix (by Pierre Matthieu) to the edition (by Pierre and François
Pithou) of the *Corpus Juris Canonici*, Ap., p. 65, Paris, 1705. Paul IV
did not specifically mention deposition and invasion; but in general he
renewed " all penalties of every kind."

appreciate that physical force was not a matter of necessity. So far no one (that the author is aware of) had enunciated the equivalent of Campion's words, and the confidence with which he declared his conviction becomes all the more remarkable, when we remember the hurricane of violence against Catholics which then raged in England. Indeed, he was convinced that he himself could not escape long. Thus may Campion stand to us for the representative of the newer and more spiritual movement, and Sander as the protagonist of the simple and spontaneous school of thought which preceded. We may consider him as the last of the Pilgrims of Grace; for he was the last English Catholic to take up arms openly for the faith.

When Sander wrote to Allen the letter on which we have been commenting, he had been just four years at Philip's Court pining and pleading for action, but without effect, and this produced in him a great longing to join Allen in his work. " I have no other thing in this world," he says, " so at heart as to be with you; nor can I get leave to depart hence." But circumstances were now shaping which were to draw him on to his last fatal journey. That summer James Fitzmaurice Fitzgerald had come to Madrid to beg Philip's aid for his expedition to Ireland, and Sander had pleaded his cause [1] with a nervous earnestness which no longer hesitated at exaggerations, in the hope of arousing Philip to action.[2] Finally he volunteered to go himself, and for reasons characteristic of his chivalrous nature.

First, he wanted to make amends for the slur which, in his estimation, Stukely's want of principle had cast on the English exiles. He had, indeed, spoken against the adventurer, and had not been listened to; but he did not dwell upon that. He wished Fitzgerald's expedition, small though it was, and little as was expected from it, to be a success; for he knew that even a small success would do more for the cause he had at heart than the best conceivable arguments and prayers. Sir Francis Englefield, too, had

---

[1] It is not unworthy of note that Sander told Philip that Ireland had been hitherto kept under because of its divisions, that a leader who would unite them would be successful, and that Fitzgerald was such a leader (Bellesheim, *Gesch. d. K. Kirche in Irland*, 1890, ii. 699).

[2] Arch. Vat., *Nunz. di Spagna*, x. 627. Dispatch of June 29, 1577.

just come to Court, and could fill his place.[1]   So he volunteered to go, and Philip, after refusing for some time, because
Sander's presence at his Court had been notorious (March 28,
1578), at last let him slip away to Lisbon (December 15,
1578) and prepare to depart from thence.   Then came more
troubles and delays, partly due to Spain's want of organising
power, partly to the haphazard, impracticable character of
the whole expedition.   Still, by the middle of July 1579
he and Fitzgerald had landed with a handful of men at
Smerwick, and before long Munster was in arms.   Yet it
hardly ever seemed likely that the rising would be finally
successful.   It was never possible (except for a time after
the defeat at Glendalough) to prevent Elizabeth's soldiers
from going where they wanted to go, and taking any place
of strength that might serve as a rallying-point; and the
slaughter at Smerwick (November 9, 1580) showed but too
clearly how utterly ineffective Spain was in sending out
naval expeditions.   Sander was not able to resist the bodily
strain of the guerrilla warfare much longer.   In his last
extant letter to Rome, January 9, 1581,[2] he confesses
that he is very, very ill; yet on the 21st of February he put
forth a proclamation which was, under the circumstances, a
wonderfully inspiriting incentive to fight on without fear.[3]
This is the last we hear of him alive.   Some time between
March and June 1581 he died; not, indeed, without the
consolations of religion and the attentions of kindly friends,
but in obscurity and destitution; and his resting-place
remains unknown.[4]

In his books, however, Sander lived on, and became
better known through them than he was during life.   He

[1] Sander to Como, February 2, 1579, Bellesheim, ii. 707.   Englefield
afterwards volunteered to go too, so convinced was he of the desirability
of the enterprise.

[2] Arch. Vat., *Inghilterra*, i. 201.   A copy among Graziani's correspondence at Florence, Bib. Marucelliana, B. iv., 5 and 6.

[3] Ellis, *Original Letters*, II. iii. 94.   Though the date, " February
1580," would naturally be Old Style, and therefore 1581 by New Style,
there is also the possibility that the year is indeed 1580; and this also
agrees well with the contents of the letter.   Sander here characteristically
reminds his hearers that, if there is "execution of the laws of the Church,
you shall for the maintenance of heresy lose your goods, your lands, your
honours, etc." (*ibid.*, 96).   There is another letter of somewhat similar
tenor in *Carew MS. Calendar*, October 27, 1579.

[4] O'Sullivan Beare, *Historiæ Catholicæ Hiberniæ Compendium*, ed.
Kelly, 1850, pp. 113, 121.

X

wrote, however, before mitigating the excommunication had been discussed, when it seemed that redress for Elizabeth's excesses could only come after they had been proclaimed loudly and clearly, with the frank fearlessness of a quasi-mediæval mind. It was inevitable that Sander's books should be attacked by the defenders of the new religion. Lord Burghley circulated extracts from them on topics like the excommunication in order to raise odium against the martyrs whom he was going to execute, though not one defended the extracts.[1]

Burnet, a century later, attempted to convict Sander's *De Schismate Anglicano* of being dishonest. This gave rise to a prolonged controversy,[2] and Mr. Froude is still earnest on Burnet's side.[3] But " Sander has been proved right in almost every disputed point," writes Mr. T. G. Law, " and Burnet wrong." Mr. Pocock and Dr. Gairdner speak in the same strain.[4] Nowadays the controversy arises chiefly about Sander's lists of the clergy who resisted Elizabeth's changes.[5] But if we keep in mind his circumstances and objects in writing, we shall always find him a witness on the Catholic side who is well worthy of attention.[6]

---

[1] The extracts are reprinted in Tierney's Dodd, iii., Ap. 4–18.

[2] Burnet's charges are summed up in two Appendices in Pocock's edition (1865), iv. 543–82, and v. 585–620. Le Grand's three volumes came out at Paris, in 1688, *Histoire du Divorce de Henry VIII, avec la defense de Sanderus.* Lewis's translation of Sander, *The Rise and Growth of the Anglican Schism,* 1877, now affords the easiest way of testing Burnet's accuracy. See also Pocock's *Introduction,* vii. 150–7.

[3] " Sander collected into focus every charge which malignity had imagined against Henry VIII and his ministers, and so skilful was his workmanship that Nicholas Sander in the teeth of Statute and State Paper, in contradiction to every document that can claim authority . . . has had the shaping of the historic representation of the Anglican Reformation," etc. (*History,* 1870, x. 550).

[4] Law in *D.N.B.,* i. 261; Gairdner in *Lollardy and the English Reformation,* 1908, ii. 71; Pocock, *Records of the Reformation,* pref. xxvi and xlii. A. F. Pollard, *Political History of England,* p. 369.

[5] Dr. H. Gee, *The Elizabethan Clergy,* 1898, pp. 221, etc., has searched the lists carefully, and in a spirit unfriendly to Sander. But the only definite fault he finds is that " a few names are given twice over." See above, Chapters III and IV.

[6] D. Lewis's translation of Sander's *De Schismate* was published in 1877 with the title *The Rise and Growth of the Anglican Schism.* Sander's letter to Cardinal Moroni is printed in *C.R.S.,* vol. i. But the bulk of his correspondence is still unpublished, and much of it is at the Vatican. If collected it might form the material for a very interesting biography.

§ 2. Marriage Negotiations of Catholic Princes with Elizabeth

In the strongest contrast to Sander's open endeavours to bring back religion by force of arms, are the negotiations of the half-and-half Catholic princes who aspired to share Elizabeth's throne. Though they were not, indeed, all nor altogether wanting in principle, those who will occupy us most belong to a class of politiques and minimisers whom one cannot pretend to respect; and their chief object was to drive a bargain on the religious question. Of Elizabeth's insincerity, consistent and unapproachable though it be, especially in this connection, we shall find reasons for a somewhat milder judgment than usual.

Of course it will not be in place here to attempt anything like a full account of Elizabeth's love affairs, even with Catholics. We are only concerned with them in so far as they involve the interests of the Catholic religion in general, or those of its followers in England. For though we know beforehand that all was destined to end in smoke, we are not thereby justified in treating the whole subject as so much purposeless flirting and foolery. We must remember that the first beginnings of toleration after the change of religion, came through the royal marriage with Henrietta Maria. The presumption is that, if Elizabeth had eventually wedded even the laxest of her Catholic suitors, little by little some diminution of persecution would have ensued.

As it was, the treaties cut both ways. They did harm in so far that the bigots, by keeping up a long agitation, won power, and did the Catholics a real injury. The apathy of the princes was discouraging, and the eventual victory of the Queen's ministers over her confirmed their influence permanently. On the other hand, Elizabeth occasionally resisted them, and relaxed at one time the severity of the persecution. Moreover, she manifests herself in various new lights. Never was she more humane towards the old religion than when under the influence of the tender passion, and her position at this period explains much of an otherwise incomprehensible Catholic optimism in her regard.

Her first Catholic suitor was Philip of Spain, and here, at least, everything was straightforward, prompt and honourable. He offered to marry her, but on condition that she should formally renounce heresy and become a Catholic, "which she has not yet hitherto been." Elizabeth's reply was almost equally frank. After a little fencing, she confessed that " she was a heretic "; and so the matter ended.[1] Then came the courtships of various smaller foreign princelets, such as Eric of Sweden and the Duke of Holstein. But the Reformation had not yet obtained possession of a single great throne which would appeal to Elizabeth's imagination; and she was chiefly interested during the years which now followed in elaborate flirtations with the Earl of Leicester. For us the main interest perhaps lies in Dudley's endeavours to win the support of Spain for his suit; and it is during this time that Elizabeth began to be occasionally more favourable again towards Catholics, as we have already seen, especially in regard to the reception of a papal nuncio.[2]

Throughout the first decade there had also been endeavours to form a match with the Archduke Charles of Austria, which became more or less serious in 1567, when the Earl of Sussex was sent to make proposals at Vienna. Confining ourselves to the points in which religion was discussed, we find some characteristic instructions given to the envoy by

---

[1] *Spanish Calendar*, January 10 and March 19, 1559, pp. 22, 37.

[2] Among Fénelon's *Dépêches* (ed. Ch. Purton Cooper, 1840, vol. vi.) occurs a long *Mémoire*, given to the Sieur de Vassal, Aug. 24, 1574, in which the ambassador gives a description of the situation in England, with explanations from what had occurred at earlier dates, and *inter alia*, vi. 221, he recounts a long story told him by Leicester, in which that courtier magnifies all that Spain had offered him, with the evident object of getting France to go one better. Amongst other offers (so he says) was that of Spanish support for his marriage with Elizabeth. De Quadra offered the whole Spanish influence in England, and even " le consentement et l'authorisation du Pape; et que mesmes, s'il voulloit incliner à la réduction de la religion catholique, que le Pape luy octroyeroit un chapeau de cardinal pour son frère, et d'establir luy et sa race pour jamais en ceste couronne. Qui avoit esté un poinct de ce dernier, qui l'avoit faict retirer de la praticque du dict d'Aquila."

Now that we have de Quadra's dispatches before us, we can see how gross the misrepresentation is. It was Leicester who was constantly offering conversion or favour to Catholicism, in return for aid in his suit; De Quadra who as constantly refused to treat of the religious subject, noting from the very first the insincerity of the actors, and foreseeing the likelihood of subsequent misrepresentations (*Spanish Calendar*, 1558–1568, pp. 182, 194, 200, 226, 234, 272).

Lord Burghley, July 20, 1567.[1] The Queen, he says, cannot allow the exercise in her realm of any other religion than that established by law. " But as there is a general toleration used to subjects who live otherwise quietly, he (the Archduke) will herein enjoy as much liberty as any other." In other words, the Archduke 'was to give up all right to his religion, and trust to Elizabeth's mercy that he should not be interfered with, so long as he practised his religion in such privacy that not even the Puritans should make a fuss about it.

This demand for practically entire outward submission was, of course, here put forward, not as an ultimatum, but to some extent as a feeler; and the real question was, what would Austria's counter-demands amount to? These counter-demands were not sent in till three months later, and to understand them we must remember what sort of Catholics Elizabeth was dealing with. Charles left himself entirely in the hands of his brother, the Emperor Maximilian II, so that we may say that on these topics there was little to choose between the two. Now Maximilian was, indeed, a Catholic, but a staunch upholder of Imperialism before all else; and hence the *Kompromiss-Katholizismus*, for which he is noted.[2] He is said to have died refusing the last Sacraments.

With such a one to draw up the religious clauses for the marriage settlement, the interests of English Catholicism were not likely to be very carefully safeguarded. In truth the proposals now made carried compromise a great deal farther than was safe, prudent or dignified; and they would have caused no little harm and scandal to Catholics. There was, indeed, no betrayal of the faith, for Charles insisted on the full exercise of his religion in private. On the other hand, he agreed to attend the Queen to the Anglican church, to forbid his followers to argue in favour of his faith, and to allow any English who came to his services to be punished by the laws of England, and, finally, to settle any difficulties that might arise in this connection through the Queen's advice. If it had not been that Lord Burghley afterwards

---

[1] *Foreign Calendar*, p. 257.
[2] *Kaiser Maximilian II und der Kompromiss-Katholizismus*, by O. H. Hopfen, Munich, 1895.

excogitated still more abject terms, one might have thought
these reached the limits to which compromise could go.
Elizabeth's envoy strongly urged her to yield, and Maximilian characteristically asked how they could know she
was in earnest unless she gave way in something.   It may
be that if the Archduke had trusted Elizabeth so far as to
come over and act with energy the part of an *enamorato*,
his suit would have made progress.   But the Austrian,
not unwisely, declared that he must at least have some
answer to his proposals before he went.   Elizabeth was too
irresolute to give one, and he never came, though Sussex
hints to Cecil that if they did get him over it was very
possible he would turn Protestant.[1]

   This period of irresolution lasted for three years.   In
1570 Sir Henry Cobham was sent to renew the negotiations,
but again without any conclusion being reached.   As to
what part the religious question played this time, I have
not found precise record.   The subject had been meanwhile
complicated by the excommunication of the Queen early in
that year.   But to Maximilian that was no obstacle.   As
an extreme Imperialist he was disgusted with Pius's action;
and told Cobham so with great emphasis.[2]   It was stated
later by the French that " liberty for exercise of religion " [3]
was offered; but until one sees the propositions in full, the
meaning of the terms is open to question.   Perhaps it was
only liberty at the mercy of the Queen, as had been offered
from the first.   Anyhow the Archduke soon declared himself
engaged to a Bavarian princess, and Elizabeth's proposals
to him were succeeded by courtships with the royal family
of France.

   These, again, began in a way that seemed to bode no
good at all to the English Catholic cause.   The first proposals

---

[1] Sussex, Dispatches of October 24 and 27, 1567 (*Foreign Calendar*,
pp. 360, 361).
[2] *Foreign Calendar*, 1569–1571, p. 339 (September 17, 1570).
[3] *Foreign Calendar*, 1571, p. 435.   The Venetian ambassador to
Austria writes, " The whole country is much opposed to this marriage,
and for this reason the negotiations are kept secret " (*Venetian Calendar*,
p. 410).   This secrecy accounts for the ambassador getting hold of unreliable reports, which we now see, with the English documents before
us, were far too honourable for Austria, *e. g.* that they were insisting on
an open chapel, etc. (p. 411, January 1568).

were made by the Huguenot leaders,[1] who were begging
Elizabeth for money to continue the wars of religion, and
the apostate Cardinal of Châtillon explained, what was
sufficiently notorious, that Henri, Duke of Anjou, was then
very close to Calvinism. This was due to the way he and
his brothers had been brought up, for his mother had given
all of them Calvinistic teachers at one time or other, probably
with the idea that this would make them better fit to get
on in the world, and they all passed through a period of
proclivity to Protestantism.[2] At the moment the Huguenots
" made no doubt of Anjou's revolt in religion," if only
Elizabeth would honour him.[3]

Now the French ambassador then in London was de
La Mothe Fénelon, who had been previously instructed to
thwart the Huguenots at Elizabeth's Court, because they
drew from her the funds on which they waged the wars of
religion; and again, at the time of the Northern Rising,
Fénelon had been told to do all he could to put Elizabeth's
Government " in confusion and trouble at home, so as to
upset their undertakings as much as possible, and thereby
to prevent them " from further succouring the French
Protestants.[4] When, therefore, Catherine de Medici wrote
(October 20, 1570) to tell him of what the Cardinal de
Châtillon had proposed, he answered in the spirit of his
previous instructions, strongly insisting that all was
insincere.[5]

But Catherine was absolutely incapable of resisting a
tempting offer when the prize to be won was a crown for

[1] The Vidame of Chartres to Montmorency, October 1570 (*Foreign
Calendar*, p. 372).

[2] A. de Ruble, *La première jeunesse de Marie Stuart* (Paris, 1891), pp.
43, 132, etc. H. La Ferrière-Percy's *Projets de mariage de la Reine
Elizabeth* (1882) is more scientific than Martin Hume's *Courtships of Queen
Elizabeth*, but cannot, of course, be considered as a final account of so
complicated a subject.

[3] *Foreign Calendar*, 1569–1571, pp. 436, 455. This correspondence
illustrates vividly the bad state of religion under Catherine de Medici, and
Walsingham's alertness to take every advantage of it. The ambassador
de Foix " secretly swore to him that Monsieur would, within a twelve-
month, be as ready to forward religion (*i. e.* Protestantism) as any man
in England " (*ibid.*, p. 477).

[4] Fénelon, *Dépêches*, vii. 70, November 1, 1569; orders repeated on
the 19th, p. 73.

[5] *Ibid.*, iii. 357, Fénelon to Catherine, November 9, 1570 : " Elle ne
se soubsmettra jamais à nul mary . . . et les siens l'en detournent
davantage."

one of her children.   In spite of a thousand humiliations and
rebuffs, she worked henceforward for years to win the
unattainable object.   To open the negotiation formally she
sent one of her much-trusted fellow-countrymen, Cavalcanti,
and Fénelon, seeing that his Court was now in earnest,
changed his tone.[1]

Cavalcanti's articles for the marriage [2] were, of course,
intended to obtain from Elizabeth as much liberty as
possible, and eventually the main point was found to turn
on the second article, that the prince should be free in his
religion.   On their side, Elizabeth's ministers absolutely
refused the Mass, but Fénelon held out hopes of Elizabeth's
relenting.   Almost the whole year 1571 was spent in
debating this point, the English demands growing on the
whole more arrogant and oppressive as time went on.[3]
On the 19th of August it was proposed that the prince
should content himself with the Anglican formularies,
supplemented by " such (Catholic) rites, prayers and ceremonies as are not repugnant to the Scriptures," by which
clause the Council would have excluded the Mass.   Moreover, even this concession was to cease " if the Council
avow of their honours that troubles do grow by occasion
of the said permission."   On the 24th of August still heavier
conditions were added : he was only to have his private
prayers, in a secret chamber, until he may be persuaded
that the rites of the Church of England are sufficient, and
the Queen is to retain the right of adding further conditions
when she thinks necessary.[4]   To Henri of Anjou's honour,
it should be added that he is reported in July as being cool
about the marriage, and by October the Court itself regarded
the match as practically given up.

The revived plan for marrying Mary Stuart to the Duke

---

[1] Fénelon, *Dépêches*, iii. 415.   Dispatch of December 29, 1570.
[2] *Hatfield Calendar*, ii. 542, etc.   The articles appear to have been
handed in April 13, 1571.   There are various forms of the answers (*ibid.*,
p. 543), dated April 16.
[3] Walsingham to Burghley : " Being assured by divers (Huguenots)
that religion would not be a cause of breach, so that the Queen (Elizabeth)
stood firm, he used some sound speeches to de Foix, whom he found
very tractable " (May 26, 1571.   *Foreign Calendar*, p. 456.   Same thing
repeated, June 21, p. 477).
[4] *Foreign Calendar*, 1569–1571, pp. 511, 515.   See also *Foreign Calendar*,
1572–1574, p. 29.

of Norfolk was discovered in the fall of 1571, and this so-called conspiracy naturally caused a renewal of Elizabeth's marriage negotiations with France, for it showed how far the Conservative party in the nation was from acquiescing in the actual state of the kingdom as final or established. Sir Thomas Smith, fresh from his inquisitorial proceedings in the Tower on the luckless prisoners implicated in the plot, was sent to press the French Court about the match, and found Catherine as obsessed as ever with desire for its accomplishment, so much so, that she tamely accepted his rude and cruel answers to her representations about Mary Stuart, without showing the least surprise or resentment. But Prince Henri had by this time made up his own mind, and refused to continue the treaty. It is a pleasure to record that the conditions he now laid down were worthy of a Catholic. If he married, he said, his religion must have in England the same honour as in France. Queen Catherine " wept hot tears," [1] and Smith was angry and aghast; but the prince carried his point, and the courtship was over so far as he was concerned. The negotiation, however, had served its purpose; for under its cover once Catholic France bound herself by the Treaty of Blois (April 1572) to aid Elizabeth in any war levied against her, even if purely in the cause of the Catholic religion. The humiliation of France as a Catholic country was complete. [2]

But before the break with Henri took place, Smith had learnt from the Huguenots of the Court that he had rallied to the Catholic side, while his younger brother François, then Duke of Alençon, was inclining to the heretics even more decidedly than his brother had done in previous years. François was, therefore, at once substituted for his brother; his mother gave the assurance that " for matters of religion the Queen of England might rule him at her pleasure," and the next ambassador, Dale, reported it as his opinion " that the Duke would become Protestant." [3] The chief objection

---

[1] *Foreign Calendar*, 1572, p. 10.

[2] With a disingenuousness characteristic of the times, this was not avowed in the articles of the treaty that were made public; but each sovereign wrote to the other a private letter, still extant, acknowledging the obligation (*Foreign Calendar*, 1572, p. 86).

[3] Dispatches of July 7 and 26, 1573, *Foreign Calendar*, pp. 385, 394. Owing to the succession of names and titles, Henri and François de

to the marriage was that he was extremely young (their ages were respectively seventeen and thirty-nine), and also that his looks were seriously marred by pock-marks. But in spite of these drawbacks he proved the most constant of Elizabeth's suitors, and the nearest to winning her, which, but for his unexpected firmness as a Catholic, he would probably have accomplished.

The ten-year-long wooing must here be treated very summarily. It was at first hoped that he would turn Protestant at once, and Elizabeth's ministers were much disappointed at finding the same demand for liberty of conscience as before, and as its pledge the same insistence on having the Mass. The massacre of St. Bartholomew, in August 1572, and the subsequent fighting, naturally caused a break in the intercommunications, which, however, were taken up again with more zest when the Duke of Alençon went over entirely to the Huguenot side. So long, however, as he dealt through Elizabeth's ministers, who were now to a man religious bigots, no real progress could be made. The Duke, therefore, sent over various agents, Maisonfleur, Marshal de Retz (Gondi) and de la Chastre, who courted the Queen herself with fervour, and this proved much more successful. The old ambassador, de La Mothe Fénelon, gave place to Michel de Castelnau, Seigneur de Mauvissière, in August 1575 [1]; and on October 27, 1578, Jean de Simier arrived, who so delighted the Queen by the vigour and

---

Valois are very liable to be confused with one another; for both were known as Duke of Anjou, and both as Monsieur, though at different times; and one succeeded the other under the same title as suitor to Elizabeth. Henri, the third son (baptised Alexandre, but called Henri after the death of his father, Henri II), was created Duke of Anjou in boyhood, and after his elder brother, François II, died, he became "Monsieur" *par excellence*, or Monsieur de France, as nearest collateral heir to the throne. At the same time the fourth son, baptised Hercules, and created Duke of Alençon, took the name François. When Henri became King of Poland in 1573, François became Monsieur de France; and three years later still (Henri having meanwhile succeeded as Henri III) he was created Duke of Anjou.

Even contemporaries (as, for instance, the Spanish ambassadors) did not change their nomenclature as quickly as they should have done with the above changes of title; and several modern historians (as Mr. Froude and Major Hume) have, with even less excuse, followed their example.

[1] Only one volume of his *Dispatches* survives, June 1578 to June 1581, Paris, *Bib. Nationale, fonds français*, 15,973. A transcript at the Record Office, Baschet, *Transcripts from Paris*, bundle 27. The condensed translations below are from this bundle. After this volume there is a protracted breach in the regular French correspondence.

freedom with which he made love to her that it really seemed as though she might, after all, break away from the influence of her Council. It was therefore then, if at any time, that there would have been a chance of favour or relief for the English Catholics, and we do in fact find in M. de Castelnau's dispatches a new gleam of hope. He declares himself satisfied that Elizabeth will eventually obtain for her husband liberty of conscience; that she will honour him for his firmness in his beliefs, and that she was actually to some extent relaxing the persecution.

It will be worth while to make some longish extracts from Castelnau de Mauvissière's dispatches, for he sets forth the side of Elizabeth's character favourable to Catholics with greater authority than any one else   It is true that he is optimistic.[1] The French Government were not satisfied with anything less, as we saw in the case of Fénelon. Nevertheless, we cannot suppose that he would consciously or grossly misinform or deceive his employers. He uses, indeed, too much *couleur de rose*, but, taking all circumstances into consideration, that was for him the safer side to err upon, and his picture probably gives us a truer portrait than the representations either of the English, which flatter grossly, or those of the Spaniards, where irony and complaint are also liable to obscure the likeness to nature.

Here is Castelnau's flattering picture of Elizabeth's arrival at an entertainment, where she was to meet him and Simier—

(f. 54 *b*.) " More beautiful than ever, she appeared like the sun ; mounted on a handsome Spanish charger, and with people before her, so many that it was a wonder to behold. They did not merely honour her, but adored, with knees on the ground, and invoked upon her thousands of blessings and good wishes."   (He then describes Simier's vicarious courtship, January 1579.)

The critical and most important point is her position in regard to Catholics, and to the liberty of conscience which is to be allowed to her husband.

[1] Mr. Butler says, " Mauvissière, good, easy man, was completely cajoled by her Majesty's professions " (*Foreign Calendar*, 1581, p. xi. n.). But this refers to a later period.

(f. 96.) "The Catholics of this kingdom are a great party, and your sister, the Queen, affords them underhand much favour and assistance, and shuts her ears to all bitter reports. People are very much afraid lest, when she shall have married a prince so Catholic as Monseigneur your brother, she may prefer to strengthen herself, and to make sure on that side rather than on the other. If I could have the honour of a three hours' conversation with your Majesty in France, I could tell you things incredible, of which, moreover, the result is sure to follow. So far would the said Queen, your good sister, be from asking from Monseigneur a religion different from his own. From her he ought to expect all contentment in respect of his said religion, provided that he acts prudently. The Earl of Huntingdon and his party say that this marriage will be the ruin of England and of religion. Elizabeth is angry and has imposed silence on them. She goes less to their services while the marriage is being discussed. All this must be kept secret, and this letter should be burnt." (May 29, 1579.)

Similar news is given on the 26th of July.

(f. 112.) "If he espouses this princess, it is certain that she will yield to him for his religion all that shall be in her power."

On the other hand, the agitation among the Puritans of London, fomented, at least in secret, by most of Elizabeth's councillors, grew ever more intense. Eventually the French prince did come over (August 17 to 28, 1579) to woo for himself. With Elizabeth his courtship was most successful; but on the zealots the effect was maddening. They believed all the scandals which were freely circulated, and seemed likely to be true, such was the laxness generally in vogue at Elizabeth's Court.

(f. 142.) They declared that all sorts of terrors would follow, especially "a massacre of St. Bartholomew, in which the Queen would be the first victim, and a thousand other villainies." Hereupon they band together in anger. . . . "Some are threatened, some driven away; while mischief is always being preached in the churches. When proof is asked of them, they misquote some text; and no one dares bear witness against them," etc. (October 29, 1579.)

On the English Catholics, so Mauvissière repeatedly assures his master, the effect has been admirable.

(*Ibid.*) At first they had feared that the marriage " would be the total ruin of the hopes they still have for their religion." But of late they have been better treated,[1] and some are heard and much favoured by the Queen. So now they are all in favour of France, and have abandoned the side of Spain. But this, far from improving the chances of the match, has " set the Calvinists into a perpetual ferment," and now [the end of October] " the Queen is much agitated and shaken by their various alarms, for fears are easy to move. She has for a time resisted courageously, threatening and attacking the most powerful of those who favoured the agitation.[2] At one time she thought of admitting to her Council four Catholic men of influence, in order to counterbalance the rest. Two, Viscount Montague and [Sir William Cordell] the Master of the Rolls,[3] had been in Mary's Council. The other two were [Henry Percy] Earl of Northumberland, and a fourth, for which post several were named."

But Elizabeth had not the decision to take such a step; nevertheless, we next find the ambassador suggesting one still bolder.

(f. 166.) The present Parliament is composed " of men of the Puritan and Calvinist religions, having been named and sent some three or four years ago [1575, 1576] by those who wanted to advance the said religions, and to destroy the Anglican, with that little residue which remained of

---

[1] It is difficult to see exactly what improvement these sanguine words of Castelnau's can point to. It is true, however, that whereas there were three martyrs between November 1577 and February 1578, there were then no more till July 1581. Strype, *Annals*, II. ii. 241, says that the Papists were " very jolly " and " on tiptoes "; but he does not cite Catholic evidence, only Protestant alarmists, whose evidence is of no value.

[2] As early as March 1579 Elizabeth " gave express commandment that none should preach upon any such text " as might lead to " inveighing against the match " (Talbot to Shrewsbury, April 4, 1579; Lodge, *Illustrations*, 1830, ii. 150).

[3] Elizabeth kept Cordell as Master of the Rolls, though she removed him from the Council. Of his Catholicity we get a confused indication in his refusal to take the Oath of Supremacy till 1569, see *D.N.B.*, *s.v.*

the poor Catholics. . . . Elizabeth recognises this, and that they have always wanted to bridle her in the matter of her religion and of her marriage." . . . So it had been suggested that the Queen should dissolve this Parliament, and have another selected "in which the said Queen might place men of her own making and at her devotion." She would present the new marriage treaty to them " and make them ratify everything at once, for her wishes would be assured from those who would be named by her for the said new Parliament." (January 27, 1580.)

Through the ambassador's rosy spectacles the suggested measures seemed simple and promising; but where Elizabeth could not alter her Council, what chance would she have of bending both Council and Parliament combined? In February she gave in to the opposition, but in a character-istically round-about way. The actual state of the question is ignored, as well as her promises to her lover when he was present, and she goes right back to the breach with Rome caused by her birth, and to the Bull of Excommunication of 1570, and thence argues that this marriage, however great its advantages, being a contract with a Catholic, cannot be without danger, seeing the multitude of Catholics there were in the realm.[1]

(f. 177 b.) " She told me she could no longer conceal the strong and poignant reasonings with which she was being vigorously assaulted. . . . And first people told her that in the Roman Church some considered her father's marriage illegitimate, and herself by consequence a bastard, and some [a hint at Mary Stuart] would have liked to deprive her of the arms of England, if they had been able. . . . Then the Pope had excommunicated her, and the Catholics of this realm (who were very numerous and some very factious) said her rule was illegitimate.

" Now Monseigneur was a young prince, gallant and ambitious, in religion a strong and constant Catholic, for

---

[1] This statement of the multitude of Catholics was, of course, an exag-geration inspired by fear, and must be discounted in the same way as the exaggerations founded on hope which are found in the calculations of the Catholic exiles, etc.

which she personally esteemed him the more. But coming to marry her, it would be easy for him in a short time to win the entire affection of the Catholics of this realm, and perhaps also of divers others, malcontents and lovers of novelty and change. These malcontents might in a year or two suggest to Monseigneur to repudiate the Queen as a bastard, a heretic, of illegitimate rule. . . . The Pope might give him the kingdom on pretext of restoring religion, and he might depose, even kill her.

" These were things constantly pressed upon her, and she could not but think of them and of the rising which the Catholics of the realm might make in favour of their religion. At the same time she would not make herself unhappy before her time, and she hoped better things of his Highness." (February 15, 1580.)

De Mauvissière made a most diplomatic answer. Leaving all her points aside, he spoke only of " choses qui luy estoient très agréables."

" Had she not reigned for twenty years without the least danger? Did not her subjects, one and all, not only honour, but even adore her, each in his own rite (*sic*). Besides, she was so admirable, so perfect, so virtuous, that for this alone she made herself everywhere beloved. It was only when she halted among apparent arguments like those just mentioned that she began to show weakness of heart, and seemed as if, in a *laisser-aller* mood, she would let droop her merits and perfections. As for dangers from the Prince, why he only lived to love her."

Under such sweet compliments the Queen took heart again, and the ambassador ends his account of the interview with sanguine words of hope. Knowing women as he did, he would warrant that she meant to persevere.

In one sense he was right; her preference was still for marriage. But in effect her long speech was a confession that she could not now adopt any other means of solving the problems that hung over her, from her birth to the present hour, except that which she had already chosen.

She had forced England to exclude or ignore those solutions to her problems which Catholics would consider honourable and effective. Would her marriage be considered honourable and valid even now, unless some solution on Catholic lines was found for the old difficulties? As it was she could neither ignore those difficulties nor face them; so the only thing to do was to give up the idea of marrying. After this Mauvissière, though too sanguine to give up hope, writes rarely about her resolution; and as we look back we see clearly that the crisis is past.

To understand the change we must look a little deeper into the fate of the two articles on religion, which were debated between the two Governments.[1] The first regarded the marriage ceremony to be used, the French objecting to any ceremony which should scandalise Catholics. In effect a formula for the ceremony was eventually found which it seems might have proved sufficient. While the civil contract was being made the parties were to stand on a platform in the centre of Westminster Abbey, without religious ceremonies, though each party was to be supported by a bishop of his or her respective persuasion. Then both were to retire to different aisles of the church, and there each was to have had their own service.[2]

The second article, about which the real difficulty lay, regarded the freedom of religion afterwards—

" 2. That Monseigneur and his servants may make free (in the Latin version, *liberum*) exercise of his said religion, without thereby in any manner infringing the order thereupon which is received and approved by law in England." [3]

As has already been said, the answers at first given were altogether negative; Elizabeth, said her ministers, could not permit another religion in England, or tolerate private Mass.

---

[1] The articles brought by Cavalcanti have been referred to above. These proposed by Simier were, says Lord Burghley, " in very deed the said nine articles brought by Cavalcanti " (*Hatfield Calendar*, ii. 291). A Latin version, dated June 17, 1579, is printed in Strype, *Annals*, II. ii. 631; but his source is not indicated. The marginal note against the first two articles is that they are to be left till the personal conference.

[2] *Foreign Calendar*, 1581–1582, p. 190.

[3] *Hatfield Calendar*, ii. 542. Hatfield is especially rich in materials about the French match.

The French ambassadors, however, discovered that the Queen herself was by no means as rigid on this point as had been alleged; so it was proposed and settled that negotiation on this point should be postponed until the two royal personages met.[1] When they did meet (August 1579) the Duke asked to have the articles granted, and Elizabeth consented. In a subsequent letter the Duke reminded her that she had done so, and Elizabeth's answer tacitly, but quite plainly, admits it.[2]

As we have heard, the visit drove the fanatical party almost to madness. In November 1579 John Stubbes, for writing a strongly worded pamphlet against the match, had his hand cut off as a punishment. But this did not calm the public mind, because it was perfectly well known that there was a very strong party in the Council itself against the match, and a few words on this division of opinion must be here given.

Except a few of her chief favourites (as Leicester and Hatton), whose power was sure to decline with any marriage, all in the abstract wished the Queen to marry. So long as she had no children, and Mary Stuart stood as next heir, every Protestant would want the Queen to have issue, in order to establish a Protestant succession. But when it came to this or that husband in particular, deep division of opinion was soon evident. The Duke of Anjou had no sincere supporters, except perhaps the old Earl of Sussex, while adversaries were numerous. To say nothing of his being French, and in character restless, ambitious, grasping and extravagant, of his being mixed up with continental wars which were no concern of England—omitting all this, and keeping to the subject of religion, we find that on this, too, he seriously divided the opinion of the Council. The zealots, under the Earl of Huntingdon and Sir Francis Walsingham, were fanatically opposed to any marriage

---

[1] " The interpretation or explanation of the doubts touching the cause of religion shall remain to be determined by her Majesty and the said Duke at their interview."—August 22, 1572 (*Hatfield Calendar*, ii. 22, 288). Same resolution April 3 and June 15, 1579 (*ibid.*, pp. 291, 293, and Strype, II. ii. 631, where it is dated June 17).

[2] Anjou to Elizabeth: " Reminds her that when in her presence one of the subjects on which he most desired her acquiescence was that of religion."—January 28, 1580, *Hatfield Calendar*, ii. 307. Elizabeth's answer, *ibid.*, p. 539, will be quoted more fully below.

with a papist, whatever the safeguards. The more moderate party, under Lord Burghley, thought that this Duke at least was not a serious foe, that the emergent dangers might be provided against by laws, articles and agreements;[1] and, finally, they held that the perils of not marrying at all were graver by far.

As generally happens, the more fanatical and excited party won a decided victory over their more philosophic colleagues, even though the latter were supported by the Queen. It is remarkable that, though she bitterly reproached her Council for not giving at least a formal support to her marriage project, not one even of the moderates would do so, probably out of fear of her instability. Lord Burghley, though in the most deferential terms, insisted on leaving the initiative to her,[2] and to take an initiative in opposition to her ministers was just what she was never able to do in a matter of importance.

Unable to find support, the next best thing was to diminish the causes of the public irritation by removing from Court the French favourites. The Duke, presumably at Elizabeth's suggestion, recalled Simier in October; and before he left he asked that the marriage articles should be " accorded," in order that both sides might know how the affair stood. This was done at the so-called Treaty of Greenwich, November 24, 1579, but, as Lord Burghley notes, " There were objections made to two of Simier's articles—concerning the manner of the marriage, and for permission of religion."[3] Simier at once made considerable concessions, with which Elizabeth's Government were for the moment satisfied. When,

---

[1] This was very possibly true, for in later years, when Anjou was Duke of Brabant, he did not prevent the persecution of the Flemish Catholics, as English Protestant observers several times reported (*Foreign Calendar*, 582–1583, p. 1259). A dissertation on the dangers expected by Protestants, with answers (*Hatfield Calendar*, ii. 242, endorsed by Burghley). Cf. p. 270, where, *inter alia*, Burghley says that " all proceedings, actions and protestations " of the Duke " manifestly testify his countenance to the Protestant religion, both in France and in the Low Countries, on whose behalf he did not hesitate to take up arms against his own brother." See also p. 272, another similar passage in Burghley's hand.

[2] Minute by Lord Burghley, October 8, 1579, *Hatfield Calendar*, ii. 273.

[3] *Hatfield Calendar*, ii. 275, 293. These were the two first articles, mentioned above. Unfortunately we do not know what changes were now introduced.

however, the Duke received the amended text, he found it—
"not exactly in such form as he would have liked for the
liberty of his conscience; his ambassador having withdrawn from many points which he had hoped with her
good favour to obtain. But having heard that they could
not be obtained, he desires to comply with her wishes,
and begs, if no further religious changes are made, for a
conclusion." [1]

But the consent, albeit unwilling, which the Duke gave
to the revised articles was not at all reciprocated by the
English zealots. Simier, with the articles in his keeping,
had sailed from Dover on the 27th of November, the plan
being that the French should next send over a body of
Commissioners, who should finally settle the form of the
articles. Early in January 1580 Elizabeth wrote that the
agitation still continued, and that she could not let the
Prince return to a people so disturbed. Either the Commissioners must make concessions, or the match must
lapse. In spite of the obscurities of her style, there is
already here a clear intimation about giving up the match.

"You do not forget, *mon très cher*, that the greatest
cause of delay is due to this, that our people ought to con-
gratulate and to applaud. To bring this about I have
let time pass, which generally helps more than reasoning.
Now that I have used both, I must tell you that, though
some are improved . . . the public exercise of the Roman
religion sticks so much in their hearts, that I shall never
consent to your coming among such malcontents. But
may it please you to consider that the Commissioners should
have power to relax the stiff terms that M. Simier offered
us; and as I should not like you to send them over unless
the cause is going to be concluded, I beg you to remember
that the matter is so bad for the English to bear that you
could not imagine it unless you knew. . . . To conclude,
I cannot and will not let this negotiation trouble us more.
Let us remain faithful friends and assured. So let me
know if you will make some settlement other than the

[1] *Hatfield Calendar*, ii. 307.

public exercise of religion, for I desire nothing but what shall please you." [1]

The Duke in answer sent a diplomatic letter, which started with (and improved a little on) one of Elizabeth's sounding phrases about the need of faith and honour.

He reminded her of the application he had made personally in the matter of religion, and that Simier has now (the words are quoted above) made all the concessions possible, " and hopes that the matter may proceed, provided no change is made in the matter of his religion. . . . He was not surprised that she put off the journey of the Commissioners under the pretext of religion. Some people have tried to persuade him that this was a device to break off the negotiations altogether. But he is unable to believe this, as her Majesty has always done him the honour to tell him her intentions candidly." Two days later (January 30) the Duke wrote again in the same sense, and even more explicitly.[2]

But though he thus ignored Elizabeth's hint about breaking off on the grounds of religion, she answered, repeating the refusal in still clearer terms. The letter, drafted in her own hand, characteristically throws on Catholics the blame for her own change of face; but it also contains a profession of her own personal tolerance, which partly justifies Castelnau, whom one might perhaps otherwise suspect of optimism.

" Monsieur, I see from your letter that you desire that the articles should pass as they were agreed to. You do not remember that my plan was not to go on until I saw all was agreeable to both of us. I cannot say this is the case, hearing, as I do, how the people are murmuring. If I had thought of this at first, I swear to you I would not

[1] *Hatfield Calendar*, p. 298, draft with autograph corrections. No date, but answered January 28, 1580. Notice that the Queen speaks of the " public (*aperte*) exercise of religion," whereas the article only spoke of its " free " exercise, not specifying whether in public or in private. It is not very likely that she was alluding to the marriage rite, for the Commissioners came to an agreement about that, so it seems likely that she was overstating, especially as the Duke's answer (quoted above) only speaks of " liberty of conscience," not " public liberty."

[2] *Ibid.*, pp. 307, 31.

have waited, and would have answered in a different fashion. But the Prince [King of Spain?] injures me day after day with *preparatifz*, and after their menaces will follow (execution) I doubt not. Then there are the sermons, and continual maledictions made to mislead my subjects in Ireland and elsewhere. Such things incite my people. They will with difficulty endure that religion, unless it were better moderated than the articles indicated.

"Now I beg you to believe that I am not such a bad Christian, and that my love for you is not so small, that I should refuse to agree, that you should have your religion for yourself, free and without let, though under such conventions that it should offend our people as little as possible. But, seeing that you insist on the articles, while I perceive such dissatisfaction as I do, I must consider myself as most unfortunate that I was [not] born for that great hour which God seemed lately to be preparing for me. Methinks my unhappiness is all the greater because it has no company; whilst you seem to have been fortunate to have escaped such evil fortune. And notwithstanding that I cannot be yours, as you desire, yet grant me at least this grace—that a friendship be accorded me the most close that ever was between princes." [1]

This letter, which is not dated, would have been written about the same time, in February 1580, as the speech made to Mauvissière, in which she dealt with the subject from a yet more fundamental point of view, and both were in reality a renunciation of the match because of religion. Not that she objected, but she felt that her ministers would not support her. A formal declaration that the engagement was ended could not be expected from her. A change, however, which was already indicated in the last sentence of the Queen's letter, was gradually made in the negotiations. Instead of a marriage, a league with France was asked for, through which the ambitions of the Duke to form a dukedom or principality in Flanders at

[1] *Hatfield Calendar*, ii. 539, undated. The modern editor refers the letter to 1582, but the old endorsement, "no. 10," rightly assigns to it an earlier place in the correspondence.

the expense of Spain was to be encouraged by French levies and an English subsidy.

In the eyes of the world this was a dishonourable slight on the French Prince, and even Catherine de Medici could not ignore it, however gladly she would have seen him sovereign of the Netherlands. Besides, France did not want a war with Spain. Elizabeth's proposals were therefore rejected, and the marriage was urged. On her side Elizabeth was quite ready to keep up talk about the marriage, while she egged on the Prince to war. He accepted, on the 12th of August, 1580, the sovereignty of the Netherlands, which the Protestant States offered him; but he was for the moment unable to do anything, because the seventh war of religion was engaging all the forces of France, both Protestant and Catholic.

Such was the state of the Catholic marriage treaties at the period to which we have followed the fortunes of the English Catholics. But before we endeavour to realise what this dallying meant for them, it will be well to follow Anjou's failing cause to its final end, and this need not for our purposes occupy us very long.

Throughout the year 1581 the French Prince was falling more and more into the position of a cat's-paw, by which Elizabeth annoyed and injured Spain without damnifying herself, except in pocket, through the subsidies she had to furnish her professed lover. In the spring of that year the French Commissioners came over to settle the oft-debated marriage treaty;[1] and now that the projects of marriage were practically at an end, there was no great difficulty found in settling all the hitherto insoluble difficulties about the religious ceremonies for the marriage and the Prince's liberty of conscience, though unfortunately no copy has yet been found or published of the terms on which this fictitious agreement was reached. The treaty, however, was signed with all solemnity on the 9th of June, 1581, or thereabouts.[2]

Almost at the same time the Duke began his campaign in Flanders, whence, after some slight preliminary suc-

---

[1] The reason given to the Commissioners to show that the articles on religion needed revision was that Jesuits had lately come into England and made divers converts (*Foreign Calendar*, April 30, 1581, p. 142).

[2] *Foreign Calendar*, 1581–1582, p. 202.

cesses, he came over to England again in November, to
make a last attempt to win the Queen; while her object in
welcoming him was probably only to maintain her personal
power over him, and so to keep him at war with Spain.
During this stay there were the same violent flirtations as
before. Once she publicly kissed him and gave him a ring
(November 22, 1581), which every one at first understood
as a promise of marriage.[1] Whatever its significance,
Campion was executed the week after, which was generally
and with some reason interpreted as the Tudor way of
showing the Puritans that no concessions to Popery were
contemplated.[2] Immediately afterwards, and in the same
way, in order to justify herself to the French, Thomas
Norton, a well-known Puritan lawyer, who had superin-
tended Campion's torture on the rack, was placed in confinement for intriguing (it was alleged for conspiracy)
against the marriage.[3]

Again befooled, Anjou left England (February 1582) to
take up the revolution against Spain in the Netherlands;
and continued to write to Elizabeth as a lover, but his
letters generally ended in petitions for more and more
money, which the Queen, however much she begrudged
the expense, found herself constrained to give.

Eventually all his projects ended in ignominious failure.
On St. Anthony's Day (January 17), 1583, he attempted to
seize Antwerp and other Flemish towns by treachery. But
the enterprise ended in disaster; five thousand of the
French, and among them many of his best and noblest
captains, were slain in the streets, while the Prince escaped
with difficulty, and was forced to retire from the country.

[1] There is, of course, no official record of this escapade, but Mendoza
at once sent his version of it to Madrid (*Spanish Calendar*, 1580–1586, p. 226),
and a French version may be found in the *Mémoires* of the Duc de Nevers.
Miss Strickland (iv. 456) quotes Aubrey's *Life of Scorey* for what seems to
be an English variant of the story, that Elizabeth brought her lover to an
English service at St. Paul's and rewarded his attendance by kissing him
before the whole congregation.

[2] According to Mendoza, Anjou promised at this time to turn Protestant and to suppress the Seminary of Rheims (*Spanish Calendar*,
pp. 238, 253). But Mendoza is throughout the episode a very interesting,
but a very prejudiced witness. Froude and Hume accept the bitter gossip
of his dispatches too easily.

[3] Fuensanta del Valle, *Documentos Inéditos*, xci. 210. Hume unfortunately omits his name (*Spanish Calendar*, p. 233, December 11,
1581). For Norton's career see *D.N.B.*

Yet he did not cease to intrigue with all sides, with Catholic and Huguenot, with Spaniard, Dutch and English; and he was planning new revolutions when he died prematurely at Château Thierry on May 31 (June 9), 1584, his last movement being one of adoration towards the Host at the Mass, which was being celebrated by his bedside.[1] Elizabeth wept at the news; but there were few real mourners, though his death, meaning as it did the eventual extinction of the House of Valois, was destined to bring on France a long and disastrous war of succession, of which we shall hear repeatedly as our history continues.

To return to the English Catholics and to the year 1580—what might they, what did they expect from this restless and unprincipled son of Catherine de Medici? Castelnau, indeed, gave repeated assurances that all Catholics were ready to welcome him, but we may be sure that their hopes were but short-lived. Among the English Catholic records of that period we do not, in fact, find any reports or calculations of good that will come to them by him; and, on the other hand, the means taken by Elizabeth to reconcile the Puritans cannot but have produced great discouragement among Catholics.[2] " Put not your trust in Princes " was the lesson which his intervention in English affairs incessantly emphasised; and, without a doubt, the total effect of his career was greatly to divide and weaken the forces of the Catholics, greatly to excite and animate those of the Protestants.

Nevertheless we must in fairness admit that his own perseverance in the faith must have done something to counteract this general want of principle. Whereas almost every one, including his mother, at first expected that he would purchase the favour of the Protestant party by apostasy, and so make sure of a high position both in

---

[1] K. de Lettenhove, *Les Huguenots et les Gueux* (1882), vi. 520, 528. The Duke's will, dictated the day before death (*ibid.*), also reflects credit upon him. De Lettenhove describes excellently the conflicts of the contending creeds and the international side of the story.

[2] Mendoza wrote, December 4, 1581 : " The Catholics have greatly lost heart at seeing that Alençon has made not the slightest effort to induce the Queen to suspend the execution of those about whom I write in another letter," that is, of Campion and his companions, who had been executed three days before (*Spanish Calendar*, p. 230). See also Simpson's *Campion* (1867), p. 317.

England and afterwards also in the Netherlands—this he would not only not do, but he expressly broke off the match by insisting on the religious safeguards, as those who read his letters must acknowledge. In the Netherlands, too, in spite of the Dutch unwillingness, he insisted on his Mass; and he won from Elizabeth (though not perhaps permanently or fully) liberty of private worship, which had at first been most distinctly refused. In all this there was undoubtedly much which would appeal to the Catholic imagination of that day; and if drowning men will clutch at straws, it would be no wonder if Catholics did from time to time build hopes upon him.

There is a curious paper among the dispatches of the Venetian ambassador at Paris, in which the advantages and disadvantages of the match are carefully set forth from the point of view of a foreign Catholic; and it is needless to add how striking the difference is between these views and those which Lord Burghley so often enumerated, for and against, but always from the point of view of a Protestant courtier. The conclusion of the acute but religious-minded Venetian is that, though the disadvantages appear on paper to outweigh the others by far, yet that this does not prevent there being room for hope. " As many things are hidden in the hearts of Princes which do not appear externally, and as their hearts are in the hands of God—so, even should the marriage take place, it may be for the service of Christendom and for holy purposes which we do not as yet perceive." [1]

The penultimate chapter of a volume is naturally one in which we begin to say good-bye to many of the characters, with whom we have had much to do in earlier periods of our story. While bidding farewell to the Duke of Anjou we are also taking leave of his unprincipled mother, Catherine de Medici. She did not die just yet, but she falls into the background and is hardly heard of again. Don John, too, has gone; the Duke of Alva has won his last victory;

---

[1] *Venetian Calendar*, 1558–1580, p. 603. There appears to be a similar paper in the Eliot MSS., vol. xiv. (*Historical MSS. Commission*, i. 42). " General heads of two orations at the college of Rheims regarding the proposed match (*pro* and *contra*)."

and Cardinal Granvelle will soon have completed his last ministry. With the Duke of Anjou the last of those phantom beliefs has disappeared, that Elizabeth would some day marry a Catholic, and that all would end happily. It is strange that such ideas should ever have gone current; but Pius IV once solemnly dwelt upon it at a public consistory. But now at least there were no more such illusions, and circumstances were shaping themselves, slowly but surely, for a straight fight between Spain and England at sea, and on land between La Sainte Ligue and Henri of Navarre.

Among the ranks of the English Catholics, too, not a few old friends have fallen out together with Sander. The old generation of exiles at Louvain is heard of no more, and Dr. Morton and Dr. Maurice Clenog are near their deaths. Stukely and Fitzgerald, too, have passed, and nothing more appears about men like Sir Richard Shelley, who, if they did not accomplish much, at least did not despair of the religious Republic in her hour of deepest darkness and amid general defection. That was certainly no trivial praise; and the men that come next upon the scene reckoned it a sure sign of their being in the right way, that, amid new and even more acute difficulties, they were faithfully following in the path trodden by their predecessors.

CHAPTER IX

THE COUNTER-REFORMATION IN ENGLAND

§ 1. *The Arrival* (*June, July* 1580)

BY the time the Jesuit Fathers were ready to start their
party had greatly increased. The missionary spirit was in
the air. Not only were five alumni of the college ready
to return, but even the old Bishop of St. Asaph had
volunteered to go, and with him Dr. Morton and four of
the late chaplains from the hospice, one of whom was over
sixty. The Bishop and Dr. Morton rode ahead, Fathers
Persons, Campion and their party, twelve in all, started
from Rome on the 18th of April and arrived at Rheims on
the last day of May. The journey had been marked by
many characteristic incidents. Some of these were full of
consolation, especially the welcome given them by Cardinal
Paleotto at Bologna, and again by St. Charles Borromeo
at Milan; some were inspired by love of adventure, as their
detour through Geneva (in order, under incognito, to beard
Beza in his den) and their pilgrimage to St. Claude among
the Juras. All was flavoured with the chivalrous spirit of
the Counter-Reformation movement, though there is no
need to enter into details here.[1]

It was not until they reached Rheims that they heard
any special news from England. But they were then informed for the first time [2] that Dr. Sander was among

---

[1] See Sherwin to Bickley, June 11, 1580, printed in *The Journey of
Bd. Edmund Campion from Rome to England*, in *The Month*, September
1897. Also Persons' fuller *Life of Campion*, chaps. xvi. to xxii.

[2] As Sander had now been ten months in Ireland, this ignorance may
seem strange. But we must remember that Sander had come in secret,
lived in hiding, and had hitherto done nothing that attracted public
notice. Even in Ireland rumours sometimes got about that he had
returned to Spain (e. g. *Irish Calendar*, August 3, 1579). Nor did either
the Pope or Elizabeth (so far) wish to give publicity to such official
information as they occasionally received. The information about Lord
Baltinglas was really fresh news, and Persons mentions that Allen had
heard it through Spain.

the insurgents in Ireland, and that they had recently been joined by Lord Baltinglas. At this Elizabeth's Government was much exasperated, and the prospect was much more threatening than before. The party resolved nevertheless to proceed, after reviewing once more the reasons for so doing, first at Rheims and afterwards at St. Omers. So the mission started again early in June; even the old chaplains went forward, and upon the whole with excellent results. We may say, however, in the light of subsequent events, that it would have been better to have sent them in more slowly, by ones and twos.

Only the old Bishop of St. Asaph and Dr. Morton turned back, and there were some, including the Cardinal of Como, who were distinctly annoyed at this.[1] But the arguments in the Bishop's defence are very strong. If even the two Jesuits, with the activity of youth on their side, were, in fact, unable to hold out for more than a year (the one being taken, the other constrained to cross the seas), what chance would an old man, in poor health, have had, whose dignity would have marked him and his hosts for overwhelming persecution?[2] Even if he had not attempted to govern, there was small chance of escape; yet what use in coming, under such restrictions?

For greater precaution, the Fathers now separated. Persons crossed on the 11th of June, and reached London a little before the middle of the month. Both he and his companion, no doubt, wished to be very cautious at first; but they knew they must run some risks, and we shall notice in all the first steps now taken a certain attractive note of boldness, which, however, was not to last, though at the moment it conduced to success.

Father Persons, on the day he landed, went to one of Elizabeth's prisons to inquire after one of the Catholic prisoners. He did not, to be sure, go the instant he disembarked; but, after walking about for some time, and

---

[1] Even Allen was a little disappointed. See the correspondence in his *Letters*, pp. 400–4.

[2] The successors of Persons and Campion, FF. Holt and Heywood, managed to survive two and three years respectively. Southwell escaped for five years, Garnet for nineteen. Of the twelve who came with Persons, not more than one-third escaped capture.

endeavouring in vain to get into touch with Catholics (this remained for years a very great difficulty for incoming priests), he recognised that his inquiries were causing him greater risk than would result from putting himself incognito into the hands of Elizabeth's officials. So he went to the Marshalsea,[1] and inquired for Mr. Thomas Pounde of Belmont, of whom we shall hear more presently. The Jesuit was admitted to see him, was recognised, and most warmly welcomed. In Mr. Pounde's room Persons met a Catholic gentleman, Mr. Edward Brookesby, who took the missionary away with him, and brought him to an old friend, Mr. George Gilbert.[2]

The first thing that Persons begged of his new allies was aid to bring in Father Campion, who had not yet arrived. It afterwards turned out that he had been in danger for a time; for the Mayor of Dover kept him at first under observation. But he was afterwards set free (June 24); and when he came up the river to London, Mr. Thomas James, who was watching for him at the landing-stairs, recognised him in the boat, and said, " Give me your hand, Mr. Edmunds; I stay to lead you to your friends."

James brought the newcomer to the Catholic circle which had already received Persons. That Father, however, was already off for three weeks on his first missionary tour, and in his absence Campion's admirers arranged that he should preach to a fairly considerable audience in the great hall of Lord Paget's house at Smithfield on the Feast of SS. Peter and Paul, June 29. This was going too fast. The attention of the adversaries was awakened, and Campion was warned by friends at Court that endeavours were being made to track him down. So he retired to a poor man's house in Southwark, and there Persons found him a week later.

The latter notes in his Memoirs that, when he returned to London, he already perceived signs of change among

---

[1] The wealthier Recusants were confined here. The fees were higher, but the surveillance much lighter. For the names and localities of the London prisons, see *C.R.S.*, i. 47. For the prisoners then in the Marshalsea, *ibid.*, p. 70.

[2] Edward Brookesby of Sholdby, Leicester, and George Gilbert of Beaconsfield, Bucks—names which frequently recur in the accounts of this time.

the Catholics. They were unusually comforted and inspired by the quasi-simultaneous arrival of so many priests, for, besides the party from Rome, all of whom had reached England by various routes, a smaller body of Rheims students had come in about the same time. But the Government (so at least Persons believed) also heard something of this influx of priests, and was "extremely stung" at the news.[1]

§ 2. *The Synod of Southwark* (*July?* 7-12)

Meantime Persons, though recognising that the sooner they left London the better, wished first to present himself to the ecclesiastical authorities and the clergy of the place. That act of deference and respect was the ordinary preliminary to a Jesuit mission, and in this case it was also very important to ensure conformity in working. But as there was then no clergyman at liberty with ecclesiastical rank, he asked the older priests to meet them in a poor man's house by the river side near St. Mary Overies (now St. Saviour's), Southwark. How many came we do not know; Father Persons only mentions George Blackwell, the future Archpriest, and already one of the most respected priests in town,[2] Edward Metham,[3] Bachelor of Divinity,

---

[1] Persons, *Life and Martyrdom of Fr. Campion* (*Letters and Notices*, 1877), p. 23. Chaps. xvi. to xxii. of this work form the chief authority for this section; and they have been freely used by Simpson and others. It is to be regretted that we have not ampler records of the other missionaries. Sherwin's letters reveal a nature intensely chivalrous and interesting. Bryant, Rishton and Cottam, so far as we can follow their lives, were also missionaries full of the religious spirit of the great revival. Lives of all three will be found in *D.N.B.*, Gillow, etc., but Allen's sketches in his *Brief Historie* give the spirit of the men in its most attractive aspect. See also Allen's *Letters*, ed. Knox, pp. 87-9, 400-4, and *C.R.S.*, vii. ix. 22-31.

[2] On the 24th of May, 1578, he received a brief enabling him to bless altars, etc. The original parchment is still in the Westminster Archives, ii. 79, printed in Dodd's *Church History*, ii. 251.

[3] But he probably means Thomas Metham, Licentiate of the University of Louvain, one of the first students of the Douay College. He was, indeed, then confined either in the Queen's Bench or in the Marshalsea at this time (*C.R.S.*, i. 68). But several instances are on record of Catholic prisoners being able to bribe their gaolers to let them out for short periods. He was shortly afterwards deported to Wisbech (Bridgett, *Catholic Hierarchy*, p. 197), where he died some ten years later. Very much drawn to the Jesuits, he had been allowed while in prison to make, out of devotion, the vows of the order. (See *C.R.S.*, ii. 279, and *Catholic Encyclopedia*.)

and Mr. Tyrrwhit.[1] There were also present some of the newly ordained priests and some of the laity.

Father Persons began on his side with a very serious protest of his entire ignorance of Dr. Sander and his expedition to Ireland, solemnly declaring under oath before the whole assembly that he had not even known the project until he heard, at Rheims, that Sander had gone. He also read out the instructions the missionaries had received against taking any part whatever in politics.

The next topic for consultation was, what rule to follow on the subject of attending Protestant services. As has been already explained, English circumstances gave to this practice a peculiar character. The Elizabethan Settlement of Religion *depended* on the participation of the people in heretical worship. Thus for a Catholic to attend them was not merely *participatio in sacris* with heretics (which does not necessarily imply renouncing the Catholic faith oneself), it was here, by force of circumstances, also an act of adherence to the system of Tudor religion; it was a participation in a tyrannical effort to put King before God, not merely in one's own heart, but in the consciences of the whole kingdom.

The questions now put related to various excuses made by occasional conformists, of which the strongest was that of those who said they went merely from external obedience. Elizabeth professed to require nothing more; why should not they, by protesting that they went from blind obedience *only*, be held clear from any real *active* participation in the heretical rite? The answer was made that—

" So public an act as is going to the church, where profession is made to impugn the truth and to deface, alienate and bring into hatred Christ's Catholic Church, is the highest iniquity that can be committed; and therefore a Catholic cannot without great impiety bind himself to be present at those acts," etc., etc. Eventually " it was concluded that this should be the sum of that which all priests

---

[1] *C.R.S.*, ii. 176. He was probably Nicholas, who left Douay in 1577 (*Diary*, p. 25), and was later on Prefect of Studies there.

should teach and insinuate unto Catholics in all places, as hitherto they had done." [1]

The third topic was, again, typical of England at that time. We, perhaps, do not sufficiently remember that if the new missionaries had been at once victorious, the Church which would have arisen would have used, not the Roman, but the cognate Sarum rite, and so far no change from it had the sanction of law. On the contrary, the Council of Trent had ordained that all ancient rites and traditions were to be preserved. Yet as things now stood it was morally impossible to maintain the old English rite in every detail. To begin with, there were no more Sarum service books printed, and the new clergy, being entirely educated abroad, would be so used to the Roman rite that a complete change to the English order could hardly be expected the moment they returned to their native shore. Some difficulty between the two rites was, therefore, to be expected, and especially in those observances which were more onerous under the Sarum than in the Roman code. Thus the Sarum practice prescribed fasting on every Friday (as well as on Vigils which fell on Saturday), whereas the Roman only enjoined abstinence. This was a point on which some people would, under the circumstances, be sure to raise doubts. It was discussed, therefore, and the decision was an extremely conservative one.

" Nothing shall be altered in the matter of fastings from the old customs; but in what shire so ever of England (for all had not one custom, but the church of York some, and Canterbury and London others) the Catholics could remember that the Fridays, or any other day or vigil was fasted, the same to be kept and continued now, and the priests always to be the first and most forward to put it in execution." [2]

There is no indication here that any change was expected. Nevertheless, in Father Heywood's time, a couple of years later, considerable modifications were admitted, as we shall see.

[1] Persons, *Life of Campion*, p. 36. [2] *Ibid.*, pp. 36-8.

The fourth topic of discussion was one that involved no serious principle, but was nevertheless very difficult to settle. How should the incoming priests be distributed among the different counties, towns and houses of Catholics? It was a most important point of discipline, but no definite scheme was, or could be, formulated until the clergy could have a head of their own, and this, in the rising storm of persecution, did not seem likely to take place in the proximate future.

Then there were some smaller matters concerning particular persons. Father Persons mentions three such, and it will be best to deal with them at once, as they are very characteristic of the times, though the case of Bosgrave, which we are now able to locate in October, cannot have been discussed in July, and that of Cottam may have been decided earlier. Thomas Cottam had been arrested at Dover and sent up to London in charge of a fellow-traveller, whom the port authorities took for a Protestant. But he was really a Catholic jurist, Dr. Humphrey Ely, travelling under the name of Havard. Ely, of course, let the priest go, but he was afterwards himself arrested for having done so when he got to London. What, it was asked, was Cottam's best course? He wanted chivalrously to give himself up to save his friend. It was a noble aspiration, and the little synod would not condemn it. So Cottam gave himself up, and afterwards won the martyr's crown; while Ely retired abroad, and eventually became a priest.[1]

The next case was that of John Hart, afterwards a Jesuit, but then a newly ordained priest of the Rheims Seminary, which he left on the 5th of June. Arrested on landing in England, he was sent up to Walsingham, who was

---

[1] A prison list gives the 27th of June, 1580, as the date of Cottam's committal to the Marshalsea (*C.R.S.*, i. 71), which seems to be ten days or so before the synod began; and if this is so, we have another case of Father Persons' memory, full and accurate as it was about facts, yet failing to arrange them in the right order, a very common defect. But it may also be that the prison list was wrong. Such lists are not very reliable; and we know that there was roguery about Cottam's capture; for Andrews the Searcher applied for and obtained £5 for bringing Cottam up from Dover. This was, of course, to disguise the fact that he had allowed Ely to bring him up (R.O., Declared Accounts, Treasurer of Chamber, 542, rot. 10, July 4, 1580). It may, therefore, be that June 27 was the day on which Cottam ought to have been at the Marshalsea, but one does not feel convinced that he was there. For Ely see *D.N.B.*

z

unexpectedly kind, and allowed him to go to his home in Oxfordshire; but under condition of holding conferences on the faith with John Rainolds, a Divinity Professor at Oxford.[1] Could that be allowed, especially as Hart did not display extraordinary learning or fortitude? We do not know what was said at the synod, but eventually Hart returned to London, was imprisoned at first in the Marshalsea, and then, in December, was transferred to the Tower.[2]

The other case which Father Persons ascribed to this time, was that of the Jesuit Father James Bosgrave. He had entered among the Polish Jesuits, and the Fathers there let him come to England for health's sake. He, too, was arrested at landing,[3] but was offered liberty if he would go to the Protestant church. Not having come as a missionary, he was not prepared for this trial, and so he yielded and went, though assuredly not meaning to deny or injure the faith. But whatever his motive, this act could not but cause some scandal at that particular crisis. After thus having regained his liberty, he endeavoured to enter into communication with his co-religionists, but he soon found what a mistake he had committed. He therefore wrote them a very handsome " Satisfaction," [4] and addressed some similar letter to the Privy Council, and his re-arrest soon followed. He was sent to the Tower (at the end of 1580) and condemned to death, but was eventually banished.

The end of the synod came suddenly. One Charles

---

[1] *Douay Diaries*, p. 166. The *Diarium Turris* (published in Rishton's edition of Sander's *De Schismate*, and probably written by Hart) begins on the 15th of June, and then breaks off for a time after the 19th. This may be due to this journey home. A warrant for £5 was given to Andrews, the Searcher of Dover, on the 4th of July for expenses in bringing Hart up (R.O., Declared Accounts, Treasurer of Chamber, 542, rot. 10).

[2] *C.R.S.*, ii. 220; *Diarium Turris*, 1628, p. 352. See Hart's " Letter to the Indifferent Reader " (July 7, 1582), in Rainolds's *Summe of a Conference between J. R. and J. H.*, 1584, p. 9. Father Persons says in the *Life of Campion* (cap. 23) that the conferences were at Oxford; in his *Autobiography* that they were in the Tower (*C.R.S.*, ii. 29). But this apparent variation really confirms the correctness of his memory, for both statements were true. For Rainolds and his Catholic brother see *D.N.B.*

[3] The date of this must have been September, for on the 4th of October Edmund Boode received under Council Warrant cxiis. iiijd. for bringing him up from Orford (R.O., Declared Accounts, Treasurer of Chamber, 542, rot. 19).

[4] Allen afterwards printed this with the title " The Satisfaction of Mr. James Bosgrave, the Godly Confessor of Christ, Concerning his Going to the Protestant Churches on his First Coming." This is appended to his *True Report of the Late Apprehension of John Nichols at Roan* (Rhemes), 1583, pp. 32, 34 (B M., 699, b. 7).

Sledd (or Slade, or Sleydon) had been a servant in Rome to Dr. Sanderson or Dr. Morton, and had there come to know many Catholics. Now he had turned traitor, and began to arrest his former acquaintances. He seized Robert Johnson, priest and afterwards martyr, and Mr. Henry Orton, who was at that time actually on his way to the house where the Jesuit Fathers were; so that if Sledd had had the patience to follow his quarry home, he might have seized the whole band of missionaries at one swoop.[1] After such a warning it was no wonder that the assembly broke up with all convenient speed. To have met at all was a brave conception, and shows how deeply every one felt the need for some sort of ecclesiastical government.

§ 3. *The Lay Workers, and the Proclamation of July* 15

On the 15th of July was issued an important Proclamation, which all contemporary writers declare to have had a great influence in aggravating the persecution. Yet none of them quote it or had it before them when writing, and when we come to look into its text we do not at once see the connection with the missionaries. This, in fact, is the Proclamation which the Government sent out on the reception of what seemed to them reliable evidence of the existence of the oft-rumoured Grand Papal League,[2] which had been supplied to the English ambassador at Paris by Mary Stuart's zealous, but imprudent agent, the Bishop of Ross. The Government were too nervous about this bogey to give it more advertisement than was necessary. So, instead of using the word League, they only aver that, whereas the Pope and the King of Spain and others were threatening the Kingdom, and diverse rebels and traitors were inciting and assisting them, it was hereby forbidden under the severest penalties to circulate alarmist rumours on these subjects. The following is a condensed version of this paper—

[1] Johnson and Orton were committed by the Lord Mayor to the Poultry Counter, July 12, 1580 (*C.R.S.*, i. 67). Persons usually connects this incident with the close of the Synod. See *Vita Campiani*, cap. 10; *Autobiography, C.R.S.*, ii. 27, and Bombino (whom he helped). Yet once (*Life of Campion*, cap. 22) he puts it earlier.

[2] See above, p. 236. Cobham had sent in the news from Paris about the 2nd of July.

BY THE QUEEN

Traitors abroad, and especially at Rome, increase in malice, and attempt to irritate all estates against her Majesty. Now they devise in writings, and some have published, " that the Pope, the King of Spain and some other princes are accorded to make a great army to invade this realm of England and other her Majesty's dominions," etc., etc., in order to comfort themselves in their undutifulness. But the Queen's Majesty, " who has never offended any foreign prince, but only for the defence or preservation of her own realm (*sic*), without seeking to usurp upon any other prince's possession " . . . hath made ready her forces, and is in readiness. Therefore her Majesty thinketh it good to admonish her good and faithful people, that they continue their dutiful service, and be in good readiness, with their bodies, arms, etc. Any " who have unnatural affections are charged not to irritate her Majesty to use the rod or sword of justice against them . . . from which, of her own natural goodness, she hath a long time abstained . . . although she knoweth that it is her duty in time to use it, and so she meaneth to do." Her Majesty warns all not to be moved by murmurers and spreaders of rumours, the dissemination of which is to be punished as the spreading of sedition.[1]

Though the Proclamation made no explicit reference to the new missionaries, it probably, for that very reason, hit them as hard as, or even harder, than if they had been mentioned by name. If a persecuting motive had been placed in the foreground, many would have been repelled; whereas the appeal to political loyalty would unite all, and the genuine persecutors would assume of themselves, and

---

[1] *Dyson's Proclamations*, B.M., Grenville Library, 6463, n. 207. The style and line of argument is throughout curious, and it might, perhaps, be useful to study the text in further detail by collating it with the drafts in the Record Office. Where blame is laid on those who have " devised in writing and published " the League, it might almost seem as though Leslie were being blamed for having given the information. But the Government probably wished people to think that they had detected the Catholics in publishing copies of the sham League. As is shown in the text little turns on the actual phrases, the general object being to arouse a quasi-patriotic animus against the Catholics.

act on the assumption that the missionaries would intrigue at all their religious meetings in favour of the Catholic Powers. Thus an increase of persecution was certain to follow in practice, and Father Persons, writing three weeks later, says that the Catholics listen eagerly to our conferences, " although by public proclamations just published, though not against any one by name, this has been forbidden under the severest penalties." [1] Persons was not wrong in the practical interpretation he put upon the Proclamation, for, in fact, the charge of advancing the supposed grand Papal League was eventually brought in their trials against Campion and the rest. This Proclamation made the missionaries decide to leave London at once.

The Fathers, however, had no intention of flying and hiding themselves in obscurity. On the contrary, they were intent on trying a new method of carrying on their apostolic work, and that was by a missionary tour. Such journeys had, no doubt, been undertaken before and would be undertaken again, nevertheless, these particular expeditions had a character of their own, due partly to the intense vigour of the missionaries, partly to the spirit of the gentlemen who organised them.

It has been already pointed out that the religious revival of this time depended in an unusual degree upon the gentry. The Crown, in these days of its greatest power, had become the fountain-head of heresy; the peerage, half exterminated with the rise of the Tudors, had been re-stocked with new men, who, enriched by the spoils of the monasteries, were pledged to the new order of things; the people and the country towns were still too untrained in the use of political power to count seriously in the great struggle. Thus it was among the country gentlemen that protectors and co-operators must be chiefly looked for; and this state of things was to continue, not only during the period of the revival, but all through the long centuries of persecution and penal laws which were to follow, until in the nineteenth century the spread of liberty and the rise of the people

---

[1] Letter of August 5, 1580, quoted more fully below.   Persons speaks of " proclamations " (*editti*) in the plural.   If this is strictly true, we should suppose that some lesser authorities were issuing proclamations or orders of their own, as was often done in those days.

enabled the Church to come out from the catacombs, and allowed all Catholics to take their part in political life.

Of the Catholic laymen who in that day played so brave a part, the chief was Mr. George Gilbert, only son of Ambrose Gilbert of Beaconsfield, Bucks, and of Grace Townsend. When he was an infant of two years, his father died (February 1554), and George passed under the wardship of his uncle, Robert Townsend of Ludlow. He was educated in London and at Cambridge on strict Puritan principles, coming much under the influence of Edward Dering,[1] a well-known Puritan divine, who died in 1576. About this very time, having presumably completed his University course, his uncle Townsend " delivered him his lands and his free marriage," and he set out for his travels abroad to complete his education. At Paris he met with Father Thomas Darbishire, by whom he was probably converted and received into the Church. Then, going on to Rome, he became acquainted with, and in time deeply influenced by, Father Persons, by whom his Catholic training was completed, at the same time that—

" he prosecuted the learning of such gentlemanlike exercises as men of his quality are wont to learn in Italy, as riding, fencing, vaulting, and the like (for he was of a most able body) ; yet did he so join therewith in secret all kind of Christian piety, both by prayer, fasting, and mortification of his body, and liberal alms, as a man might easily see that the true Spirit of God had laid hand fast on him." [2]

In this spirit of fervour Gilbert thought of making a pilgrimage to the Holy Land; but Persons advised him rather to go to England and devote himself to succouring priests. This he did with fervour, and having sufficient money, he boldly bribed the chief pursuivant of the Bishop of London, viz. his son-in-law, Adam Squire, and took lodgings in his house in Chancery Lane. Then, having " drawn divers principal young gentlemen to the same purpose," he had " sundry Masses said daily, until the Jesuits came in, when times grew to be much more

---

[1] *C.R.S.*, ii. 201.   For Dering, see *D.N.B.*   [2] *Ibid.*

exasperated." He also at this time, "being incited by
his chiefest friends," made " propositions of marriage to a
certain gentlewoman." But upon hearing that Fathers
Persons and Campion were coming to England, he broke off
the treaty, and henceforth devoted his mind entirely to aid
this mission, and wished to take a vow never to marry.
But Father Persons would not allow this, permitting him,
however, to vow chastity so long as England should not
return publicly to the Faith.[1]

Now that the Fathers were about to start they were
equipped with princely generosity by this man, whom
Persons calls " the good angel, which God in His Eternal
Providence had appointed should be the chief temporal means
of assisting the first mission of the Society in England."
He provided for each the complete outfit for a gentleman
of means, that is, two horses and a servant, and sixty
pounds in money.[2] What was more, he proposed to ride
with Father Persons, and he " entreated another gentleman
like himself, and his dear friend, to accompany the other
Father," that is, Campion.

We do not know who this friend of Gilbert's was, but
Persons has left us the names of nearly thirty gentlemen
who took their share in Gilbert's good works. He notes,
however, that there were many others whose names he had
by then forgotten ; and many more still whom he remembers
but cannot mention, partly because they would themselves
prefer not to have their good works published, partly because
there was still danger of their being persecuted for the help
then given. So he confines himself mostly to such as were
already dead (12) or had entered religious orders (6), or were
in exile, or who, having already paid the full penalty of
imprisonment, had nothing more now to fear. Three of
them, Arundel, Tresham and Tylney, were once gentlemen

---

[1] Evidently Persons thought there was a good chance of its return.
[2] So in the *Life and Martyrdom of Campion*, cap. 21, Persons' letter
of August 5, 1580, does not mention the exact sum of money. Sixty pounds
was, of course, a very large sum indeed for those days, when the multiple
for the buying power of money, as compared with that of our own day,
was about six, eight, and sometimes ten. One must remember, however,
that Persons, at least, kept lodgings in London, and had to send letters
abroad by special messengers. Gratuities, too, had often to be given
suddenly and on a large scale.

of the Queen's Court, others were heirs or sons of peers or knights, as Vaux, Stonor and Throckmorton.

They were all, as Persons says, "young gentlemen of great zeal and forwardness in matters of religion, who, in respect of their estate and parentage, and for that they were more free and able than others (the most part of them being unmarried and without charge) to advance and assist the setting forward of God's cause and religion, it seemed that His Divine Majesty made choice of them for the same, and put into them such extraordinary joy and alacrity to be employed therein—which in truth was so great as cannot be well expressed, every man offering himself, his person, his ability, his friends, and whatsoever God had lent him besides, to the service of this cause." [1]

It is not, of course, to be imagined that the missionaries were perpetually accompanied by these fervent assistants. That would have attracted notice and created a new danger. Even when they were on their journeys, the greater part of the time was passed in the houses of gentlemen, where a guide would not have been needed. One of Campion's journeys was deliberately made from inn to inn, partly for the sake of a change, partly also for safety's sake. Still, in any case, the care, the good example, the sympathy shown by these young men must have had a wide and deep influence. A more striking proof that the ardour of the Counter-Reformation was actually spreading in England itself could not be expected.

But human nature being prone to excess in almost every mood, is notoriously most of all liable to go too far, when elevated by excitement and strained by the presence of danger. There will be later on extravagances among the missionaries themselves in the direction of exorcising and witch-finding; and among the laity there will be cases of rash recourse to illicit proceedings in politics. The matter must be discussed fully later, and even here we should notice that amongst the dead whom Persons thought it safe to mention occur the names of four out of the fourteen who had been executed for participation in the so-called Babington conspiracy. Persons, indeed, like most con-

---

[1] *Life and Martyrdom of Campion,* p. 28. A similar passage in the letter of August 5.

temporary Catholics, believed that the initiative in the plot had been Walsingham's, and that those who suffered were clearly his victims. Now, though this is certainly not the complete and final truth about the case, still much may be said for this way of looking at it, and we cannot be surprised at Father Persons taking that view. It is clearly unreasonable to take Persons' words in a sense not only not intended by him, but which even excludes his declared meaning. Nevertheless, this has been done, and the group of deeply religious Catholics who were the foremost in spreading knowledge of the aims of the mission have been called the Jesuits' Secret Society, that is, a secret society for political purposes. In reality this is pure myth. There was neither a society, nor a secret, nor a policy. Gilbert and his friends were not united in any sort of club or association; and in their mission-journeys, the object of which was purely religious, they aimed at all the publicity which the circumstances permitted.

The error originated with Mr. Simpson's *Life of Campion*. He appears to have imagined that, as Jesuits were fond of Sodalities, he would be right in supposing that all co-operation among their friends must have been executed under the sanction of a sodality or guild. This, however, is plainly no more than a surmise. Moreover, the ground on which the surmise is ultimately based is historically unsound. In Gilbert's time Sodalities had been in existence for a few years only and for strictly limited purposes, they did not until the next century reach that vogue of which Simpson was thinking.[1] Nor were they ever so numerous that they could be called into existence for co-operative work, so transient and casual as that of Gilbert and his friends.

The *à priori* reasoning is, therefore, quite inconclusive, and of *à posteriori* or documentary evidence there is none whatever. No mention of it in any contemporary letter, journal, biography or State-paper. Yet had such a Sodality existed, Gilbert's Jesuit friends would have been the first to praise and proclaim it. They all praise his spirit of

---

[1] The first English Sodality was founded among the students of the English College, Rome, in 1581; the second (so far as we know) among those of St. Omers College, in 1609 (*The Month*, February, March 1912).

fellowship and zeal for organisation; but no one hints that he acted under ecclesiastical direction, or by any fixed rule. It was true of him what Father Weston said of Babington, "he gathered round him various young men of his own rank *by force of his mental gifts and moral superiority*." [1] Until some actual evidence for the existence of this alleged secret society is produced, it seems unnecessary to elaborate further negative arguments against it.

To return to the two Jesuit missionaries who, accompanied by George Gilbert and his friend, were about to leave London. The persecution being so strong that they could not live together, they agreed to meet for the last time at Hoxton, then a village in the country, at the house of a Protestant gentleman whose wife was a Catholic. They came at dusk on the 18th of July,[2] and were about to start early next morning when another Catholic layman of note rode down from London. This was Mr. Thomas Pounde, of Belmont, near Bedhampton, Hants, a man born to considerable estate, and closely connected through his mother with the Earl of Southampton, who is said to have befriended him in his various troubles. These were so characteristic of the times as to require a brief description.

Thomas Pounde had at first been "a gentleman of the body" to the Queen, and had been one of the gayest of her courtiers. In a masque given to the Queen at Kenilworth he had acted the part of Mercury, and he had also something of a reputation as a dancer. On one occasion the Queen asked him to give some specially intricate measure before her, which he did with such grace and spirit that the Queen was delighted, and made him repeat the performance. But this time, whether it was that he was now somewhat fatigued, or from some accident, he missed his footing in the middle of a difficult figure and came down with an ignominious crash at her feet. At this her Majesty roared with laughter and promptly kicked him in the ribs, crying, with mock allusion to the ceremony of knighthood, "Arise, Sir Ox!"

---

[1] Morris, *Troubles of our Catholic Forefathers*, ii. 182. Mr. Simpson's error has been fully discussed in *The Month*, January 1905.

[2] Writing on the 5th of August, Persons says it was eighteen days ago.

At that period and in that Court such unqueenly action did not by any means signify what it would have meant in times such as ours.   But even so, it did mean something, and Pounde was not the man on whom the lesson would be lost.   He arose, bowed, and left the hall, saying, " *Sic transit gloria mundi !* "   Returning home he began to devote himself with all his old enthusiasm to a life of austerity and devotion, and for a while he became a hermit.   Then he became more and more drawn towards a life of active apostolic work, and resolved to become a Jesuit.   But the persecuting Government, after many fines and other annoyances, finally threw him into prison (1574) and kept him in confinement, first in one place, then in another, for almost all the rest of Elizabeth's reign, so that there was no chance of his going abroad to enter the Jesuit novitiate, as he would have liked to do.   The Father General of the order, however, under such circumstances, took the imprisonment in lieu of novitiate, and admitted him to the religious vows during his confinement.   So he was already in an especial way bound to the new missionaries,[1] though in his circumstances he lived, and went on living till the end, as other imprisoned Catholic or Recusant gentlemen might have done.

Of tried faith, witty, generous, with considerable literary powers and respectable abilities as a controversialist, he had nevertheless some of the peculiarities which often characterise men who have been forced to live long in solitude, especially when this is the result of injustice and cruelty.   " He is very fervent," wrote Father Garnet, April 10, 1605, " but somewhat abounding in singularities." For instance, he would reward his gaoler handsomely when he was put into irons or otherwise harshly treated, but when freed from bonds he would (contrary to custom) give the expectant locksmith nothing.   His love of controversy was also intense.[2]

But though " somewhat abounding in singularities," the chivalrous spirit which animated him was not singular

---

[1] Father Persons brought him from the General a special letter; printed in Foley, iii. 586, with much other matter for Pounde's biography.

[2] This will be seen below, and in the interesting autobiography of Henry Chaderton, Foley, iii. 545, etc.

at that day, and we find the same spirit henceforward working high and low among the Catholic laymen. The pages that follow, the correspondence of Father Henry Garnet and the autobiography of Father John Gerard, which continue our story in the next generation, will show us many examples of the persistence of this courageous and devoted type of men. What a contrast to the laymen at the time of Elizabeth's accession, who stood tamely by, while the residue of the ancient hierarchy faced the incoming heresy almost alone, and practically unsupported.

§ 4. *The Challenges* (*July* 19, 1580)

So far we have not heard why Pounde took the considerable risk of bribing his keepers in the Marshalsea to let him ride away at dawn. His explanation was that he and his fellow-prisoners had come to the conclusion that the missionaries ought to take an important precaution. There was evidently a grave risk of one or both being captured at any moment. Once captured they would be buried in seclusion, then examined, and malignant reports would be spread abroad about their confessions, which no one would be able to answer. Therefore prepare now, he said, some protest or declaration, which may be published by your friends as soon as you are taken.

The advice was obviously sound; indeed, the forecast was, in Campion's case, fulfilled to the letter. Though neither had as yet written a word with a view to publication, both Fathers agreed to delay their departure, and do what was advised. They must also have decided to write on the same lines, for the series of points in their respective papers are very similar one to the other. This settled, they both began to write, and in half an hour Campion had finished. Then, a copy having been taken and committed to Pounde's charge, and the original being consigned to Campion's valise, he rode off westwards in the direction of Oxford, where he was to turn north and make a long circuit back to London. Persons, whose paper bears the title, *A Confession of the Faith, addressed to the Magistrates of London*, wrote at somewhat greater length, and he would not have finished quite so soon, but he, too, was off ere long, riding northwards.

Persons had taken the precaution of sealing his paper before he gave it to Pounde, while Campion gave in his unclosed, though with the proviso that it should be kept secret. This, however, did not necessarily prevent Pounde from reading the paper, and he was altogether delighted with what he found. It was, indeed, an unexpectedly felicitous treatment of the subject he had proposed, *i. e.* to explain who the Fathers were and why they had come.

The explanation, in fact, is one which should be read by all who wish to understand the spirit of the Counter-Reformation. The obstacle which the missionary saw before him was that of religious prejudice. Prejudice asserted that the Jesuit could not possibly be heard, because he would malign the Queen, and deny her authority. Campion showed by the very idea of his writing that this preconception was entirely wrong—that he would appear at Court, in the Universities, anywhere, ready to be heckled and examined about the most burning questions to any extent. What test more easy, more searching, more convincing? Prejudice, too, asserted that he would reject free discussion, and would be unable to face the test of Scripture. Yet here he stands, ready to be examined by all their learned men, and to bear questioning from all their books. Then, too, there is an entire absence even of spiritual threats. There is no calling down of fire from heaven, nor imprecation of punishment hereafter. The only terror was that of innocent hands lifted in prayer, and of zealous hearts who will never despair of " winning you heaven, or of dying on your pikes."

To the Right Honourable Lords of Her Majestie's Privy Council [1]

" Right Honourable,

" Whereas I have come out of Germanie and Boëmeland, being sent by my Superiours, and adventured myself into this noble Realm, my deare Countrie, for the

---

[1] The principal texts of this document are R.O., *Dom. Eliz.*, 142, 20, Harleian 422, 12, and 422, 13, Stonyhurst *Coll. P.*, ii. 583, etc., the editions of Charke, Hanmer, etc.

glorie of God and benefit of souls, I thought it like enough that, in this busie, watchful and suspicious worlde, I should either sooner or later be intercepted and stopped of my course. Wherefore, providing for all events, and uncertaine what may become of me, when God shall haply deliver my body into durance, I supposed it needful to put this writing in a readiness, desiringe your good Lordships to give it ye reading, for to know my cause. This doing, I trust I shall ease you of some labour. For that which otherwise you must have sought for by practice of wit, I do now lay into your hands by plaine confession. And to ye intent that the whole matter may be conceived in order, and so the better both understood and remembered, I make thereof these ix points or articles, directly, truly and resolutely opening my full enterprise and purpose.

" 1. I confesse that I am (albeit unworthie) a priest of ye Catholike Church, and through ye great mercie of God vowed now these viii years into the Religion of the Societie of Jhesus. Hereby I have taken upon me a special kind of warfare under the banner of obedience, and eke resigned all my interest or possibilitie of wealth, honour, pleasure, and other worldlie felicitie.

" 2. At the voice of our General Provost, which is to me a warrant from heaven and Oracle of Christ, I tooke my voyage from Prage to Rome (where our said General Father is always resident) and from Rome to England, as I might and would have done joyously into any part of Christendome or Heathenesse, had I been thereto assigned.

" 3. My charge is, of free cost to preach the Gospel, to minister the Sacraments, to instruct the simple, to reforme sinners, to confute errors—in brief, to crie alarme spiritual against foul vice and proud ignorance wherewith many my dear Countrymen are abused.

" 4. I never had mind, and am strictly forbidden by our Father that sent me, to deal in any respect with matter of State or Policy of this realm, as things which appertain not to my vocation, and from which I do gladly restrain and sequester my thoughts

" 5. I do ask, to the glory of God, with all humility, and under your correction, iii sortes of indifferent and quiet audiences : *the first* before your Honours, wherein I will discourse of religion, so far as it toucheth the common weale and your nobilities ; *the second*, whereof I make more account, before the Doctors and Masters and chosen men of both Universities, wherein I undertake to avow the faith of our Catholike Church by proofs innumerable, Scriptures, Councils, Fathers, History, natural and moral reasons; *the third* before the lawyers, spiritual and temporal, wherein I will justify the said faith by the common wisdom of the laws standing yet in force and practice.

" 6. I would be loth to speak anything that might sound of any insolent brag or challenge, especially being now as a dead man to this world and willing to put my head under every man's foot, and to kiss the ground they tread upon.   Yet have I such a courage in avouching the Majesty of Jhesus my King, and such affiance in His gracious favour, and such assurance in my quarrel, and my evidence so impregnable, and because I know perfectly that no one Protestant, nor all the Protestants living, nor any sect of our adversaries (howsoever they face men down in pulpits and overrule us in their kingdom of grammarians and un-learned ears) [1] can maintain their doctrine in disputation. I am to sue most humbly and instantly for the combat with all and every of them, and the most principal that may be found : protesting that in this trial the better furnished they come, the better welcome they shall be.

" 7. And because it hath pleased God to enrich the Queen my Sovereigne Ladye with notable gifts of nature, learning and princely education, I do verily trust that— if her Highness would vouchsafe her royal person and good attention to such a conference as, in the ii part of my fifth article I have motioned, or to a few sermons, which in her or your hearing I am to utter,—such manifest and fair light by good method and plain dealing may be cast upon these controversies, that possibly her zeal of truth and love of her

---

[1] The meaning is : " The ministers tyrannise over us, as if we were schoolboys and unlearned folk, who could listen only, not speak."

people shall incline her noble Grace to disfavour some proceedings hurtful to the Realm, and procure towards us oppressed more equitie.

" 8. Moreover I doubt not but you her Highness' Council, being of such wisdom and discreet in cases most important, when you shall have heard these questions of religion opened faithfully, which many times by our adversaries are huddled up and confounded, will see upon what substantial grounds our Catholike Faith is builded, how feeble that side is which by sway of the time prevaileth against us, and so at last for your own souls, and for many thousand souls that depend upon your government, will discountenance error when it is bewrayed, and hearken to those who would spend the best blood in their bodies for your salvation. Many innocent hands are lifted up to heaven for you daily by those English students, whose posteritie shall never die, which beyond seas, gathering virtue and sufficient knowledge for the purpose, are determined never to give you over, but either to win you heaven, or to die upon your pikes. And touching our Societie, be it known to you that we have made a league—all the Jesuits in the world, whose succession and multitude must overreach all the practices of England— cheerfully to carry the cross you shall lay upon us, and never to despair your recovery, while we have a man left to enjoy your Tyburn, or to be racked with your torments, or consumed with your prisons. The expense is reckoned, the enterprise is begun ; it is of God, it cannot be withstood. So the faith was planted, so it must be restored.

" 9. If these my offers be refused, and my endeavours can take no place, and I, having run thousands of miles to do you good, shall be rewarded with rigour, I have no more to say but to recommend your case and mine to Almightie God, the Searcher of Hearts, who send us His grace, and set us at accord before the day of payment, to the end we may at last be friends in heaven, when all injuries shall be forgotten."

Such was Campion's high-spirited and magnanimous conception of his swan-song, but his words were destined to serve a somewhat different purpose. Through Pounde's enthusiasm they became known to the public in a few weeks, and this premature publication completely changed the feeling with which they should have been read, and threw into quite unintended relief the offers of disputation. Campion had strongly denied his intention of " anything that might sound of any insolent brag or challenge." But early publication gave such emphasis to the idea of a challenge (which was originally quite a subordinate issue) that the name of " The Challenge " was immediately applied to the paper itself, and so it is called still. That there was some little loss here is certain, but the compensating advantages turned out to be very great indeed. The best judges, Campion and Allen among them, thought the publication most fortunate, and this because its daring gave to his terribly oppressed fellow Catholics the greatest encouragement they had received for a generation.

Hitherto the Catholics in England had not had a single external success to cheer them in their painful and humiliating struggle against an overpowering, ever-present enemy. There had, indeed, been examples of patience, of firmness, and other unostentatious virtues. But how little these, in comparison with the vast superiority of their enemies' forces, the saddening remembrance of many falls, and the ever-disappointed hope of help to come. The controversy twelve years earlier no doubt had cheered them, but since then how little to give them heart or courage ! But now this fugitive has actually issued a challenge " to all and every " of the enemy " and the most principal that may be found." Its verve, its inoffensiveness, the recollection of its author's old academic triumphs, made it greedily read by Catholic and Protestant alike. It was a bright literary success, a welcome presage of superiority.

The Protestant pulpit soon began to answer by protests and counter-defiances. That, of course, only increased Campion's triumph. If they professed to be able to meet him in debate, any hesitation to do so must be ascribed to cowardice, unless their professions were false pretences. " The error of spreading abroad this writing hath much advanced the cause," wrote Campion later, and no doubt with perfect truth.

A A

Still a drawback made itself felt later on. Protestant controversialists began to represent the Jesuits as perpetual disputants, and ill-wishers to the order afterwards took up the cry. Later on, too, when the persecution grew still hotter, it was found more prudent for the Catholics to avoid every manifestation whatever, even of high spirits, let alone of readiness to dispute; and this change of policy naturally appeared like a reflection upon the bolder line taken by the first missionaries at the beginning of their campaign. But, as the reader has already seen, all these objections are only surface deep. It was not the original intention of the Jesuits to encourage disputations. Their instructions dissuaded them from such a course; their intended last speeches were written with a very different object in view. There is no need, for the present, to pursue this side of the subject further. It is more important to consider in detail the increased rigour of persecution which led Pounde to publish the Challenge prematurely. Persecution is the characteristic note of English Catholic history at this time, and we have already followed its course down to the slight mitigation, or pause in growth, which accompanied the more active negotiations for the French match in 1579. We must take up the story from that time.

Note on Father Persons' *Confessio Fidei ad Magistratus Londini.*

This paper now only survives in a Latin translation, so that an elaborate comparison of his work with Campion's is no longer possible. Some description of it, however, should not be omitted. It is a good deal longer than the Challenge, the Latin version being at least twice the length of Campion's English. The substance of both the papers is very much the same, so much so that we must suppose that they both had the same ten or twelve points in their heads when they began to write, but they are worked out and expanded differently. Persons' Introduction is three or four times the length of Campion's. He declares, like Campion, that he is a Catholic, a priest, and a Jesuit. But he adds to the declaration of his Catholicism a paragraph on his conversion. Though this is well done, Campion's reticence is distinctly better. That he came as missionary because he was sent is explained exactly as Campion had done, but as usual, more diffusely. The paragraph about avoiding politics is again longer, and the additions, though not important, are naturally interesting. He says that Jesuit Superiors, even when Catholic Princes have begged them to attend to some of their own political matters, have refused to do so; and how much more in this case, where they are not even informed as to the principles at stake.

The only point in which Persons is perhaps superior is this, that he is somewhat less high-flown and more practical. Thus Campion's proposal to give three different sorts of discourses for three different sorts of audiences, may sound perhaps a trifle overdone. Persons makes a simple request for disputation, and there leaves the subject.

On the whole, then, we may say that Campion's *Challenge* represents all the important points of Persons' paper, and generally in a better form.

§ 5. *The Recrudescence of Persecution (June to December, 1580)*

The relaxation of severity, which lasted from the spring of 1579 till April or May 1580, was by no means a deeply-marked change, nor did it ever seem likely to be permanent. No laws were repealed or modified; no prison was closed; there was no declaration of clemency. Catholics do not mention it at all, and the only person who speaks about it clearly and positively is the French ambassador, Castelnau, to whose good offices it was presumably due. Yet even he does not insist much upon it, for it was not a primary object of French policy. It seems, in fact, to have depended solely upon Elizabeth's whim. The persecuting party resisted the match with Anjou, which she was then anxious to bring about. So she retaliated by going less often to the Protestant services, and giving the Catholics some " underhand " assistance. The relief afforded, though not extensive, was no doubt real, and to prevent overstatement it will be well to resume a few of the dates, from Castelnau's correspondence, which has been quoted more fully above.

The ambassador's first hints are very slight. On the 22nd and 25th of February, 1579,[1] he reports from the Earl of Leicester, that Lord Huntingdon, the head of the Puritans, has been won to the match, and about the same time Elizabeth remarks that she gave no support to any minister, " of whatever religion he might be," who used her service to cloak his ambitions. The remark may be of little importance in itself; still, indirectly, it includes a

---

[1] R.O., *Transcripts from Paris*, xxvii., ff. 62, 65. The news of Huntingdon's support is not reliable, or at least it only lasted a short time.

recognition of Catholics as well as of Protestants, and implies that the latter are losing favour. This is the starting-point. In March we read that Mary Stuart is to be better treated, and on the 29th of May, Castelnau says that the Queen " gives underhand much favour and help to Catholics, and closes her eyes and ears to all the evil reports made against them." By July the ambassador, knowing how easily a reaction might ensue, says that caution must be used, as the Catholics are a trifle too forward on behalf of the match.[1]

Once we have got the date of the relaxation from the French ambassador, and an idea of what to expect, we can find illustrations in other quarters. Thus the keeper of the *Douay Diaries* was wont casually to chronicle in it news which he received of special sufferings. He makes no such notes between March 1579 and September 1580. Similarly the Spanish ambassador reports no outrages from February 1579 to June 1580. The Acts of Privy Council do, of course, record many cruel orders issued between those dates, but when one sifts them carefully, one finds that the relaxations of imprisonment were more frequent then than before, and that the general orders to exert pressure show a distinct falling off.

Again, it is remarkable that no fresh severities were ordered immediately upon Sander's landing (July 1579), though this may also be attributed in part to the slight success of the rising in the first year.

During the winter of 1579–1580 Elizabeth was struggling hard with her ministers to obtain their support for the match. But with the Puritan party behind them in an open ferment the Tudor Queen could not constrain them, and by February 1580 it was clear that she would not insist on the marriage. Nevertheless, in March she scolded some of the bishops for too much zeal against the papists.[2]

This is the last we hear of her intervening on the side of the Catholics. The change to positive disfavour must have come in April or May, for Persons and Campion were

---

[1] R.O., *Transcripts from Paris*, xxvii. pp. 72, 96, 112.

[2] Mendoza, March 23, 1580, in *Spanish Calendar*, p. 20. Mendoza, however, ascribes this, to her fear at the position in Ireland, which he thought, August 15, 1579, would make her agree to toleration (*ibid*. p. 686).

told of it when they reached Rheims or St. Omers (May 27 to June 4). But the first dated orders which we have for renewing severity were letters sent out to the bishops by the Privy Council on the 18th of June, ordering renewed proceedings of the Ecclesiastical Commission against Recusants, and that special vigilance should be used against Catholic " schoolmasters, both public and private " (that is tutors), because of " the daily corruption grown thereby in teaching and instructing of youth." [1]

Next week (June 26, 1580) Mendoza gives further details about the increase of rigour. Those released have been recalled to prison, but the number of Catholics continues to grow. He has heard that the cause of the outbreak may be due to some one having scattered in the streets copies of the crusade indulgence granted to Fitzgerald's followers,[2] but feels doubtful about it. King Philip, in his reply to the ambassador (August 15), notes the renewal of persecution and asks for further information. I do not find any distinct answer to this, but the question of itself marks the fact of the change.

From now onwards the downward course is all too clear. On the 15th of July came, as we have seen, the Proclamation against traitors in foreign parts, for which the immediate occasion was given by the Bishop of Ross's indefensible error of sending in an information against the Papal League. Though this Proclamation stimulated the persecutors to fresh activities, and provided them with specious arguments for their cruelties, there are no distinct orders for severity in the document itself. On the contrary, when one recollects the character of the previous relaxation, one may well believe the declarations made here of " her Majesty's reluctance to use the rod, or sword of justice, from which she hath of long time abstained, although she knoweth that it is her duty in time to use it, and so she meaneth to do." No doubt Elizabeth would have been glad to use no further violence if Catholicism would but expire under the laws already passed. But rod and sword she meant to use, if necessary,

---

[1] Dasent, *Acts of Privy Council*, xii. 59.
[2] *Spanish Calendar*, p. 38; Philip's reply, p. 49. This Indulgence was probably akin to those attached to Stukely's crucifix, June 13, 1575, the list of which is in *Westminster Archives*, ii. 15.

to obtain her ends; and, in truth, violence was immediately applied with vigour.

There is no question that the increased persecution during August exceeded everything heard of before. Beginning with July, but almost daily throughout August, we find the Privy Council issuing orders to almost all parts of England for severe proceedings against Recusants, who were everywhere to be thrown into the common prisons and fined, while those known to be constant were to be interned in retired castles or other places of strength. Of these Wisbech Castle, though already for some time devoted to this purpose, became henceforth notable as the place of perpetual confinement for the clergy of highest name. Framlingham Castle, too, was now set apart for lay Recusants, and the Catholic prisoners there will doubtless have remembered that Framlingham had served as a refuge for Queen Mary Tudor in 1553, when Cecil's party was attempting to drive her and her house from the throne.

The letters of the Spanish ambassador help to realise the picture. After sending on the Proclamation of the 15th of July, he continues (July 23)—

" All the Catholics of London and in the whole country who had been released on bail, or had given sureties to appear when summoned, have been ordered to surrender themselves in the London prisons within twenty days under pain of death. A great number of them have already done so, and it is a subject of heartfelt gratitude to God that they bear with joy and confidence this travail and persecution, such as they never have been afflicted with before."

On the 7th of August he notes that imprisonment continues, and on the 21st of August he wrote—

" When the Catholics here are summoned before the Council and are asked why they do not attend the preachings, they answer that it is against their conscience to do so, and they are then sent to prison. They have given the nobles who have hitherto presented themselves a month to make up their minds which they will choose, either to hear the

sermons or to stay in prison, where they would like to keep
them during the sittings of Parliament, to prevent them
from opposing a bill which they are determined to pass
against the Catholics. This is to the effect that any Englishman who will not openly attend the preachings shall be
punished by a fine of 40 l. sterling for the first month,
80 l. for the second, and so on, doubling the fine for each
month. This is Cecil's idea, who says it is much safer for
the Queen thus to deprive the Catholics of their property
than to take their lives.[1]

In spite of these great severities the French ambassador,
Castelnau, can still find a sort of excuse (based on his belief
in the false reports from Rome), though it is the last time
that he attempts one (August 30)—

" For some little time back there has been some distrust
of the Catholics here. An adverse conclusion has been
passed against them in full Council, and even their friends
have not been able to defend them against the charge of
having had intelligence with the Pope, and of his Holiness
having had sundry Bulls, pardons, plots and other dispensa-
tions to trouble. It is by the means of these said Catholics,
who are in number infinite [something seems missing
here]. But eventually the storm is appeased, after some
of the chief Catholics have been examined and sent to
prison. The said Queen does not wish to force their consciences, but she does mean to make them obey the laws
and customs introduced since she has been Queen. In fine,
the said lady, according to her natural inclination, wishes
nothing but entire friendship to the said Catholics, and
finds them her best subjects. True it is that the marriage
has inspired them with too much confidence and boldness,
but this lady does not esteem them the less, and defends
them almost alone when several people bring charges
against them." [2]

---

[1] *Spanish Calendar*, pp. 43, 45, 50, 51. The law, alluded to in the
second extract, eventually inflicted a fine of £20 per lunar month. Those
who heard Mass were considered as " compellable " to take the Oath of
Supremacy, and the second refusal of this was High Treason (5. Eliz. c. l.).
On the 23rd of October Mendoza announces that five hundred gentlemen
have been imprisoned in the last six weeks. On the 11th of December he
adds that the goods of these prisoners were to be confiscated (*ibid.*, pp. 62,
69).   [2] R.O., *Transcripts from Paris*, xxvii. 257.

These phrases are all characteristic of Elizabeth—the fictitious stories of new Bulls; the imprisonment of Catholics in spite of her entire friendship for them; her reluctance to force consciences, but insistence on obedience to her religious laws. Even the hope that the storm had passed was, alas, unfounded. Individuals here and there received lenient treatment for a time, but, broadly speaking, the persecution was steadily growing worse.

In September Mr. Pounde allowed Campion's Letter to the Council to go from hand to hand, and in their irritable frame of mind the persecutors were hereby still further aroused. In fine, it was not until the final destruction of San Joseffe's force at Smerwick was known in London (about the 6th or 8th of December) that there was any prospect of greater moderation being shown. But by that time many permanent changes had occurred in the political state of Europe which would tend to keep Elizabeth's mind embittered. Spain had conquered Portugal, and was clearly on its way to recover the Belgian Netherlands. Mendoza and Philip had constantly made the mistake of endeavouring to alarm Elizabeth with the prospect of what Spain would do when she became more powerful. Though the Queen was notoriously liable to be influenced by such alarms, still, on the war party in her Council, whose influence would eventually predominate over her, Mendoza's bluster made just the wrong impression. The return of Drake from his long, buccaneering expedition among the Spanish colonies, tended to create still further dangers for peace. On the 8th of December Castelnau announced the news of the fall of Smerwick, and that, whereas [false] news from Rome had previously made Elizabeth's advisers fear that England was to be attacked after Ireland, now a reaction had set in, and Elizabeth wanted to be revenged on Spain all the world over. On the 13th Herle wrote that "the Queen is sharply set against papists." [1] The persecution was now fully alight.

Looking back on the renewal of the persecution, we see that it is due to many causes, more disparate and varied than was suspected by those who had not our advantage of

[1] R.O., *Transcripts from Paris*, xxvii. 291; *Domestic Calendar*, p. 690.

studying the confidential papers of all parties. Most
Catholic writers have assumed that it was simply due to
the success of the new missionaries, and especially to the
Jesuits.[1] But not only is this an unproved assumption,
but, if we look closely to the chronology, we shall find that
the relaxation came after the first successes of the Douay
priests, and the recrudescence a little before the preaching
of the Jesuits. The most important factor in the situation
was, no doubt, Elizabeth's position *vis-à-vis* to the French
match, the waxing and waning of severities varying directly
with her keenness or nonchalance in its regard. Irritation
at the Irish expedition was also a most important factor,
the great severities of August corresponding clearly with the
Irish successes, which began in July. As to the rumours
of the Papal League, and of a renewed excommunication,
it is more difficult to trace their effects. They did not lead
to particular acts of persecution, but helped to build up
that fatal tradition of religious prejudice which was the
source of such appallingly widespread evils. To the minds
of those already warped by prejudice, the successes of
the missionaries were, of course, as gall and wormwood,
and we cannot wonder at their being among the first marked
out as victims. But this is not at all the same thing as
saying that they caused or occasioned a renewal of the
persecution.

§ 6. *The Counter-Reformation under Persecution*

The conflict that now ensued was horrible. Families
were to be broken up, the children taken, the property
confiscated, the master of the house imprisoned, the priest
murdered. That was what the Catholics were now called
upon to face. Not that the laws as yet enforced regularly
each and all of these barbarities, but all had even now to
be reckoned with. There had been examples of all, there

---

[1] The Privy Council had issued orders against Jesuits in 1578, two years
before any had landed. After they had landed their name does not
appear in the *Privy Council Registers* for another three months, *i. e.* not
till the 6th of September, 1580. Dasent, x. 426, xii. 194. Campion was
probably the person then aimed at.

was no protection from any. The rapidly-rising tide of cruelty would certainly lead to all those excesses. There was no escape, no chance of mitigation.

Could any one stand against that? For those, at least, who had been worsted in the first encounter when they had numbers on their side, what probability would there be of successful resistance? The age was one when submission to the Crown had grown and grown, until it had become an article of faith, and the Catholics were the party out of whose exaggerated loyalty this abuse had sprung. To make a stand for liberty was hard indeed for men with traditions like that.

Humanly speaking, the cause was hopeless. But if there was to be a presage of providential delivery, it would be found in the arousing of strong religious enthusiasm, and our attention must now be chiefly directed to the re-enkindlement of devotion. This was exactly what the Counter-Reformation was achieving so successfully on the Continent. In England the Douay priests had already begun to fan the sacred fire; and now the burning words of Campion, and the cogent, practical reasonings of Persons, soon set it aflame.

Religious enthusiasm is a difficult subject to describe precisely, and yet it is so important that a correct idea should be formed of the feelings, aspirations and motives of the Catholics at this crisis, that it will be worth while to quote at considerable length a letter of Father Persons, and afterwards another letter of Father Campion. No one could speak on this subject with more authority than they.

" I wrote last hurriedly, about eighteen days ago, as I was setting out from London . . . for we have both left town, and mean to stay away for two or three months. We believe we can do more good in the country, for almost all the gentry are now living there, and the persecution in London is worse than ever. At our departure we were abundantly supplied (through God's goodness) with all things necessary, for both of us were freely offered clothes, money, two horses and a servant. Moreover, certain young men of birth and fortune offered to accompany us wherever we

wanted to go, intending to participate in all our dangers.[1]
Even before Father Edmund arrived, I managed to gain
divers friends and places of shelter, during a short visit to
the country.

" We were together in London before we left, and
even gave exhortations and took counsel together. Though
we have neither seen nor heard anything of one another
since, I do not doubt that he is succeeding as well as I have
done hitherto. The reason is that good men, of whom
there are many here, are most desirous of our company,
and listen to our instructions with great avidity, although
this is most strictly forbidden by public proclamations,[2]
lately published, which, however, do not mention any one
by name.

" To be brief, there is a vast field here in which to labour
with fruit, if only there were enough men of our company.
So that before all things else we must beg you to send us,
as soon as possible, a good number of efficient men. The
duty which falls to us is of the greatest moment, not only
for the reputation of the Society, but also for the recovery
of this kingdom, and for the common cause of the Catholic
Church.

" Against us a most grievous persecution has already
broken out, so that no day is safe from peril. Still, this is
only what was reckoned with when we were with you, and
we may hope that nothing unforeseen will occur. We and
our friends are all convinced that (happen what may to us)
the Pope and his Paternity will never give up this mission.
. . . I see that the continuation of it is of first-rate importance for the conversion of the whole North, and cannot be
abandoned without great loss to many souls, and to the
Catholic religion in general. Catholic preachers have already
given out that the Jesuits have begun this war by order
of his Holiness, that no danger will stop them, that sooner
shall the power of the enemy to torture fail than the readiness of the men of the Society to endure for the honour of
Christ and of Holy Church.[3] Nay, we are in greater perils

---

[1] It will be noted that nothing is said of a Sodality.   [2] See above.
[3] This paragraph corresponds, *mutatis mutandis*, to § 8 in the " Letters "
both of Persons and of Campion. To the first, of course, more closely
than to the second. " His Paternity " is the Father General of the
Jesuits.

than those of our successors will be, partly because they will find safe places ready prepared by us, partly because the adversaries are especially angered against us as first comers. Still the dangers are not such but that we may escape them for many years, or at least for many months; and I hope we shall, though we are never safe for one single day.

" Meantime we are full of happiness, and our Lord consoles us so much on every side that it seems as if we were in a delightful paradise. The reasons of this are : first, the peril itself will bring with it the highest of all God's blessings—that of suffering something for His Holy Name. If God should bring us to that, we hope that not only our courage, but also our answers, which we have ready in writing, will be such that no loss shall ensue to the honour of his Holiness, nor to the reputation of the Society.

" Then, while our Lord leaves us free, the hope of fruit is very great, for we are so welcomed, so occupied, that both time and strength fail us. I am obliged daily during my journey to make two or three discourses to gentlefolk, who are so affected by the Spirit of God that they are ready for any enterprise, however signal. On almost all occasions they offer themselves and all their property, and their zeal and fervour is wonderful, especially in three respects.

" *First* in hearing Mass, at which they assist with such sighs and frequent sobs that, dry though I am, it moves me to tears despite myself. The *second* is their reverence and zeal towards the Holy Father. For, greatly as they should and do appreciate his authority, this is not so great as their love. Hence it comes that as soon as they hear these words : ' Let us pray for our Pontiff Gregory,' in the litany, they raise their hands and voices to heaven with an unanimity that is wonderful. The *third* is their wonderful fortitude of mind and readiness to suffer any travail on account of religion. A notable example of this occurred to me lately. A knight,[1] a man of birth, education and intelligence, and in his country ranking as rich and powerful, heard, three weeks after he had been reconciled

---

[1] "*Cavalier.*" In his *Autobiography, C.R.S.*, ii. 27, Persons enumerates Sir William Catesby and Sir Thomas Tresham as the first knights reconciled. But "Cavalier" might also mean a gentleman or esquire.

by my means to the Church, that letters had been sent
him by the Privy Council, either to return to schism or
to be committed to prison.   He immediately put his affairs
into order; and sending for me, gave me a certain portion
of his goods to distribute to the poor; then with happy
face and heart, assured me he was ready to enter any
prison whatever.   His example will, I know, be followed
by many.

"The persecution is now very grave.   New prisons are
appointed in every county, as the old ones are full of Recusants, as they call those who will not go to their churches
and sermons.   But these measures, and the others they
are designing against us, will end eventually in our advantage.   For there are to be imprisoned all the best and
wealthiest gentlemen, who have dispensed hospitality
before the eyes of either the parents, or the brothers, or
the relatives or friends (of every one), and it is easy to
conjecture what sympathy this will give rise to.

"But no more of this.   My companions are in a hurry
and I am being called away.   Only I beg you to procure
from his Holiness and Father General a reinforcement of
men from the Society.   They should be learned men, not
less than four or three, one a Spaniard and one an Italian,
if possible; but let them be capable men, and men of letters,
so that they may be placed in London, where they may live
quite safely,[1] and there settle cases of conscience and difficulties that may occur.   I should be glad if some priests
of the English College were sent separately, so that they may
travel more secretly, and that nothing may be known of
their coming.   Pray consider it a matter of great importance
that this fresh reinforcement should arrive before we are
shut in.   I greet all.   On my way, the 5th of August, 1580."[2]
(No signature.)

One sees distinctly in this letter the figure of a great religious leader who has succeeded, despite a thousand dangers,

[1] *Saranno sicurissimi.*   The idea was that they should not be missionaries, but only chaplains, confessors, consultors.   Even so, the statement
would only be true in a very broad sense, and the idea was soon abandoned.
[2] This letter survives in a transcript at the Vallicelliana Library, N. 23,
f. 179, a copy possibly supplied to St. Philip Neri.   A quotation is made
from it in the *Douay Diaries*, p. 171, under date October 4.   There is
also a Latin version in *Anglia Romana*, i. 154.

in animating his followers to true heroism. They are ready "for any enterprise, however signal"; while he has his plans, some long prepared, some lately formed, but all progressing steadily. Though he is fully conscious that he never has a day of safety, he is looking forward to victory, not in England only, but to the re-conversion perhaps of the whole of Northern Europe. His enthusiasm, as that of his followers, is purely religious. There is no trace of self-seeking or of private interest. Though hunted for his life, he feels as if he were already in paradise. The thought of future suffering has no terrors, and he is buoyed up by the self-devotion of those amid whom he lives, who "on almost all occasions offer themselves and all their property" to advance the cause.[1] Without a question the fire of the Counter-Reformation is now burning in England as brightly as ever it did in Rome, or in any of its acknowledged centres.

It is true that, as is usual with enthusiasts, the plans do not all seem to have been either adequate or secure. Really safe plans there could not be. More will be said about this later. For the moment the important thing is that there were plans, hopes, offers of "signal enterprises." This indicated the true conquering spirit, and formed of itself a presage that, if help from above continued, final victory was not impossible.

It may have been noticed that there is in this paper, though written nearly three weeks after the *Letter to the Council*, etc., no mention whatever of disputations. The *Letters* are not expected to see the light till after the fathers chance to fall into the enemy's hands. A very few days later, however, a considerable change took place, and Catholics as well as Protestants were all talking of Campion's "great brag and Challenge."

This was due to Thomas Pounde, to whom, it will be remembered, Campion had handed his paper unsealed. It is not known when he first began to pass it to others or to get it copied, probably soon, but perhaps not until after the order for his confinement in Stortford Castle.

---

[1] One negative is worthy of remark. There is no attempt to explain the reasons of the increased persecution. It is not till November that the endeavour will be made.

We have already heard that the Government had made a plan of interning firm and resolute Catholics in solitary or distant places, to prevent their contaminating others; [1] and in accordance with this order, Pounde was destined for Stortford about the 1st of September; and it would then at least have become his duty to hand on his precious document to others, if he had not done so already.

Nor did he stop there. He set to work to bring about a disputation as soon as possible. The very circulation of the *Letter* would have caused such a demand, and he himself boldly wrote various still extant letters to the Bishop of London to prepare the way, while he composed and sent in a paper of " Six Reasons," which he would be ready to defend himself.

These cartels he delivered in a quaint and highly characteristic fashion. Approaching Tripp and Crowley, two well-known Puritan ministers, who came to the Marshalsea to harass the Catholic prisoners there, he fell upon his knees before them, a demonstration the more remarkable as no one had hitherto treated those foul-mouthed fellows with more boldness or disregard. He had, however, previously explained that the reverence was not to them, but for them to witness; so that they might testify that these offers of disputation made to the Queen's Council were preferred with all possible deference and obsequiousness. Chivalrous as the idea was, it, of course, failed in its main object. Instead of being allowed free speech, Pounde was sent off to the ruinous keep at Stortford, even though his former friend, Sir Christopher Hatton, spoke in his behalf and procured a few days' delay. [2]

The demand for Campion's *Letter* or *Challenge* was growing steadily, and in the course of September and October it acquired a wide circulation for those days. Though the *Letter* lost something of its simplicity and charm by this premature publicity, as has been already explained, still the gain far exceeded the loss. For eventually, in any case, the *Letter* was addressed over the heads of the Council to

---

[1] Dasent, xii. 124, under date July 26, 1580.
[2] Pounde's *Six Articles* and the letters connected with them are printed in Foley, iii. 632–44.

the public, and the public now read it with avidity. The reasonableness and moderation of its demand could not fail to make its effect on all moderate men, To the Catholics the idea of meeting their foes on equal terms was intensely encouraging, and we find repeated attempts made by them at this time to arrange for a disputation. This had not been done before, and the idea of it would soon pass; but its presence indicates that we have arrived at a moment when hopes were running more than usually high.

Meanwhile, both Campion and Persons had practically disappeared. Country life in those days was so quiet and retired that it was hardly affected by what was passing in town, and the two missionaries found themselves able to devote themselves quietly and without interruption to their work for two or three months. It was only when Persons came up to London in October that he realised how things had been moving. Instead of quieting down, the persecution was worse; and yet the Catholics were more animated than ever, and they were now calling out that Campion must write again. Persons would not let Campion come to town, but made him stop in Uxbridge, and rode out there to arrange measures together, perhaps early in November. What they then agreed upon must be discussed in some detail in a subsequent chapter, when we consider the new enterprises then undertaken. Suffice it, at the end of this volume, to say that they were making plans, and bold ones. Campion was to address a new appeal to the public, in a book to carry on the discussion adumbrated in the *Challenge;* and Persons, undismayed, undertook to print the work in England and to circulate it there. Thus boldness was still on the increase.

Then they separated again, and not long after, according to agreement, both sent to Rome full accounts of what was going on. These are extant, and afford us a most valuable survey of the effects produced so far by their missions. Both, indeed, have been used before, but must be quoted again here. However, as we have just cited Father Persons fully, we may be content with a shorter summary of his letter.[1]

[1] The original of this letter from Father Persons to Father Agazario, London, November 17, 1580, was once preserved in the English College,

Persons begins with an analysis of the situation, and gives four causes for the growth of persecution : 1. The war in Ireland ; 2. The rumoured demonstration of the Spanish Fleet against England (this never, in fact, took place; the rumour was akin to that regarding the Grand Papal League) ; 3. The advent of the Jesuits and their success; 4. *The Challenge.* He says that the number of Recusants known to the Government has increased to fifty thousand persons, and " you may guess how great the Catholic total is, if so many offer themselves to suffering and ruin on its account." He repeats the prayer for more Jesuits, and speaks enthusiastically of the encouragement and support he received from the secular clergy. " We have many most generous helpers. The secular clergy is everywhere at one with us. Nay, with every demonstration of affection, it defers to us, so that it makes one anxious about living up to the reputation of the Society, which is everywhere so high, while we feel ourselves so far from that degree of virtue which they reverently look for in us. So much the more, then, do we need your prayers."

From Campion's letter I must transcribe enough to give some idea of his individuality, of the courage he breathed into his hearers, of the spirit with which he regarded the future.

[After describing his arrival, he continues] " I ride about some piece of the country every day. The harvest is wonderfully great. On horseback I meditate my sermon; when I come to the house, I polish it. Then I talk with such as come to speak with me, or hear their confessions. In the morning, after Mass, I preach.

Rome, and Father Grene made some extracts from it now in Stonyhurst, *Collectanea P.,* i. 299.

From the original a somewhat ciceronic version of the paragraphs on the persecution was made, at once, to show to friends at Rome, and there is a copy of this in Arch. Vat. Castel. S. Angelo, xiv. c. 11. n. 42 (erroneously dated September 17). It is printed hence by Theiner, iii. 216, and translated by Simpson, p. 172 (with note, p. 376). There is another copy, *Anglia Necrolog.* 1576–1651, and another, *Anglia Rom.* i. 155.

Father More (*Historia*, pp. 52, 78) has copied a good deal, and perhaps from the original text, but, according to the custom of this day, he amends the Latin of his text very freely.

B B

" They hear with exceeding greediness, and very often receive the Sacraments, for the ministration whereof we are ever well assisted by priests, whom we find in every place, whereby both the people is well served and we much eased in our charge. The priests of our country, themselves being most excellent for virtue and learning, yet have raised so great an opinion for our Society that I dare scarcely touch the exceeding reverence all Catholics do unto us. How much more is it requisite that such as hereafter are to be sent for supply, whereof we have great need, be such as may answer all men's expectation of them. Specially let them be well trained for the pulpit.

" I cannot long escape the hands of the heretics; the enemies have so many eyes, so many tongues, so many scouts and crafts. I am in apparel to myself very ridiculous; I often change it and my name also. I read letters sometimes myself that in the first front tell news *that Campion is taken*, which, noised in every place where I come, so filleth mine ears with the sound thereof that fear itself hath taken away all fear. *My soul is in my own hands ever.* Let such as you send for supply premeditate and make count of this always.

" Marry, the solaces that are ever intermeddled with these miseries are so great that they do not only countervail the fear of what punishment temporal soever, but by infinite sweetness make all worldly pains (be they never so great) seem nothing. A conscience pure, a courage invincible, zeal incredible, a work so worthy, the number innumerable, of high degree, of mean calling, of the inferior sort, of every age and sex. Here, even amongst the Protestants themselves that are of milder nature, it is turned into a proverb that he must be a Catholic that payeth faithfully that he oweth; insomuch that, if any Catholic do injury, everybody expostulateth with him as for an act unworthy of men of that calling.

" To be short, heresy heareth ill of all men; neither is there any condition of people counted more vile and impure than their ministers. And we worthily have indignation that fellows so unlearned, so evil, so derided, so base, should in so desperate a quarrel overrule such a number of noble wits as our Realm hath.

" Threatening edicts come forth against us daily ; notwithstanding, by good heed and the prayers of good men, and (which is the chief of all) by God's special gift, we have passed safely through the most part of the Island.   I find many neglecting their own security to have only care of my safety."   [*He then gives his account of* " The Challenge " *and its publication.*]   " The people hereupon is ours, and that error of spreading abroad this writing hath much advanced the cause.   If we be commanded and may have safe conduct, we will into the Court.

" But they mean nothing less ; for they have filled all the old prisons with Catholics, and now make new ; and in fine, plainly affirm, that it were better to make a few traitors away, than so many souls should be lost.

" Of their martyrs they brag no more now.   For it is now come to pass that, for a few apostates and cobblers of theirs burned, we have Bishops, Lords, knights, the old nobility, patterns of learning, piety and prudence, the flower of the youth, noble matrons ; and of the inferior sort innumerable, either martyred at once, or by consuming prisonment dying daily.   At the very writing hereof the persecution rageth most cruelly.   The house where I am is sad ; no other talk but of death, flight, prison or spoil of their friends.   Nevertheless they proceed with courage.

" Very many, even at this present, being restored to the Church ; new soldiers give up their names, while the old offer up their blood.   By which holy hosts and oblations God will be pleased ; and we shall, no question, by Him overcome.

" You see now, therefore, Reverend Father, how much need we have of your prayers and sacrifices and other heavenly help, to go through with these things.   There will never want in England men that will have care of their own salvation, nor such as shall advance other men's. Neither shall this Church here ever fail, so long as priests and pastors shall be found for the sheep, rage man or devil never so much.   But the rumour of present peril causeth me here to make an end.   *Arise God, His enemies avoid.*   Fare you well.[1]

" *Edmund Campion.*"

[1] Allen, *Brief Historie of the Martyrdom of XII Reverend Priests,* 1582, reprint of 1908, p. 21.

BB 2

" This Church here shall never fail, so long as priests and pastors be found for the sheep, rage man or devil never so much."

This prognostic, from one so capable of judging as Edmund Campion, we may take as marking the close of the hour of greatest darkness in the history of the English Catholics, as showing that the prospect of inevitable extinction had passed. We have watched the dying down of corporate life, we have witnessed its gradual recovery; but no one has yet said, " We shall, no question, by God overcome."

The grave crisis is now passed, and a new phase begins. There is still, indeed, to be a battle for life, a battle even more painful and cruel than before, but the danger of extermination was over. Henceforth there would always be life to fight for life. A new period in the history of the English Catholics is now opening.

INDEX